THE MINER'S CANARY

Based on The Nathan I. Huggins Lectures

THE MINER'S CANARY

ENLISTING RACE,

RESISTING POWER,

TRANSFORMING

DEMOCRACY

LANI GUINIER and GERALD TORRES

HARVARD UNIVERSITY PRESS

Cambridge, Massachusetts

London, England

First Harvard University Press paperback edition, 2003

Library of Congress Cataloging-in-Publication Data
Guinier, Lani.
   The miner's canary : enlisting race, resisting power, transforming democracy /
Lani Guinier and Gerald Torres.
      p. cm.
Includes bibliographical references and index.
ISBN 0-674-00469-8 (cloth)
ISBN 0-674-01084-1 (pbk.)
   1. United States—Race relations—Political aspects.   2. Political participation—
United States.   3. Minorities—United States—Political activity.   4. Coalition
(Social sciences)   I. Torres, Gerald.   II. Title.
E184.A1 G94 2001
323.1'73—dc21   2001039629

In 1953 Felix Cohen wrote: "Like the miner's canary, the Indian marks the shift from fresh air to poison gas in our political atmosphere, and our treatment of the Indian . . . marks the rise and fall in our democratic faith."

In 1967 Dr. Martin Luther King, Jr., said to his staff: "We're going to take this movement and . . . reach out to the poor people in all directions in this country . . . into the Southwest after the Indians, into the West after the Chicanos, into Appalachia after the poor whites, and into the ghettos after Negroes and Puerto Ricans. And we are going to bring them together and enlarge this campaign into something bigger than just a civil rights movement for Negroes."

Inspired by the work and the words of Dr. King just before he was killed, and building on the insight of Felix Cohen's powerful metaphor, we hope to show that Cohen's canary is not alone. All canaries bear watching. Our democratic future depends on it.

CONTENTS

On the computer screen, the letters were pulsing. I wrote: "At a talk in Chicago one wintry afternoon a middle-aged, very attractive black woman from Texas asked to take a picture with me. She proudly, almost defiantly, turned to the woman waiting in line behind her and announced, 'I'm going to hang this picture in my office. Ain't nobody gonna mess with me then!'" I sat back and lifted my hands from the keyboard, lost in thought, when my eight-year-old son, Nikolas, came into my office. He started reading aloud over my shoulder: "At a talk in Chicago one wintry afternoon a middle-aged, very attractive black woman from Texas asked to take a picture with me." He carefully reread the sentence, pausing at the phrase "black woman." Then he instructed me to change the sentence immediately. "Take out the word 'black.' It doesn't matter, Mom."

Somewhat surprised by Niko's demand, I tried to explain to him that the adjective was useful because it linked back to an incident in 1993, when President Clinton nominated me to be Assistant Attorney General for Civil Rights and then pulled my nomination without a Senate confirmation hearing, following controversy about law review articles I had written. I explained that because I continued to speak out in the face of criticism, I became an unexpected symbol to many black people who wanted to associate themselves with my refusal to be silenced.

Niko persisted. So I asked my son: "Well, what should I say? Would you feel better if I had written: 'An attractive person from Texas asked to take a picture with me'?" He said, "No, she is a woman." "Why," I asked, "does it matter that she is a woman but not a black woman?" Niko did not hesitate to draw a distinction. "You cannot just write 'a person,' because there is still sexual abuse." He had learned all about sexual abuse in school, and he offered to demonstrate what he meant. "Pretend we are walking down the street," he said, swaggering toward me. "If I touched you in ways you didn't like, that would be sexual abuse. I shouldn't do that to you."

"Okay," I said. "Now let me demonstrate racial abuse. Let's walk back down that same street." Just as I passed Niko, I looked him straight in the eyes and almost spit out, "You ugly nigger!" He jumped backward, afraid. "You called me the 'N' word, Mom," he said, accusingly. "Yes, I did. That's racial abuse." He paused, reflecting a moment. Then he almost whispered, "Mom, will someone ever call me that?" I was torn. I did not want to mislead my son, yet I was sad to scare him so early in his life. Reluctantly, I said, "I'm afraid that is possible." Niko whimpered, "Mom, you just made me wish I was white!" "Why?" I asked. "Because if I was white, no one would call me nigger."

My son was able to see "woman" as a real category in part because his Germantown Quaker education schooled him to take seriously sexual but not racial differences. He, as a male, was being trained about sexual abuse. In the context of gender relations, Niko's teachers were imposing boundaries, not erasing them. But while the Friends School Quakers were using boundaries to articulate difference and clarify "rules" of conduct between boys and girls, when it came to race they were teaching Niko that the category itself should be erased. He was being educated to internalize the colorblind norm: race somehow was different. Gender roles, gender differences had borders that must be policed. As with any border, there were clear rules about permissible crossings. But unlike gender, racial identity or racial difference was not supposed to exist and thus needed no fences.

In fact, what was being policed here was noticing that there were differences at all. He could confront the limitations of his privilege as a boy toward girls, but neither he nor his teachers wanted to be reminded of his differences as a black student in a majority-white environment. If we were to make people aware of racial differences, simply by noticing we would reintroduce the illusion of race and thus inevitably polarize and divide or, perhaps even worse, stigmatize. With race, difference—which was to be feared—had to be negated and conflict thus avoided.

Many whites, like U.S. Supreme Court Justice Anthony Kennedy, invariably express "grave concerns" with naming race as a legitimate public identity.[1] Those who oppose race-consciousness believe that highlighting the racial distribution of social goods invites invidious comparisons between groups. These comparisons are politically dangerous because they expose the inherent vulnerability of political minorities. This fear is magnified, these critics contend, because race-consciousness legitimizes white race nationalism as well.

In light of these unpalatable alternatives, many well-intentioned whites choose a colorblind vision. Except for gender, we are all the same.[2] I, on the other hand, wanted to prepare my son for the real world. My first response to Niko's effort to censor my manuscript was that a failure to acknowledge difference is a failure to prepare him for a world in which his differences may matter—a world in which when he walks down the street, white cops may stop him or other young black males may resent him, in both cases because of a potentially deadly combination of racism and machismo.[3] I wanted to teach my own son that in a very few years, when he would walk the streets of his community, the burden of his race might be reflected in the caution or fear he sees in the eyes of others.[4]

Yet, in some way, my response was just a mirror image of the colorblind Quakers. I was schooling my son to see race as stigmatizing. I was making my son visible in ways that made him want to be *in*visible. I was teaching my son that the only way to see racial difference was in the negative, to be called the "N" word and then to wish he were white. I was reinforcing hierarchy, not resisting it. In an effort to make his difference apparent to him, I had resorted to calling him names. Like Zora Neale Hurston in her essay "How It Feels to Be Colored Me," I was telling my son that he was black only in contrast to being white. Hurston exposed this move when she wrote, "I do not always feel colored. Even now I often achieve the unconscious Zora of Eatonville before the Hegira. I feel most colored when I am thrown against a sharp white background."[5]

On some level I too was trapped in the categories. I was teaching Niko to counter the Quaker idea that race is an illusion with yet another illusion—that because race can be manipulated to stigmatize and oppress, race is therefore concrete. I had neglected to emphasize that race—and racial identity—is always relational, not inherent. By relational I did not mean oppositional. Being black has meaning not just in opposition to white but in relation to others that are similarly situated. Thus, understanding Niko's identity as black is also about seeing him as a part of a community of people who are similarly defined or situated. Race is many things, not just a single thing.[6] It can be stigmatizing, but it also can be liberating.

If we think in categories, and think about race only as if it were a single category, we conflate many different spheres of racial meaning. We fail to specify if we mean biological race, political race, historical race, or cultural race. We simplify race as a fixed category from which many people want to escape. They seek exit, not acknowledgment; they want choice, not voice. The category becomes a barrier, a fenced enclosure, and transgressing the boundary becomes an act of rebellion and self-definition. These negative aspects of race do not stand in for the entire experience of being "raced." And yet, despite knowing this, I found myself re-enacting all the fears of difference.

What was missing from my conversation with my son was recognition that being forced to identify with a group of people can be an unexpected blessing. Those who are racialized by society may miss out on a specific kind of individual liberty, but they gain a different perspective on wholeness and its relationship to freedom. They learn to appreciate the importance of friendship, of solidarity, of connection. They also may learn from a place at the bottom or on the margin to be skeptical of authority, to distrust hierarchy, to find comfort in community.

At eleven years old, Niko moved to Cambridge, Massachusetts. His new school, though also Quaker, had a very different approach to teaching about race and racism. It had a curriculum that used the *Autobiography of Malcolm X, To Kill a Mockingbird,* and *Betsy Brown*—three books about race in America—to teach the history of the United States, not just the history of blacks. The school had a contemporary issues class that tackled race and racism directly. The teachers encouraged students of color to join affinity groups, where they could talk about their feelings, unobserved by others.

In the middle of seventh grade, Niko announced to me that he was going to tell his classmates he no longer wanted to be called African American. He had been thinking about this, and he realized, he said with great authority in his voice, that it bothered him every time someone white said "African American." It bothered him for three reasons. First, white people seemed to have trouble getting their mouth around the words. It seemed to take too much effort for his white teacher and some of his white classmates to say the seven-syllable term. Second, and more to the point, it reminded him that he did not know where in Africa his ancestors had lived. African American was the best they could do because the history of human bondage and the Middle Passage had deprived him of any direct connection to his country of origin. Third, because the word "American" so often ignores Central and South America as well as Canada and Mexico, "African American" ignores the African people who live in other parts of the Western Hemisphere, outside the United States.

"Just call us black," he told one classmate, who had just commented, "All African Americans seem to have dark hair." "You took too long to say 'African Americans,'" Niko explained. "You hesitated before you could even say the words." "Yeah," a black girl echoed after Niko spoke. "Just call us black."

When Niko recounted this story to me, I experienced a mixture of awe and uncertainty. I was proud that he was willing to speak up in a predominantly white environment, with the obvious support of another black classmate, about what he thought was right. I was pleased that he had found a way to articulate his concerns to his classmate that was honest, not threatening. But I was also admittedly confused. "Remember," I asked Niko, "when you were in third grade and you didn't want me to put the word 'black' in a sentence describing a woman who wanted to have her picture taken with me?" "No, Mom. I don't remember that." I tried to prompt his memory, to no avail. I replayed the scene we had scripted in my office about sexual and racial abuse. Niko still had no recollection.

But then he got very quiet and said, with a note of sadness in his voice, "I am ashamed of myself." "Why?" I asked, "What are you possibly ashamed of?" "Well, I don't remember when you pretended to call me 'nigger,' but I do remember that when I was in third grade I wished I was white just like the rest of the kids in my class. I remember that I wanted," and here he paused, took a breath, and then resumed so as to emphasize the next word, "the *benefits* of being white." He was suddenly able to summon up his third-grade perspective—looking at whiteness as a privilege, the ability to be an anonymous individual. "I just didn't want to draw attention to myself, to emphasize the ways I was different."

So which way feels more comfortable? "Just call me black," Niko replied, a confident smile filling his face. "I know who I am now, Mom. I don't want to be anyone else."

LANI GUINIER

California in the sixties was emerging from the postwar boom, and a feeling of optimism and openness about the future was everywhere. I attended San Bernardino's only inner-city high school, which was about equally divided among Chicano, black, and white students. One of my best friends there was a Chinese-American student named Stephen.[7]

Steve was the son of a prominent doctor and lived across town. In San Bernardino High School, Steve and I were part of the small percentage of the graduating class who went on to a four-year college. Most of my Chicano friends went either to Valley (the local community college), to work, or to Vietnam. When I was a child, my neighborhood was predominantly Chicano, and my family had remained there as it changed from Chicano to black. By the time I was in high school, I was enough a part of the black community that my English teacher felt a need to take me aside to correct the "black mistakes" in my usage.

Our girl friends were best friends and white, from that part of San Bernardino where motorcycles and chickens negotiated an uneasy peace in the front yard. Out back, a pig destined for a family roast could usually be found rooting around in a pen made of chicken wire and scrap lumber, while acrid trash burned in a pit in the far corner of the lot. An overlay of working-class life and fruit-stand capitalism contributed to the tension in this part of town, where rural and urban poverty, with their different rhythms and rituals, frequently collided.

Steve and I knew that even in the mid-sixties people found our inter-racial romances odd. We knew that we were in the vanguard. The problem was color.[8] We thought that the children of mixed unions were clearly the hope for the future, and thus black people should be prohibited from marrying black people and white people should be prohibited from marrying white people. Chinese and Mexicans, however, could marry whomever they chose. We would be the agents of a raceless society.

In our youthful view, race was reducible to color. We thought that by mixing the colors together we could eliminate invidious distinctions drawn solely on the basis of appearance. We knew that color could one day bar us from things we wanted. We had the same middle-class dreams as most of our white classmates. Wendell, the one black kid they let into the college prep courses, did too. Being in the "honors" class may have re-inforced our belief in transcendence of color, by creating the illusion that we were honorary whites.[9] But in our youth and naiveté, we did not fully comprehend the implications of this belief. What we did not understand was that transcendence would eliminate the positive content of race as well as the negative.

I felt more strongly than Steve the sense of values and community that flowed from a specific racial identity. Chicanos shared a feeling of solidarity that stemmed from the Spanglish we spoke, from the extended families that filled our neighborhood, and from the inchoate recognition of Indian culture at the root of Chicanismo. The Catholic Church also was a source of unity and strength, and its values animated our lives. In some sense there were no strangers in my neighborhood and parish, we had so many different links.

We had black Chicanos and blonde Chicanos, with some of each in my own family. Before there were Hispanics there was *raza*, which of course means race and not ethnicity. Two dominant myths pervaded my Chicano identity, completely apart from encounters with Anglo culture. First was the myth that a new race had been created in the Americas and that Mexicans were the instantiation of that race, and second was the myth of Our Lady of Guadalupe. That God had chosen to be made manifest in the New World in the form of an Indian woman worked a powerful sense of belonging to this new earth. Both of these ideas are part of the general theme of the *mestizaje.*

Not to paint a too-rosy picture, I must confess that Steve and I projected our youthful romantic fantasies against a backdrop of race riots in our high school. The police forcibly evacuated our classrooms by spraying them with pepper gas, and the rural white kids formed a White Leadership Council. During the riots I remember talking to my Chicano friend Fat Boy as he was on his way to his car to get his jack, telling him, "Don't call them niggers, man. That is what those gabachos are saying about you." That I would know what the white kids were saying about Chicanos and what the Chicanos were saying about blacks and what the black kids were saying about the others demonstrates how implausibly situated I was in the middle of this mess, but there I was.

In trying to figure out where I fit after high school, I rejected the cultural nationalist line that denied Chicanos our racial connection to blackness. But I struggled with whether the solution was the polyglot mixture that Steve and I had fantasized about as boys. A new politics based on cultural affinity felt right to me; but whereas Chicano nationalism would have separated me from my best friends, the pan-ethnic, nonracial category of Hispanic would separate me from my own Mexican culture. I could observe it, even celebrate it, from a distance, but no longer would it be who I was. Yet cultures are not so easily eliminated. Even as Mexican culture was minimized, it was simultaneously romanticized.

Chicano nationalism as a liberatory moment exists for me now only in reveries of a specific period in the past. In its place, we who are neither black nor white are now seduced with a simple two-part offer. In the first step, we can trade in our Mexican culture and our sense of local connection with black people and Indians. In exchange, we get a chance to share a language and a national identity with others across the country who have also grasped the name Hispanic. Then, if we agree to become Hispanic, as a second step we are promised a chance to trade up. We are offered the possibility of joining a new paradoxical category: Hispanic whiteness.

I could not be both Mexican and white when I was in high school, even though I dated white girls. Now that I am an adult, being Hispanic and white is apparently no problem. Despite my dark Indian features, as a Hispanic I am promised the possibility of joining a new nonracialized category: whiteness of a different color.[10]

This offer suggests the erasure that Steve and I daydreamed about. It was an erasure that I enacted in romantic liaisons. But I now see that maximizing my romantic options does not transform the borderland where I have always lived. This borderland is a wonderfully rich and complex psychological and social space. The offer to erase it produces more anxiety than relief. It is a relief to experience free and easy wandering. The anxiety arises because that freedom says there is no space between white and black. I must choose to be "either" black or white.

Steve and I shared a fantasy that gave us a different freedom and a larger power—not just the power to choose mates but the power to make everyone else look like us as well. Our vanity reflected our adolescent narcissism, but it also surfaced a profound insight—that in order to create a potential force for far-reaching social change, we would have to find a way to give greater voice and choice to those on the bottom of the racial hierarchy. Indeed, fundamental change required that eventually we topple the hierarchy itself.

This is a third way. I now realize that this way is not through physical attraction or regulation. It will be through political action that builds from the liberatory energy of culture and community. This alternative approach does not attempt to hide the heavy social lifting that clear black and white categories do. Those categories are political, not just physical. And they call for a political response, not a physical erasure.

This third way navigates the shoals of identity politics and the fantasies of colorblindness. It is a political project that does not ask who you married, or what your daddy was. At its core it does not ask what you call yourself but with whom do you link your fate. It is a fundamentally creative political project that begins from the ground up, starting with race and all its complexity, and then builds cross-racial relationships through race and with race to issues of class and gender in order to make democracy real. We call this project *political race.*

GERALD TORRES

POLITICAL RACE

1

AND MAGICAL REALISM

Race, for us, is like the miner's canary.[1] Miners often carried a canary into the mine alongside them. The canary's more fragile respiratory system would cause it to collapse from noxious gases long before humans were affected, thus alerting the miners to danger. The canary's distress signaled that it was time to get out of the mine because the air was becoming too poisonous to breathe.

Those who are racially marginalized are like the miner's canary: their distress is the first sign of a danger that threatens us all. It is easy enough to think that when we sacrifice this canary, the only harm is to communities of color. Yet others ignore problems that converge around racial minorities at their own peril, for these problems are symptoms warning us that we are all at risk.

Achieving racial justice and ensuring a healthy democratic process are independently knotty problems; at points where the two problems intersect, they have seemed intractable. Yet we believe progress can be made. Our goal is to explore how racialized identities may be put to service to achieve social change through democratic renewal. We also seek to revive a cross-racial project of social change. Toward these ends, we link the metaphor of the canary with a conceptual project we call *political race*, and in so doing we propose a new, twenty-first-century way of talking about this distinctly American challenge.

The metaphor of the miner's canary captures the association between those who are left out and social justice deficiencies in the larger community. The concept of political race captures the association between those who are raced black—and thus often left out—and a democratic social movement aimed at bringing about constructive change within the larger community. One might say that the canary is diagnostic, signaling the need for more systemic critique. Political race, on the other hand, is not only diagnostic; it is also aspirational and activist, signaling the need to re-build a movement for social change informed by the canary's critique. Po-litical race seeks to construct a new language to discuss race, in order to rebuild a progressive democratic movement led by people of color but joined by others. The political dimension of the political race project seeks to reconnect individual experiences to democratic faith, to social critique, and to meaningful action that improves the lives of the canary and the miners by ameliorating the air quality in the mines.

The miner's canary metaphor helps us understand why and how race continues to be salient. Racialized communities signal problems with the ways we have structured power and privilege. These pathologies are not located in the canary. Indeed, we reject the incrementalist approach that locates complex social and political problems in the individual. Such an approach would solve the problems of the mines by outfitting the canary with a tiny gas mask to withstand the toxic atmosphere.

Political race as a concept encompasses the view that race still matters because racialized communities provide the early warning signs of poison in the social atmosphere. And then it encourages us to do something dif-ferent from what has been done in the past with that understanding. Polit-ical race tells us that we need to change the air in the mines. If you care to look, you can see the canary alerting us to both danger and promise. The project of political race challenges both those on the right who say race is not real as well as those on the left who say it is real but we cannot talk about it. Political race illustrates how the lived experience of race in Amer-ica continues to serve an important function in the construction of indi-vidual selves as well as in the construction of social policy.

Political race is therefore a motivational project. Rebuilding a move-ment for change can happen only if we reclaim our democratic imagina-tion. Because such a project requires faith in the unseen, we find an in-spired comparison in the literary movement known as *magical realism.*

This movement also began as a project to liberate a democratic imagination. We will explore the connections with magical realism shortly, but first we would like to explain the genealogy of the concept of political race.

At its genesis, we referred to this concept as "political blackness." Our effort to develop a terminology arose in reaction to the neoliberal and neoconservative attempts to reduce race to its biological and thus scientifically irrational and morally reprehensible origins—that is, to eliminate race as a meaningful or useful concept. But it was also a reaction to the civil rights advocates' inadequate response, which tended to embrace race as skin color and thus to limit the radical political dynamism of the civil rights movement to persons "of color." In the view of the neoconservatives, race is merely skin color and is thus meaningless and ignorable. In the view of the civil rights advocates, race is skin color plus a legacy of slavery and Jim Crow that is now realized through stigma, discrimination, or prejudice. But to those outside this subtle debate, it often appears that both sides see race primarily as being about skin color. They differ simply on whether such a definition of race is meaningless and thus should be abandoned or is meaningful and thus should be at least temporarily acknowledged. The word "political" in the term political blackness was an attempt to dislodge race from this color-of-one's-skin terminology and to extend its social meaning from a moral calculus that assesses blame as a precondition for action to a political framework that cultivates and inspires action directly. It was also an attempt to dislodge race from simple identity politics; it was a reaction to the cultural or race nationalists for whom one's personal identity constitutes one's political project.

We sought a phrase that would name the association between race and power that is lost in the current debate. But in responding to inquiries about the meaning of political blackness, we found ourselves bombarded by boundary questions: Who is inside and who is outside the category? For example, one graduate student persisted in seeing political blackness as a membership category. "Is a black woman lesbian middle manager inside the political blackness idea?" she asked. We responded that the term covers three elements: it has a diagnostic function; it embraces an aspirational goal; and it hopes to jumpstart an activist project. We then insisted that it was up to each person to determine whether she was part of this project. Action and commitment, not predetermined descriptors, would be the guide. We were not gatekeepers.

Meanwhile, we also discovered that many black Americans were offended by the substitution of "political blackness" for "race" because, by opening up the category "black" to anyone who wished to enter, this semantic move discounted the material reality black Americans faced every day and misappropriated the cultural community they experienced. In our view, these were all substantial reasons to find another term. Thus we substituted the term *political race project*. This terminology is also subject to ambiguity, but it seemed to minimize these specific confusions and liabilities. And while we moved to the more inclusive nomenclature of political race, blackness—and the experience of black people—is nevertheless at the heart of our argument.

Political Race as a Diagnostic Tool

To the extent that individuals have common experiences of marginalization, those experiences often function as a diagnostic device to identify and interrogate systemwide structures of power and inequality. When these experiences converge around a visible group, they can raise our awareness about that collective phenomenon. This consciousness, when it helps us identify structural inequalities, becomes a potential catalyst for changing those structures. This claim was made in 1967 by Dr. Martin Luther King, Jr., in *Where Do We Go from Here: Chaos or Community?* "Negroes have illuminated imperfections in the democratic structure that were formerly only dimly perceived, and have forced a concerned reexamination of the true meaning of American democracy. As a consequence of the vigorous Negro protest, the whole nation has for a decade probed more searchingly the essential nature of democracy, both economic and political."[2]

We use the term "political" to mean collective interaction at the individual, group, and institutional level. In order to understand the multiple levels at which race and power intersect, it is necessary to move from the primacy of individual status to a focus on group interactions and their relationship to power. We do not, however, mean either exclusively or primarily those activities associated with electoral politics. Nor do we mean up/down voting in the legislature or the control of state apparatus more generally.

The political race project is an effort to change the framework of the conversation about race by naming relationships to power within the context of our racial and political history. This approach reveals race as a political, not just a social, construction. It does not suggest special access to an essential reality; neither does it describe a state of nature; nor is it motivated primarily by some conception of enlightened self-interest. Instead, it offers a method of analysis to signal systemic failure and to catalyze institutional innovation.

In saying that race is linked to power, we suggest that it is linked to more than the way an individual experiences power. We mean that the distribution of resources in this society is racialized and that this racial hierarchy is then normalized and thereby made invisible. Race can be about putting people into powerless positions, but it is also about putting people into powerless positions which they accept as unchanging even though they recognize the injustice. A response to these processes of racializing power and then normalizing that racial hierarchy is inherently political.

We are concerned with the public and political meanings of race in this country. By public meaning we refer to the ways in which race is tied to many socioeconomic factors such as life expectancy, health, accumulated wealth, likelihood of completing a number of years of education or likelihood instead of spending a significant amount of time incarcerated, and so on. We describe these objective manifestations of race in Chapter 2. Readers who are more interested in the practice of political race may want to skip ahead to Chapter 3. There we explore how political race affirms the value of the group to see and to name these barriers to mobility, hierarchies of privilege, or other defects in the way that power organizes social and political relationships. We show political race in action in Texas, where black and brown colleagues used their common experiences as a tool for critiquing structures of power.

Similarly, political race affirms the value of the individual's choosing to affiliate with the named group as a way of making sense of—or even reframing—the condition in question and then organizing both within and without the group to do something about it. Unlike identity politics, political race is not about being but instead is about doing. Political race configures race and politics as an action or set of actions rather than a thing.

People in our society are *raced*. In this sense political race takes on the attributes of a verb, not just a noun. People are raced multiple times and in multiple ways, often asymmetrically. Political race, as a diagnostic tool, seeks to get at the way people are placed—and place themselves—in powerful or powerless positions depending on both the historical context and their given relationships at a personal, group, and institutional level. Race, in other words, is an ideological position one holds as well as a social position one occupies.

For example, *The New York Times* reported the story—no longer atypical—of Michael Gelobter, who, despite his mixed-race family, marked the category "Black" on his U.S. Census form. In 2000, the census for the first time invited respondents to check all races that describe them by marking one or more of fourteen boxes, representing six races or categories. The six categories offer 63 possible combinations of racial identity. Yet many who could legitimately check a number of boxes opted, like Gelobter, simply to call themselves black. Gelobter says that by checking black, he is preserving the efficacy of blacks as a political group. He and many others see black as a political and not just a personal referent.[3]

There are, of course, private or individual meanings to race, as the movement toward multiracial classification exemplifies, but those dimensions are not what we use the concept of political race to explicate. Those private meanings are certainly real, but they are not the focus of political race except insofar as they are a component of political identity. Political race is not a theory of racial group membership, skin color, or other individual attributes traditionally associated with race. Instead, political race identifies a specific form of public meaning that is tied to the distribution of social goods and is thus intrinsically political. Race both reinforces hierarchies of power and, simultaneously, camouflages those hierarchies.

Political Race as an Aspirational Project

To merely critique the status quo is not by itself political or transformative. The miner's canary metaphor alone is not the full expression of the political race project. Race becomes political when those who have been raced black in this society not only experience their identity in the form of what Michael Dawson calls "linked fate" but then act accordingly.[4] They see that their fate is linked to others who are like them. They see that what happens to one happens to many others, if not to most others, who are similarly situated. Race becomes political in the sense of generating collective action only when it motivates people to connect their individual experiences to the experiences of others and then to act collectively in response to those experiences.

By focusing on the relationship between race and power, we use political race to suggest the circumstances through which people, without regard to their skin color, can join together to transform that relationship. Political race posits that those who have been raced as "losers" or marginalized will often be among the first to see the pernicious effects of normalized inequality. Its premise is that those who have been so raced will also be more motivated to understand those patterns of access to social power. As a result, those who have been marginalized or left out could be well-positioned to lead a movement for social justice that others will want to follow if they can frame that movement to speak to conditions of injustice that disfigure our social institutions more generally. It is at this point that political race shifts from description to prescription, from what we see to what we would like to see.

This aspirational and motivational project—the subject of Chapters 4, 5, and 6—focuses on political action rather than on legal reform. It emphasizes bottom-up movements rather than top-down technocratic policy solutions. We are not opposed to law reform, nor do we dismiss all public policy agendas or bureaucratic reform movements as optimistic or naive, although we do worry about their often unintended consequences.[5] Our concern is that law reform and technical fixes have claimed too much of our attention. Our goal is to restore some balance to the dynamic relationship between insider strategies that depend on elites manipulating zero-sum (I-win/you-lose) power and outsider strategies that emphasize the role for grassroots organizations to experiment with alternative forms of resistance leading to greater access and accountability.

To move toward the goal of rebuilding a social movement, we borrow from the French philosopher Michel Foucault the idea that identity is both a target of power and a vehicle for resistance. We explore a post-postmodern idea of power that highlights human agency within relationships that narrate rather than simply observe change. By narrate we mean an active process of creating a story that is both explanatory and motivational, as opposed to merely descriptive. This concept of power is explicitly relational, but it is not confined to relationships of domination or coercion. It is independent of zero-sum outcomes, although it may coexist with a structural analysis that points out the ways in which human beings are often constrained by forces beyond their control. It emphasizes an element of power that is potentially generative, that can be exercised by those who create it within groups. It enables those who resist zero-sum outcomes to initiate new forms of interaction. To those who say that all power eventually becomes determinative of those individuals who create it, we respond that here the power being exercised is generative of new forms of creativity.

Not all members of a racial minority, as defined in census terms, admissions applications, or other arbitrary categories, are willing or able to generate such power. We recognize the many intragroup problems that disable mobilization and collective resistance—issues such as color hierarchy, class divisions, self-hatred, and internalized racism. We explore some of those issues in the chapters that follow.

An individual in isolation cannot constitute or define the meaning of a political space. Only when individuals freely join together to resist and transform the forces of conventional power which named them as part of a group in the first place can the possibilities emerge for generating new forms of collective and democratic struggle. Those intermediate spaces defined by this reconceptualization of post-postmodern power offer the opportunity for individuals to share their stories and construct relationships that reinforce a more systemic and critical social understanding.

The effort to expand our readings of race and power beyond strictly win/lose outcomes is not explanatory as much as it is motivational. It describes, from the inside out, what it feels like to experience the joy of human solidarity when mobilized to generate new and unexpected outcomes. Thus, political race builds from inside the lived experience of a marginalized community and uses that experience as an imperfect but valuable lens through which to view and possibly enhance an individual's political status. The lens on that experience can be stretched and even re-shaped when human beings join together to engage in diagnosing and organizing through the multi-step process that we imagine. When and if it is acknowledged, groups may move from this vantage point to join with others in free spaces of participatory democracy that resist authority and challenge the status quo.

As we illustrate in Chapters 5 and 6, these free spaces are usually outside the formal public sphere of legislative decision-making; they are also not the same as the public sphere of communitarian literature. They are instead intermediate or in-between places in which a marginalized group can share their experiences without interference from the dominant group.[6] The interstices are practice fields or training sessions for an eventual engagement with various hierarchical sources of power. They are laboratories as well as launching pads.

The black church served just such a function during the civil rights movement of the 1950s and 60s. Septima Clark's citizenship schools in Alabama, where blacks learned how to read and write in order to pass literacy tests for voting, were important sites for building community. Clark's work provided the foot soldiers of the civil rights movement, who could now not only read and write and pass literacy tests but march forward with a newly empowered sense of their own capacity. Clark's participatory approach helped others develop a vision of the possible and a resistance to the present. By using literacy to cultivate this resistance, Clark's citizenship schools demonstrate the value of power-sharing and offer a potential antidote to the internalized racism that often plagues the black community. Within these free spaces, networks of relationships are built, cultural rituals are developed, shared meanings are facilitated, and strategies are rehearsed, thus making social movements possible.[7] This is a potentially transformative experience for individuals as well as society.

Political race does not require or assume a biological understanding of race to define collective action. But it recognizes that the impetus for seeing patterns of injustice usually comes from the group that has the greatest connection to this experience. It may be that those who are thrust together by their experience of being raced will act first and lead. Indeed, it is probably critical for people of color to lead this movement. But it is equally critical that they find allies if a movement for social justice, and not just for racial justice, is to succeed. In this way, political race is similar to feminism; it may be more likely that women consider themselves feminists and lead the struggle for gender equality, but there is nothing about the term feminism that excludes men from also claiming the form of analysis and critique it embraces. Political race has the potential to be an even more transformative force than conventional feminism, however, because it seeks to use the experiences of people of color as the basis for fundamental social change that will benefit not only blacks and Hispanics but other disadvantaged social groups.

Political race suggests that patterns which converge around race are often markers of systematic injustice that affect whites as well, and thus disclose how institutions need to be transformed more generally. Our premise is that current institutional arrangements do not work for people of color, and that it is not possible to address the present racial hierarchy without addressing these institutional arrangements. By attending to this larger critique, one gains the critical insight and motivation necessary to change institutions to benefit others. Thus, a politically raced perspective would look at the ways that race camouflages unfair resource distribution among whites as well as blacks.

That whites would immediately see themselves as disenfranchised in ways that are similar to those who are raced black is unlikely. Certainly, as presently constructed, race offers poor whites an excuse *not* to mobilize to fight the larger injustices in this society. Yet, we are envisioning a "fantastic" shift in the social psychological orientation of progressive movements in the United States. We suggest that some people who are raced white in this country might eventually join with others in a social movement led by people of color.

If whites join the political race project under the leadership of people of color, they would not become "black" in the conventional sense of the term. To be part of the project of political race, it is neither necessary nor sufficient to take on black cultural styles or aspire to identify with blacks and other people of color. Culture does not do the work of politics.

Rather, whites would become invested in addressing race as part of their own social justice agenda. They would begin to understand that those who are raced black have much to teach about the distribution of social resources in this society. They would see how the construction of race shaped their own access to those resources, or perhaps constrained it. They would start to critique systems of power, rather than seeking just to exercise more power themselves. They would become part of a group of people who identify race or its impact as constructed by power in ways that are integral to their own aspirations for social change. As a result, they would realize, perhaps for the first time, how conventional zero-sum hierarchies trap even the most privileged among them in units of autonomous individuality. This entrapment precludes the formation of an organic community capable of resisting injustice and mobilizing around a collective and transformative response.

We can imagine at least three reasons why others who are not raced black may choose to participate in this project. First, race is becoming less rigidly constructed by pseudo-scientific certainty. The "one-drop rule,"[8] which traditionally dictated that anyone with one drop of black blood was necessarily black, has been officially discarded by the Census Bureau, which gives individuals many options for racial and indeed multiracial self-identification. The softening of census designations also means that the choice to associate with people of color becomes just that, a political rather than a false biological choice.

The second reason to believe that people who are not black will join the political race project is that it does not valorize each participant as a symbol of the group. No individual alone stands in for the group or speaks for the group. Thus, individuals who do not share characteristics traditionally associated with biological race may, through their conscious association and participation, identify as members or allies. In our usage, the project defined as political race has an evolving collective reality which, although influenced by its individual parts, is greater than their sum.

Third, political race permits the individual not only choice but also voice. Individuals benefit when they transform the ways in which the group responds to perceived injustices. They also benefit from association with others who reinforce a positive sense of self, connect them to larger issues by providing sources of pride rather than shame, and enhance their sense of belonging and optimism about the future. These benefits are not unique to political race; they occur in any form of good group deliberation.

The dynamic of the political race project grows out of education and participation, as happened in Septima Clark's citizenship schools. Through internal deliberation and self-conscious reflection, individuals can work together to develop a framework within which to critique existing power structures. Political race is thus a richly complex project organized around both race *and* democratic politics. And those who identify with the project of political race are challenged to move from a politics based primarily on a narrow definition of group or individual self-interest to action in service of a transformative vision of social justice.

The Magical Realism of Political Race

We have been urged to compare the political race project to a religious conversion. That comparison is intriguing because it suggests that more is required than merely an intellectual commitment or choice. Political race, like religious experience, may start with a personal insight, but it is reinforced only through community. The experience may start with race, but it does not end with race. The comparison to religion is intriguing also because it recognizes the importance to our project of faith. We are democratic idealists who imagine a new social movement that seems well beyond our present reach. We are deploying the concept of political race to identify what appears utopian and utterly implausible.

But while religious experience may touch recesses of the spirit that political race can never reach, it does not, for us, capture nuances of political race that are critical to the project. To help narrate the use and meaning of race that concerns us, and especially to capture the link between race, power, and democratic representation, we are drawn instead to secular literature, especially magical realism. Magical realists infuse ordinary situations with an enchanted quality that distorts both physical and temporal reality. This allows the narrative to take paths that would ordinarily fall outside the range of acceptable accounts. In Freudian fashion, magical realists explore the realm of myths, fantasies, and dreams. But unlike Freud, for whom the importance of dreams resided in their distinction from waking reality, magical realists dissolve that boundary and narrate fantasies, myths, and quotidian life in the same frame. The reader sees previously familiar things in a completely new context. The change in context is critical, for it provides the foundation for radically different meanings. Though the new reality may astonish and disorient readers, the characters in the story react to it with curiosity and faith rather than with confusion, uncertainty, fear, or disbelief. This discrepancy between the reader's and the character's reaction is key. The reader enters a reality that is fantastic yet remains empirically grounded through the actions and reactions of the characters.

Although magical realism's roots can be traced back to early twentieth-century Europe, it is most closely associated with Latin American authors, notably Gabriel Garcia Marquez. Magical realism challenges social realism and other traditional Western representations of what is real and what is not. Dream life, fantasy, and indigenous mythology intrude into and illuminate daily life in order to engage the complications and confusions of political reality in contemporary Latin America. By liberating the imagination, magical realists give voice to the possibilities of futures that are not held hostage to either the military juntas in power or the juntas' neoliberal defenders.

The juxtaposition of plausible and implausible events stretches and invigorates the reader's conception of reality. The narrative technique evokes qualities of metaphor and parable, but it goes beyond simply attributing something mystical or elusive to the concrete or familiar. The movement from the plausible to the fantastic disrupts and surprises the reader against all expectations. This constant imbalance then makes possible a willingness to question, reframe, and experiment.

In *Beloved,* Tony Morrison recognizes that realism alone cannot convey the experience of an African-American runaway slave who chooses to slay her baby daughter rather than return her to slavery.[9] By destabilizing the physical and temporal world of the novel, Morrison carves a free space for her readers to reconceptualize their assumptions about maternity, morality, and history. The reintroduction of the slain child into the story first as a ghost, then as Beloved, a physical being simultaneously the specific dead daughter and every child abandoned by the slave trade, forces the reader to question her original reaction to the infanticide. Reinvigorated by the possibility of redeeming herself to her dead child, Sethe allows herself to confront the horror of slavery and her decision to kill her Beloved. Morrison reframes the novel's question in Sethe's practiced justification of her action to Beloved: "I'll explain it to her, even though I don't have to. Why I did it."[10] What initially looks to the reader like unconscionable slaughter now looks like an action that has saved a life. Morrison's experimentation with the definitions of life, death, and killing destabilizes the reader's real-world assumptions. The impact of slavery becomes more powerful when what seemed clearly wrong—the ultimate maternal betrayal—now seems its opposite.

Morrison uses magical realism to imagine America's racial past. We will use similar techniques in some of the chapters that follow to imagine our racial future. We hope to destabilize assumptions about race relations to allow a questioning of current boundaries and a reconceptualization of political strategies. The idea of building a progressive democratic movement led by people of color but joined by others may also require a certain suspension of disbelief. We find the comparison to magical realism applicable on two registers.

First, it is applicable to us as authors. Some will say that political race is a ridiculously optimistic exercise of our imagination. But in magical realism we see a provocative comparison that connects us to others who share the faith that change is possible. The stories of resistance that we retell in this book help us put race and power into a different narrative frame. Most important, they reveal points of resistance that might be obscured with a conventional reading.

Second, magical realism is relevant to the application of political race in practice. Political race suggests that those who are raced white in traditional terms will join with people of color and by that act disrupt common assumptions about movements for social change. It is that move across conventional racial boundaries that creates a full flowering of new possibilities. Thus, magical realism has traction both as an idea and as an application.

Although we are not magical realists ourselves, we believe the technique to be powerfully illuminating. It took incredible will, but also belief and imagination, to challenge the racial status quo that defined reality in the United States prior to the civil rights movement. The shade trees and beauty shops where Septima Clark set up her schools became the chapels and charmed circles of democracy. In the same spirit, we use the miner's canary metaphor to show blackness freed from the framework of individual moral culpability or the pseudo-scientific straightjacket that has constrained both the social and legal meaning of being raced in America. Through magical realism, we imagine future strategies for a progressive movement that would not be held hostage to conventional understandings of what is happening now in the mines. Certain promising political dynamics may be invisible to most of us at the moment because the categories we have for naming them make them invisible. Step outside the categories and suddenly there are new things to see. This claim appears magical only because so many of us have been imprisoned by what Professor Kendall Thomas terms the rigid moral grammar of legal analysis; but like magical realism, political race has its roots grounded in empirical reality.[11]

Political race, in other words, involves several dramatic dislocations in conventional wisdom. The first will occur when white progressives recognize a more complex notion of racial consciousness that exists outside of, yet is connected to, conventional class analysis. They will come to understand that energy for social change is often created when blacks and other racial minorities are encouraged to organize as a group without merely retreating into an exclusionary racial consciousness. The second disruption involves moving away from the anti-discrimination model that has dominated the discourse of civil rights. This discourse, in fact, sometimes inhibits the development of a broader coalition to challenge the status quo. Such a change might require black leadership and the leadership of other marginalized communities of color to articulate the consciousness of a racialized identity in broader terms than the current remedial strategies of the civil rights paradigm.

Political Race in Practice

When Niko—Lani Guinier's son—turned thirteen, he was brown, thin, and well-proportioned for his age, though he still had the doe-eyes and ready smile of a youthful boy. To get home from middle school, he had to walk half a mile from the subway stop through a racially mixed and so-cioeconomically diverse section of Cambridge, Massachusetts. He was usually stooped over from the weight of a backpack heavy with books. Walking down Pearl—a well-traveled but narrow one-way street—he no-ticed that sometimes white people crossed to the other side as he ap-proached. He watched them cross the street, apprehensive as he drew near, and he was not sure what to do, if anything.

A colorblind approach to this situation might have offered Niko some solace. A colorblind solution might have trained the white people who crossed the street not to notice Niko's brown skin color. They should not have noticed that he is raced black in this society or that, by his clothes and style, he is gendered male. They should not have noticed that his baggy jeans and loose-fitting shirt—the uniform of his generation of teenage boys—give no clue to his middle-class status. Instead, they should have disciplined themselves to walk on the same sidewalk with this black boy. They should have treated Niko the same way they would have treated a thirteen-year-old white girl walking home from school.

Meanwhile, what should Niko's parents have said to him as they waited for these white people to train themselves to ignore his skin color? Should they have said: We know this is a humiliating experience for you, and so we'll pick you up from school to avoid the situation. We know that wait-ing for white people not to be afraid of you may take your entire lifetime. We know that these are well-intentioned people who choose to live in a racially mixed neighborhood, but they are also watching television, where most portrayals of crime are gendered male and raced black. They proba-bly believe racial profiling by police is wrong, but they cross the street themselves, nevertheless.

Or should Niko's parents have said: Don't worry about ignorant white strangers on a busy street. Instead, associate only with white people who already know you. Walk home from school only with other white friends so you are not targeted. Make your race a different shade of whiteness. Or should they instead have focused on ways to make Niko's middle-class sta-tus more visible? Should they have said: Dress in a suit when you go to school or wear clothes that are ironed and fit properly to show you are not threatening? Or perhaps they should have said: We will bring a lawsuit against the people who refuse to share the public street with you. We will affirm your pride even if we lose the case.

None of these options satisfies the theorist or the parent. Political race would follow another course. It would see the issue not as a function of Niko's individual skin color or the particular way he dressed and walked down the street. Nor would political race support the argument that the solution is better law enforcement, since criminal law enforcement is part of the problem here. Instead, proceeding from the perspective of political race might have helped Niko to learn from this experience, rather than run from it. Of these potential lessons, one of the most important is the lesson of solidarity that he was beginning to experience with other black boys, regardless of their economic status. From that lesson, he would realize that the problem is not about him, but he would continue to notice the pattern, so he could understand better what it says about the association of race, gender, and crime in this society. And then he would reach out to others who also notice that pattern to try to do something about the way the criminal justice system has been misused to racialize both crime and poverty.

These multiple steps would represent the development of a mature oppositional consciousness that is different from adolescent rebellion, individual resistance, or collective anger. Many American blacks, those whom the sociologist Mary Waters calls "involuntary minorities," have an oppositional orientation.[12] They take the perspective that the rules of the game governing both social relations and access to social goods are stacked against them and are deeply ingrained. Don Terry, a reporter for *The New York Times* and the child of a black father and a white mother, writes about the moment, as a college student at Oberlin, in which he developed an oppositional consciousness. He signed up for a course on black nationalism, and the decision turned out to be one of the most important developments of his life. "Black studies saved me," Terry claims. It gave him a "sense of discovery both academically and personally."[13] Terry had been raised as mixed but chose blackness as a shield and a cause. It helped him understand the world around him, especially his anger, which he later discovered he shared with his absent black father.

When the explanatory power of a collective consciousness joins with its cathartic and empowering sensibility, people like Don Terry voluntarily identify with others whom they see as similarly oppressed or marginalized. Those who develop a sense of collective identity see that what they are experiencing is reflected in the conditions of the group of which they are a part. They are able to see that as a group they are dominated and exploited; they reject the legitimacy of their subordinate position, which they are able to understand as a function of a system created by others; and they come to believe that collective action is their best form of resistance.

In *Beloved,* Morrison narrates the development of an oppositional consciousness in a community of ex-slaves in rural Ohio. When the reappearance of Beloved subverts the slave-owning reality, the black community comes together to save Sethe from the grip of her all-consuming memory of slavery. The ex-slaves in the novel struggle to understand the structure of the oppressive slave culture that extended beyond emancipation. They recognize the scars left from slavery. Morrison's characters succeed in a project that resembles political race when they are freed from the limits of a reality prescribed by the slave-owning culture. And just as the fantastic helps Morrison's characters save themselves, the technique of magical realism enables Morrison's readers to consider the actions of her characters freed from the assumptions of the culture that surrounds them and thus to imagine a reality undeformed by the history of slavery.

The magical-realist potential within a mature oppositional consciousness is not limited to people of color. In an intriguing study, Sharon Groch identifies the Deaf community as having a strong oppositional consciousness, attributable in part to the fact that many of the Deaf live a more physically segregated life that allows them to create a shared meaning of their situation through images, slogans, literature, humor, rituals, and other cultural expressions. Because deaf and blind people are often placed in residential schools at a young age, their interactions create a "sense of collective identity, an injustice frame, and a belief in the power of collective action." But the Deaf perpetuate that oppositional consciousness more deliberately and develop it further through participation in various collective struggles. These include what some have called the Selma of the

Deaf: when Gallaudet University students forced the newly appointed hearing president to resign and replaced her with a Deaf president—the first in the history of this leading university for Deaf students. Many in the Deaf community consider themselves a linguistic minority that is not disabled; many Deaf people say they do not wish they could hear. Groch suggests that the Deaf are therefore more like blacks than are other oppressed but physically integrated groups like white women, because the Deaf have developed a stable oppositional culture.[14]

An oppositional orientation is not without its difficulties. Sometimes it leads to despair, alienation, and dysfunction. It may be confused with excuses for unpleasant circumstances that pacify rather than mobilize. It can be dismissed as adolescent rebellion rather than accepted as a mature political engagement that would take the data of lived life as more significant than ideological explanations of it. But it is also the case that, in particular contexts, an oppositional consciousness can motivate people to participate in movements for social change. It can unleash individual creativity and arouse people to challenge what they come to see as systemic unfairness. It can create and reinforce social and political bonds, a sense of linked fate.

In other words, a political race project, infused with a magical-realist spirit and an oppositional consciousness, would help Niko name what was happening to him and then help him begin to act politically to change that experience. He could begin to describe what it feels like to be raced black in his own mind and in the minds of the people who cross the street. A response to the experience of being raced black would be to see himself as an advocate for change rather than as a helpless victim of the status quo. And he would be encouraged to see his experience as a warning to others. To act on that insight necessarily involves working within groups to challenge the hierarchies of power that reinforce and create the experience of marginalization in the first place.

This kind of racial literacy would, however, reach beyond the initial descriptive step of an oppositional consciousness to identify patterns of injustice that link race to class, to gender, and to other forms of power. Niko's experience has wider implications than the social conditions of thirteen-year-old urban black boys. His experience can serve an important diagnostic function for assessing the health of both our public institutions and the quality of our public responses to the conditions identified by racialized groups. Guided by a more inclusive vision of both democracy and justice, the political race project seeks to mobilize people initially around a frame of racial inequity and then move them beyond their starting point. By reframing their initial insights, the protests lodged first by people of color become catalysts for a larger, cross-racial coalition dedicated to changing zero-sum hierarchies of power.

As we detail in Chapter 8, experiences with structural racism can become a potent force for exposing structures of power and inequality that implicate issues of gender and class as well. This involves noticing the link between race and gender and between race and class and showing how poor white men are also victimized by a criminal justice system that tracks young black boys from kindergarten to prison rather than to college. Those whites who cross the street are not afraid of Niko but of the position his race, gender, and age occupy in a system that uses criminal law enforcement as our major instrument of social control. Yet even middle-class whites are forced to pay as education budgets shrink and prison budgets expand to accommodate this ill-informed public policy. Thus, Niko's political race project would start with race but then use race as a lens to understand better the signifying role of young, black boys. It would move from race to class to assumptions about masculinity, but it would never lose sight of race.

At age thirteen, Niko had not yet participated in this kind of organized collective action. Yet, the experience of sharing his story with other students of color would be a start because it would transform his and their understanding of their own experience. In that sense, political race as an aspirational and motivational project is not simply about changing society. It is also personal in the sense that it changes the stakes for connecting with others around an understanding of the world that race has revealed. And it is interpersonal in that it seeks to create and sustain democratic relationships in the service of social change.

For these reasons, we argue for a more populist response to hierarchies of power, but we identify the initial leadership for this social justice agenda within communities of color. Unlike other populist coalitions that have been organized first within white working-class communities and then were splintered by racism, or women's groups that focused initially on the concerns of middle-class white women, we advocate a coalition that explicitly starts first with race and then moves to class and gender while never losing sight of race. For a progressive cross-racial coalition to emerge, whites need to engage with race, and blacks need to engage with a more inclusive vision of social justice. Both types of engagement require a different understanding of the meaning of race and its relationships to power.

This new racial literacy should be flexible enough to apply to different contexts without forcing everyone's experiences into a single explanatory narrative. In Chapter 7 we explain how, for example, the political and legal category "Hispanic" was originally constructed by elites to unify the major ethnic and linguistic groups that count Spain as their European referent. The Hispanic category may have created a name more than an identity; yet, having a common name encouraged people to rethink their political allegiances across local and national dimensions. Thus, the term Hispanic functions as a powerful racial grouping within the taxonomy of American law and politics. We are not arguing that the experience of Hispanics mirrors the experience of African Americans. We are not trying to instantiate race as one fixed thing. What we do argue is that racial self-awareness and solidarity, for both Hispanics and African Americans, can to varying degrees be both a diagnostic tool and a mobilizer.

This is our realist critique. Although we are committed to what we call social justice, we are not saying that we know what social justice looks like in every case or for every historical period. We do know that it does *not* resemble the racially coded distribution patterns that mark our current social institutions.

In the end, we are not proposing a full-blown theory of social movements. We offer less an explanation than an imaginative accounting. We use the metaphor of the miner's canary and the project of political race, enhanced through the insights of magical realism, to explore a social psychology of one version of a progressive political movement. In our own concededly optimistic view, this just might work in the twenty-first century.

A CRITIQUE

2

OF COLORBLINDNESS

In a 1995 article in *Dissent*, the political scientist David Plotke made an argument for masking race in political discussion.[1] In his view, a frank engagement with race would only heighten social divisions, making progressive alliances harder to achieve. Moreover, racial politics had descended into a corrosive kind of identity politics, often with no empirical referent.

As evidence for this position, Plotke presented an experiment he conducted with graduate students in Hungary. He showed the students a picture of Lani Guinier and asked them to guess her ethnicity. They concluded that she might be North African but was probably Italian. This experiment demonstrated, for Plotke, the coercive power of American racial categories. The students failed to authenticate Guinier's black American identity. They were viewing her from a perspective that started with ethnicity, not race. In Hungary, physical characteristics marked a national identity, but not necessarily race. Only in America, Plotke noted, would Guinier, whose father was a first-generation Jamaican black and mother a second-generation Jewish immigrant, be considered black. Plotke concluded that the rigidity of racial categories in the United States, where Guinier self-identifies as black, means that progressive coalitions can form only if people practice racial deceit or racial denial in the form of colorblindness.[2]

On a sunny late-spring day in Philadelphia, not too long after Plotke published his findings, Guinier was crossing a parking lot to retrieve her car. From across the lot at a distance of about 200 feet, the attendant, a dark-skinned black man, yelled out, "Aren't you the one that was supposed to be in Clinton's cabinet?" She smiled at the recognition even though he had the job title wrong. When Guinier nodded yes, the attendant got very excited and continued the exchange, pumping both his arms in the air for emphasis. "I know why you didn't get that job," he announced. "You were *too black!* You were just *too black!*"

What explains this paradox? How is it possible for a person to be both not black and too black? Is race a switch that was "off" in Hungary and "on" in Philadelphia? In crafting a response to the *Dissent* article, Guinier realized that potential progressive allies like Plotke were laboring with limited conceptions of the role that race can and does play in American politics. Plotke wanted to see race as an objective category, based on physical characteristics alone, whereas the parking lot attendant apparently understood blackness as an internal signifier of something else, such as identification by one group member of another.

How would Plotke's Hungarian graduate students have explained the greeting from the parking lot attendant? They might say the man was confused or, worse, was so fixated on race that he could turn anyone into a black person. Perhaps they would say that the parking lot attendant was merely a black nationalist who was eager to include Guinier as a member of his racial group while carefully patrolling its boundaries. Alternatively, the parking lot attendant may have been condemning Guinier, suggesting that if she had not been preoccupied with race she would be in government today.

Whatever the interpretation, Plotke's experiment with his graduate students reflects the classic effort to limit the meaning of race to superficial physical characteristics. The parking lot attendant, in our view, was using racial markers in a different way. He was framing a political moment through his identification with Guinier's experience in Washington. In our view, the parking attendant's comment went to what Guinier stood for—her politics—rather than what she looked like.

The Genealogy of Our Project

This book project began in discussions of what we might learn from the intriguing juxtaposition of graduate students in Hungary and the parking attendant in Philadelphia. We were particularly interested in the way white progressives seemed to be reading race. We wanted to help them recognize the reality of race while challenging the idea that race is a fixed category. We also wanted to show that the boundaries of historically fixed racial categories can be fundamentally refashioned without discarding race. We sought to articulate, from our own experience, the ways that race has multiple meanings, including positive ones that make race an asset, not just a disability.

Let us be clear: we are not saying there are no problems associated with race and racism.[3] We are asking a different question: How do we harness what is constructive about race? Race is a social and political construct that has been used for both good and evil. How do we separate what is evil about the uses of race from its unappreciated creative and critical power?[4]

Finally, with this project we want to move critical race theory forward. CRT is an outgrowth of the critical legal studies (CLS) movement, a group of leftist activists and scholars who sought to expose the deeply imbricated relationship between law and the routine practices of social life. Critical race theorists concerned themselves with the marginality of racial analysis within judicial opinions and legal doctrine. This group of legal scholars largely came of age after the civil rights movement. Appreciating the gains that the demise of Jim Crow occasioned, they experienced a growing sense that the structure of conventional doctrinal analysis could not come to grips with the continuing problems of deeply embedded racism.[5] We acknowledge our roots in CRT and seek to build on two major contributions of that movement: its distinctive and complex racial perspective and its methodology of storytelling, which suggests in its concreteness the pragmatic roots of CRT's inquiries.

Before the advent of CLS and CRT, most critics of racial injustice spoke as though the idea of race was unambiguous. This was not without good reason. From the late 1940s until the middle 1960s much of the civil rights and equal protection jurisprudence operated as though there were a fixed meaning to the word race. Race meant black or Negro.[6] Blacks or Negroes were disadvantaged because of their race. Race was a biological category and thus a simple legal category. If you had a black ancestor, you were black too and were therefore subject to all of the legal disabilities that attended that designation.[7] The law determining race was formally neutral. For the leading constitutional lawyers of the time, the moral implications of such a classification were subsumed within a simple logical exercise.[8] The challenge for the law was to treat people of different races the same, and thus treat them fairly. Thus, defenders of the anti-miscegenation statute in *Loving v Virginia* could argue that the law was constitutional because it prohibited whites from marrying blacks in the same way that it prohibited blacks from marrying whites.[9] CRT's first major contribution was to destabilize this fixed idea of race within legal discourse and to link ideas about race to ideas about the way power constructs relationships.[10]

The second important contribution of critical race theory was its methodological commitment to what Jerome Bruner has called a "narrative construal of reality."[11] The narrative effort of CRT is to destabilize doctrine so that law may be engaged as a tool of progressive change. In telling stories, CRT was making the point that context is essential for understanding both doctrine and theory. This narrative effort was premised on the need to challenge the conventional constructions of meaning in legal discourse. It is a way of getting at competing normative standards and exposing the limitations in existing legal doctrine and theory, both of which depend heavily on stock stories.[12]

Stock stories are those ways of explaining and interpreting the world that embody received understandings and meanings.[13] For example, the stock story of colorblindness is that the only motive of the civil rights movement was to free individual black people from state-sponsored discrimination. This depiction of the civil rights movement put assimilation (an option primarily available to middle- and upper-class blacks) as the engine that drove the civil rights movement. After formal, state-sanctioned barriers to individual mobility are removed, any continuing inequality must result from the personal failure of individuals or, in its modern iteration, the dysfunction of black culture. The story of the heroic actions of Rosa Parks and the vicious racism of Bull Connors fit within that understanding of racism. They are stock stories about how America put an end to racism.

While most mainstream legal scholarship consists of describing and justifying the role of courts in our liberal democracy, CRT asked whether that ought to be the primary task for those interested in racial or social justice. For example, in one of the first articles in what has become the CRT canon, Derrick Bell argued that the integrationist ideal in school desegregation cases may not represent the true interests of black clients, even as it served the development of conventional antiracism legal doctrine.[14] By asking what the interests of the black community might be, Bell was able to show that the assimilationist strand that flowed out of *Brown v Board of Education* was not the only or even the most important story that could be told about that case. Bell told the story of the school cases from the perspective of members of the plaintiff class rather than just from the perspective of the lawyers. He argued presciently that it was necessary to tell stories about the real world within which legal rules are reduced to practice.[15]

Though we are sympathetic with the CRT project, we think it is time to move beyond sophisticated rejoinders to conventional legal doctrine. Both legal doctrine and theory are unable to address the condition of racialized groups in our culture. Legal institutions construct a form of social solidarity that, in our view, inhibits the development of robust democratic counterweights to the agglomeration of private power. The debate about race that has been raging within academic circles on the left is too often disconnected from the material reality of being raced in the United States.

Given a federal judiciary increasingly dominated by ideological conservatives, we believe that progressives need to focus on politics, not just law, and to engage politics in small laboratories of democracy that exist below the radar of the national media, the federal judiciary, and the traditional theaters of power. By advancing CRT's analysis into political theory and democratic practice, we hope to go beyond the efforts of critical race theorists to reformulate legal doctrine, in order to explore the critical meaning of race for progressive politics.

Thus, this book is a work in critical race theory, but it is not about critical race theory.[16] It is a project that seeks to apply some of the theoretical insights of CRT academics to reconceptualize politics at the level of social movements. We aim to enlarge the idea of what is possible and to study the ways that race can signify differently as a political instrument for social change. In other words, the rich history of the concept of race and its uses informs much of what we do, even if it is what we are writing against.[17]

The Ideology of Colorblindness

We began our political race project by formulating responses to the conventional discourse of colorblindness within which Plotke hatched his Hungarian experiment. We concluded that the colorblind paradigm has led to paralysis rather than action. Perhaps a more important conclusion than that, however, is that ideological colorblindness inhibits the kind of democratic engagement necessary for confronting some of the most deeply entrenched problems facing our society.

ASSAULTS FROM THE RIGHT

For the last part of the twentieth century, the neoconservative agenda successfully set the terms of the public debate in the United States about race. Using the discourse of colorblindness, the right signaled the arrival of a just society with the dismantling of the formal system of Jim Crow laws. In this view, all that remained was the problem of the "bad heart," a province beyond law. As a consequence, the rhetoric of colorblindness came to dominate the debate over racial justice.

Conservative critics such as Stephan and Abigail Thernstrom reject race as a meaningful political or social category. Whether this is from a fear of race, from the privilege of their own racelessness, from a strategy of public invisibility that limits the celebration of difference to the private sphere, or from assimilation of race as the remnants of a peculiar social and scientific pathology makes little difference. Race, for these conservative critics and others, can only produce identity politics, balkanization, and a world where government control of social life and its benefits is premised on arbitrary and pathological ascriptive categories. The person who notices race in the United States "refuses to let race go and thus jeopardizes the possibility of a society in which race doesn't matter," according to one critic.[18]

The discourse of colorblindness focuses on managing the appearance of formal equality without worrying overmuch about the consequences of real-world inequality. Proponents of a colorblind ethos define freedom and equality exclusively in terms of the autonomous—some would say atomized—individual.[19] This individual has no historical antecedents, no important social relationships, and no political commitments. By structuring the primary concerns around the idea of freedom for an everyman or everywoman, proponents of colorblind analysis locate that atomized individual in an abstract universe of rights and preferences rather than within an obdurate social structure that may limit or even predetermine a person's choices. In relationship to the state and to the market, the paramount virtue of the colorblind universe resides in treating each abstract individual the same as every other.[20] By subjecting rules to this metric of simple sameness, people are legitimized through the appearance of abstract fairness.

Three rules seem to govern this colorblind universe. First, race is all about skin color. It is not a marker for social status, history, or power but is simply a false construction of phenotype that relies improperly on ascriptive physical identifiers of "blood" or ancestry. This is what some commentators call "formal race." Others refer to it as "biological race."[21] Formal or biological race treats all race as pigmentation and grants all racial classifications symmetrical status. When race is only pigmentation, all racial classifications are equally bad, despite hierarchies of privilege or disadvantage that accompany the racial assignation.

Thus, the second rule of colorblindness is that recognizing race is the equivalent of holding onto unscientific notions of racial biology. If race is essentially "made-up," with no scientific basis, then critics of race argue that treating people differently based on these made-up categories is unacceptable. Even if members of different "races" are treated "the same," each person so identified is denied his or her essential individual humanity. Moreover, when one notices race, one is implicitly manifesting racial enmity or racial preference. Since racial classification enabled a Jim Crow legal system to perpetuate false assumptions about biological inferiority, noticing race is in essence a throwback to racism.[22]

The third rule is that racism is a personal problem. Unlike capitalism or socialism which are economic systems, or democracy which is a political arrangement, racism, racial hierarchy, or any institutionalized racial discrimination is not an economic or historic system, political arrangement, or social structure. Under the third rule of colorblindness, racism lacks any necessary nexus to power or privilege, and any observed connection is incidental, merely a result of the actions of people with a bad heart. Racism is a psychological disease of individuals, not a social plague. Racism is not produced by environmental toxins, nor is it reinforced by cultural forms or institutional practice. It is simply an irrational defect of the individual mind. It afflicts the aberrant soul who is vulnerable to prejudice or even self-hatred. The challenge for the judiciary, therefore, is to discern and eliminate to the greatest extent possible any public identification of race, since the identification is per se stigmatizing.[23]

For those who believe we are already close to a colorblind society, formal fairness outweighs other concerns. They prefer rules like colorblindness even when such rules hide or reinforce relationships of privilege and subordination. The dangers of continuing to notice race are so profound that they justify doing nothing about the historic and present effects of the nexus between race and political and economic power. Not only is it wrong for the government to notice race, it is wrong for the political system to permit racially affected groups to mobilize in either their own self-interest or the larger public good.

ASSAULTS FROM THE LEFT

The rhetorical force of the colorblindness argument soon overwhelmed many of the traditional liberal supporters of the early civil rights movement. Colorblindness became the rationalization for a loss of momentum to carry forward the movement's social justice program. Largely because of the success of conservatives' assault on race-consciousness, liberal progressives have also embraced race neutrality as a new approach for ameliorating the condition of poor whites and black people. Some of them hold deeply to the principle that race-talk is inherently malignant. Others have a more instrumental view that race neutrality is necessary for building progressive coalitions. The idea is simply that black advancement will come only through social programs with universal appeal that minimize or eliminate overt discussions of race.[24] They fear balkanization—they worry that frank engagement with the continuing legacy of race can only lead to polarization and never yield the progressive programs that a universalist appeal could achieve. So long as the polity views social programs and transfer payments as government aid to blacks and other communities of color, popular support for such programs will decline. To protect those programs and to provide a foundation for progressive coalitions, there must be racial denial or racial silence in political discourse.[25]

Using this line of argument, Plotke, Mark Graber, and other well-intentioned progressives have in essence joined conservatives and neo-liberals in proposing a political strategy that reduces blackness to a mere individual characteristic.[26] Plotke argues, for example, that the Democratic Party has to retain black voters and keep them turning out at the polls. But to be seen as tailoring programs directly to meet the needs of black people or those like them leads to electoral disaster because of the disaffection of white voters. To reconcile these competing impulses, Plotke concludes that the racial politics of the Democrats must be one of silence and amelioration through universal programs. In this way, the Democratic Party can capture the white vote, to the extent that it can, *and* have policies that keep black Democrats coming to the polls.[27]

The logic of these universalist arguments, though not all the same, follows a similar pattern. First, they tend to suggest that the era of overt racism is over. The problems of black people are no longer those traditionally associated with prejudice but instead are more clearly related to the human capital within the black community and the nature of the economy. Second, popular animosity toward programs that are regarded as "special" to black people means that targeted programs will increasingly fail politically.[28] The reality of that backlash, so this argument runs, will doom any program, regardless of its virtues, if it can be characterized as one designed to address problems that are peculiarly or primarily related to one (usually black) racial group.[29] On the other hand, there is evidence that

Americans as a general matter would support programs aimed at helping all people in need, instead of a subset of those people.

Third, such universal programs would reinforce the idea that the government is committed to middle-class values, as against the social pathologies of disadvantaged groups. Finally, by rejecting measures that are targeted for the nonwhite poor, the programs would, as Theda Skocpol puts it, "speak with a consistent moral voice."[30] This makes them more durable in design and defense.

Plotke asserts that procedural remedies will not solve the problem. Cumulative voting, for example, will merely allow intensely felt majorities to prevail. Or, as Graber argues, in the U.S. context, systems of proportional or semi-proportional representation will more likely disaggregate the white majority into right or far right factions that do not identify with, or reject, the progressive policies with which members of the black community are more likely to agree.[31] Blacks will continue to lose either way. According to these commentators, the only way (without antidemocratic procedures) to achieve the support of both blacks and whites is to increase the number of black officeholders *and* construct issues in ways that garner support across racial lines. Progressive politics cannot afford to talk directly about, or to, racial interests.

Plotke and Graber do not represent the entire spectrum of liberal opinion. Some progressives advocate race-consciousness as a temporary utilitarian intervention. They believe that colorblindness is the appropriate ideal but that the legacy of less-enlightened times has not allowed our society to reach that point yet. While we await transformation to a raceless society, these liberals continue to endorse race for purposes of distributing goods and services, and thus defend transitional measures, such as affirmative action, that are based on phenotypic racial categories. These liberals have remained committed to legal action as the ultimate weapon, but as colorblindness has become the national mantra, many have found themselves unable to defend their race-conscious, litigation-oriented methods in the face of the judiciary's increasing commitment to colorblindness as both the means and end of racial equality.

Indeed, as was evident in the success of Proposition 209 in California, which led to the abandonment of affirmative action in university admissions, defense of race-consciousness has become more and more difficult. Proposition 209 was a political initiative, yet the terrain of the public debate had been defined by the Supreme Court's view. All along the political spectrum, more and more people have adopted the Court's majority view that race itself is the problem. Both sides of the debate are united by a normative vision, what Kendall Thomas calls the moral grammar of racial justice. Consequently, many liberals have ceded the definition of race, as well as other important rhetorical and substantive points, to those whose project is to purge legal and political discourse of all racial reference and who may be indifferent to whether this move preserves unjust hierarchies.[32]

A very different group—black nationalists—want to preserve race permanently on the theory that there *is* an irreducible essence of race that is biological and thus natural. Cultural nationalists, by contrast, do not believe in biological essentialism, but they do hold to the idea of a racialized community whose members are presumed to share a common culture—a presumption that may be no longer consistent with the history, class, gender, and ideological differences within such a community.[33]

A Response to the Contemporary Discourse on Race

In response to the claims of those who take a colorblind approach, we argue, as a practical matter, that it is impossible to be colorbind in a world as color-conscious as ours. Moreover, efforts to be colorblind are undesirable because they inhibit racialized minorities from struggling against their marginalized status. The rule of colorblindness disguises (sometimes deliberately) or normalizes (sometimes unwittingly) relationships of privilege and subordination. It gives those who have enjoyed little power in our society no mechanisms for understanding and challenging the systemic nature of their oppression. It affirms the existing imbalance in power relations; all that must change is for the privileged within the society to learn to tolerate on an individual basis those who were previously raced black or brown. Racial difference is relegated to celebratory holidays that capture the nostalgia of a time when we once thought we were different, but whose celebration reaffirms how essentially "the same" we truly are.[34] This approach does not involve any fundamental rethinking of how race has socially and politically constructed privilege. The way race has been used both to distribute resources and to camouflage the unfairness in that distribution remains invisible. And the political space, where groups come together to give voice to their collective experience and mobilize to engage in fundamental social change, vanishes.

In the sections that follow, we will examine three major flaws in the colorblindness approach: (1) it assumes that racial inequality is a problem of individuals; (2) in so doing, it masks entrenched racial inequality; and (3) it acts as a brake on grassroots organizing.

RACIAL INEQUALITY IS NOT A PROBLEM OF INDIVIDUALS

Most people who oppose racism today believe that it is a psychological condition which distorts a person's thinking about people of a different "racial" phenotype. They believe in the changing-people's-thinking approach to racism.[35] This approach, we argue, poses several dangers.

First, it reaffirms an essentialist view of race as merely a biological holdover from a less enlightened time that lacks any present political or social meaning. It suggests that racism is simply an inappropriate way that some individuals categorize groups of people who are in fact phenotypically different but whose physical differences amount to nothing important. This approach does not leave any space for other kinds of differences that people of color do in fact experience. These experiences are written off as some aberrational individual commitment to racialism that is obsessive and negative.

Second, the changing-people's-thinking approach not only locates the problem in the individual but it locates the remedy there as well. All that is necessary to overcome racism is for an individual to become better informed about different racial groups.

Third, in the changing-people's-thinking approach, either not speaking of race at all or speaking of it as a uniformly bad thing trumps all other options. This so-called neutral stance becomes almost inevitable after one has defined racism solely as an individual problem and an aberrant one at that. Racism is chased into the closet, and we are surprised when someone openly expresses intolerant views. Conservatives and progressives alike get caught in this trap and end up as speaking police, monitoring what people may say but feeling no compulsion to do anything about the racial hierarchy that shelters the root sources of bigotry. What surprises us about open bigotry is that it is public, not that it exists.

If we do not shift the locus of conversation to make visible the effects of such deeply held but unspoken attitudes, they will tend to normalize inequality. We will all then be tempted to explain the terrible condition of people of color as resulting from the behavior of the victims themselves.[36] Having cleansed the social discourse of any mention of race and having policed expressions of bigotry, we will come to view any remaining racial dimension to observed injustices and inequities as a function of the way "those people" of color conceive of and structure their social life.

COLORBLINDNESS MASKS ENTRENCHED RACIAL INEQUALITY

The colorblindness doctrine assumes that race is an individual attribute that should be of no consequence. For that reason, those advocating colorblindness as both means and end fail to recognize patterns of racial inequality and perceive no need to look more closely at data associated with these collective accidents of birth. They fail to see that an economy which is largely unaccountable to democratic institutions and principles of justice merely compounds inequality through the generations.

Stripped of concrete features like race, a black family earning $50,000 a year, for example, seems financially identical to a white family with the same income. Yet, this assumption of sameness does not take into account the effects of structural inequality compounded over time. Data on the generational effects of inequality show that blacks earning $50,000 or more have a median net worth that is barely one-half the median net worth of their white counterparts.[37]

Most Americans have difficulty accumulating wealth. Income, understood principally as wages and salaries, does not easily convert into wealth because immediate necessities deplete available resources. Although income is distributed in a highly unequal manner in the United States (the top 20 percent of earners receives 43 percent of all income, while the poorest 20 percent of the population receives 4 percent of the total income), the distribution of wealth is even more unequal, and that inequality grows with each succeeding generation. In 1900, 39 percent of the wealthiest men in America emerged from wealthy families; by 1950, 68 percent of the wealthiest were born into wealth. By 1970, this figure climbed to 82 percent. That same year, only 4 percent of the richest men came from modest origins.[38]

Income has been used as a surrogate for wealth at least in part due to the existence of little reliable data on wealth accumulation.[39] But income alone offers an incomplete, skewed assessment of the inequality in life chances among different individuals and groups. The reality for most families is that while income may supply basic necessities, wealth is a critical resource for improving life chances, securing prestige, passing status along to the next generation, and influencing the political process. Wealth also provides financial stability during times in which needs overwhelm income.[40]

Even at a time when the economy is good and when the unemployment rate for people of color is at an all-time low, blacks will not be able to sustain their economic gains until they can convert income into asset accumulation.[41] Yet as the sociologist Dalton Conley points out: "At the lower end of the income spectrum (less than $15,000 per year), the median African American family has no assets, while the equivalent white family holds $10,000 worth of equity. At upper income levels (greater than $75,000 per year), white families have a median net worth of $308,000, almost three times the figure for upper-income African American families ($114,600)." The median net worth of whites is twelve times that of blacks. Similarly, the average white household controls $6,999 in net financial assets while the average black household retains no net financial assets whatsoever.[42]

Owning a home is the primary method of equity accumulation for most families in the United States. Not surprisingly, disparities in home-ownership rates contribute to the black-white wealth disparity. As of 1997, only 44 percent of blacks owned their homes, in contrast with 71 percent of whites. Not only are blacks less likely to own homes, but when they do own homes, their asset is less likely to accumulate value than that of white homeowners. The value of housing in black neighborhoods increases at a lower rate compared with similar units in predominantly white neighborhoods.[43] Black households are less likely than white households to have their wealth invested in financial assets, rental property, and businesses or farms that are likely to produce income. Black assets more often are tied up in a home and consumables, such as a car or household goods. As a result, black families are less able to expand their income than white families, and thus the disparity in wealth perpetuates itself.[44]

What these comparisons of income and wealth illustrate is not just the effects of historical discrimination in particular cases but the effects of an entire complex of social relations, reflected in poorer housing markets, less adequate schools, reduced access to banks and other sources of capital, hostile relations with police authority, and increased crime. The cumulative impact of these disparities requires an explanation that does not merely excuse the current distribution of assets.[45]

Efforts to pass these effects off to class are unavailing. When trying to explain the wealth gap between blacks and whites, Melvin Oliver and Thomas Shapiro used a large number of controls in their work—income, age, sex, marriage, children, number of working people within the household, education, occupation, work history, and region. With these controls, Oliver and Shapiro confirmed that nonracial factors standing alone cannot explain the black-white wealth gap.[46]

The status of both the black poor and the black middle class is much more precarious and unstable than that of their white peers. Between 1980 and 1996 the absolute incomes of the poorest blacks declined dramatically, as compared with a small decline in the income of the poorest white families. Even as poverty in the black community declined overall, those who remained poor became poorer still. The percentage of black men between ages 25 and 34 who earn less than the poverty line for a family of four jumped from about 20 percent in 1969 to just over 50 percent in 1991.[47]

Even among blacks and whites who both start at low socioeconomic positions as measured by parental occupation, whites who make it into the middle class accumulate more wealth than blacks who have traveled the same path. Blacks' middle-class status entirely depends on income, whereas the status of the white middle class rests on the stability and security of assets. The writer DeNeen L. Brown illustrates this marginality and fragility when she explains what it means to be first-generation black middle-class: "To me that term doesn't mean anything other than someone who is one step out of poverty and two paychecks from being broke. I have income but not true wealth."[48]

The average net worth of middle-class whites is nearly four times that of comparably situated blacks, and their average net financial assets are nearly 55 times greater than that of their black counterparts. This is true even within the context of real economic success. As Oliver and Shapiro note: "No matter how high up the mobility ladder blacks climb, their asset accumulation remains capped at inconsequential levels, especially when compared to that of equally mobile whites." As a result, each generation passes on a form of "asset poverty" regardless of the level of mobility or occupational attainment achieved. Social mobility does not fully counteract the effects of the intergenerational transmission of wealth.[49]

Access to higher education has always been an indicator of both social mobility and the capacity of families to transfer wealth across generations. What we find when we compare the opportunities of white and black people is a continuing gap in access to higher education between these two groups. Because of the dramatic changes occurring in our economy, what this differential means is that the distribution of access to our knowledge-based economy will be color-coded.[50]

Most people believe (and the data confirm) that education positively affects wealth accumulation: high educational achievement typically leads to better-paying jobs, which in turn result in greater wealth accumulation.[51] What is less clear is the affect that wealth has upon education. While ample research has explored the effect of family and neighborhood income upon student performance and attainment, few studies have focused on wealth. The studies that do exist provide some insight into this relationship. Conley found that financial contributions of parents to their children's educational expenses have strong effects upon children's educational expectations. Yet African-American young adults receive less financial help from their parents and return more money to their parents' households than their white counterparts during the period immediately following high school. These data suggest that African-American young adults are substituting work for schooling.[52]

Conley found that the most significant wealth-based predictor of educational performance is parents' liquid assets. (The most significant *over-all* predictor, according to Conley, is parental educational level—another instance of the compounding of wealth over generations.) From this he infers that family-based educational financing is "probably more important than the differences in school districts associated with housing values." Conley states that wealth-based resource disparities at the district level (created by reliance on local property taxes, which fund the schools) account for approximately 10 percent of the gap in black and white standardized test scores.[53] Furthermore, a decline in our social commitment to providing access to higher education for people of color is widening the gap. The declining support for public education compounds the problems in higher education. Black and other nonwhite communities feel the impact of this decreased support first and most powerfully, but it will affect all poor communities, regardless of color, in the long run. Everyone who depends on public education for upward mobility will suffer. Recent dramatic changes in the economy promise to magnify this disadvantage.[54]

When Conley incorporated wealth factors into traditional educational analyses, a number of important elements in the cultural-deficit model for explaining educational disparities disappear. These include the pathologies supposedly created by female heads of households, receipt of welfare payments, parental age, parental occupational prestige, and parental income level.[55] As the economist Marcellus Andrews puts it: "Working-class black people are muddling through an economy that no longer offers the prospect of middle-class life to hard working but modestly educated adults."[56] There is a simple way to look at the confluence of these facts. Black people as a group not only have lower incomes than whites but also reduced access to the major avenue of wealth creation and transfer in the middle and working classes, namely high-quality higher education. Race in this society tracks wealth, wealth tracks education, and education tracks access to power.[57]

Race provides an analytic tool for understanding significant dynamics of American economic life, such as the largely unremarked upon absence of any automatic escalator from one class to the next, despite the Horatio Alger myth. The linkages between race and black poverty tell us more about race than they do about individual black people. Moreover, the linkage between race and poverty tells us as much about white people as it does about black people. It tells us that the most potent determinant of economic success lies in the accumulated assets that are passed on from one generation to the next. Racial disparities cannot be explained by reference to any simple binary in which blacks are poor and whites are not. Instead, the mechanisms making it so hard for black people to accumulate assets in a way that changes their life chances are the same mechanisms that keep poor whites poor. These mechanisms are compounded by race, but they are not totally explained by race. Race is instructive in identifying the workings of class, but it cannot be swallowed up into class.[58]

Hugh Price, President of the National Urban League, challenged us in his 1999 State of Black America address to look at race as "endogenous," that is, "something that is defined within a political-economic system and not at all natural or immutable." Race cannot be defined outside the economic or political system; "it is defined by the economic system, to grant or deny access to wealth accumulation."[59] For the individual who is raced black, Price is pointing out links in a chain that may provide an important context for what otherwise might be interpreted as individual deficits, behavioral flaws, or cultural pathology.

COLORBLINDNESS ACTS AS A BRAKE
ON GRASSROOTS ORGANIZING

By strictly limiting the legitimacy of certain types of collective action, especially action organized around racial groups, the discourse of colorblindness inhibits grassroots organizing around local, political, and collective interests. The colorblindness critique discounts the idea that black community groups ought to be directly engaged in the politics of basic (as against cosmetic) institutional change.

A commitment to formal equality above all, rooted as it is in a structure of legal and political-philosophical formalism, narrowly interprets the goal of civil rights. Indeed, the entire enterprise of civil rights is limited to creating opportunities for individual advancement for those talented enough to take advantage of a new colorless order. By not talking about race, colorblinders believe we are taking giant steps toward the elimination of the corrupting influence of racism. This silence is a strange strategy for change. It is as if those who object to capitalism simply declared that we should stop discussing wealth and those who fought communism did so by refusing ever to mention their distaste for centralized planning or statist bureaucracy.

As Jodi Dean writes in *The Solidarity of Strangers,* colorblindness promotes a laissez-faire attitude—that people should just be people instead of members of a single- or multiple-identity grouping. While it attempts "to drape itself in a politically correct rejection of labels," it adopts its own politically coercive approach that celebrates the rugged individual at the expense of the potential harmony or well-being of the group. It "views social progress and change through the individualist lens of competitive self-assertion." In so doing, Dean observes, "it fails to acknowledge the sense of community and responsibility underlying the hope for a 'we.'"[60]

The conservative and neoconservative colorblind critique disables the civil rights community from mobilizing its supporters to become full members of the polity in all the ways that social citizenship requires.[61] Instead of struggling for the right to become active citizens in a public and participatory democracy, movement activists and their beneficiaries are invited to become private careerists and individual consumers.[62] Their insistent focus on atomized individuals leads conservative colorblind advocates to ignore the collective aspects of democratic participation, preferring to focus on the importance of individual choice. For example, a federal district court recently held that it was constitutionally inappropriate for the Alabama legislature to take into consideration the interests of a black political organization in gaining political power. The constitutional disability arose solely because this grassroots organization, advocating on behalf of its black members, successfully influenced the drawing of election district lines.[63]

Consistent with this view, Justice Clarence Thomas condemns judicial enforcement of Section 2 of the Voting Rights Act of 1965 as a "disastrous misadventure in judicial policymaking" because the act should only reach "state enactments that limit [an individual citizen's] access to the ballot." The Voting Rights Act should not be "a device for regulating, rationing and apportioning political power among racial and ethnic groups." For

Justice Thomas, racial groups cannot and should not be conceived of "largely as political interest groups." Thomas condemns the "drive to segregate political districts by race" because "it can only serve to deepen racial divisions by destroying any need for voters or candidates to build bridges between racial groups or to form voting coalitions."[64]

Or as Justice Sandra Day O'Connor writes, a "reapportionment plan that includes in one district individuals who belong to the same race, but who are otherwise widely separated by geographical and political boundaries, and who may have little in common with one another but the color of their skin, bears an uncomfortable resemblance to political apartheid. It reinforces the perception that members of the same racial group—regardless of their age, education, economic status, or the community in which they live—think alike, share the same political interests, and will prefer the same candidates at the polls. We have rejected such perceptions elsewhere as impermissible racial stereotypes."[65] In other words, race is something that good people simply do not notice and would not use as a basis for political association. As we discuss in Chapter 6, the Court's race-blindness masks the more fundamental ideology of individualistic democracy. This ideology measures the quantum of democracy in terms of the individual's ballot access rather than her capacity for political mobilization. Within this democratic project, the people themselves play a very small role. The morality of individualism becomes the fig leaf behind which naked elitism hides. Not surprisingly, such a move eliminates the very site of politics that people of color could use to transcend the unconscious essentialism and paternalism that co-exist at the core of the colorblind critique of race and race politics.

Moving from the conservative to the liberal version of colorblindness, let us put aside for the moment the discontinuity that sits at the center of the progressive universalists' claim: namely, the view, on the one hand, that the age of overt racism is over and the fact, on the other hand, that most Americans oppose programs aimed at specifically ameliorating the condition of black people. This inconsistency aside, we think that universalism exhibits two additional, fundamental flaws that weaken it and strengthen our own project of political race. First, the argument assumes, similar to the neoconservative argument for colorblindness, a discontinuity between the legislated racism of the past and the racially identifiable socioeconomic inequalities we observe today.[66] Second, their prescription is a recipe for ensuring that issues specific to the condition of black people and other marginalized or racialized minorities will not find a political voice.

The reality is that agitation by people of color has made this a freer and, in a strict sense, more liberal culture.[67] The political form of the colorblind critique ignores this insight; instead, it delegitimizes all racial politics as the mere politics of identity or, worse, brands them as racist.[68] The universalists' claim has to be that continued organizing around race will retard the liberal development of society and thus should be stopped because it has lost its liberatory thrust. Yet if that is the essence of their claim, the question remains: What is the mechanism that will continue the project of creating a society of greater freedom and solidarity where black people do not suffer injustice merely because of their blackness? All we are told is that the logic of liberal democratic theory drives the rhetorical and ideological movement toward colorblindness.[69] We are not told whether it makes us capable of being more democratic.

When presented by progressives as a political program, universalist arguments call for a focus on class in lieu of race. But these same progressives offer no mechanism for explaining how social solidarity will emerge to eliminate the remaining inequality. Phil Thompson points out, for example, that if racial groups are an impermissible unit of analysis, how can we be sure their interests are considered and incorporated in a manner acceptable to black people?[70] Universalism's paternalism makes all of its beneficiaries objects rather than subjects of policy. It fails to name the conditions in the mines in ways that empower those most likely to challenge or resist those conditions. By substituting public policy programs for public policy movements, it undermines the enforcement of political choices that democracy contemplates. It undervalues the need to anticipate resistance among those who resent the agenda and also fails to provide a truly transformative conception of power that begins to change not only the immediate conditions of some poor and working-class people but also situates their conditions within a larger vision of social justice.

In order to create a progressive political movement, universalists must locate a space where some democratic organizing can occur. Though they strongly suggest top-down elite-driven solutions, to the extent that they identify a space for political organizing, it is with poor and working-class people generally. One of the problems with this argument is that it does not explain how to get from poor people's identity to their interests without falling prey to attacks by conservatives claiming that poor people are instigating class warfare. Moreover, asking black people to submerge their interests into the generalized interests of working-class, mostly white, people requires from them a level of trust in the political process that its current paralysis does not warrant. It requires that black people willingly remain objects of the politics of others, rather than subjects of a politics of their own making.

At this point, our putative progressive allies become, instead, allies of the status quo. The fact is that race is already a part of the political discourse, whether it is a coherent analytic category or not.[71] Moreover, for all its rhetoric of "integration" and "coalition bridges," the ideology of colorblindness fails to acknowledge that blacks do in fact, when given a choice, vote cohesively.[72] That does not imply a monolithic or essential quality to black political interests. However, if history and recent electoral results are any evidence, there is substantial overlap between the social and political identities of most blacks. Consequently, those who deny the political valence of black social identity ignore the political consequences of that identity, too.[73] If you have to run from being identified with blacks socially, you have to run from being identified with them politically as well. This is precisely because of the racially charged structure of political debate in our culture. The top-down elimination of racial discourse as a form of stereotyping then leaves a vacuum that is filled by cultural nationalism and its twin, identity politics. One twin occupies the space of "culture" and the other of "self," each relying on some notion of an essential and decontextualized identity.

Into this opening, advocates of political biology, who are commonly known as racial nationalists, assert essential connections from which political positions are supposed to arise but which are not predicated on democratically driven positions. One of the perils of the nationalist/essentialist position is that its assumption of a pre-political solidarity may be used to repress the development of democratic mechanisms *within* the racially marginalized but electorally powerful groups in a given district. As a result, a paradox emerges from the ideal of colorblindness. If progressives ignore race, the only groups left that are willing to speak to the experience of being raced in this society are the cultural nationalists. And the only words or ideas that will be spoken are racial stereotypes. The very thing colorblinders seek to avoid is what they end up resuscitating.

As should be clear, we challenge the racial essentialists as well as the advocates of race-blindness. We disagree with the essentialists that race, by itself, is an adequate basis for political mobilization or political resistance. We reject the idea that personal identity derived from a belief in biologically assigned race or the cultural experience of being raced is, alone, sufficiently political. Though essentialists may organize around race, the politicization of race as essence is not what we mean by political race. Their organizing tends to focus only on step one: remediating racialized grievances. While they understand the capacity of racialized groups to galvanize around such grievances, their exclusively race-based vision tends to reinforce in others the general view that race is a liability.[74] They fail to take either the second or third step that we argue is critical for enlisting race in progressive reform: moving from their own grievances to articulate a larger social justice critique and organizing relationships democratically to resist both horizontal and vertical hierarchies of power.

We are starting from the same insight that our progressive allies have identified—that race has been deployed to polarize, marginalize, or distract a multiracial coalition from pursuing a social justice agenda. But unlike others who advocate targeting within a framework of universalism, we make a strategic as well as a social justice claim as to why it is necessary, affirmatively, to recognize race. The justice claim is that neoconservatives and their allies to their right have used race to obscure their agenda of dismantling government. The strategic claim, considered at length in Chapter 3, is that racially marginalized individuals are more likely to mobilize to resist systemic patterns of unfairness when it is presented to them, at least initially, as a racial injustice. And without their initial energy and resistance, progressive social movements will lose their most dedicated base of support.

Thus far we have shown three flaws with the ideology of colorblindness by both neoconservatives and progressive liberals in the United States. To reiterate: colorblindness misdiagnoses racial inequality as a residual individual problem; it masks systemic racial injustice; and, perhaps merely the precipitate of the first two, it cripples the capacity for collective organization and democratic mobilization.

The Abandonment of Politics

In addition to our critique of the ideology of colorblindness, we were moved to begin this project by two related concerns. First, we felt that the moral and analytic vision which motivated the civil rights movement had run out of steam. The ideas of liberation and community that emerged with the legal demise of Jim Crow were increasingly under ideological and political attack from the right, but the responses to those attacks from the left were insufficient. The courts, not just conservative commentators, now promulgated the corrosive and co-opting ideology of colorblindness. The civil rights struggle, which had become mostly a legal rather than a political movement, was losing its moral and analytic authority because of this judicial takeover by the right.

Second, in a related development, we witnessed the mainstreaming of an increasingly impoverished concept of public life.[75] The commercialization of politics accompanied the mounting contempt for governmental authority.[76] With the cooperation of some liberals and many "New Democrats," conservative and neoconservative legal and political thinkers convinced the rest of us that genuine broad-based efforts aimed at fundamental social change are pointless. According to this view, only individual initiatives can make a difference, and the only difference that matters comes from providing opportunity to those individuals with initiative. A harshly inequitable regime is left undisturbed.

Federal judges appointed by Presidents Ronald Reagan and George Bush shared this skepticism about the role of the federal government even to remedy racial discrimination. Dominated by a radically conservative mindset, the federal judiciary has largely abdicated legal responsibility for enforcing public laws to ameliorate racial injustice. The reconceptualization of racial discrimination as being merely the personal prejudice of individual white people or the cultural pathology of black and brown people justified judicial withdrawal from a remedial role.[77]

This conservative doctrinal retreat from the task of eliminating racism was the sharp edge of the wedge that splintered our conception of the public sphere. The political scientist Luis Fraga, building on the work of Tom and Mary Edsall, argues that small-government conservatives and opponents of civil rights joined together in a long-term strategic plan to reduce the legitimacy of governmental action through the use of coded language linking "race, rights and taxes."[78] Defenders of the status quo effectively deployed the symbolism of race to silence their opposition by claiming that "whoever mentions race first is the racist in the room."[79] They then moved on to their real target: the break-up of a mobilized cross-racial coalition that might melt the congealed concentrations of wealth, power, and privilege in our society.

In other words, they used the discourse of race-blindness to disguise the privatization of public power. Their commitment to speaking only in terms of the individual allowed them to mask the structural patterns of inequality. In the case of striving black people who overcome the odds or the case of those irresponsible black people whose poverty is self-inflicted, isolated individuals are the unit of analysis, in this view, and structural patterns that affect both people of color and poor whites can be safely ignored.

By embracing the formal rhetoric of colorblindness, conservatives succeeded at "blackening" poverty. This has had two effects. By linking general social problems of poverty with a specific group, efforts to ameliorate poverty are made to appear as special pleading for that particular interest group. The interests of the poor are reduced to the interests of blacks as an interest group no different from, say, the gun lobby. In fact, there are many more poor white people in America than there are poor black people.[80] But by first thinking about poverty as a black problem and then structuring social policy around the goal of eliminating all solutions that target race, the degree, nature, and vast scope of inequality within our

economy is elided and then ignored. When the New Right gives poverty a
black face, they are suggesting that one can safely ignore poverty because
it is a largely intractable problem resulting from pathologies of black individuals or the black community as a whole. It is a problem that poor black
people have created for themselves and that they alone can solve, if anyone can.[81]

There is a paradox in imagining that race divisions can be eliminated
by ignoring their continued material reality. On the one hand, we are not
supposed to notice that the general poverty rate is, in fact, racially linked;
to do so, we are told, would simply reinforce negative stereotypes about
poor black people. Consequently, references to poverty are translated into
disparaging comments about the culture of poverty. But (and this is the
paradox) the ideology that spawned the idea of a culture of poverty essentially uses that language as code for "under-socialized poor black people."[82] By ignoring the social and economic dimensions of race, race-
blindness merely forces racialized thinking into the closet. This move
neglects to interrogate the foundations of negative stereotypes or to admit
that they still exist, even if they are unspoken.[83]

When we think of high poverty rates as somehow pathologically tied to
race, we tend to ignore the high rates of poverty among other nonwhite
groups such as Hispanics (including Cubans) and Asian Americans.[84] In
fact, one of the odious consequences of colorblindness ideology in analyzing the inequalities of our economy is that it permits policy analysts to ignore the high poverty rate among Asian Americans because *it is not supposed to be there.* Efforts to blacken poverty must therefore be challenged
directly by reinterpreting the link between race and poverty. The alternative is to ignore poverty by ignoring race, and in the process to leave unnoticed the complex generational dynamics between poverty and race.[85]

We maintain that one can identify race affirmatively in order to mobilize both a critique of the connection between race and power and to
identify a base of support for changing the status quo.[86] Focusing attention on the distress of the miner's canary does not mean that one must locate the pathology within the canary itself; one can still locate the problem
in the atmosphere of the mine. Using race as the miner's canary allows us
to depathologize conceptions of race, poverty, and powerlessness.

This is a moral as well as a pragmatic response. By using the term "moral" we do not invoke the restrictive moral grammar of conventional racial discourse, in which contemporary legal analysis limits action to punishing those isolated individuals who intentionally discriminate. Here, in stark contrast, the moral imperative is to do something about the legacy and current structural effects of racism; in its pragmatic articulation we are reminded that we can best do something about that continuing legacy by starting with those who are racialized. But then we must help them to enlarge their claims in service of a larger social justice vision that will reach out to more than just the racially marginalized.

The pragmatic point is that if we do not—if we maintain silence on race—we allow conservatives to define the agenda, not just about explicitly racialized issues like affirmative action and racial profiling but also about health care, education, economic policy, immigration policy, labor reform, gun control, the war on drugs, and crime. The failure of progressives to engage directly with the way each of these topics is racialized permits conservatives to occupy and define the available political space. Historically, they have done this by isolating black voters, marginalizing the allies of blacks, and stigmatizing reform efforts that go beyond blaming the individual for social ills. Then they explain the continued marginality of people of color as some version of the black dysfunction thesis. Rather than identify the conditions in the mine that are affecting working-class people of all races, the universalists' silence on race reinforces the view that the entire problem resides in the canary, not in the mine—and that poor whites should locate in the canary, rather than in the mine, any problems they may be experiencing as well.[87]

Conservatives have employed the rhetoric of colorblindness to mask their effort to limit the authority of the state, and conventional racial discourse has reinforced that tendency by elevating private activity over collective public engagement. The market is the source of all solutions, and it will function better if it is free from democratic interference, they claim. Among progressives, talk about race has to take the form of "Let's talk about proposals for reducing racial inequality without increasing racial polarization." This also means racial silence, and it, too, is a recipe for black invisibility rather than for an honest confrontation with the political dimensions of black interests.

The Brazilian Experiment in Race-Blindness

Let's now return to the experiment with which we began this chapter. What if, instead of showing Guinier's picture to graduate students in Hungary, Plotke had instead shown it to graduate students in Brazil? What would their reading have been? This is not an idle question. Those who worry that race is the great divider in American culture often point to Brazil as an example of a racially complex democracy that has moved past the problem associated with race-consciousness. Brazil is a racially mixed nation that has maintained a formal post-slavery ideology of race-blindness. To many American observers, Brazil moved seamlessly from an economy and society based on chattel slavery of Africans (and Indians) to one where race does not matter.[88]

As in the United States, there was intellectual opposition to the inclusion of a race question on the Brazilian census, predicated on the idea that "the question was unnecessary, because Brazilians were simply Brazilians. Each had transcended his or her consciousness of racial origin and become a member of a Brazilian meta-race."[89] But, as in the United States, the structure of distribution of social goods defies the formal claim of racelessness in Brazil. Blacks occupy the lowest strata of the sociopolitical and economic hierarchy.

Ignoring the material reality of racial inequality, American political observers have long been fascinated with Brazil because it allows them to imagine the possibility of a colorblind yet multicultural future for the United States. The attraction stems in part from the belief that Brazil, the largest former slave-owning country in Latin America, has solved its race problem. If a country with the largest black population outside of Nigeria can become a racial democracy then surely we can as well.

What would the Brazilian graduate students have done with Guinier's picture? Unlike the students in Hungary who started from a frame of ethnicity, Brazilians would likely have started by looking at color. Color matters a great deal in Brazil, despite the official racelessness of public policy.

Unlike the United States where there is essentially a racial caste system, in Brazil there is a color caste system. As Melissa Nobles puts it, "In the United States, race trumps color: in Brazil color trumps race. Although hardly unambiguous, that distinction is the key to Brazilian racial discourse."[90]

To understand Brazilian racial discourse, we need to remember that, unlike the United States where the issue of slavery was integral to the founding of the republic and where a bloody civil war was required to end it, Brazil abolished slavery peaceably by decree. The abolition of slavery in 1888 first put the question of race on the Brazilian national agenda. Postemancipation, the major theorists of race in Brazil worked out elaborate explanations for the ideology of racelessness and the mechanisms for eliminating observed distinctions based on color. There were no Jim Crow laws to extend the conditions of subordination past slavery. Racial discrimination was, according to the government, foreign to Brazil.[91] As one commentator summed up the early twentieth-century formulation of this position: "There are no inferior and superior races, only advanced and retarded races."[92] That formulation, of course, suggests the possibility of advancement and does not admit of immutable differences between the races. This is radically different from the idea of race in the United States, which has maintained both the inherent inferiority of black people and the immutability of the category.

Yet, it turns out that the ideological differences are mostly superficial. The spinners of rhetoric in Brazil dealt with the presence of large numbers of Africans as well as widespread miscegenation by avoiding the question of inherent racial superiority in favor of a whitening thesis.[93] The whitening thesis held that the more advanced races (meaning, of course, the European Brazilians) would succeed in whitening the general population. According to race theorists of the time, Negro blood would disappear in the fifth generation. This pseudo-scientific theory was predicated on two "facts." First, whitening would occur because whites had a higher birth rate. Second, miscegenation naturally produced a lighter population, because white genes were "stronger." Because people were presumed to want to choose partners lighter than themselves, a higher percentage of the more marriageable lighter-skinned people would reproduce, passing along their strong white genes.[94] Furthermore, the pseudo-scientific racist writers of the immediate post-abolition period continued to speak in terms of "blood," as if there were a deeply biological content to the division in society that color marked.[95] The solution to the race problem is the erasure of blackness through its dilution with white blood. As Theodore Roosevelt remarked at the time about Brazil, "The idea looked forward to is the disappearance of the Negro question through the disappearance of the Negro himself—that is, through his gradual absorption into the white race."[96]

The whitening thesis has not lessened an obsession with color or superior or inferior races. The continuing influence of the idea of whitening could be discerned at the First Brazilian Congress of the Negro that was held in Rio de Janeiro in 1950. Suggestions for a national confederation to organize black communities and unify black organizations throughout the nation were rejected because organizers feared that whites would oppose such a body as racist.[97]

Interestingly, the obsession with color persists even though Brazil, unlike the United States, does not have a one-drop rule. In Brazil race is a continuum, based on phenotypic characteristics (skin color or tone, hair texture, facial features). Blood quantum is not the measure of either whiteness or blackness. So Brazilians do not conflate colorblindness with race-blindness, and this distinction, they argue, permits a social democracy where hereditary lineage is not determinative of social status. The social science data suggest, however, that this may be a distinction without a difference.[98]

Because ancestry is not determinative, a person is placed in a social hierarchy based on both skin color *and* class, a phenomenon Charles Wagley defines as "social race."[99] The mulatto category occupies a social space between black and white that creates an escape hatch for blacks to move from the bottom of the social hierarchy by virtue of an economic free space dictated by the historic necessities of the Brazilian economy. Marvin Harris developed a Brazilian taxonomy that reflects mobility within the color/class categories. A "Negro" includes a poverty-stricken black person, a poor black person, a black person of average wealth, a poverty-stricken mulatto, a poor mulatto, and a poverty-stricken white person. A "white" includes a poor but not poverty-stricken white person, a white person of average wealth, a wealthy white person, a mulatto of average wealth, a wealthy mulatto, and a wealthy black person.[100] What this taxonomy demonstrates is that while the solvent of class status may loosen social categories, there is still an essential divide between the very rich and the very poor, and it parallels the divide between white and black. The middle space occupied by mulattos is mediated by both color and wealth. White persons do not sink into blackness unless they are destitute, and black persons (as opposed to mulattos) do not rise to whiteness except through above-average wealth.

The disadvantage flowing from race or color, despite the absence of an official language to name that disadvantage, remains apparent in Brazil. As in the United States, the facts are clear. Kathleen Bond describes it this way:

> Skin color profoundly influences life chances. According to a 1992 study by Carlos Hasenbalg and Nelson do Valle Silva, Brazilian nonwhites are three times more likely than whites to be illiterate. The numbers deteriorate in the high echelons of academic study. Whites are FIVE times more likely than people of mixed ancestry and NINE times more likely than Blacks to obtain university degrees. This pattern repeats itself in the work force where according to government statistics whites have access to the highest-paying jobs, earning up to 75% more than blacks and 50% more than people of mixed ancestry. Brazil's prisons and youth detention centers are bursting at the seams. The vast majority of detainees and victims of police brutality are non-white Brazilians. Not surprisingly, health statistics paint a similar picture. For example, non-white Brazilian infants are almost twice as likely to die as their white counterparts.[101]

Yet, many blacks in Brazil express uncertainty whether the disadvantage they experience is because of race or class. According to Degler, there is very little consciousness of the connection between the two, although this may be changing.[102] Just as we struggle in some quarters of the United

States to speak of the racial dimensions of class, whites in Brazil are suspicious of any political organization predicated on race. As with the current version of the American rhetoric of colorblindness, in Brazil the dominant ideology of race-blindness has long denied that race has any relevance as a social, political, or economic marker.

Most of those who experience marginalization in Brazil because of their prior condition of servitude or their color have no words for what they know. They are told that it is not because of their "race" as such. It is because they have not yet "advanced." The irony of the whitening thesis and official race-blindness ideology is that you can look at a dark Brazilian who does not possess great wealth and tell that he or she is not "white." What you notice is that they are not yet "white," but what you can *say* is that they are not yet advanced.

If Plotke had shown graduate students in Brazil the picture of Guinier and had made clear that she is a law professor, it is entirely possible that she would have been declared white. Yet, if our hypothetical Brazilian graduate students had chosen white as the proper description for Guinier, would their views have changed if Plotke had then added that she has defined her life through advocacy for black people and others who are systematically disadvantaged? Would her politics have colored her black, even as her social class and skin tone made her white?

The lessons of social race in Brazil are not completely lost on the United States. Recently, we have witnessed a new openness among elites to include, as if "white," people with dark skin. This is a subject to which we return in Chapter 7. To those espousing the ideology of colorblindness, Guinier would just "happen" to be black and would be encouraged to identify simply as a human being without racial affiliation. As in Brazil, her refusal to do so would make her "too black," in the words of the Philadelphia parking attendant.

Taking seriously the lessons from Brazil, we see that the cost of "racelessness" is not born evenly. For blacks it is measured in both individual and collective terms. Those who are black by virtue of origin and phenotype and who are "whitened" through social class have an incentive to disassociate themselves from the black community. Even the blackest Brazilians avoid the stigma associated with blackness by claiming Indian ancestry as the explanation for their dark coloring.[103] Brazil has, like most of Latin America, adopted the mythology of the *mestizaje* to deny the continued salience of unassimilated groups.[104]

In addition to the social distance between "whitened" blacks and the black community, racelessness requires the denial of race or color as a problem, and this move prevents political organization around race even where racial designations are the clearest markers of social position from which a politics could be developed. The most significant casualty of this official race-blind, color-conscious discourse is the inability of those most disadvantaged by it to organize. In 1968, at a meeting commemorating the 80th anniversary of the abolition of slavery in Brazil, one participant, Souza Dante, commented: "We know the Negro is relegated to a situation of social inferiority and every time he rises up against the state of things he is taken as subversive, as forward, and particularly as a Black racist."[105]

Whereas in the United States organizations such as the NAACP were once seen as the center of black activism, no comparably powerful organization has existed in Brazil.[106] Many Brazilians ascribe this absence to a lack of racial tension. This is true only in so far as the absence of these organizations removes the possibility of overt struggle and merely hides the underlying racial structuring of the society.[107]

What we see in Brazil is not the elimination of the effects of race by officially declaring its irrelevance but the elimination of race as a site of democratic and progressive political organization. Rather than permitting greater social and economic equality, the ideology of social race has prevented anything other than class-based resistance, leaving intact the color-based inequalities buried within the classes themselves.

There is evidence, though, that even the official denial of material reality has its limits. In describing the emergence of a black consciousness, one reporter notes that "during the annual, statewide Black Movement Conference in September 1999, more than 100 activists from these [minority] groups gathered for three days in the capital city. With Brazil approaching in April, 2000 the anniversary of the Portuguese colonization, this year's theme was '500 Years of Black Resistance.'"[108] Perhaps these primarily cultural organizations may serve to generate a language that can empower citizens politically to repudiate the racial hierarchy that also defines economic inequity.

Conclusion

The Brazilian experiment with social race teaches an important set of cross-cultural lessons about the disabling elements embedded in the ideology of colorblindness. First, colorblindness disables the individual from understanding or fully appreciating the structural nature of inequality. Second, it disables groups from forming to challenge that inequality through a political process. The denial of race not only reduces individuals' psychological motivation for challenging unfairness but also contributes to their internalization of it as a purely personal problem. Either one of these effects is a deterrent to collective political action.

What the experience of Brazil also demonstrates is that the rhetoric of colorblindness can be deployed to polarize, marginalize, or distract a multiracial coalition from forming and pursuing a social justice agenda. It locates social ills in the disadvantaged rather than in the political and economic system. In both the United States and Brazil, such an ideological approach guards oligarchs from moral reproach and promotes a popular disengagement from politics. While it has allowed various white supporters of movements for social change to justify their fatigue in recent times, the colorblindness attack has destabilized the movement for transformative social change within communities of color as well.

The way to combat this fatigue is to reinvigorate race as a political category, not just for analysis but for action. Race is useful to explain a material reality in which blacks, other people of color, and whites who are otherwise socially positioned in the same way have less social, political, and economic power than others. What we are calling political race is also useful (and perhaps necessary) for collective organizing to change, through political action, the reality of racialized injustice. Political race is both a critique of the status quo and a space for action to change it. It helps locate a problem in a way that allows those most directly affected to function as a catalyst for reform. And it draws on psychological strengths that are already present in the black community. From segregation can come congregation.

This is not an argument that everyone should become black or that all blacks should feel connected as a result of a common oppression. But it does interpret the psychological connection many blacks feel as a source of strength that can be tapped for democratic activity.

In 1996, to the shock and consternation of many and the joy of some, the federal court of appeals for the Fifth Circuit declared unconstitutional all race-conscious admissions programs at the University of Texas Law School and, by extension, throughout the entire state system of higher education.[1] The case had become a staple of the right-wing attack on efforts to remedy the effects of past racial injustice. It told a stock story of individual disappointment at the hands of race-obsessed social engineers in government, and the eventual triumph of so-called merit-based, colorblind criteria in school admissions.

Cheryl Hopwood, the named plaintiff, was the vehicle for this stock story. She was a white applicant denied admission by the university's Law School. She complained that she was rejected even though she had a higher Texas Index score (a composite of undergraduate grade point average and LSAT score) than some black and Mexican-American applicants who were admitted. The university had awarded seats that should have been hers to less-qualified candidates, she claimed. Since these candidates were admitted solely because they were members of a minority, this violated the norm of race-blindness and made the process unfair. As it happened, Hopwood also scored higher than over 100 white applicants who were admitted; but because they were white, their acceptance did not raise the constitutional question of race-blindness. The unfairness for which she sought redress rested in the method used by the university to supplement the Texas Index scores for black and Mexican-American applicants.

At the largest mass rally in the history of the university, the Reverend Jesse Jackson voiced the assembly's opposition to the actions of the Fifth Circuit and the Texas attorney general, whose unusually expansive interpretation of the court opinion swept away every race-conscious criterion within its broad compass. As the afternoon progressed, the mood of resistance boiled over into an occupation of the University of Texas Law School. Activists focused attention on the long-ignored fact that the state's flagship university served only a thin slice of the Texas population. And historically, it was always the same slice. Not only did the University of Texas stand at the pinnacle of a segregated educational system that typically excluded blacks and Mexican Americans, it excluded poor and rural whites as well.

In the name of "merit," the university was using a selection process that guaranteed spaces to more affluent students whose parents could afford test coaching, private school, or a resource-rich environment. Although these selection criteria—primarily the SAT and the LSAT—were supposedly merit-based, they actually failed to predict the college or law school performance of those who did well on the tests beyond the first year of school.[2] And they were not even terribly good at predicting that limited information. As one professional who worked on the LSAT admitted, the test was only 9 percent better than random at predicting classroom performance nationwide within the six months to a year following the test.[3] Test scores tended to correlate better with parental income (and even grandparents' socioeconomic status) than actual student performance in college or law school.[4] Yet, few people at the time knew these facts about the limitations of the testocracy then in place, and the legal process in the Fifth Circuit Court had failed to make the point that Hopwood's complaint could have been used to raise fundamental questions about the way the law school was admitting everyone.

Leadership to resist the resegregation of Texas higher education quickly emerged from the Mexican-American caucus in the Texas Legislature and from civil rights activists. State Senator Gonzalo Barrientos and Irma Rangel (chair of the Higher Education Sub-Committee of the Texas House of Representatives and the first Mexican-American woman elected to that body) gathered activists and academics from around the state to discuss possible actions. In a series of meetings convened by Senator Barrientos, participants focused at first on litigation strategies that would preserve affirmative action. Lawyers did most of the talking, parsing the court's opinions carefully for those assembled. Although the legislative leaders produced a number of proposals, they too were part of an overall strategy aimed at legal solutions. Since litigation had ended affirmative action, it seemed logical to pursue legal strategies to challenge that outcome. All members of the group identified the general problem as the exclusion of people of color from the main institutional gateways to social mobility, and they framed the options in terms limited to preserving affirmative action.

Unfortunately, in the reading of the university's history supplied by the Fifth Circuit, affirmative action had lost its moral footing. Race neutrality trumped racial remediation and racial diversity. What was worse, even the activists most in favor of affirmative action still viewed it uncritically as a thumb on the scale. They, like the admissions board, considered the test-centered techniques used to ration access to elite higher education as appropriate measures of merit. At no point in these early discussions was any attempt made to reconcile the mission of the university with this elitist rationing process. Only through intense meetings and discussion among activists inside and outside the university did the selection criteria themselves finally become the subject of critical scrutiny.

Simultaneous with research and brainstorming meetings, Representative Rangel asked for meetings with the governor's staff and the conservative opposition. Her desire was to map the landscape of possibility and to construct a framework for legislative alternatives. She proved to be a master of the politically possible. Meanwhile, David Montejano, a historian and the Director of the Center for Mexican-American Studies (CMAS), convened a group of academics from a variety of disciplines to continue the discussion begun at the larger meetings. Sociologists, demographers, education experts, and historians, as well as legal and political experts, attended these meetings.[5] Smaller groups were organized to investigate specific options; each group comprised a number of different kinds of experts ranging across academic disciplines and activist bases. One of these smaller groups together with some graduate students met with legislative staff and with representatives of the Mexican American Legal Defense and Education Fund (MALDEF) and the Texas NAACP. Even as participants argued over the options, they continued to assemble data about the state of education in Texas.

The initial work of the meetings was to get past two ideas: (1) that litigation was the best remedy, and (2) that the remedy should focus only on supplementing conventional test scores in order to provide access for black and Mexican-American students. After much arguing, the issue of race was finally joined to issues of class and democratic access to public education more generally. Race became a lens through which to focus on the way the university was admitting everyone. The research from the working groups revealed that black and Mexican-American students were not the only ones who did less well on high-stakes aptitude tests than middle-class and upper-middle-class white applicants. Poor and working-class white students also lost out because the SAT and LSAT so influenced admissions decisions.

Another factor that adversely affected Cheryl Hopwood's particular application was the Law School's policy to include in its admission equation the median LSAT of all those who took the test from the applicant's college. The rationale for this was, presumably, to give students from more demanding—and higher scoring—schools an advantage over students from less demanding schools, on the theory that all A's on coursework are not the same. Hopwood, at the time a single mother raising a child with a disability, had attended a community college and a state school where the median LSAT was lower than at more prestigious and expensive private undergraduate schools. The formula penalized Hopwood because she could not afford to attend a more elite school where the higher LSATs of her classmates would give her a leg up on the Texas admissions ladder. When this piece of the formula was applied to Hopwood's application, it was downgraded from the presumptive-admit category to the discretionary category, and the final result was a rejection.[6]

This devaluation of the grades of students from less rigorous, usually public institutions may have been an effort to level the playing field with respect to grade point averages, but the premise that median LSATs function successfully as a leveling agent for GPAs was never explored in court.

Hopwood's complaint that she should have been admitted could have been based on a class issue as well as a race issue, but only the race aspect was raised. The focus on race alone successfully camouflaged the underlying economic disparities involved in the use of the LSAT and blinded the litigants to the connection between class-based and race-based arguments.

The researchers also discovered how poorly the SAT and LSAT functioned to predict academic success. Indeed, though touted as a merit-based standard, these tests are often arbitrary and exclusionary. They are arbitrary when they do not correlate well with what they are supposed to predict, which is college and law school performance. And they are exclusionary since they correlate so very well with parental income. Indeed, the researchers identified high school grades as a better predictor of college grades than the SAT, despite the uniformity of the SAT and the wide variability in local grading practices. Moreover, reliance on high school rank alone excludes fewer people from lower socioeconomic backgrounds than does reliance on test scores or test scores in combination with class rank.[7]

The activists at the meetings also identified the dual role of the University of Texas at Austin, one of the state's two flagship schools. These elite public institutions were not funded merely to prepare students for subsequent employment; they also trained a huge proportion of future Texas leaders in both the public and private sectors. It became obvious that admissions criteria should be linked to both of these important missions.

Over the course of much discussion, those in the meetings came back around to the long-ignored fact that the state's flagship university served only a thin slice of the Texas population. Research that was initially focused on race revealed the important discovery that 10 percent of the high schools in Texas routinely filled 75 percent of all freshmen seats at the university. These high schools were predominantly the more affluent suburban and private schools. Thus, the conventional admission criteria had failed to serve the public mission of the university to train citizens and leaders from the entire state.

Three proposals emerged from these brainstorming sessions and community meetings. The first was for the state, in essence, to confess error.

This proposal was for the legislature to find that the racism of the Texas school system continued to disadvantage black and Mexican-American school children and thus justified race-conscious remedies. No one gave that proposal much of a chance. The second proposal, crafted largely by Al Kaufman of MALDEF, created a menu of variables that admissions officers would have to take into account in their admissions decisions at the undergraduate and graduate level. Finally, one idea raised in the larger meeting and refined in a smaller group was a plan to admit to the flagship state university a fixed percentage of graduates from all high schools in the state.

Thus, out of all these meetings, a remedy emerged that was consistent with the stated goals of the university and with the idea that hard work ought to count for a lot and that hard-working students should not be punished for the failure of politicians to meet their state's constitutional requirement to provide equal educational opportunity within high schools throughout the state. What has come to be called the Texas 10 Percent Plan offered admission to the flagship campuses to *all* high school students who graduated in the top 10 percent of their high-school class, regardless of SAT scores.[8] Many conservative rural white legislators, recognizing that the systematic class bias in the traditional admission procedure had harmed their white constituents, joined in to support this populist measure.

This new plan was not a compromise between race-conscious admissions processes and merit-based criteria. Although it started with a focus on race, it moved to incorporate issues of class and democratic opportunity. It also moved from the assumption that tests are meritocratic for everyone except people of color to a larger critique of the way in which the conventional admission testocracy denies opportunity to many deserving white applicants as well. It changed the definition of merit.

The new rule promised to reintegrate Texas higher education and make the university more economically diverse. With a more diverse undergraduate body to draw on, the graduate schools would become more diverse as well. It also promised to begin a debate about how to measure the quality of public secondary education in order to preserve the high quality of Texas higher education. It acknowledged the importance of drawing future leaders from all sectors of the population, not just the affluent or well-endowed. It provided access to the flagship schools to citizens throughout the state and not just those from the resource-rich suburbs of Dallas, Austin, and Houston. And finally, it recognized the valuable role that the flagship schools play in creating a network of public citizens who will serve the state and its taxpayers and whose tax dollars provide the public subsidy that makes the state university affordable.

The proposal that finally went before the Texas legislature incorporated both the factors approach favored by MALDEF and the automatic admission vision of a straight percentage plan. Although the group struggled hard to illustrate the fundamental fairness of the proposal, as well as the other salutary benefits it could have, creating a coalition in the legislature to get the plan passed was an uphill battle. Because the leadership for this reform came from people of color, opposition to it followed familiar patterns. One of the important breakthroughs occurred when the advocates of reform revealed that some counties in West Texas had *never* sent a high school graduate to the University of Texas. Reformers could point to this fact and state forthrightly that the plan would help poor rural white as well as nonwhite students. The new law passed the legislature by a single vote.

Importantly, however, it caused a split between conservative rural representatives and their conservative suburban counterparts. This division remains a source of tension today. By linking the fate of rural and poor whites to that of blacks and Mexican Americans, the debate over the Texas 10 Percent Plan revealed that what had been thought of as a racial divide also masked a historic class divide in the provision of elite higher education. This is especially critical in Texas, where the University of Texas plays such an important role in the development of state leadership.

By laboring under the burden of conventional affirmative action programs, the early analysis had fallen victim to the ideology of colorblindness. Colorblindness, compounded by thinking within the conventional racial categories of affirmative action and equal protection, closed down a space for progressive democratic experimentation. A consciousness of the racial differences that were manifest in the functioning of social institutions, without the correlative claim that the racial differences were the sole measure of the institutional pathology, was required before a break-through could occur. What this experiment also revealed was that, like civil rights reform in the South, the preservation of the leadership role of people of color in progressive experiments was critical to their success.[9] Indeed, this breakthrough turned the logic of colorblindness on its head: instead of promoting balkanization, racial consciousness among people of color was a crucial element in crafting a cross-racial coalition to make Texas's educational system more just for Texans throughout the state.

The effort to enact the 10 Percent Plan was part of a series of experiments launched by the civil rights movement to assess critically the content of democratic equality in the post–Jim Crow era. Many of these experiments were local initiatives. Some were nationalist in orientation, while others were aimed at economic vitalization. Many arose around faith communities. But all were concerned with translating the promise of equality into a social reality. While the leadership of people of color was critical in each case, for the Texas experiment to succeed in the long run it had to draw in white people from the larger community, and it had to draw on connections between the interests of people of color and those of their white supporters.

Coda: The academic performance of the 10 percenters, as those admitted under the new plan are called, surprised even the architects of the plan. The freshman GPA of those admitted under the 10 Percent Plan exceeded that of students admitted in previous years under test-based criteria, and this occurred across all racial groups—white, black, and Mexican-American.[10]

Racial Group Consciousness as a Political Asset

The dramatic way in which Mexican Americans and blacks in Texas moved quickly to respond to a legal ruling against affirmative action serves as a vivid introduction to the political dimension of race, which we will explore in the sections that follow. Like critical race theorists, those involved with the Texas 10 Percent Plan changed the terms of the race debate by shifting the ground away from race as a biological category toward race as a political space for pursuing a democratic agenda. Their activism showed how collective racial identity can operate within the American paradigm, not as the limiting essentialism denounced by conservatives and neoliberals but rather as the locus for individual and communal participation. In this chapter we will use their example to ask two questions: In what ways can racial group consciousness function as a political asset, rather than a liability, in an ongoing struggle for social justice? And how does being raced black or brown in the United States affect one's motivation to engage in this kind of transformative political activity?

In Chapter 2 we discussed the direct material linkage between race and power, in the form of poverty rates, wealth accumulation, and access to higher education and jobs. What we found was that, by all of these measures, people of color—and blacks in particular—continue to be socially, economically, and politically marginalized. Consequently, they pay an exorbitant price in the form of incarceration, morbidity, and mortality. In this chapter we focus on the way many—though by no means all—people of color respond to these political and material relationships. Rather than internalizing this social dysfunction as being their "own fault," many blacks have developed a critical perspective on "the system." Refusing to swallow the American Dream that those who succeed or fail invariably do so according to their individual merit, they understand that people of color face challenges beyond the capacity of personal effort, and they appreciate the necessity and efficacy of collective political struggle.

Aldon Morris and Jane Mansbridge call this "empowering mental state" an oppositional consciousness. That it would coalesce around racial group consciousness makes sense, since an oppositional consciousness "is often based on righteous anger on the part of the group and is prompted by personal indignities suffered through membership in the group. At a minimum, oppositional consciousness includes identifying with members of a subordinate group, identifying injustices done to that group, opposing these injustices, and seeing the group as having a shared interest in ending or diminishing those injustices."[11]

When a racial hierarchy is in plain view, an oppositional consciousness comes almost effortlessly to many people of color. Witness the contrasting reaction of blacks and whites to the racial hierarchy that dominated the Smithfield Packing Company near the Cape Fear River in North Carolina. It is the largest pork production plant in the world and the biggest employer in the region. Whites, blacks, American Indians, and Mexicans are assigned to different jobs—a pecking order described in stark detail in a *New York Times* story by Charles LeDuff entitled "At a Slaughterhouse, Some Things Never Die: Who Kills, Who Cuts, Who Bosses Can Depend on Race."[12] LeDuff got a job at the hog plant, and his report is based on inside experience. "The few whites on the payroll tend to be mechanics or supervisors. As for the Indians, a handful are supervisors; others tend to get clean menial jobs like warehouse work. With few exceptions, that leaves the blacks and Mexicans with the dirty jobs at the factory."

Even criminals are racially categorized. "Apparently inmates were on the bottom rung, just like Mexicans," LeDuff reports. For example, Billy Harwood worked at the plant when he was on work release from the Robeson County Correctional Facility. Unlike free white men, he was assigned to work the cut line with the Mexicans. Harwood complained that the work stinks "but at least I ain't a nigger. I'll find other work soon. I'm a white man." To which a black worker responded, "You might be white, but you came in wearing prison greens and that makes you good as a nigger."

Of the thirty new employees hired at the same time as LeDuff, the black women were assigned to the chitterlings room, where they would scrape feces and worms from intestines. The black men were sent to the kill (butchering) floor. The kill floor set the pace of the work, and individuals in those jobs could earn a relatively high wage of up to $12 an hour. Two white men and an Indian were given even more prestigious jobs making boxes. LeDuff declined a box job and ended up with most of the Mexicans on the cut floor, doing knife work—cutting sides of pork into smaller and smaller products.

> It is mostly the blacks who work the kill floor, the stonehearted jobs that pay more and appear out of bounds for all but a few Mexicans . . . The cut floor is opposite to the kill floor in nearly every way. The workers are mostly brown—Mexicans—not black, the lighting yellow, not red. The vapor comes from cold breath, not hot water . . . People on the cut lines work with a mindless fury. There is tremendous pressure to keep the conveyor belts moving . . . There is no clock, no window, no fragment of the world outside. Everything is pork. If the line fails to keep pace, the kill men must slow down, backing up the slaughter. The boxing line will

have little to do, costing the company payroll hours. The blacks who kill will become angry with the Mexicans who cut, who in turn will become angry with the white superintendents who push them. The Mexicans never push back. They cannot. Some have legitimate work papers, but more . . . do not . . . The Mexicans are so frightened about being singled out that they do not even tell one another their real names. They have their given names, their work-paper names and "Hey you," as their American supervisors call them.

Signs of a race-based hierarchy were everywhere. At the local court-house, according to LeDuff, a plaque commemorating World War I sol-diers listed the dead veterans by color: "white" on top, "Indian" in the middle, and "colored" on the bottom. In the hog plant, that same hierar-chy still governed. People were assigned to the hierarchy by race, and when the results proved unsatisfactory, they were encouraged to direct their anger at one another rather than at those in charge. Even the way the Smithfield plant operated kept people isolated. "If it's not the language barrier, it's the noise—the hammering of compressors, the screeching of pulleys, the grinding of the lines. You can hardly make your voice heard."

Within the group of workers who understood the need to organize in order to resist this hierarchy were many black workers. According to Wade Baker, a 51-year-old black man who worked at the plant, "Socially, things are much better . . . But we're going backwards as black people economi-cally. For every one of us doing better, there's two of us doing worse." Baker acknowledged the improvements in the South since his youth, when Jim Crow prevailed, but he also realized the limitation of social changes that helped advance a few while leaving the many behind. Unemployment in Robeson County, where he lived, was twice the national average. He shared the understanding of his black co-workers that "the system" is "antiblack and antipoor." One of Mr. Baker's co-workers called the factory "a plantation with a roof on it."

"We need a union," Baker said to LeDuff. He knew that in the late 1970s the meatpacking industry, then located in northern cities like Chicago, was unionized, and people got $18 an hour for work that Baker was now doing for slightly more than $9 an hour. To cut costs, many of the pack-ing houses moved south, where they could pay lower, nonunion wages.

But everyone believed that talk of a union was dangerous. The Mexicans feared that a union would force them out because of their illegal status. Others were intimidated, too. The last organizing drive had failed in part because the factory supervisors saw blacks as too closely identified with the union. "When workers arrived at the plant the morning of the vote, they were met by Bladen County deputy sheriffs in riot gear. 'Nigger Lover' had been scrawled on the union trailer." The union was voted down nearly two to one.

Sherri Buffkin, a white woman and the former director of purchasing who testified before the National Labor Relations Board in an unfair-labor-practice suit brought by the union in 1998, said in an interview with *The New York Times* that management had kept lists of union sympathiz-ers during the 1997 election, firing blacks who spoke up for the union and replacing them with Latinos. "I know because I fired at least 15 of them myself." In essence, the factory supervisors detected and feared an impulse for collective action among the black workers, who saw their own struggle in the context of a larger racial hierarchy.

Scholars studying the trade union movement more generally have found evidence that racial solidarity among black people has often been the source of political or social activism. Many working-class blacks have been among those most likely to join labor unions, and throughout the South, black workers have been the backbone of the union movement. The strongest support for CIO organization was found not among white workers on better-paying assembly lines but among the lowest echelons of the black working class such as sanitation workers.[13] Black workers saw systemic failure for what it was, and they struggled together to make their case. Dr. Martin Luther King, Jr., died while on a mission in Memphis to get a contract for garbage collectors. He had already made the connection between race, poverty, and class identity by drawing out the analytic link-ages that came directly from the civil rights movement.[14]

Even today, blacks are more likely than whites to support unions and to embrace social democratic views.[15] Industries with higher numbers of black workers have had higher levels of labor-conscious activism as well. For example, at a South Carolina textile mill in 1984, the Amalgamated Clothing and Textile Workers Union was faced with the possibility of decertification because only 43 percent of the employees belonged to the union. That was because only 12 percent of the whites joined—but 63 percent of the black workers were members.[16]

Black workers as well as Latino immigrants and other people of color have shown themselves more experienced at organizing or more willing to mobilize than white workers.[17] The resurgence of the labor movement in Los Angeles, for example, was tied to enthusiasm among immigrant workers of color. In 1999 labor experienced the largest successful organizing drive in the country since the 1930s, when 74,000 home-care workers in Los Angeles, most of them Latino, voted to unionize. Dora Guzman, an immigrant from Guatemala who worked as a food server at the Los Angeles International Airport, told a reporter, "The union is very important to me. With unions you get your managers to treat you with respect, and you get a worthwhile salary."[18]

Other immigrants of color have turned to ethnic workers' associations to pursue their grievances. Worker associations are community-based organizations that, unlike unions, possess more than a workplace orientation and tend to be rooted in ethnically or racially marginalized constituencies. The Workplace Project on Long Island, for example, seeks to convert the daily experiences of immigrant workers into a theory for future action. As its founder, Jennifer Gordon, explains, "Organizing workers goes far beyond a strike for a better contract. It must be the conscious development of a worker-led movement for better communities and better lives. The first step in achieving these goals must be to build centers of workers who learn what it means to be leaders by participating in a democratic organizing process."[19] The Workplace Project seeks to build an independent movement of low-income workers, composed disproportionately of people of color, to lead a struggle for better lives for all working people.

Racial bonds that are enhanced by cultural bonds can also connect people of color to common social identities and mobilize them to political action. Cultural bonds create cross-class convergence within a racial group which helps it resist the dominant culture's justification of the group's subordination. As Cornel West points out, a group's cultural resources and resiliency shapes and molds its political consciousness.[20] Group identity motivates individuals to join a social movement. When their group identity becomes a political identity, people are more willing to participate in the group's activities, to identify with its practices, and to make sacrifices for its cohesion.[21]

Religious associations that link the individual to a community of people who share a common culture or similar experiences can also engender feelings of political efficacy. Fredrick Harris describes the importance of faith-based organizations within the black community as sources of macro and micro political mobilization. Harris calls these religious resources "an oppositional civic culture." Contrary to those who view religion as a conservative force to accommodate believers to the status quo, Harris finds that the cognitive, discursive, and cultural resources of the black church are as important as its institutional networks for social movement and political mobilization. Churches give ordinary people the opportunity to make speeches, contribute money to a candidate, and work for a political campaign. But even more important are the simple acts of "collecting money, preparing food, setting up chairs and tables, performing a song, or leading a prayer." These activities, normally thought of as routine events in church life, are relevant skills that provide active church members, many of whom are black women, the political education necessary to challenge their marginality.[22]

Andrew Young affirms that religious rituals and symbols were critical to black political mobilization in the Mississippi Delta:

> Nobody could have ever argued segregation and integration and gotten people convinced to do anything about that. But when Martin [Luther King, Jr.] would talk about leaving the slavery of Egypt and wandering into a promised land, somehow that made sense to folks. And they may not have understood it; it was nobody else's political theory, but it was their grass roots ideology. It was their faith; it was the thing they had been nurtured on. And when they heard that language they responded . . . I think it was . . . when they saw in their faith also a liberation struggle that they could identify with, then you kinda had 'em boxed . . . And when you finally helped them to see that religion meant involvement in action, you kinda had 'em hooked then. You had a ready framework around which you could organize people.[23]

Religious beliefs and practices helped link faith to action not only for blacks but for white West Virginia coal miners, whose prayer meetings, biblical interpretations, and sacred songs strengthened their bond in the struggle for better working conditions.[24] Similarly, Latin American organizers used religious symbols in faith-based communities to interpret and legitimize political action. Marshall Ganz, in his study of the United Farm Workers' efforts to organize Mexican-American immigrants, also notes the importance of cultural rituals in strengthening bonds of solidarity and, through their familiarity and association with moral righteousness, lending legitimacy to the struggle. These rituals provided a defense against fear and reinforced a sense among participants that they were not alone as they embarked on risky ventures that challenged fundamental social or political institutions.[25]

Whether organizing a coalition to confront an educational hierarchy in Texas or organizing a union to confront a labor hierarchy in North Carolina, racial group consciousness can lay the foundation for democratic participation that makes blacks and other people of color more politically effective, not just politically active. Racial solidarity gives those who may feel racially marginalized the political confidence to organize and take risks. The bonds of trust that form around common cultural rituals and practices also help them transcend class differences and gain confidence. A collective awareness of systemic racial injustice can move those who have been marginalized to participate in public life rather than withdraw from it. The process of participation itself becomes an act of discovery, offering the rewards of fellowship and community awareness that come from being a part of joint decision-making.

In these ways, racial group consciousness becomes a form of cognitive, political, and moral literacy. It can excite people to participate in public forms of collective action. It is a key source of political energy that can ultimately be tapped for social change. Those progressives who deny its significance—as both a window on exclusion and an entryway for political activism—are ignoring an opportunity to rejuvenate a movement for social justice. Indeed, those trying to organize low-wage workers who are predominantly people of color may have no choice other than to meet these individuals "where they are at." By taking advantage of the pre-

existing institutional infrastructure and energy of race-based mobilization, progressives would have the opportunity to help more people practice the skills of political engagement.

Racial Group Literacy as a Psychological Resource

Racial group consciousness not only makes blacks more politically active
and effective as a group; it also helps make individual blacks more psychologically resilient. As such it becomes an important resource in the black
community, independent of the practical outcomes from political activism. Race-consciousness can affirm the individual's ability to cope with
the challenges of discrimination. It can offer solace to people who might
otherwise individuate the stigma of being positioned at the bottom of a
racial hierarchy, by granting access to a sense of community and not just
critique.

In a law school class, students were assigned to read an article in which
Peggy McIntosh lists 46 ways her white skin gives her the ability and the
freedom to be an individual.[26] Many white students identified with the article—it helped make them race-conscious in ways that they could relate
to. But many students of color resisted the idea of white-skinned privilege.
They worried that calling individualism a privilege means not only that it
is a preference or an unearned entitlement but that it is always better than
the fraternity or sorority that comes with being a member of a group.
They worried that it valorizes personal liberty in ways that are conformist
rather than reformist; that it reinforces rather than challenges hierarchy;
that it tells people of color they will be complete only when they acquire
those things that white people take for granted.

What was missing from the initial portion of the class discussion of
white-skinned privilege was the same thing missing from many conversations about race—the recognition that being forced by circumstances to
identify with a group of people can be a blessing in disguise. For instance,
one black woman described the experience that she and many of her black
women friends have in living without husbands or partners. Whereas the
overwhelming majority of white heterosexual women get married by the
time they are forty, that is simply not true for the black middle-class
women in law school.[27] The question the student raised, however, is this:

Who is truly freer in this situation? Is it the white women, who feel so-cially and culturally compelled to get married early; whose families worry that "there is something wrong with them" if by the age of twenty-eight they are not married; who feel like a personal failure if they cannot hold their marriage together? Or, this student suggested, is there something to be gained, an insight to be learned, from being involuntarily liberated from those cultural obligations? She pointed out that as an unmarried black woman she has experienced a certain freedom from cultural coer-cion, as well as a sense of community with many other black women who share her condition.[28]

This student's response may be an idiosyncratic reaction to a difficult reality. Nevertheless, similar to the relationship between black Americans to art forms such as jazz or the blues, this student found new forms of in-dividual redemption in what others might interpret as collective suffering. Emerging from the "oppressive experience of blackness," jazz and the blues are hybrid forms that exemplify a balance between the individual and the collective. They are American originals that use sites of oppres-sion to unleash the creativity of the individual. They represent a different kind of wholeness, the connection of being together in a small but famil-iar "partness."[29]

"Joined at the Stoop" is the phrase used in a *New York Times* headline to describe the way working-class elderly black women in a poverty-stricken section of Philadelphia looked out for one another.[30] When people in their neighborhood were getting robbed after they cashed their social security checks, the women all walked to the check-cashing office together. Having lived on the same block for thirty or forty years, these women resembled in their interdependence the interconnected structure of the front porches of their row houses.

The psychological value of expanding one's vision from individual iso-lation to group identification is illustrated in another story, this one from Brunswick, Maine. When in third grade, Jackson Stakeman, who is black, had a white classmate who called him a "darkie."[31] Jackson complained, and the teacher admonished the white student that what he had done was wrong: "If someone were in a wheelchair would you point it out? Would you tease that person about it?" This analogy—insensitive both to people of color and to people with disabilities—did not ease the situation for Jackson or his parents, who addressed their concerns to the administration. The school responded to their distress by bringing the two boys into separate meetings with a guidance counselor. The counselor proposed that the white classmate prepare a collage with images of black people. When the collage was presented to Jackson, he did not feel mollified, since all of the images were of black sports stars.

A few months later, Jackson wrote an essay for school, and in bold letters at the top of the first page he proudly dedicated the essay "To Black People Everywhere." His dad explains, "We tried, in raising him, to remind him that he was part of a greater collective. He may be a minority in Brunswick, Maine, but he needed to reach out to a larger identity that would be a source of support for him. Here he was definitely a minority, but if he expanded his vision he could link up with others like him." Like Wade Baker at the Smithfield factory, Jackson was getting the message: at the core of being strong enough to oppose powerful people allied against you is the feeling that you are not in this alone.

Resistance fosters resilience, the social psychologist Janie Ward explains. Black children who are encouraged to identify and then fight systemic oppression are less likely to internalize feelings of helplessness and are better prepared to withstand racism.[32] Race becomes a signifier of cultural heritage, not biological inferiority, of kinship and not just discrimination, of survival against the odds through mutual support and reciprocal connections to others. In these ways race simultaneously serves "the voice of black oppression and the voice of black liberation."[33]

As Beverly Daniels Tatum points out, opportunities "to come together" can enable blacks, especially young black teenagers, to talk about the issues that otherwise hinder their performance—racial encounters, feelings of isolation, test anxiety, homework dilemmas—"in the psychological safety of their own group." Tatum was describing the Student Efficacy Training (SET) program within the Metropolitan Council for Educational Opportunity (METCO) in Boston. SET required black students who were voluntarily bused into white suburban high schools as part of the METCO program to meet each day as a group with two staff members. At first, many of the student participants resented the meetings, which used up a study hall or a free period. But over time they eventually began to see their group as being "like one big family," and they started "looking out for each other with homework and stuff."

Not only did the students begin to share their own fears in ways that helped them bond, but the faculty noticed improvement in their academic performance and participation in school life. One classroom teacher said, "My students . . . aren't battling out a lot of the issues of their anger about being in a white community, coming in from Boston, where do I fit, I don't belong here . . . I think [because these issues] are being discussed in the SET room, the kids feel more confidence." Students who had been getting D's and F's starting getting B's and C's and an occasional A. The teachers were enthusiastic because the program produced immediate results. Tatum recognizes that "it might seem counterintuitive that a school involved in a voluntary desegregation program could improve both academic performance and social relationships among students by *separating* the black students for one period every day." But it did.[34]

Like race itself, solidarity in the form of community is not just one thing. It has the potential to free its members from externally imposed stigma. But it may also reflect back an externally generated and internalized inferiority that undermines political assertiveness. Assertiveness or commitment to collective struggle is not a worldview shared by all those who have been raced. Many blacks suffer at the hands of other blacks from the stigma of race that is shared by both blacks and whites. Indeed, relationships within communities of color may mirror the hierarchies observed in the larger society, in which the individual voice is stifled. As Frank Michelman has observed, in a winner-take-all society there is a strong resistance to being on the bottom. People in a position to keep someone beneath them will do so—including other people in their same racial group.[35]

Thus, the individual who is raced as dark-skinned and classed as poor may simply be trapped and made to feel less worthy not just by those in the white majority but by others in the community of color. Blacks who feel loyalty as blacks may be pressured to deny the problems of gender, class, and sexual orientation that exist within the black community.[36] Resolution of these problems will not come easily. Yet, before whites join a movement led by people of color, the damage done to the black community itself must be repaired. It may be necessary, as Tatum observes, to set aside room for restoring a sense of affinity that directly addresses feelings of social isolation. Self-contained spaces, which allow communities of color to become whole within hostile environments, may also furnish opportunities to address internal fragmentation along the lines of gender, class, skin color, and sexual orientation. In recognizing and coping with those fissures, some community members have been prompted to invent new forms of leadership (a phenomenon we explore further in Chapter 5). Forging a democratic, egalitarian community of color is not sufficient to change the conditions in the mine, but it is often necessary to help individuals within that community survive.

Turning a Psychology of Weakness into a Politics of Strength

Thus far we have tried to show, through a variety of stories, that those who have been raced black in our society are more likely than others to develop an oppositional, collective consciousness and to engage in political action, and that individuals whose political identity grows from awareness of their racial group identity and its implications often become more resilient in the face of racism. In other words, we have argued that a collective consciousness rooted in a racial oppositional consciousness can be both a political and a psychological asset.

In this section we will take this argument a step further, to explore the psychological links in a chain that connects race, power, the construction of the self, collective identity, and political activism. We will argue that in our current racial hierarchy, social and political power is distributed to blacks and whites asymmetrically, and this asymmetry of power leads to asymmetrical concepts of the self. Asymmetrical concepts of the self, in turn, have implications for the way people engage in political activities. Reduced access to individual power may lead to a heightened awareness of alternative methods for accessing collective power. To put it another way, racial group identification can turn a psychology of perceived individual weakness into a politics of collective strength.

As Janet Halley suggests, power names and positions people, and in so doing it constructs the self. "Power can be exercised not only to make people do things they would not otherwise do, but to make them become people they would not otherwise be."[37] This can have good and bad consequences. The bad consequences often occur when those in power act to name others without power. At the Smithfield hog factory, as we have seen, the Mexican workers had their birth names, their work-paper names, and "Hey you," the name their supervisors called them. To avoid being harassed by those who run things at the meat plant, the Mexican workers did not even tell one another their real names. But "Hey you" not only named them as anonymous, it also raced them as black and poor or its equivalent. "Hey you" became part of a "very precise operation" which the Marxist political theorist Louis Althusser has called "interpellation."

Interpellation is the act of defining someone's identity for him or her, including naming someone as being so insignificant that what they call themselves no longer matters. By diminishing the sense of self of those at the bottom of a racialized hierarchy, the act of naming transforms isolated individuals into racialized subjects.[38] Whether hailed by a supervisor or a law enforcement officer, "Hey you" can transform an individual with agency into an insignificant subject who is lumped with all others at the bottom. Some may respond to the "Hey you" of a police officer by running for dear life. To them, "Hey you" is too often accompanied by a willingness to shoot to kill. Others may turn around, compliantly. Either way, the officer's "Hey you" races them black and names them as a criminal, whatever their "biology" or actual innocence. Those who turn around have learned their "real" name and social position; the power of others has constructed their sense of who they are.[39]

The transformation from someone with a name to someone with only a race can occur through simple verbal hailing or it can take place with social policies that accomplish the same thing. In Oneonta, New York, for example, an elderly white woman who was assaulted could describe her assailant only as having a dark-skinned hand with a cut on it. When the police decided to investigate and detain all black men in the town, they were naming blacks in the community as criminal suspects.[40] This form of interpellation has entered popular consciousness in the dispute over racial profiling.

People respond to interpellation in different ways, depending on their social roles. When a police officer shouts "Hey you" on a street crowded with white people, it is quite conceivable that no one will respond. Most white people do not recognize themselves as the types of subjects who can be made into criminal suspects just because a cop yells "Hey you." In their minds, the policeman is not talking to them because he has not called out any specific identifying features like "Hey you in the red plaid shirt." Whereas a black person might respond to the officer's hail and thus see himself as a raced subject, white people in this society enjoy a certain racial invisibility and are not raced by the officer's call.

But even among blacks, there is not a one-way, negative relationship between power and the construction of the self. As black people have demonstrated throughout history, and as the stories in this chapter make clear, the self can also react affirmatively to the conventional exercise of power with various forms of collective resistance. From coded spirituals of slave defiance in the middle of the nineteenth century to nonviolent acts of civil disobedience in the middle of the twentieth century, blacks have created spaces where they can define themselves, instead of being totally defined by those at the top of the racial hierarchy. Within those spaces, they have shared their critique and constructed their own forms of power.

Such identity constructions, predicated on situating the individual experience within a collective reality, is what Charles Lemert has termed a "weak-we" relationship. Weak-we individuals construct their conception of self from their local experience of material reality, and they locate their conception of justice in tangible social practices rather than in an abstract universal truth. Identification with their local group is the primary psychological resource for weak-we individuals, however oppressed and stigmatized that group may be by the larger culture. A person with a weak-we identity is much more likely to develop a sense of group consciousness than a person with a strong-we identity. The strong-we conception of self is constructed out of an abstract notion of an autonomous self that one then projects onto all humanity. Strong-we individuals trust that their "intuitions are reliably in tune with certain universal human essences."[41] Strong-we individuals tend to value their autonomy more than their relationships; weak-we individuals tend to do the opposite.

This theory is consistent with research by the sociologist Michele Lamont, who conducted in-depth interviews with thirty black and thirty white blue-collar workers. She selected the workers randomly from phone books of working-class towns in New York and New Jersey and matched them by occupation and age (all had a high school diploma only). Although Lamont's sample was not scientifically selected, her interviews lasted two hours and enabled her to "develop a complex view" of these plumbers, electricians, truck drivers, letter carriers, and factory workers.[42]

The black workers Lamont spoke with emphasized group loyalty and egalitarianism, whereas white workers emphasized personal responsibility and the work ethic. According to the black workers, it was important to "show solidarity," by which they meant fighting daily for social justice, helping "the brothers." White workers had a more individualistic orientation. One black worker defined all black people as his kin and wanted to have enough money to help people: "They don't have to be our relatives, just be black and need it." A phone technician described his goals in life: "I'm more interested in things that are going to help minorities. I've always been for the underdog because of my upbringing when you're discriminated against." Their egalitarian impulses were reflected in their greater reluctance to describe themselves as feeling superior or inferior to others. More than twice as many blacks as whites said that they never feel superior to people. But these simple statistics do not fully capture the depth of the feelings of camaraderie and generosity that characterized the black workers. For these men, blackness was not so much a drop of blood as a state of mind.

Another way to appreciate the asymmetry in the way power constructs individual identity among blacks and whites is to imagine the experience of race as being like water. The constituent elements of water do not change with temperature, but the state of water differs profoundly. Similarly, the experience of having a racial or ethnic identity is common to all, but consciousness of that identity and its relative importance differs profoundly.[43] Minus the heat source of privilege, race for many poor black people is like water in its frozen state. The crystalline structure of race locks many poor black people into a set of local relationships that have to be negotiated regardless of their social position as defined by other factors. These preconditions are often associated with a weak-we identity. For poor blacks, identity is a function of their neighborhood and their race. Although their individual education or family background influences their self-conception, they are less likely than more privileged individuals to project out from their own experience to claim the right to speak for humanity as a whole. Their "we" is a local, community-bounded, or at most racially affiliated aggregation. It is a small-scale rather than a grandly universal conception of the self. Yet when weak-we individuals coalesce in weak-we groups, their collective experience has large-scale implications.

By contrast, for most white people, including many who are poor, race is experienced more like a vapor than like ice. Water in its gaseous state is not constrained. It is functionally formless. It does not inhibit movement. Liberal theory defines race—based on the experience of those doing the defining—as vapor. These liberal theorists assume, based on their personal experience as whites, that race should be a nonconstraining factor. Their experience permits them to assume an essentially evanescent quality for race. Yet for people who have been raced black, those vaporous conditions do not come about by mere declaration alone. Only political struggle or propitious access to huge amounts of wealth can turn race from ice into vapor for people who have been raced black.

The asymmetry of racial self-understanding that we have tried to capture with the water metaphor has important consequences. The asymmetry of race helps explain, for example, why the colorblindness thesis appeals to so many white people. Colorblindness as an ideological and emotional position "names" race for many white people, because it explains the way they experience race.[44] It names race as an arbitrary category that can simply be ignored. If you just refuse to see it, race becomes like vapor. If the white experience of race is invisible, and this becomes the norm, it is easy to see the basis for the moral content of the colorblindness thesis as expounded by liberals and conservatives alike. The small "l" liberal theory of race is, in short, the white theory of race, based on the construction of self as an autonomous and anonymous historical actor.[45]

In a class taught at Harvard Law School, students were invited to create a visual image of what race would look like in their ideal world. Two white students, independently of each other, constructed their image by holding up a blank sheet of white paper. One accompanied her image with a verbal explanation that in her view "race is silly." Neither seemed to assign any significance to the fact that racelessness in their ideal world assumes by default not only a blank slate but a completely white universe. This is the classic strong-we identity—projecting out from an individual experience a claim about the experience of humanity as a whole.

For those who experience race as ice, or for those who move back and forth between ice and water, depending upon their specific context, the experience of race is both relational and definitional. It defines itself in relationships to others—in relationships both to those who are raced invisible and autonomous and to those who are raced visible and interconnected. This relational sense of self views with suspicion hierarchies of power that consider a vaporized state superior to a frozen one, or that profile and discipline those groups whose very visibility makes them targets. It also creates bonds and feelings of solidarity among similarly situated targets whose fate seems linked. The weak-we conception of the self describes the experience of many people of color in the United States, who fluctuate *between* independent and the interdependent notions of self.[46]

Sometimes people who escape the frozen state that characterizes blackness still carry traces of that frozen state with them, in the form of what the psychologist Claude Steele calls the "stereotype threat." This combination of hypervisibility and invisibility can have a negative impact particularly on the academic competitiveness of high-achieving black schoolchildren and college students.[47] Even for those who leave the structure of their in-group, their newfound mobility may be experienced not as walking through vapor but as walking backwards up a cheese grater. Sociologists and psychologists have labeled this phenomenon the "token effect." Because a token black is the only person like herself in the new environment, she may have a sense that the price of becoming invisible is the loss of her identity. The new environment forces her to shed what makes her who she is.[48]

A weak-we identity may respond to such competing pressures by focusing on opportunities for collective resistance. This phenomenon helps explain the "irrational" commitment of blacks to the political process. If one controls for class, blacks participate in politics at a higher rate than whites. Poor blacks vote at higher rates than poor whites, and black women have higher levels of interest in politics than women generally. In 1998, voter turnout among blacks was slightly higher than the level for voters overall, even though income alone would predict that they would be less likely to vote. Black voter turnout is actually increasing at a time when general voter turnout is declining consistently. The same seems true of Latinos, especially if the 2001 mayoral election in Los Angeles is evidence of a trend.[49] Explaining why this is so is complex, but in our view it has as much to do with the sense of community fate bound up in public decision-making as it does with any abstract belief in the virtues of exercising one's democratic rights. This notion of linked fate may also explain why black and Latino graduates of law schools show a greater commitment to public service than white graduates.[50]

Even within communities of color, however, race is asymmetrical in the way that each racial or ethnic group experiences it. By this we mean that race for Latinos does not function the same as for blacks or for whites; race for Asians does not function the same as for blacks or Latinos; and so on. But while cultures as a whole can be categorized along a continuum from strong-we to weak-we, individuals should be analyzed in terms of both. This means that there are conventional understandings of race constantly in play, while at the same time those understandings are highly context-bound and imbricated by specific histories and discursive practices.[51]

Despite the importance of local context, the asymmetry between a weak-we and a strong-we self is particularly revealing for our political race project; it identifies the democratic potential in the way many people of color use race as a site for contestation and exchange, structuring and modifying their public engagement.[52] Because of its hybrid nature, the weak-we group often engages in a politics based on group fulfillment as a principal means of individual fulfillment.[53] As Martin Luther King, Jr., recognized, "We [blacks] have many assets to facilitate organization. We band together readily, and against white hostility we have an intense and wholesome loyalty to each other . . . Solidarity is a reality in Negro life, as it always has been among the oppressed."[54] The public dimension of a weak-we identity exists because the way you relate to others and your sense of connection to others helps to define "who you think you are." The connection with group members comes from a sense that others share a common fate with you. The result is a relational and public version of the self.[55] It is a peculiarly American variant of reality for a group of people whose self is defined by local circumstances that disable individual choice and mobility, within a larger culture that celebrates those very virtues.

The democratic potential of a racial group identity was evident in Lamont's interviews with black workers. She found that these workers valued friendships and the ability to socialize with one another. They often expressed worth on the basis of altruistic concerns as well as the quality of their interpersonal relationships. Their preference for fraternity had a fragile but real participatory dimension. It helped socialize them to listen, collaborate, delegate tasks, and share authority—all crucial democratic practices.[56]

Having the support of others makes getting things done a lot easier. People who are disenfranchised or dispossessed can also be angry together in ways that channel their anger to propel forward motion. On the other hand, groups can exacerbate passion and irrationality. But when the danger of group polarization is balanced against the alienation of isolated individuals, we agree with Michael Walzer that the individual acting alone is often more of a threat to democracy than the individual who interacts with others.[57]

By contrast, many of the white workers Lamont interviewed were more likely to define themselves by reference to the meta-narrative of universal access to the American Dream. This view of self creates a comparably individualistic notion of democracy. The political theorist Judith Shklar locates this American version of an independent self and the notion of citizenship attached to it in efforts to create an identity in contradistinction to slavery. To have a self, you must "own" yourself. To be a liberal self is to be differentiated from others—to enjoy a freedom from group constraint, coercion, or external definition.[58] It is encouraged, indeed made possible, by the capacity to be both personally visible yet collectively invisible and remain an autonomous, freely choosing, independent individual.

The strong-we conception of the self, for example, helps explain why a white felon at the Smithfield meat plant who was treated "like a nigger" nevertheless could fail to see his local reality and instead could connect himself to the universal signifier "white." By adopting a strong-we position, however, he put himself in a bind. If everyone is an independent individual who "owns" himself, then how does Billy Harwood explain his personal failure? In contrast to the willingness to join a union that we associate with the weak-we identity of Wade Baker and other blacks at the hog factory, Harwood's strong-we position offers little comfort. He can either internalize his failure as an individual or blame someone else—most likely a person of color. His choices are constricted to the extent he lacks a sense of community that might provide a more critical analysis of the bottom rungs of the social hierarchy at the hog factory that he too occupies.

From Racial Group Consciousness to Democratic Practice

Most observers and commentators now recognize that race does not have a fixed meaning, even though the dominant discourse on race still depends upon the fiction of such a stable meaning.[59] In the Texas coalition that organized in the wake of the *Hopwood* decision, race became a proxy for one's political and socioeconomic status rather than merely denoting an individual's biological ancestry. Mexican Americans and blacks came together by using a different language both to discuss race and to construct a coalition. They started with consciousness of the unfair effect of admissions criteria on black and Mexican-American students. They then engaged with social and not just racial justice critiques as they discovered that rural white students had also effectively been raced black or brown and thus excluded from the flagship schools. As they linked race to class, their story became a parable of how race-consciousness can evolve to embrace a social justice critique and inspire a broader democratic experiment for distributing educational opportunity.

This multi-step progression from race-consciousness through social

justice critique to democratic experimentation is what we are calling political race. Political race is a lens through which to see and address injustices to people of color and, beyond them, injustices to other oppressed
groups such as poor whites. It is an evolutionary process.

The first step involves recognizing as an asset the potential solidarity
and connection that those who have been raced often experience. In
Texas, race became not just a position of disadvantage but a position from
which to critique the status quo. Blacks and Mexican Americans started by
first privileging race but found there was not just one single injustice tied
to race. Race had located them socially and politically in a space from
which they could perceive the intergenerational structure of injustice in
the way educational opportunities were distributed in Texas. They demonstrated, by their insight, our epistemological claim that without access
to race others are unlikely even to recognize the ways in which many of
our civil institutions are undemocratic.[60]

But perception is only the first step. Race-consciousness alone would
have limited group members to an awareness of the admissions monopoly
enjoyed by the suburban high schools. An exclusively race-conscious position would have promoted solutions that benefited only group members
or, even worse, provided benefits only in the form of ethnic tokenism or
racial symbolism.

Step two of political race entails articulating a broader social justice
agenda. Blacks and Mexican Americans began to take this step when they
shifted from mere solidarity and group consciousness to the development and strategic deployment of a political race-consciousness. They explored how the construction and uses of race have historically operated to
prevent authentic and strategic linkages between communities that have
more in common than is normally supposed. Progressive reformers in
Texas started with groups most likely to mobilize and then challenged
these groups to expand their critical analysis to precipitate transformative
change. By channeling their anger about the demise of affirmative action
into a larger critique of high-stakes admissions policies generally, they
energized and emboldened even rural white legislators to support their
effort.

The third step of political race, which we develop at greater length in later chapters, entails a willingness to experiment with new democratic practices. In Texas, black and Mexican American professors, activists, and elected officials engaged in popular education and critical reframing, linked ultimately to the democratic idea that education at a state university should serve all the residents of the state. Theirs was not just a plea to exercise state power to redistribute resources. Instead, they applied theories of democracy to the processes of participation and mobilization. They came to understand that democracy and justice are interlinked substantive goals. Each has many local expressions that flow from collective experiments, large and small.

Rather than resisting the implications of the 10 Percent Plan, the leadership at the University of Texas took new responsibility for the system of K–12 public education to which they now were demonstrably connected. The net effect has been a more diverse campus and a greater concentration of university resources on improving elementary and secondary education in the state. But without the leadership of people of color, the systematic unfairness that characterized the conventional ways of selecting classes would have remained invisible. Their success reinforces the idea that progressive reform needs a politics. By politics, we mean a strategy for directly and continuously engaging the energy of local communities and political activists to mobilize a transformative social justice movement.

In subsequent chapters we shall show how our present conception of democracy is failing not only people of color but poor and working-class whites as well.[61] For now we merely draw attention to a few experiments that showcase the democratic potential of collective action among racially defined communities. Archon Fung uses the term "street level democracy" to describe local communities of democratic practice.[62] In his model, the "atom of social action" is a small, coherent group of lay citizens and professionals who govern themselves through a deliberative problem-solving process that Fung calls "learning by doing." These groups are deliberative, pragmatic, and experimental. Their decisions reflect the "best guess" of the participants; they often change in light of new information or feedback that reveals flaws in the analysis; and they are considered good because they work. Only when conflicting opinions cannot first be settled through opportunities to deliberate over time do these local "communities of inquiry" vote to arrive at the single opinion that collective action may require.[63]

Fung spent eighteen months observing community policing boards which met regularly in Chicago, as well as local school councils. He found that these local, deliberative bodies produced outcomes that were often better than what the police commissioner or school principals identified as a priority in a command-and-control model. Poor neighborhoods seemed to exhibit slightly better collective problem-solving skills than those neighborhoods with median incomes in the upper three quartiles. Three of the four police programs ranked as excellent by the Chicago Community Policing Evaluation Consortium in 1997 came from poor neighborhoods with what academics would call "relatively little community capacity."[64] Indeed, people who lived in high-crime areas turned out at community policing meetings in greater numbers than did people in low-crime areas—a finding which weighs against the notion that disadvantaged groups "lack the resources to participate in decentralized democratic institutions."[65]

In every neighborhood, substantially more women participated than men. Whereas white men tend to dominate in more formal, conventional political arenas, Fung found that participation in local deliberative bodies was much more egalitarian, as measured by race and gender, than he expected. Approximately 70 percent of local school council members were women.[66] Both blacks and Hispanics participated in the local school governance councils in proportion to their presence in Chicago's population.[67] Moreover, Fung's findings show that blacks and Hispanic parents are somewhat more likely to turn out to vote in local school council elections than others. They are also as likely as their white neighbors to run for office. In Fung's words, "Disadvantaged citizens will overcome quite substantial barriers to participate in institutions that credibly promise to reward such activity with concrete improvements to the public goods upon which those citizens rely."[68]

Fung's research found that blacks and Hispanics, especially when they made up at least half of the community, participated in community policing meetings at higher levels than would be predicted from their income or class position.[69] By contrast, when Hispanics constituted a minority of a neighborhood's population, they tended to be under-represented at community policing meetings.[70] This key finding supports our claim that race may function for people of color as a place for political mobilization and solidarity. At these organized and local sites of deliberation, the willingness of blacks and Hispanics to participate rose as attendance by members of their racial group went up. This likely reflects an increase in confidence that their participation is welcomed and valued.

In these many ways, Fung's study of street-level democracy confirms our claims about the potential significance of race to progressive and democratic transformation. First, he shows that racial solidarity can be a positive condition for democratic participation. His findings in Chicago's local school councils suggest the importance of a critical mass of participants of color. In integrated settings in which whites dominate, both black and Hispanic parents often do not show up or talk at the meetings. Second, he demonstrates that racial solidarity alone does not produce systemic change. Only when it is linked to democratic participation broadly conceived can racial solidarity produce ongoing and sustained relationships in which the people work with, rather than under or for, their government officials. This kind of meaningful representation is a form of communication and movement that is horizontal as well as vertical, and it does not reduce to mere symbolism or status.

Political Race Is Neither Identity Politics nor Class Politics

Political race is distinct from identity politics, simple race-consciousness, or, for that matter, class. Identity politics is consumed in a single step—the personal *is* political. In identity politics, the subject position is simply affirmed and legitimated by virtue of its recognition of that identity. Political race is not simply a more militant form of identity politics. In fact, political race is a critical lens on identity politics, to the extent that identity politics is a thin version of both politics and identity.

The Workplace Project on Long Island illustrates the difference between identity politics and political race. As Jennifer Gordon explains, shared ethnic background among the mostly Hispanic workers was not sufficient to make internal participation work. "For one, non-Salvadorans made up a disproportionate part of the organization's member-leadership. For another, the Salvadorans sometimes were divided along Salvadoran political allegiances, which was not constructive for the group. The fact that everyone spoke the same language and was having some similar experiences as immigrant workers was critical to being able to build a solid organization—but that kind of linguistic/experience shared identity is present in a lot of organizations that don't have strong internal democracy."[71] For the Workplace Project to succeed, it had to go beyond thin ethnic solidarity to develop strong democratic structures. It had to move beyond identity politics to political race. For the immigrant workers, political leadership solely premised on ascriptive characteristics would have been corrosive of the vitality of their community.

We also want to emphasize the distinctions between our project of political race, on the one hand, and the idea that racial consciousness is reducible to claims of racial superiority, with the politics that flows from those claims, on the other. We fear that some readers will equate our commitment to race-consciousness with the bigoted forms of white supremacy that define for so many the exclusive meaning of race. We are here making a crucial distinction between race-consciousness and racism.[72] While political race is a form of black race-consciousness, we do not reduce it to its biological expressions nor to its expression as "anti-whiteness."[73] Confusion on this point inevitably leads to the call for race-blindness or colorblindness as the only political position consistent with liberalism.

In almost every instance in our history, movements based on white race-consciousness have endorsed racial supremacy, whereas movements based on black race-consciousness have not.[74] For nonwhites, race-consciousness was more often a door into political participation that was not destructive of the idea of a polity within which issues that divided the "races" could be constructively addressed. There are, of course, exceptions, but their very marginal or exceptional status simply proves rather than refutes the main point we have been making. Moreover, we are arguing that political race consciousness is not restricted to those people who are phenotypically black.[75]

Our thesis is diametrically opposed to notions of biological essentialism. It is the very antithesis of the fear of ethnic or racial balkanization that troubles the neoliberals or those we have called progressive universalists. Balkanization depends upon a conception of essential differences between people and groups of people. Without some form of biological or cultural essentialism as a fundamental axiom, there is less possibility of using racial separatism as an organizing political principle.

Our thesis does not support claims of white nationalism either, because we are directly challenging the idea of race as a biological category or nationalist concept. Yet, we argue that, in part because of their collective experience of being marginalized, racialized groups have much to teach us about the positive values of a collective identity as a site for democratic participation. Our strategic claim is that people who feel marginalized need to have a political space before they can be mobilized for political action. We also claim that it is easier to mobilize those who feel marginalized when their specific claims or perspectives are addressed. We are faithful to the basic liberal view when we say that the individual participant must feel that his or her conception of self is respected, in order for that individual to have a stake in the process. If the process is destructive of that conception, a rational individual might ask: Why participate in one's own disintegration? Finally, we shall argue in Chapters 5 and 6 that the experience of trying to incorporate racially marginalized groups suggests the importance of rethinking issues of representation in particular and democracy in general to emphasize community-based, dynamic, and site-specific opportunities for voice and choice. Racialized communities can represent sites for democratic renewal and resist the pressure to become part of a system of patronage that merely reinforces racial divisions. Yet this risk can be avoided only with deliberation within the community that is both democratic and transformative.

With the political race project, we propose a vision of political organizing that puts the democratic process in direct opposition to the dominant ideology of individualism, as reflected in the consumerism of the market, in order to articulate the needs of those whom the market neglects. We note that this is especially important for those groups for whom the market has never been intended to work. Some commentators on the right talk about ending self-imposed "racial apartheid"—of rescuing black men and women from their dependence on group affinity so they can participate in democracy as individuals of various ethnicities and races. By joining the market economy, they would be put right. If young black men would just get to work in the pork plant, at $9-an-hour doing jobs that paid $18 an hour ten years ago when the plant was unionized, everything that is "wrong" with them would be fixed even if everything that is wrong with the Smithfield Packing Company would stay the same.

This example, among the others that we have used, may lead some to ask: Why political race and not political class? Political race builds on a sense of linked fate that, as a general matter, white working-class people simply do not currently have, largely because social policy has actively opposed the development of such a consciousness. Despite the obvious energy and potential for change that is pooled within the community of blacks or Latinos, some progressive universalists argue that emphasis on race is counterproductive because it undermines the working-class base of the Democratic Party. Racism, in their view, pulls white working-class voters to the Republican agenda.[76] These commentators advocate programs in which the race of the intended beneficiaries is not mentioned. These approaches potentially undermine the very groups that would be most likely to campaign aggressively for a progressive agenda.[77]

Indeed, this is exactly what happened after World War II, when the CIO dealt with the danger of racism by de-emphasizing race and not making strong appeals to black workers.[78] Fifty years later, in Miami, Florida, deference to fears of white racism in the nation's largest textile plant caused the union organizing effort to fail among whites and left black employees with no sense that the union was concerned with them and their interests.[79] It was only when union organizers found they could draw on the strengths of Chicano and black communities that the organizing effort made progress. By highlighting the willingness of blacks and Chicanos to work together and take a stand, the organizers helped white workers see that the racial pride of minority communities strengthened the coalition.[80]

When racial justice issues were ignored, blacks felt that the campaign was unresponsive to their concerns. Racial pride became a vehicle for building worker, and ultimately community, solidarity. It was seen not merely as a formula for advancing self-interests but as an appeal to their best instincts. Indeed, many white workers "came to believe that greater working class unity could be built by confronting rather than avoiding issues of discrimination, race and racism."[81]

When white former SNCC organizers created the Grass Roots Organizing Work (GROW) Project in Laurel, Mississippi, and helped organize black and white pulpwood cutters and later woodworkers at a Masonite plant, they confronted race bias head-on. Martha Mahoney described the conflict this way:

> The organizers told the white woodcutters that they could hold any attitudes or beliefs they chose about black inferiority and white superiority, but regardless of their beliefs, their behavior must change completely. They had to work on a basis of genuine equality with blacks if they wanted to make any progress with their union. This strategy reflected their belief that shared interests could quickly mobilize changed behavior, but that rhetoric would probably be the last vestige of white racism to change. The result was organizational growth, and also surprisingly rapid, explicit changed beliefs. One former Klansman commented, after a few years of work in the union, that he had now "joined the civil rights."[82]

The argument for race-consciousness as an organizational asset does not mean blaming white workers but advocating conscious coalition-building while acknowledging existing racial divisions. The race-consciousness of black and brown workers makes their political consciousness more likely. But even more than making race visible so as to reach out to workers of color, organizers have to engage in a democratic project of education, analysis, and mobilization. It is not enough to identify leaders of color with the ability to articulate the concerns of their racial constituency. It is necessary to involve that constituency in the process of decision-making and strategic planning. Here, we begin to see the importance of moving from race-consciousness to political activism and a participatory vision of both social justice and democracy.

Another answer to "Why not class?" is that we are working with categories that people understand. There is simply no American vocabulary for class as a linked fate or as a basis for critique of systemic failure. Class does not appear to affect identity in qualitatively the same way as does race. In a study of white working-class women, Beverley Skeggs reports that while they were highly conscious of class, they refused to identify as working-class and adopted various strategies of dissimulation to avoid feeling and appearing working-class. She writes, "It thus seems unlikely that the actions of these women are likely to lead to class politics, to class organization or even to class consciousness of a directly articulated form."[83] Such a rejection of one's class position prevents formation of a weak-we identity and precludes the kind of group-based effort we argue is central to democratic participation.

Class is often an unnamed, intentionally unnoticed variable in the lives of Americans, who are taught to identify individual hard work as the primary explanatory variable for social mobility. The narrative of the American Dream—if individuals work hard and play by the rules, they succeed—invariably trumps other explanations, such as class structure. When working-class and poor whites fail to get ahead, they often turn to racial stereotypes as a way of explaining their own powerless condition. "Other" people, black people, have simply stolen the American Dream, by getting undeserved benefits such as welfare or quotas. Because class is not named in this society, to collapse race into class would be to make *both* invisible, disabling a social movement from forming around either variable.[84]

This leads to yet another answer to the question: Why political race, not political class? Unlike race, poverty is not something that most people are proud of. In this sense we do rely on cultural (as opposed to biological) nationalism to do the work for us. Cultural nationalism has reinforced ideas of solidarity and has affirmed for many people of color a collective pride in their identity. This response builds on the asymmetry of race without locating itself exclusively within a race-based identity or critique.

Indeed, a political race analysis can help identify class barriers. For example, at the hog plant, blacks who wanted a union understood that "the system" was "antiblack and antipoor." Their insight is consistent with Charles Tilly's research, which shows how those with power in organizations often solve pressing organizational problems by creating unequal work-related categories (different jobs connected to different promotion lines and commanding very different rewards) and matching them to exterior categories of race, ethnicity, or gender. In places like the hog plant, therefore, race-based mobilization can draw attention to large inequalities in the distribution of job types as well as to the huge disparities in rewards associated with particular job categories themselves.[85]

Billy Harwood did not share that understanding. His strong-we position encouraged him to identify more with white elites than with other workers in the plant. As a felon, he was not given the good jobs set aside for free white men; yet he seemed oblivious to the fact that the racial hierarchy at the factory raced him black. Beth Roy has described the effects of "the myth of American classlessness" on black and white graduates of Central High School in Little Rock, Arkansas.[86] Many working-class whites did not see themselves as members of "some group bound to a 'place'" but as unfettered humans who could scale whatever heights they were willing to challenge. When they failed, they were left angry and frustrated as individuals, with a Hobbesian understanding of society. Their racial group "privilege" gave them a temporary psychological boost, but it also left them bereft of the tools to engage in progressive critique or social change. By focusing on white-skinned privilege, for example, "white workers hear only about the qualities they share with whites from other classes and higher socioeconomic status—not about interdependence, mutuality, nor the many ways in which people of color have brought militancy" to the defense of working-class people.[87]

By contrast, consciousness of race has, for many people of color, functioned as a form of political literacy, both affirmatively connecting individuals to a group and critically assessing the conditions of the group in light of larger structures within the society. It may encourage them not only to see but also to act. Race-based mobilization highlights the existence of, and also aims to eliminate, the multiple forms of race-based exploitation. But it can also move to name larger democratic principles.

The oppression of black Americans can spark political engagement with democracy in a way that class does not. The early civil rights movement, for example, moved from explicit consciousness of race to reach for the moral high ground. In *Why We Can't Wait,* King wrote, "American politics needs nothing so much as an injection of the idealism, self-sacrifice and sense of public service which is the hallmark of our movement." And in a 1959 speech he eloquently gave voice to this seemingly contradictory theme of victimization and transformation:

> For the southern Negro is learning to transform his degradation into resistance. Nonviolent resistance. And by so doing he is not only achieving his dignity as a human being, he is helping to advance democracy in the South. This is why my colleagues and I in the Southern Christian Leadership Conference are giving our major attention to the campaign to increase the registration of the Negro voters in the South to three million. Do you realize what would happen in this country if we were to gain three million southern Negro votes? We could change the composition of Congress. We could have a Congress far more responsive to the voters' will . . . A new era would open to all Americans. Thus, the Negro, in his struggle to secure his own rights is destined to enlarge democracy for all the people, in both a political and a social sense.

King's message was that we must acknowledge the experience of racial exclusion to remind us about the need "to enlarge democracy for all the people." The experience of the dispossessed in general and blacks in particular can be politically inclusive if racial justice is a window enabling us to see the larger injustice instead of a plea for succumbing to it. In this way, King claimed race as a starting point for systematic reform.

In our view, one of the reasons political race occupies a theoretical space that can promote and sustain vital coalitions is that the very movement to political race represents a commitment to change. The very opening within a culture that makes change possible also has a transformative effect on the culture. Points of resistance, large and small, become clear. Perhaps more important, a change in the political dimension of a culture changes the aspirational horizons as well. One of the things that the civil rights movement did, and changed for all time in American politics, was to tie political struggles to what have conventionally been seen as social and cultural struggle. Culture is not politics and we do not pretend that cultural activity is a substitute for political activity, but we understand the critical relationships.

Conclusion

In this chapter we contend that the impetus to change a failed set of practices will likely come from people of color. The weak-we construction of nonwhite groups helps explain this category of activists. Because they see their fate as socially linked to others like themselves, democratic organization makes sense for them. It is, in its finest articulation, doing with and for others.

The activity generated by those who are most likely to think of themselves as disenfranchised can be a catalyst for the independent dispossessed if two things happen: (1) if the weak-we groups, by communicating their critique in a larger vision of social justice, invite others to join with them; and (2) if potential allies—watching those who have hope in the future act on the basis of that faith—then feel encouraged to transform witness into action.[88] When those two things happen, the conditions are set for the development of what we are calling political race.

We use the word "race" in multiple ways within our political race project. First, as we discussed in Chapter 2, the term race is an empirical diagnostic to assess the material conditions of a group of people. Second, the term describes those who identify with the struggles of racialized groups, usually including people conventionally defined as racial group members but not limited to them. For us, the term connotes those who have made a concrete choice—or whose material conditions can encourage such a choice—to engage in transformative political struggle.

For those in Texas who saw the experience of race as political, it was not simply a sign of conflict, black versus white, invisible versus stigmatizing. Rather, race named the status of marginalized groups in relation to power, and then became—as evidenced in the development of the 10 Percent Plan—a source of oppositional consciousness. Under the leadership of Mexican-American and African-American legislators and activists, the Texas coalition used the state's rigid residential segregation as a vehicle for reallocating the scarce and valuable resource of higher education in a more democratic way. This strategy not only built on the racial reality of Texas but also produced a more diverse student body in a way that was fair both to people of color and to poor and rural whites. Although it did not remove the structural components of inequality that disadvantage all students in rural or urban schools, the elegant simplicity of the plan benefited the entire state.

The story of the Texas 10 Percent Plan illustrates that political race is not defined exclusively by constructing a series of oppositions based on color or genealogy. It may be transformed into a site of oppositional organizing, but that does not mean organizing in opposition to white people. Black is not the opposite of white; it is not a color at all in any essential sense. Instead, it describes a social, cultural, and political space that is tied both to self-identity as well as to the capacity for political action. There is no essential morphological or biological basis to the construction of racial groups, but the existence of such groupings continues to have roots in both the empirical history of white supremacy and in the discursive structure that supports it. The project of political race is a direct challenge to that discursive structure. It does not depend on the substitution of another discursive framework, such as class-based inequality, but looks instead to the places where race, politics, culture, and economics intersect. Political race is not something you are; it's something you do. It's a decision you make.

Some, like the sociologist Todd Gitlin, think that we obsess about race.[89] They worry about the negative political consequences of focusing on race. They cannot imagine a benefit to American democratic life flowing from racially self-conscious groups. We respond to their fear by pointing out the potential richness of the democratic contributions that racialized groups can, do, and should be encouraged to make.

We started our inquiry in Chapter 2 by asking the question: Is there a racially identifiable way the social goods of this nation are distributed? In asking it, we used conventional understandings of race, and we discovered that the answer is yes. But as the story of the Texas 10 Percent Plan and many others make clear, there are more "black" people in America than can be accounted for using ordinary definitions.

RETHINKING CONVENTIONS   4
OF ZERO-SUM POWER

In the summer of 1998, one of us observed a golf-ball relay race involving children, ages nine to eleven, at a going-away party. The two teams were organized by gender: boys against the girls. The object of the race was to carry a golf ball on a teaspoon for a specified distance and then transfer the spoon to the next child, without either dropping or touching the ball. Both times the children played the game, the girls won. They "kept their eyes on the ball," according to the analysis of the adults present. Slow and steady. The boys focused instead on "the outcome" and assumed that raw speed would get them to the finish line first.

As the boys realized they were losing (because speed alone does not keep a golf ball on a teaspoon), they experimented with different—and devious—strategies. They catapulted the golf ball forward to the finish line, for example, thus technically complying with the rules because they did not actually touch the ball with their hand. They palmed the bowl of the spoon in their hand rather than holding the stem of the spoon as they had been instructed. Despite their efforts to bend the rules, however, the girls' team still won.

The adults watching the race, many of them academics, then began to "deconstruct" the game. The initial interpretation was that the game illustrated conventional views of contemporary gender dynamics—differences stemming from either cultural or natural tendencies of boys and girls at play. Girls possess superior fine motor skills; boys have better gross motor skills. Girls are more people-oriented and value their relationships more highly.[1] Girls don't cheat but instead follow the rules and cooperate with authority rather than challenging or resisting it. Because they are traditionally considered less powerful in a culture in which power is both zero-sum and controlling, girls find alternative ways of establishing connections with one another to substitute a network of relationships for their otherwise individual weakness.[2] As with all first impressions, however, a lot more lay beneath the surface.

The grandmother of one of the children, a high-school English teacher now in her early 80s, observed the game with the other adults. She interrupted the conversation to ask, "Who designed the game?"[3] As the official hosts of the party, the girls did. The girls designed the game to play to their strengths, and the boys mistakenly assumed that the game (like most games involving physical activity) favored *their* strengths.[4] The girls enjoyed a preferred position from which they could defend or promote their particular skills, and they did so in a way that allowed them to dominate their opponents and consistently win a zero-sum game—a characteristic traditionally associated with males.[5]

Indeed, when the girls were asked to pose for a picture of the winners, they assumed the muscle-flexing winner's stance of a male bodybuilder—in other words, they acted like boys. And when the girls exercised their power as winners to select the next games to be played, they chose activities that did not appeal to, or that even excluded, the boys.[6] At this point, the guest of honor at the party—a boy—got upset. After all, he was, in his mind, entitled to have at least some input into the terms of engagement. When asked why he cared that the girls were excluding him, he said, "Because they are in the majority." There were in fact more girls.[7]

In this game, the girls subverted traditional gendered norms of power to prevail in the competition. Conventional ideas about power suggest that it invariably involves control, domination, or force.[8] But power occupies and functions in different spheres. John Gaventa, Steven Lukes, and others who have explored theories of power articulate three dimensions of power, as we conventionally conceive it:[9]

- *First dimension:* Direct force or competition, typically in a winner-take-all context;

- *Second dimension:* Indirect manipulation of rules to shape the outcome of such competition;

- *Third dimension:* Mobilization, often through psychological means, of biases or tacit understandings that operate to exclude or to include individuals or groups in the collective decision-making or conflict.[10]

The first dimension can be directly observed by simply watching who wins and who loses in an arena of conflict.[11] The second dimension involves understanding how the underlying rules and structures that play to the strengths of the winners were created.[12] The third dimension requires exploring the cultural narrative that the powerful develop in order to "sell" those underlying rules and structures to the powerless. This meta-narrative perpetuates the existing hierarchy because it elicits the cooperation and ultimately the passivity of the powerless.[13] A meta-narrative is merely a legitimating background story that "can reveal the meaning of all stories."[14]

In short, there are "winners"; there is a bias in the rules that defines "winning"; and there is a narrative that justifies both the winners and the rules by which they win. All three dimensions are variations on a theme that configures power as control. Those with control maintain control because they set the agenda. With no voice in the process that distributes power, those out of power have a hard time wresting control. And they become further isolated and alienated because the stories that the winners tell the losers make the losers feel as though they deserve their condition and do not have a legitimate right to complain.

These three dimensions of zero-sum power are closely interrelated, but each dimension possesses important independent explanatory value.[15] Each reveals different ways in which the powerful and powerless understand and respond to the conventions of power. We often pay attention to only what we see in the open conflict and ignore the role played by the second-dimension rules, even as the outcome in the first dimension is inexorably dictated by the rulemaking power of the second dimension. Similarly, the exercise of power in the first and second dimensions may be rendered invisible if we cannot identify the stories being told by those in power. The cultural mythology of the third dimension is critical to the maintenance of domination.

Within each dimension, however, one group's benefit comes at another's expense. When a person or group possesses power in a zero-sum world, it means they gain control of a bounded "thing" that is then denied to others. Power becomes necessarily something one has *over* either others or oneself, and thus we will refer to this zero-sum conception of power as *power-over*.

Returning to our relay race, we see that the girls exercised all three dimensions of power-over in a stereotypically male fashion. They prevailed in a competitive, winner-take-all struggle (the first dimension); that is, they exercised power directly: they won, the boys lost. They constructed the rules in favor of their participation (the second dimension) by devising a game with requirements that favored them, and they disguised the built-in preference of the game for finesse rather than speed by calling it a "relay race." When the girls consistently won the game that they themselves had structured, they proceeded to exercise their power as winners to determine the next game; they leveraged prevailing cultural assumptions—"to the winners go the spoils" and "the majority rules"—into continued dominance (the third dimension), to which the boys, though grumbling, nonetheless acquiesced. The boys were unhappy because they lost in the direct conflict (first dimension), and they had no opportunity to participate in defining or changing the terms of engagement (the second dimension). The boys' conception of their own relative powerlessness also led them to feel alienated as they submitted to the story being told by the girls (the third dimension). By manipulating cultural symbols and rules, the powerful convinced the powerless it was futile to resist.[16]

Two weeks before the relay race, at a faculty meeting in an elite law school, adults played their own version of the golf-ball relay race. The person running the meeting was outlining his strategic plan, which included a role for members of the faculty through advisory committees. Several faculty members then raised their hands to inquire about the process. One of the inquiring faculty members—we'll call her Martha—teaches civil procedure and is well known for her scholarly explorations of deliberation and difference. Martha asked: Why should she or other professors invest time and energy in any of the proposed advisory committees? Why should she, in other words, "play this game"? The person running the meeting turned to Martha and said, "I know you are a process person." Martha quickly interrupted to correct him: "I am a power person."

Like the golf-ball relay race, this exchange illustrates the way categories of exclusion or under-representation, in this case gender, may help us see the relationship between the three dimensions of zero-sum power. In both the relay race and the faculty meeting, the gender of those with power is a lens through which to understand the dynamics of power more generally. Like race, gender can help expose the ways in which the pervasive hierarchies of power are often perpetuated. We can interpret Martha's response three ways, in light of the three dimensions of power.

In the first dimension, she wanted to change the vocabulary from process to power to gain authority and thus more effectively compete and win within the existing game. Because those in authority respect power but not process, she wanted to use the right nomenclature, to show that she understood the rules and would therefore be given authority to exercise power or to participate as an equal with those who are tougher or bigger and who are currently exercising power.[17]

In the second dimension, she recognized the power that resides in the process itself. That is, the person who controls the agenda controls the outcome. Just as the child's grandmother observed in the context of the relay race, the architect of the game constructs both the barriers to entry and the terms of engagement, either of which often is outcome-determinative.

In the third dimension, Martha saw the powerful manipulating the less powerful by providing empty opportunities for formal participation and through this participatory process constructing a narrative to which the powerless meekly subscribe. Thus, she wanted some assurance that the less powerful would enjoy real power through their formal participation, rather than merely giving sanction to a process structured to exclude or ultimately ignore them.

All three understandings track the modern idea that power is about domination by those with power over others. The first dimension, the visible conflict, requires a certain amount of puffing as verbal armor. In an openly zero-sum competitive situation, it is better to present oneself confidently as a power person—someone who plays to win—than timidly as a process person, especially if the latter suggests someone who is simply not tough enough to play, or even understand, the game in the first place.

The second interpretation of Martha's "I am a power person" reply reveals that the issue here is not just formal authority but the power to shape outcomes under the camouflage of participation. Using second-dimension analysis, some scholars have argued, for example, that simple majority rule may not be a fair method of deciding conflict when the majority is homogeneous, cohesive, and prejudiced against the minority, as the girls in the relay race clearly were. What is particularly pernicious about such systems is the ability of the cohesive majority to exercise power by devising procedural rules that completely shut out or trivialize the contribution of minority groups. These scholars have tried to render visible the ways in which the exercise of rule-making, agenda-setting power has created and then maintained hierarchies. They have proposed alternative rules and innovative procedures that would allow a minority a fair distribution of chances to win. Both proportional representation systems and interactive forms of leadership, described in Chapters 5 and 6, are examples of such alternatives.

The third dimension of power is the most complex because it recognizes the power of true participation to change people's understanding of their lives even when their daily struggles remain very much the same. Power stretches in the third dimension to become autonomy. It extends to the many the idea of control of their own destiny.[18] But too often third-dimension power is simply a right to participate, even though one has no resources to make one's participation affect important policy outcomes. When those in power structure opportunities to participate as hollow rituals, the powerless ultimately lose confidence.[19] This may be the more traditional view of power in the third dimension—power is a form of false consciousness created by institutional arrangements that structure opportunities which are in fact inaccessible to the powerless yet maintain the fiction that opportunity exists.[20]

A Critique of Power-Over Strategies

Seth Kreisberg poses the following question: Have empowerment theorists made a wise decision in avoiding power as a central concept in their work?[21] Kreisberg's question suggests that examining the concept of power itself may help us understand the way the three dimensions of power-over interact with race-conscious or gender-specific strategies for social change. The aim of policies such as affirmative action or race-conscious districting is to advance deserving individuals who then have an opportunity to exercise first-dimension power differently. Kreisberg's query raises the possibility that success in the first dimension may lead theorists to fail to question the second-dimension rules and third-dimension narratives underlying the game. These theorists may even adopt and replicate those biases in their own analyses.

Most liberal strategies for social change, for example, are premised on the modernist idea that *all* power is power-over. They focus their energy almost exclusively on changing the most obvious manifestation of power-over: winning in first-dimension contests. Hierarchy—that is, a pyramid-like structure of permanent winners and losers—is seen as a normal and necessary outcome. Within hierarchy, upward mobility is a good thing. The goal is to repopulate hierarchies of winner-take-all power to include more people of color or women in the arena of visible conflict.[22] Conventional strategies for social change proceed as though a change in who administers power fundamentally affects the structure of power itself. Putting the girls in charge of designing the games will make the outcomes fairer, they imply. Previous outsiders, once given a chance, will exercise power *differently*. Who is included at the top of the hierarchy—that is, who is dominant—really matters, they say. It makes a difference not just to the individuals involved or to others for whom the involvement is symbolically significant (most notably their fellow minority group members) but also to substantive outcomes.

This view underestimates the co-opting effect of what Randall Kennedy terms "robust tokenism," or superficial diversity in leadership roles. Token participation may not properly account for the second dimension, in which less visible rules are more important to the allocation of power than are more visible individuals. It tends to ignore as well the third dimension, which includes the ability of the powerful to discourage others from acting in their own self-interest. As happened in the relay race, those who win also get to dominate the next game, and the winners explain the outcome in ways that justify, and ultimately exploit, their success.

There are three additional points to this argument. First, the access of outsiders to an existing hierarchy stiffens the resistance of those already in power, who typically see the claims of outsiders as threatening. A zero-sum paradigm in which someone must lose if someone else wins strengthens the impulse to exclude. Second, cosmetic diversity, which focuses on providing opportunities to individual members of an under-represented group, diminishes the possibility that unfair rules will be challenged. As long as there is equal access for a few, rules that exclude the many will remain intact. Third, the existing hierarchy disciplines newcomers who, although they look different from traditional incumbents, learn to exercise power in the same old ways.

Even advocacy groups whose focus is race and gender often engage in elite decision-making that does not foster give-and-take conversations or organizing efforts to involve those directly affected.[23] The access of insiders undermines the ability of blacks and other outsiders to use community dialogue to shape their understanding of their collective interest.[24] Without an informed and networked group of outsiders, even the few individuals who are successful at penetrating the hierarchy are then disabled from protecting the gains they achieve when such gains are subsequently under attack.

As we will see in the sections that follow, a strategy which emphasizes individual access can create, within those still on the outside, a psychological barrier to opposing a system that now includes at least some of "those who look like you." Access for a few individuals may demobilize the majority of outsiders in another way—by failing to lead to concrete improvements in their lives. Seeing that nothing has changed but the token advancement of individuals, many who would be inclined to support continued reforms withdraw from civil society or at least remain aloof.

Problems with the Individual-Access Model: First-Dimension Rules

The guiding assumption behind affirmative action—bringing more people of color or women into previously all-white or all-male domains of power or opportunity—is that an inclusionary approach has many beneficiaries: the individuals involved, others whom they represent either actually or symbolically, and society as a whole.[25] This idea is also the guiding assumption behind race-conscious districting—namely, that creating opportunities for communities of color to elect representatives of their choice benefits the system on many levels. It enables minority voters to gain access to legislative policy-making and thereby gain a voice in democratic politics. It benefits the larger society as well because it brings new perspectives into the public policy arena. And, applying a utilitarian calculus, advocates note that redistributing legislative seats to a few deserving individuals limits the clash for power to the first dimension. Those who are still excluded from power will buy into the game and not question the dominant second- and third-dimension biases that strengthen the legitimacy of the existing system of power distribution.

Thus, policies like affirmative action tend to reinforce rather than upset the underlying structures of power. In that sense, they are conservative. Despite this, conservative critics oppose these policies on the grounds that "quotas" distort achievement, diminish true merit, overemphasize statistical under-representation by reference to an elusive pool of genuinely qualified applicants, and, perhaps most damning, treat individuals simply as members of a racial, ethnic, or gender group. In Chapter 6 we will examine this specific critique as developed by the Supreme Court in its voting rights jurisprudence, in which the current majority of justices target majority-minority districting as emblematic of the evils in what they perceive to be a rigid focus on apparently monolithic racial groups.

Those sympathetic to affirmative action have sought to defend it by collecting data about the actual experiences of affirmative action beneficiaries.[26] They contest the critics' claims that the "wrong" people are in fact benefiting from improved access to the first dimension of power.

Similarly, voting rights advocates have analyzed the actual consequences of creating majority-black districts on the registration and participation rates of black voters and the legislative votes of representatives in selected southern states.[27] From the work of those studying women in politics, black and Latino law school, medical school, and college graduates, as well as from our own work and experience and the research we have undertaken with others, we are convinced that those with newly acquired power do, in fact, exercise it in ways that are different from standard behavior.[28] When measured over their full career, beneficiaries of affirmative action not only succeed in ways similar to their white counterparts but also exceed the performance of their white peers in public-spirited contributions to the community.[29] It is often the black elected officials who stand alone to protest obvious injustices, while their white colleagues, though sympathetic, sit back, constrained to follow the rules.[30] The data also suggest that women politicians often have an approach to politics that is more participatory, inclusive, and collaborative than that of their male colleagues, and their policy priorities are frequently different.

Those who focus on changing particular first-dimension outcomes within the existing hierarchy produce very real short-term gains, especially to the immediate beneficiaries. But they often limit themselves to challenging outcomes only as they affect women and people of color. They do not mount a sustained critique of the rules that shape those outcomes for everyone, and they fail to imagine a larger—rather than merely reallocated—quantum of benefits.[31] In this sense, conventional empowerment strategists lock out any possible transformative vision of social justice by restricting the game to a win/lose paradigm. They also proceed on the basis of an essentialized conception of race. In this rigid definition, "all" whites are "winners," as though working-class or poor whites benefit when rich whites succeed.[32] The same logic is applied to blacks: When a few blacks are allowed to become rich, poor blacks somehow benefit.

Because working-class whites imagine that all blacks get an unfair advantage when a few blacks reap the benefits of affirmative action, conventional approaches that rely on biological definitions of race tend to incite opposition on the right. Whites construe their interests as threatened by people of color, no matter how powerfully the data argue otherwise, and conservative activists then use this resentment as an excuse to oppose traditional civil rights claims for special treatment.

Yet surprisingly, strategists on both the left and right, despite their differences, converge on the individual as the unit of power. The conservatives argue that the group, as well as society at large, will benefit when more group members achieve power as individuals; the best empowerment strategy, they argue, is entrepreneurship and individual initiative. They challenge the very legitimacy of the category of group rights or race-consciousness. Civil rights advocates argue that individual group members "represent" the race and that hierarchies of power that lack diversity are illegitimate. When black individuals achieve power for themselves, black people as a group benefit, as does our society as a whole. Here we see both liberals and conservatives endorsing the same meta-narrative of American individualism: When individuals get ahead, the group triumphs. When individuals succeed, American democracy prevails.

Race-conscious or gender-specific strategies focus almost exclusively on distributing benefits to members of these categories, conventionally defined.[33] They often fail to identify the ways in which others who are not racial minorities or women are also made powerless by the rule of winner-take-all. Thus, they do not appeal to a potentially broad multiracial coalition. By framing the debate in terms of compensation for racial groups, any possible energy for struggle that might exist within poor whites is extinguished. Many poor whites might in fact feel alienated from white elites and might self-identify not even the least bit with "privilege." Yet, civil rights activists do not question the way the rules that exclude blacks or women from participation adversely affect poor whites, too.[34]

Whatever the merits of the current anti-discrimination approach, and there are many, it is a difficult strategy to defend in the long term when only the visibility of race itself is put before the public. Using divide-and-conquer politics, those in power pin blame for the condition of white workers on the race-conscious remedies they have been forced, against their will, to adopt. A coalition between poor whites, women, and people of color never emerges in part because empowerment strategists fail to expose the second and third dimensions of power as they affect all people, not just people of color or white women.

We do not advocate abandoning efforts to include more women and racial minorities in the established arenas of power. The redistribution of outcomes in zero-sum power struggles definitely has some trickle-down effect in constructing more effective narratives for social change, as many studies indicate. But we suggest that a more innovative approach is necessary if we wish to move beyond the distortions of individual-access models of remediation.

Problems with Outsider/Insider Dynamics: Second-Dimension Rules

When subjected to the backlash of incumbents seeking to protect their power, the actual gains made by the few individuals from marginalized groups who are admitted to arenas of influence are fragile. Even if the initial program of affirmative action or special access for racial group representatives is successful, further social change is unlikely. As blacks or women achieve fairer ways of executing the existing rules, they risk legitimating a fundamentally unjust status quo in which resources have been historically hoarded or distributionally distorted in other ways. The girls may now win for the first time in the relay race, but the relationships among the children are still predicated on a conception of power that requires excluding *someone*. Gains, even for mass movements, are translated into access for the elite within the movement. This admittance to the corridors of power is meant to pacify the activists and mollify their base.

Some black leaders, for example, push for access to elite decisionmakers as their first priority. The "real deal," one black powerbroker explains, "is accessibility."[35] This is an insider strategy in which outsiders either become insiders or enjoy one-on-one access to traditional insiders. Access is important in the short-run. Sympathetic insiders do play an important role when they work in conjunction with those on the outside. But long-term success can be measured only by whether insider access brings about fundamental social change.[36] Unless the rules of engagement are constantly interrogated, those already in power may seek to protect their own power by encouraging a handpicked group of former outsiders to participate in a rigged game. The danger is real that such participation simply camouflages hierarchy.[37]

For example, in retail workplaces, clerks are now "partners" or "sales associates." In offices, secretaries are now "assistants." In universities, staff members are now "officers." The changes in terminology alter the story being told about the relationship between management and labor, but the fundamental nature of the relationship itself often remains unchanged. Thus, labor theorists have concluded that despite this new collaborative and empowering vocabulary, no genuine power has been surrendered.[38] While manipulation of the symbols of power may alter the psychological framework, the existing hierarchy remains unchanged. Through this re-naming phenomenon or "conceptual co-optation," the less powerful are tricked into identifying with the values and goals of the more powerful.[39] As this softening of rhetorical opposition illustrates, what appears as a form of second-dimension participation may not influence the agenda or alter the relationships in the first and the third dimensions of power.

Gerald Frug makes a similar argument about the bureaucratic state. Bureaucratic states justify their power by claiming that their rules con-strain arbitrary power through the enforcement machinery of objectivity and neutrality. Yet, the story goes, bureaucratic states also allow for the presence of personal self-expression and individuality. Frug says that such "mechanisms of deception" foster the illusion of human freedom and au-tonomy when in fact this coercive system narrows democratic possibili-ties.[40] Bureaucracy is supposed to ensure that ordinary politics will not in-fect the basic interactions of the citizen with the state. But, according to Frug, the bureaucratic state controls both access and options in ways that thwart individual agency. Bureaucratic insiders often choose to resist this subtly coercive system through forms of passive subterfuge and acts of in-dividual sabotage. While micro-resistance enables the less powerful em-ployees or workers to express dissatisfaction or alienation, it leads to di-minished commitment and withdrawal on the one hand or internalized oppression on the other.

The possibility of coercion exists even between people who occupy structurally equivalent positions and who are not in a hierarchical relationship with one another. Even within horizontal relationships, the exercise of power can take on aspects of domination. As Susan Sturm and others report, many workplaces are in the midst of reorganizing production and employment into self-directed work teams that make decisions as a group.[41] While these work teams have been hailed as successful in improving employee morale and productivity, they often reproduce the dynamics of race and gender found in the larger culture. Within these teams, exclusion and bias may take forms that are difficult to identify and expose. Decentralized authority—which invites greater participation from those situated lower down in the management hierarchy—does not, therefore, by itself, resolve the dilemma. Race and gender conflict remain salient in many of these work groups. Even peer relationships may reflect a kind of flattened hierarchy, where power-over is "encoded and implemented" in participatory settings. According to Orly Lobel, this would most likely occur when the horizontal relationship essentially serves a vertical purpose.[42]

The predicament of outsiders who become insiders is a complex and longstanding problem. In legal and business contexts, it has generated a significant literature about "regulatory capture"—the process by which those who administer and make bureaucratic decisions are captured by external and internal forces. All the efforts of newcomers to think and act independently are slowly constrained by increasingly limited choices and the pressure exerted by those most invested in their producing certain outcomes.

In the civil rights context,[43] J. L. Chestnut, the only black lawyer in Selma during the critical early days of the civil rights movement, recalls in his memoir *Black in Selma* the consequences of converting a movement for social change into a set of opportunities for well-meaning individuals to help manage the status quo. Chestnut noticed they were "letting the protests die while messing around with biracial meetings, thinking [they] could negotiate change on the basis of [their] personal skills." In his view, "this wasn't a matter of personal skill." He realized later that what he had witnessed was the beginning of "a transformation from civil rights leaders to politicians, from outside protestors to inside manipulators."[44] How, Chestnut wondered, could we maintain a culture of struggle necessary to sustain and continue the real progress that had been made?

Activists often ignore Chestnut's question. Instead, they commonly seek to advance the appointment of individuals with a "different" perspective. They expect that this different perspective will have a transformative effect. Sometimes it does. Yet once an outsider is put in such a position, the key to resisting power—to the extent it is a zero-sum resource—is to remain "critical." In the words of W. E. B. Dubois, to be critical means one is capable of experiencing double consciousness. It is not impossible to be an insider and an outsider simultaneously. But if outsiders who have become insiders desire to retain their critical double consciousness as they exercise power or authority within the status quo, they need an alternative or independent source of power. In other words, if one is an outsider now operating as an insider, unless mechanisms are in place that give other outsiders power, the insider's power will come to depend increasingly on the views of other insiders. This makes it less likely that an insider, acting alone but in good conscience or with good intentions, can simultaneously enlist and resist authority.[45]

Thus, infiltrating hierarchy in order to redistribute power usually will not succeed unless the new insider has an energized or powerful base of outsiders as support. In fact, only by having a real and vital connection to such a base can a new insider remain politically or intellectually independent of the enormous pressure otherwise to conform. Marooned individuals, cut off from their base, may be reluctant to push for change; or they may be marginalized and unable to do so.[46]

One might ask, therefore: once you enlist power, do you forfeit your ability to resist it? Although Chestnut initially posed this dilemma about the civil rights movement, his questions are fundamental to most social movements, especially after the more spectacular manifestations of the protest have passed. The structure of power itself, more than the ideology or personal inclinations of each newly powerful individual, defines how power is exercised in the long term. Insiders do not permanently forfeit the ability to resist zero-sum power, but they are less inclined to develop such capacity over time.

One of the reasons insiders are less able to ward off the conventions of power is that part of their energy is devoted to maintaining the source of their individual power. If the source of their power comes from acquiescence and cooperation, then they are not only less likely to resist but they are less capable of exerting counter-pressure. As they lose an objective position from which to judge the workings of power, they become less critical. On the other hand, they are paradoxically dependent, at least in the long term, on some efforts to gain credibility with those still outside the circle.[47]

The Australian political scientist John Dryzek notices the substantial loss of political power that disaffected groups experience when they move from social protest to formal entry into party politics. Dryzek concludes that unless their political objectives happen to fit with a larger economic or social imperative of the party in power, such groups pay a high price for acceptance: "They may be allowed to participate in the policymaking process, but outcomes will be systematically skewed against them." Without a democratic culture of citizen-initiated mass protest, public officials have less to fear. As a consequence, disaffected groups experience loss in terms of "a less vital civil society, erosion of some existing accomplishments, and reduced likelihood of further democraticization in the future."[48]

Dryzek gives the example in the United States of leaders of environmental interest groups who were brought into the Clinton administration at high levels but then were unable to achieve much change in substantive policy. Jay Hair, leader of the National Wildlife Federation, the largest of the groups Dryzek describes, concurred: "What started out like a love affair turned out to be date rape."[49] By seeking appointments within the first Clinton administration, environmentalists achieved symbolic rewards that have intrinsic value, but they lost out on opportunities to gain more tangible goods and services.

In Dryzek's view, movement concerns can be incorporated within established public policy channels only if citizen-initiated protest efforts continue to fight for substantive policy changes and sustain the energy vital to their own success as well as to democracy itself. That was the lesson, as well, in David Ost's important observations about the political evolution of Solidarity in Poland.[50] Solidarity began when Polish intellectuals and labor activists realized that the most effective way to open up the political system "was for citizens to engage in unsupervised public activities of any kind." They worked to recreate the classic institutions of the modern public sphere, what many now call civil society. They created places to meet; they organized interest groups; they convened open forums for education and discussion of public policy; and they defined political engagement to include social activism and cultural creation. Solidarity's early goal was somewhat utopian. It sought to create an engaged citizenry in a free society. Its goal was to allow everyone to have a say in public policy.

Ost explains that this "anti-politics" ideology shaped Solidarity when it came into existence in 1980. The union was committed to a rhetoric of public democracy, democracy as "many publics." When the government wanted to negotiate with strike representatives in secret, strike leaders demanded that negotiations be public. They insisted that loudspeakers broadcast the negotiation proceedings to the workers occupying the shipyards.

But Solidarity's very success changed its approach. Once the government relented and held formal elections, over 250 Solidarity leaders successfully ran for Parliament in 1989. Their departure helped engineer a reconsideration of their original idea of "many publics." Now, in order to maintain their own credibility as leaders, the interest of Solidarity officials shifted, according to Ost. They no longer encouraged workers to protest. They no longer worried about creating a free society; their election presumably embodied it. Yet their very electoral success depleted Solidarity's ability to organize and mobilize and left efforts at social change exclusively in the hands of public officials, albeit officials with historic sympathies to the movement. Those officials began to define their goals in terms of what *can* be done rather than what *should* be done. And they began to see their own political survival as paramount.

The danger comes when, instead of incorporating movement ideas, government incorporates movement leaders. This gesture creates a set of successful individuals whose role-modeling increases the psychological investment of previously disenfranchised members of the group. But when the leadership of a social movement leaves the sphere of "many publics" to enter electoral politics or to gain appointive office, their departure creates a vacuum. One kind of public success usually means another kind of public loss. The dilemma remains: How does a social movement enlist formal authority while resisting conventional means of distributing power?

Loss of an Outsider Role: Third-Dimension Problems

The insider-access strategy may be purely symbolic, a legitimating ritual that permits neither influence nor genuine agency. Such a strategy promotes opportunity for the few in the name of the many, but it may fail to consider how the few are changed by their own opportunity. The girls may simply become "boys," and the original boys may resent their displacement. The insider-access strategy is troubling for another reason. It functions as if existing forms of hierarchy are acceptable and merely need to be inclusive of a more diverse group of participants. This acquiescence in zero-sum power, while offered presumably as a practical and realistic short-term reform, may contain the seeds of its own demise. It fails to mobilize a broad-based coalition to support the gains it does realize. Without an activated outsider-based movement, the successful insiders are less able to continue the struggle. In other words, participation by a few may mean isolation of the many. The few may fail to question whether the many ever benefit, and they may put whatever gains they do realize at risk because the many are disabled from joining in their defense.

A pragmatic social-change strategy that accepts the rules as given and then seeks to manipulate them on behalf of the less powerful is too often accompanied by the increasing quiescence of those on whose behalf the civil rights or the women's rights movements claim to operate. We suggest there is a relationship between a pragmatic social-change strategy and the withdrawal or passivity of those most likely to benefit from such a strategy. The third-dimension meta-narrative conditions our response to assertions of authority and defines the boundaries of legitimacy in more ways than even the first-dimension construction of power was able to do.

Especially for those who occupy subordinate positions within a zero-sum hierarchy, the absence of opportunities to participate in the development of policy may deny them a chance to formulate and identify their interests either as individuals or as members of a group. The political scientist Melissa Harris-Lacewell points to black organizations, black public spaces, and black information networks as distinct and critical forums where black people meet as equals and talk openly and "where leaders try to persuade and mobilize the community" to produce a "distinct African American discourse." What is crucial about the opportunities provided by black churches, black barbershops, and black media outlets, Harris-Lacewell contends, is the chance to learn what "one's preferences are." Rather than seeking out groups who share their preformed views, many blacks develop their views by deliberating with others within the black community. Black engagement around ideology "helps African Americans to understand persistent social and economic inequality, to identify the significance of race in that inequality, and to devise strategies for overcoming that inequality."[51]

The participation of those previously excluded or under-represented not only catalyzes opinion; it also creates it. This is true even for whites within a racialized hierarchy.[52] Insider-access strategies, by contrast, undermine the potential of those left behind to critique or defend strategies for reform. Even when the symbolism of inclusion is communicated through the advancement of a few individuals, the powerless may simply end up feeling better without actually doing better. Even more, as the link between their participation and their expectations, or between participation and outcome, becomes more attenuated, so do the incentives for their continued participation.

In other words, Kreisberg's question asking whether empowerment strategists make a wise decision in avoiding the concept of power in their work pushes us to do more than prop up outsiders who become insiders, even through rules that permit greater access to, and more accountability from, those representatives. We take his question to suggest limitations to conventional ideas about power that lead people to misapprehend both the problem they are confronting as well as its solution.

As Ronald Heifetz points out, in a challenging environment, a command-and-control model of power that is legitimated by elections or mechanisms for informing outsiders and holding insiders accountable may reinforce existing authority (at least temporarily), but it will not necessarily prepare the primary stakeholders to do the work necessary to adapt and change.[53] If we want to do more than simply get better jobs for a few good people, we need to think more critically about power in all three dimensions. An insider-access strategy organized in strictly power-over terms is problematic because it valorizes insider access, to the exclusion of grassroots mobilization rather than in concert with it.

Jose Calderon tells a story about racial and ethnic hierarchy in the early 1990s in the Alhambra School District in California.[54] At that time the district served a student population that was 51.2 percent Asian, 39 percent Latino, 8.1 percent white, and 0.7 percent black. As the demographics of the community continued to shift from what was once a white majority, tensions mounted and numerous racial incidents involving Latino, Asian, and Anglo students occurred. In 1991 protests were organized when the school district asked the district attorney's office to file charges against Vietnamese students involved in a fight with an Anglo student whose father was a local policeman. When the Asian Coalition complained, the district attorney's office responded by filing charges of battery on school property against Latinos who had been involved in a previous fight that same year.

The Asian and the Latino communities organized their own coalitions of parents, educators, and bilingual social workers. Although professionals dominated both groups, the groups mistrusted each other. The Latinos resented the Chinese businessmen, whom they suspected were of a "higher class than themselves." Their suspicions were fueled by local media reports that made it sound as though the Chinese-American PTA had been responsible for filing the charges against the Latino students. The Asian coalition saw the Latinos as better positioned to wield political power because they had "a good number of visible politicians and established organizations that could represent their interests."[55]

The competing ideologies and separatist inclinations were neutralized when the leadership in both coalitions succeeded in reframing the question away from a competition between groups to a challenge of the status quo in the school district. The separate coalitions evolved into one coalition, the Multi-Cultural Association, when they came to understand that ethnic/racial tensions in the school district involved larger inequities that required multiethnic collaboration. Instead of channeling their separate grievances into a claim to integrate the schools' decision-making elite, the coalition used their experience of mutual marginality to challenge the exclusionary power held by those in authority. They resisted the conventional hierarchy and experimented with something new.

For example, they discovered that Latinos had an unusually high expulsion and dropout rate in the school district. Latinos comprised 56 percent of all student dropouts, a pattern that had been going on for twenty years. The Multi-Cultural Association organized the various ethnic groups to oppose and eventually abolish a tracking system which grouped Latino students at lower academic levels. They also pushed for adoption of a policy requiring all principals to develop school-wide plans for "creating an environment which allows all persons to realize their full individual potential" and to promote conflict-resolution techniques that included a voice for the students in the process. Previously, the school district had resorted to expulsions, arrests, and policing to deal with increased tensions at the high school.

Rather than focusing on cultural and class differences, the multiethnic coalition united around efforts to identify the structural foundations of conflict in the high school. Calderon concludes that the real problem was the traditional top-down hierarchy of decision-making in the school. The Multi-Cultural Community Association identified the need for reform to diversify the school curriculum and governance so that parents, teachers, and students would have a stake in, and the opportunity to influence, the decision-making process.

Conclusion

What if social-change strategists like those in the Alhambra School District proceeded to interrogate, as Kreisberg urges, the concept of power itself? What if progressive thinkers and activists developed a more dynamic and pluralist accounting of the interaction between outsiders and insiders? Might they succeed in enlisting race to resist power in its conventional, zero-sum terms? The metaphor of the miner's canary suggests the possibility of interrogating the three dimensions of power more deeply than as simple expressions of race or gender exclusion. The metaphor enables us to use race or gender as fundamental tools of analysis, to understand how hierarchies of fixed and interlocked power work. But deployed in conjunction with a more critical meta-narrative, the metaphor pushes us to try to transform the atmosphere in the mines as well as the miners themselves. It reveals that the asymmetrical distribution of conventional power implicates the existing hierarchy of power more generally. It helps us assume a more skeptical stance toward zero-sum hierarchy.

Sixty-nine percent of black Americans think the current income gap is morally wrong. Women, more than men, are also more likely to think there is something morally problematic about income inequality, as do 60 percent of those earning less than $30,000 a year, compared with only 37 percent of those making more than $75,000.[56] Our miner's canaries— women and people of color—are sending us a signal about the health of our sociopolitical environment. Their experiences can enable them to see fundamental flaws in the way the second and third dimensions of power give those who already hold power inordinate control over "the system." An alternative social-change strategy might be to plumb the views of both women and people of color about their experiences and then develop advocacy centered on the problems they diagnose.

Such an alternative strategy would need to move beyond the weaknesses of the walking-backwards-up-a-cheese-grater approach. Cosmetic diversity fails in at least four ways to achieve racial and social justice. First, allowing a few individuals access to power buttresses the notion that committed individuals working within the contours of existing institutions most effectively achieve change. This strategy supports the idea that individual success is the best measure of reform. A more thoroughgoing institutional critique never gets off the ground.

Second, incorporating outsiders into the existing hierarchy prevents former critics from confronting the fundamental ways in which that hierarchy is organized, including its claims for legitimate authority. Once a space is made for critics within the dominant institutions, any failure to deliver substantive goods is not a failure of the institution but their own personal failure. External critics are encouraged to blame the internal players; the community from which the critics emerged is demoralized.

Third, selective incorporation of individuals, even if compelled by a mass movement, does more than disarm the critics by trading action for access. It also eliminates or at a minimum inhibits the creation of a vital social space for resistance to occur. This is what J. L. Chestnut complained about in Selma and what David Ost observed in the domestication of Solidarity through its incorporation into the Polish state bureaucracy. For resistance to emerge that has the strength to construct competing meta-narratives and sustain critique, it must have a space for democratic, economic, and critical social experimentation. While leaders, now incorporated into the hierarchy, will claim that institutions must be engaged on their own terms, an in-between space outside conventional hierarchies can give a marginalized community a critical place to assess the changes that these newly "pragmatic" insiders propose.

Finally, strategies of cosmetic diversity pit potential allies against one another. The third dimension of power-over is a divide-and-conquer strategy: it disguises points of collective engagement and separates logical allies. But when groups engage with one another explicitly around questions of how to define power, they may discover that the hierarchy of power itself is their common antagonist, rather than one another.

The hierarchy of power that is most effective in separating potential allies in the United States is race. Tackling the role that race plays in our social institutions is a way not just to improve the lot of racialized groups but to confront the ways in which power operates and circulates throughout our society and culture. Race reveals the distributional inequities within our various social institutions—in employment opportunities, educational chances, medical care, and democratic representation. But race can be more than a diagnostic tool. Relegated to the margins of society, communities of color can find there a "free space" from which they can critique established hierarchies and creatively imagine a new way.

5

The struggle in the 1990s to unionize the K-Mart distribution center in Greensboro, North Carolina, and secure a wage contract started with the energy of black workers and the vision of black ministers. But the key to the success of this labor struggle was bringing the larger community into sympathy with the issues that animated the workforce at the plant, which was over 65 percent black. This would mean not just emphasizing the plight of the workers and their families but demonstrating that K-Mart's resistance to the union's demands was tantamount to ignoring the needs of the larger community as well.[1] In an anti-union right-to-work state and in a community with a history of racial divisions, this would not be an easy task.

The pressure point for the union was the Greater Greensboro Open, a PGA golf tournament that K-Mart sponsored. The Open gave Greensboro national media attention, and many people outside the immediate union struggle viewed disruption of the Open as a threat to the local economy.[2] The union clearly had work to do in the community, and they turned for help to the Pulpit Forum, an association composed mainly of black pastors who served churches in the greater Greensboro area. The Pulpit Forum had been organized in the 1960s to provide shelter for political activists and to ground the civil rights struggle in the moral foundations of the churches. One of the leaders of the Pulpit Forum, the Reverend Nelson Johnson, had been a labor and community organizer before he became a minister. Because so many K-Mart workers were members of the congregations that made up the Pulpit Forum, persuading that organization to lend its initial support to the union effort was relatively easy.

But other problems quickly arose. From the perspective of the Pulpit Forum, the union's approach to the community was "Help us do what we've already decided to do," rather than "Help us think through the issues together."[3] The pastors wanted a partnership, not a master–servant relationship. The coalition broke down.

A stalemate in negotiations became the wake-up call for the union. Organizers realized that if they were going to secure a contract with the company, they had to enlist community support. So the first thing they did was to gather facts showing that the Greensboro plant—the only K-Mart distribution center with a majority nonwhite workforce—received the worst wages and benefits of any center in the country. With this information they went back to the Pulpit Forum.

At this point Reverend Johnson took the lead, reminding his fellow pastors that the union members were members of their own community and not just representatives of an organization the pastors did not trust. As he expressed it, support for the workers "had to grow out of this soil. It has to come up out of this earth, and the people here have to claim these workers as their brothers and sisters."[4] But what would it mean to form a coalition with the union? Who would get to call which shots? What was the Pulpit Forum's moral responsibility to the community, including its responsibility to those who are not part of the coalition? In the words of Reverend Johnson: "We built a good relationship . . . but we didn't build it by skinnin' and grinnin' and waving at each other. We struggled."[5]

From the beginning, two stock stories framed the dispute. One claimed that this was a unionizing effort, and therefore the struggle was correctly understood as a labor problem. The other story claimed that this was a civil rights matter that only involved issues of race. Reverend Johnson knew that they would have to get beyond both of these stock stories if organizing was to succeed. The Pulpit Forum reframed the question to ask not just whether K-Mart ought to negotiate with the union but whether it was just for K-Mart to pay wages that are lower than they pay at other plants, merely because the workforce in Greensboro was mainly black. Although the majority-black workforce was making $5.10 less per hour than workers at comparable K-Mart centers, the losers were not just blacks but all of the K-Mart workers, including white workers.

Both labor and their allies in the Pulpit Forum were convinced that K-Mart management believed it could get away with underpaying workers at the distribution center because the black workforce would passively accept this treatment. But they worried that framing a labor struggle as a case of race discrimination would hinder rather than help contract negotiations. Reverend Johnson pointed out to union leaders that black workers were among the first to organize and that their status as a racialized minority helped them see the collective unfairness of their situation and act to resist it. Denying the salience of race would risk losing the black workers and the black community. On the other hand, organizing the union effort solely around the issue of discrimination would alienate some whites and play into the divide-and-conquer strategy that opponents of the organizing effort were counting on.

Once again, Reverend Nelson Johnson put the problem succinctly: "You have to walk through race, you have to work through race."[6] What he meant was that you have to engage race as an integral part of the story about what was going on in Greensboro. But you have to realize—and help others realize—that the ill effects were not limited to the black community. By focusing on the racial dimension of the resistance to K-Mart's tactics, the threats to the broader community would become visible. The Pulpit Forum never discussed the cause as simply a racial issue or a labor-management dispute. Instead, they described K-Mart's refusal to pay a living wage as a threat to all those in Greensboro who wanted to build a sustainable community.

The pastors decided to assert their leadership by staging an act of civil disobedience at the plant. Every Sunday for several weeks black ministers went to the distribution center and prayed, prepared each time to be arrested for trespassing. While their presence supported the mostly black workforce, their prayers also expressed concern for all workers in Greensboro who relied on wages that were no longer sufficient to support their families. Up to this point, local business and civic leaders had claimed that the union organizers were outsiders, even though the rank-and-file were local. By linking the struggle to area churches and to the willingness of community leaders to be arrested for supporting this cause, the Pulpit Forum muted the press's criticism of meddling by outsiders.

Some whites were reluctant to join the movement because they did not want to share power with blacks. At least initially, they construed sharing power as losing control or being controlled by others. To highlight the importance of sharing and rotating power within the community, the Pulpit Forum cast their prayer vigils as efforts to start "a discussion about this community." Before the ministers would leave for the plant on Sundays, "we held church." They had a mass meeting each Sunday at church services, preparing the congregation spiritually to go forward.

The transformation of the resistance from a purely labor struggle to one implicating the welfare of the larger community inspired further civil disobedience, but with a crucial difference. This time, white workers and community members became part of the resistance. Although the leadership remained in the partnership forged by the Pulpit Forum and the union people, white workers, members of white churches, and other members of the white community soon joined the black clergy and the black workers at the site every Sunday. The white workers would gather first at their union hall. The black workers would gather at church. Then the groups would meet at the plant for prayer and protest. Reverend Johnson also reached out to the local business community and to white and black politicians. Eventually some white ministers, a few white college professors, and others joined in.[7] Even white merchants who "didn't start getting arrested until way down the road" finally joined the crusade to redeem the dignity of their community against the predatory logic of the prevailing wage.

On the day that the protesters were arrested for criminal trespass, the state governor's aide stood behind the black parishioners and workers as they prayed in front of the K-Mart plant, and she got arrested too. K-Mart then filed civil suits against the protesters and sought an injunction to prevent them from entering K-Mart property. Yet, even this tactic yielded a lesson in cross-racial politics. K-Mart's civil suit named only black workers and the black ministers in its complaint. At that point a remarkable thing happened. Rather than complain that this was further proof of racial discrimination, Reverend Johnson conferred with the white ministers and white workers who were part of their struggle. Going to jail or getting sued, he explained, is "the opportunity to really help share the faith."

The white workers then held a news conference, asking why their names were not on the complaint. "Why weren't we sued?" they demanded to know. After all, they had done everything the black workers had done. K-Mart's wage structure had raced them as black, too, and in response they had not only joined with black workers to resist the unfair wage structure but they had also stepped up to be arrested and sued, because they saw their fates as linked to the black workers. They felt the camaraderie of their collective struggle, and they wanted to participate in the consequences. The fight for a sustainable community was their struggle, too.

Two images are foregrounded by this story. One is the image of the black workers and black ministers kneeling to pray in front of the K-Mart distribution center. The other is the image of the white workers holding a news conference demanding to know why they were not sued along with their black co-workers. The black workers met in church to gain the courage to move forward. They came forward first. The white workers met at their union hall and began to forge an internal sense of solidarity. But then both groups of workers came together to engage in acts of civil disobedience that galvanized the community.

The idea of a sustainable community had taken hold in the minds and hearts of the citizens of Greensboro. It summarized their concern about the vitality of local institutions and the dignity of each member of the community. The redefinition of the public that began with a labor struggle led to a larger transformative effort. The response of the white workers was emblematic of a struggle that was defined by race, and led by people of color, but not limited to grievances solely oriented to problems of the black workers. The K-Mart unionization effort was more than merely an episode in labor history. It was a story about the creation of what Martin Luther King called a "beloved community." Without the politics of black and white, however, there would have been no space for this democratic community to grow.

The Affirming Power of Struggle

When the labor struggle at the K-Mart plant became a movement led by black churches and the civil rights community, the conventional hierarchy of power-over would not work, because race and racism had made that model suspect in Greensboro. In the struggle to create a unified movement, all of the participants had to wrestle with their own conceptions of power and racial hierarchy. At the moment when the white workers came forward to assume responsibility for their part in the civil disobedience, they demonstrated the power of political race to overcome these internalized barriers.

After the issues became joined in K-Mart's lawsuit, Reverend Johnson and the Pulpit Forum saw the courtroom as "just another staging area" in their effort to build community. Of course, Reverend Johnson hired a lawyer—James Ferguson of Charlotte, North Carolina—but even in court, Reverend Johnson did not want Attorney Ferguson simply to win a legal case; he and his fellow defendants wanted a broad public education strategy focused on civic rights and responsibilities. As intent on relationship-building within and among the people in the community as they were on winning the case, the defendants challenged assumptions of hierarchy between their lawyers and themselves. Reverend Johnson did not want the judge to rule against him, of course; but he also wanted his lawyer to use his argument to help the people who were crowded into the courtroom to better understand the proceedings and to feel that it was "their whole story" being told. And Attorney Ferguson cooperated. Reverend Johnson and his lawyer were determined "to tell the world" about the legal issues in a way that made plain what was really at stake. They sought to transform the courtroom into a place for collective struggle, almost literally as a mass meeting.

Reverend Johnson tells the story of going to court:

> The court was just full of people, and an old black woman stood up and started singing in this judge's court, "Ain't Going to Put My Religion Down," and the judge left the court. He came outside and asked us to ask her to stop, and she did. When she finished the song. After that,

somebody stood up and prayed . . . This lady was not asked to sing. She just did because she felt safe doing it, and my own view was the judge felt unsafe, actually. What do you do with an 80-year-old lady who does not quite know she is even in court? She's just with the people she usually sings with, and expressing her desire about all of this.[8]

According to James Blacksher, an NAACP Legal Defense Fund cooperating attorney, a former marine, and a native white southerner, "When that woman stood up and started singing in that courtroom, it became a different place." What Blacksher saw was the success of the leaders of the K-Mart struggle in framing the issues in a way "that moves the people, that mobilizes people."[9] Rather than seeing power only in the labor unions or the black church or even the civil rights lawyers who defended them in court, Johnson brought together the power of each in order to mobilize the entire community of Greensboro. By moving back and forth between the black workers and the white workers, between the workers and the community, between the church that restored their courage and the courtroom that tested it, they reconfigured traditional power relations and forged new relationships with others in the community as well.

The Pulpit Forum used the methodology of political race to begin a much larger conversation about the possibilities of structuring a political group consciousness. Their organizing strategy freed the "miners" from the burden of believing that their actions alone can create a just system. They identified the way in which the miners, too, have been trapped by the excesses of individualism and disabled from pursuing a more transformative vision. They developed a meta-narrative inviting those who are strong-we identified to join in a set of circumstances where interdependence is understood as essential both for getting work done and for a fuller conception of individual agency in community.

Their story reminds us that collective action that is cross-racial and sustainable ultimately depends on three key ingredients: (1) a reconceptualization of the meta-narratives of power-over, (2) a commitment to sharing power in ways that are generative, that build from familiar settings, and that emphasize human agency within an organized community, and (3) a willingness to engage with internally embedded hierarchies of race and class privilege. By building up the power that each person has to act and engage with the world, the Pulpit Forum helped others to follow the leadership of people of color who were working at the grassroots level. But this was not a leader-centered struggle. This was group-centered leadership that used direct action as an answer to fear. After K-Mart settled the lawsuits, the Pulpit Forum continued meeting in the black community with a biracial group of concerned citizens. To this day, they persist in building collective power through grassroots involvement of people in the decisions that affect their lives.

In the 1970s the French postmodernist philosopher Michel Foucault developed a tremendously influential conception of power that is reflected in the creative thinking about hierarchy in evidence during the K-Mart struggle.[10] Foucault recognized the need to create loci of power where, in a zero-sum conception, power could never exist. In trying to conceptualize the alternative way that Reverend Johnson used power, we think it helpful to build on (but not completely adopt) the Foucaldian view of power.

Specifically, Foucault argued first that the modernist conception of power as something that operates only top-down to oppress and repress is inaccurate and misleading. In Foucault's view, power can be exercised in ways that coerce from all sides, from the bottom as well as from the top. Power is a pervasive force that constructs all aspects of human interaction.

Second, Foucault challenged the modern idea that knowledge and power are separate entities. Instead, he argued that the construction of knowledge is necessarily tied to power. Because of the spread of scientific knowledge in particular, from the moment of birth a person is examined and measured against standards of normality and appropriate behavior, and the measuring stick for this evaluation is provided by the human sciences. Foucault used an allegorical device he called a panopticon to illustrate the effect of being always in the gaze of these evaluating and disciplining forces. We are not free to determine ourselves; rather, we are constructed from the bottom up through largely invisible mechanisms of power that at every turn create norms and measure us against those norms.[11]

Foucault suggests that to see power at work, we should pay attention to the subtle effects of many private relationships.[12] Power for Foucault is not just an expression of authority; the pervasive constitutive effects of power are not merely effects that dominate or oppress. Part of his postmodern critique is a rejection of the idea that power is inherently bad. For him, the ethics that govern social relations can be a source of strength that enables people to *oppose* the forces of repression. Foucault used the image of capillaries to capture this operation of the ever-present, intricate structure of power and to suggest that power is not merely repressive but can be a lifegiving force. For Foucault, the flow of power can either repress or liberate, depending on how it is deployed.

This structural interpretation of power has generated two divergent views of human agency among postmodernists. In one view, human agency is limited and political struggle is hollow. Ideas such as liberation, equality, emancipation, and progress are subject to the same critique that applies to power. Because power operates everywhere, any critical stance has to take account of it and is itself subject to the interrogation of power/knowledge.[13] Essentially, all power becomes determinative of those who seek to exercise it, which limits the possibility of collective struggle to make any difference. In the face of pervasive power, the only political response possible is irony, which gently subverts the disciplinary structures of power but does not attempt to change them fundamentally.

There is a second view of human agency, however, that is more hopeful. In the 1970s feminist scholars, working out the links between the personal and the political, began to redefine power as collective energy and realization.[14] Resisting the idea that feminists should address only questions surrounding personal change, they called instead for recognition that change takes place along multiple axes of human interaction. They began to rethink the concept of power consistent with their understanding that social change and personal change are intimately connected. Because the social world is a human creation, we constitute it through our relationships. Thus, feminists saw that it is critically important to change the context within which those relationships occur. Others suggested as well that power is the producer and product of every social system and cannot be done away with as an organizing principle. But what we can imagine is the transformation of the relationships and interactions among human beings. To imagine that such a transformation would eliminate the circulation of power is fantasy; rather, this reorientation seeks to capture power's generative capacity.

In sum, modernists, postmodernists, and some feminists construe power differently and thus advocate different strategies for resistance, struggle, and social change. Modernist political analysis has a fixed view of power's boundaries and focuses strictly on the struggle in arenas where those in authority exercise traditional first- and second-dimension power—whether it is the authority that comes from running a faculty meeting at a fancy law school or designing a child's relay race.[15] Power is usually seen as power-over, the ability to control others. Even when participation is linked to power and offers a mechanism to bring about different outcomes depending on who is exercising formal authority, it, too, still assumes at base that power is about dominance or control.[16]

If, as the modernists claim, power is structured to make all those who occupy a certain social or political position function similarly, then challenging the outcome really becomes an ironic stance with no concrete payoff. In this regard, the modernists and postmodernists effectively do not differ. The modernists seek to redistribute existing power in a more benign or inclusive fashion. They busy themselves building sandcastles on the beach even as the tide comes in to demolish the structures. The postmodernists dismiss such efforts as ineffective but see no alternative other than to remark upon their labors for history or, in Austin Sarat's phrase, to "remember the future."[17]

From the perspective of those who lack much opportunity to control or affect outcomes, power might be viewed very differently, however. Instead, power might take the form of autonomy or dignity. Such nonconventional engagements with power can include what we label the affirming power of struggle. It can reinforce the value of human agency especially when exercised in relationship with others.

The English word "power" derives from the Latin "posse," meaning "to be able."[18] Power does not always require control or domination. When Seth Kreisberg asked a group of tenth graders to express their images of power, power-over words predominated, but terms such as "life" and "happiness" were also mentioned, as were images of the sun and the earth. The power of life or happiness, or images of the sun and earth, suggest a shape or form of power that derives from a common source but moves in a direction different from zero-sum power. This power is generative, it involves sharing something or becoming something, not just giving or demanding or consuming. It expands in its exercise. It finds a way to call on people to connect with something larger than themselves.[19]

This interpretation of power is about the life-affirming force of resistance as well as the sustaining effect of mutual support. It suggests that the powerless, despite their dominated state, can still find meaning in collective acts of resistance and through struggle can create symbols and narratives that justify and support the vitality of their efforts.[20] One way to resist power-over is to lay its narrative bare.

Power-With

We call this generative and engaged version of the modernist's third dimension *power-with*.[21] Power-with is the psychological and social power gained through collective resistance and struggle and through the creation of an alternative set of narratives. It is relational and interactive. It requires participation.[22] As the colleague we called Martha in Chapter 4 explained, "Participation affords power even aside from direct results . . . [it offers] a chance for claiming dignity even at the moment that it is at risk of being denied."

Return, for a moment, to the ritual of building a sandcastle. Imagine that the participants understand the project's transient state, but the very fluidity of the project attracts many different people with a range of skills who experiment with alternative architectural forms. Their goal is not to participate in a sandcastle competition but to learn how to work together under stressful circumstances to keep the sandcastle standing as long as possible. The mere fact that the inevitable tide will eventually wash away the effort does not destroy the learning and satisfaction that are generated by this collective and creative activity. The community spirit built in this process will withstand the tide. At some point, the participants may need to learn how to stop the tide, but there is also value to creating small laboratories of experimentation until that happens.

This image of power as collective resistance and struggle differs from the modernist view, in which the powerful continually shore up their authority to keep rewards for themselves. The modernist concept of power is concerned with explaining particular outcomes. It suggests that persons or groups wield power with the intention of bringing about results that other groups would not have preferred. But our image of power also differs from that of postmodernists who see all relations disciplined by structures of power that operate like force-fields over every human interaction. The postmodern view introduces structural features to explain the effects of power on the relationship of groups to one another and on the internal configuration of the group. The postmodernists understand power as a general structural feature of social life that constrains the nominally dominant groups as well as the nominally subordinate groups. We caution against overemphasizing either the top-down understanding of power or the view of power that denies human agency in the face of domination. Instead, we are searching for an understanding of power that will allow individuals to resist false inevitability and to rebuild political solidarity.

Power-with—the alternative vision we are describing here—is a vision of how power can be exercised apart from the vertical arrangement that modernists use to describe power-over. It rejects the sense of futility evoked by the postmodern concept of diffuse, defining, and debilitating power. We use the idea of power-with to question existing outcomes and to explain alternative sources of motivation for action. Power-with teaches us to value a variety of outcomes that are outside either of the existing models of power-over. The contribution of power-with is to reassert the importance of human agency without retreating to an individualist position and to broaden the range of ends of power from those suggested by either the modernist or postmodernist views.

Still, power-with is not innocent of power-over. A certain element of winning and losing will remain and will make certain outcomes more likely than others. For example, the K-Mart story reveals some of the same liabilities that we critique in traditional power-over strategies. The case was still litigated in a courtroom in which—aside from the woman singing—most of the verbal advocacy was done by lawyers. Although the lawyers were accountable to an organized constituency and used the legal strategy to help educate, not just litigate, nevertheless the lawyers played an enhanced role in speaking "truth to power."

In the K-Mart story, however, participants valued the role of resistance and brought to light power relations, such as those between the lawyer and his client. Their interaction suggests, as did the early feminists and as did Foucault in his later work, that power has an under-explored social aspect that is creative, generative, and conscious of domination while resisting domination as a primary goal. They confronted the tension between domination and resistance as people committed to using power-with to mobilize community-oriented change. The Pulpit Forum leadership nevertheless negotiated from positions which reflect the exercise of conventional power. In order to bridge such tension, their creative conception of power exhorted individuals who could exercise conventional forms of power instead to emphasize and cultivate the power generated with, rather than over, others. They evoked a critical yet imaginative reconstruction of leadership and not just a collective consciousness. Their coalition's success has the potential to become a long-term and sustainable strategy for building social justice movements.

If power-over, in the modernist view, can be symbolized by a pyramid, then power-with might be symbolized by an egg. Because of its oval-shape, an egg has two centers of gravity, suggesting the possibility of shared and circulating power. Rather than focusing on a single apex of control or influence, like an egg the K-Mart struggle generated dynamic, revolving synergies. An egg's oval shape makes it strong and highly resistant to force when evenly applied. And eggs get even harder when subjected to high temperatures—evidence of strength under adversity. Finally, an egg is also the seed of life, reinforcing the idea that power-with is generative.

The resilient, co-active, and generative qualities of power-with make it a less grating and oppressive conception of power than power-over. The K-Mart story shows, however, that power-over and power-with can coexist simultaneously and can change in association with each other. Prospects for social change do not always depend upon strategies that pit one oppression against another in a competing hierarchy of power. Rather, those who hold a vision of transformation can learn ways to move outside and apart from the current models of power-over.

For example, the fact that the K-Mart struggle was built on a vision of sustainable community rather than the short-term goal of getting a few good jobs for deserving "outsiders" increased the possibility that this democratic experiment could endure over time, as indeed it has, in the form of biweekly meetings which try to extend the relationships that first developed around the K-Mart struggle. Although the activists' efforts included challenges to external hierarchies, they also located—outside and under the radar of conventional power—primary sites for engagement, including church and union meeting halls. They affirmed the importance of sharing power in an atmosphere that prepares people to oppose external oppression while also struggling with internal conflict. They recognized the need for cultural rituals that create trust and familiarity while also challenging embedded internal hierarchies. They directly undermined the mythology that those already in power have earned or deserve their power, especially if they hoard it, use it to coerce others, or waste it. Instead, they told new stories that demonstrated a commitment to struggle toward a larger vision of sustainable community. Their stories told of resistance that affirms the agency of the outsider participants as well as the insider elites, reminding both of the importance of finding allies. Their stories told of people with a cause, perhaps born of a grievance but not limited to that. Their stories measured progress by looking forward, not backward. They eventually settled the lawsuit with K-Mart, yet the Pulpit Forum continues to work to construct enduring relationships and enhance the participation of key stakeholders.

Uri Treisman teaches mathematics to college undergraduates. Among his students were a number of African Americans who were having difficulty learning calculus. Treisman's faculty colleagues assumed that these difficulties stemmed from the students' "underprivileged" backgrounds, low motivation, poor academic preparation, and lack of dedication. To determine if this was so, Treisman examined the behavior of these students and compared it with the behavior of their Chinese-American classmates who were excelling in math. He found that his colleagues' assumptions were incorrect: the black students were actually studying as much or more than the Chinese-American students. What the black students were not doing, however, was studying in groups. The Chinese-American students were reinforcing what each had learned individually by constantly talking about math in group settings—over lunch, while walking to class, even while studying.

Treisman concluded that learning calculus was often best accomplished as a cooperative venture. And to prove it, he designed a program for his African-American students using group sessions and peer study.[23] During the first semester of the program, the math scores of the black students went up dramatically, and by the end of the second semester they were among the highest scoring students in Treisman's first-year calculus course.

At that point the light went on. Treisman realized that it was not his African-American students who were the problem. It was the way he was teaching calculus to *all* his students. Individuals learn differently, and some learn much better when their peers are their teachers.[24] Treisman discovered that it is impossible to use a single set of criteria or a single pedagogical style to measure or teach a complex set of skills to a diverse group. Many students learn best by asking questions, which turns out to be a skill that is useful, yet also neglected, in fields other than calculus.

Successful performance among many highly competent professionals often depends on a team of individuals, no single one of whom possesses all of the necessary expertise but all of whom, working together, are able to accomplish their task in a reliable way. Recognizing this, some airlines sent their cockpit crews to training sessions that encouraged them to question authority. After the training, 94 percent of crew members disagreed with the statement that junior team members should not question decisions made by senior members. By contrast, surgeons—who commit large numbers of errors during operations—do not encourage questioning by others in the operating room. "Things should be reviewed by an entire team," says Elise Becher, M.D., an assistant professor of pediatrics and health policy at Mount Sinai School of Medicine, who has extensively researched medical errors. "There should be constant checking and discussion."[25]

The importance of democratic leadership that encourages critical interaction within small groups extends beyond the work of educators and professionals. Kurt Lewin's empirical research was motivated by concern that the trappings of democracy in Nazi Germany—such as its high rate of voting—did not assure democratic decision-making. Lewin's studies compared authoritarian, democratic, and laissez-faire leadership styles. He found that "democratic leadership resulted in less hostility, was liked the most by the group members, and produced the most original work." Democratic leadership views participation by group members as part of an act of mutual discovery. It "encourages thought, reflection, and analysis of the issues at hand."[26] This kind of interaction contrasts with centralized communication, in which authority resides with elites who use rewards to preserve their rule and where rigid group boundaries are maintained to censor minority opinion and maintain the status quo. In democratic leadership, authority and rewards are used to stimulate debate; a system of checks and balances is employed to limit the aggregation of power and ensure decentralized communication. Group boundaries are flexible to allow the expression of minority viewpoints that might aid problem-solving. When power is shared in this way, it often increases group cohesion and sustains commitment and involvement. It can also produce better solutions to complex problems, because it respects minority viewpoints as a means of testing popular hypotheses and making better decisions.

Consistent with models of democratic group leadership generally, Treisman's approach also shows that power can be exercised by those in authority as a dynamic and expanding rather than a static and individualistic resource, especially when the background narrative is transformed. By investigating the assumptions of his colleagues, Treisman resisted the stock story that his black students were not well suited to learning calculus. By organizing to overcome the difficulties of this marginalized racial group, conditions improved for math students more generally in Treisman's classes.

Elements of power-with revealed in Treisman's experimental pedagogy and in the K-Mart struggle include: (1) working together over time in groups rather than as individuals in isolation; (2) seeing problems in context rather than as small units independent of the whole; (3) approaching problem-solving in ways that spark joint participation from diverse perspectives; and (4) defining problems locally, by the immediate stakeholders, and then networking to similar efforts going on elsewhere. But these elements are not a primer of specific rules or practices. They represent a larger democratic ideal that values collective action and collective decision-making. However, for all its emphasis on community, power-with requires individual creativity and sometimes individual decision-making before the more transformative moves take place. For example, Treisman's effort began from his perch as an individual atop a vertical learning relationship who then altered students' study habits and ultimately his own techniques of pedagogy. Similarly, the black ministers did much of the initial work to reframe the stock story in Greensboro. While the role of such individual leaders might be crucial during the initial stages of any movement toward power-with, the movement can ultimately succeed only if individual leaders are willing to yield their zero-sum authority in exchange for true power-sharing arrangements. Political transformation occurs, in other words, when we *change* asymmetrical power relationships, rather than merely struggle for the right to *participate* in them. As the feminists whose work we draw on recognized, change is the "process of creating new problems out of our solutions to earlier problems," using strategies to build organizations and interventions that redefine political power itself.[27]

Laboratories of Democracy

In creating a peer workshop to study calculus, Treisman chiseled a physical space into a psychic empowerment zone. He lowered the barriers to entry and made access inviting, even familiar to students who often felt too demoralized by the traditional power-over format of classes to participate in learning. He created what Jane Mansbridge might call an "enclave of resistance" in which the black students collaborated to learn effectively together. Rather than reproducing the chalk-and-talk hierarchy of the typical classroom, Treisman invited students to pull their chairs around a table so that they could share their questions and solve problems together. To enhance the informal atmosphere, he served food to his students while they talked about calculus. Reverend Johnson, too, created a racially self-contained space by meeting with black K-Mart workers in church prior to every act of civil disobedience. Singing familiar songs or practicing rituals known to the community helped build courage and affirm trust. Joined in song within this enclave of resistance, the black workers and their supporters honed oppositional ideas about racial justice on the whetstone of democratic capacity.[28]

Race was an important variable in determining who was initially drawn to both of these "in-between" spaces, which were neither wholly private like someone's bedroom nor formally public like a legislature. But while they occupied a racially defined hybrid space, many other people besides African Americans eventually benefited. An analogy can be seen in the sidewalk cuts that are now familiar features of urban landscapes. This innovation was originally mandated for people with disabilities, but then parents wheeling baby carriages, children on tricycles, movers rolling heavy furniture, and teens on skates and scooters found their own mobility increased.

Within many free, in-between spaces like Treisman's workshop or Johnson's church, people have begun to build laboratories of democracy where they can experiment, reflect, self-correct, and share information. These self-consciously committed democrats attend to internal and external sources of power (including racial identity, gender, and social class) as they recruit members, shape the dynamics of group interaction, and interrogate the content of the inquiry. They realize that race, gender, and class can influence how individuals participate and which assumptions they will bring to issues such as distributive justice. These differences in perspective are examined out in the open to develop greater insight, stimulate constructive disagreement, and spark innovation. Having discovered allies and learned important coping skills, participants can then leave these intermediate spaces better equipped to exert collective counter pressure to oppose the dominant norms.

Septima Clark's citizenship schools are a wonderful example of laboratories of democracy in action. By helping illiterate blacks register to vote, Clark's workshops provided the seeds for rural mobilization during the early years of the civil rights movement.[29] In kitchens and beauty parlors and under shade trees in the summer, respected members of the community taught adults how to read and how to write their names in cursive on voter registration forms. But these schools were not just about the mechanics of literacy. People from the community would talk about whatever they had done that day; their stories would be written down and would become the text for the reading lesson. Discussion deliberately emphasized "big" ideas—citizenship, democracy, and the powers of elected officials. Adults were taught to read newspaper stories critically and to be skeptical of politicians' promises.[30] Participants began to see themselves as members of the public, whose opinion was just as important as that of the white people who always ran things. The citizenship schools helped to establish a sense of collective consciousness and solidarity that bridged the gap between voting rights and the everyday realities of constituents.[31]

One local sharecropper told SNCC organizer Bob Moses that the most important accomplishment of the civil rights movement, as far as blacks in Mississippi were concerned, was not the vote.[32] It was the opportunity to meet. Coming together in small groups at citizenship schools or attending large mass meetings in black churches gave people a way to tell their stories and speak their minds. Voting alone could never substitute for the process of formulating, articulating, or pursuing a citizen-oriented, community-based agenda. The vote was crucial, but it was not all. In retrospect, maybe not even most.[33]

The lesson of the citizenship schools proved enduring. In the early 1990s, a group of community organizations in the Delta region of Mississippi, led by Southern Echo, held workshops to inspire local black residents to get involved in redistricting efforts. According to Southern Echo's executive director, Leroy Johnson, "Fear is the first and deepest obstacle." Southern Echo confronted that fear by producing training workshops for community residents. By arming them with much-needed information and working through role-playing exercises, they first confronted the intimidating presence of white officials indirectly.

In the workshops, some residents would play the role of white members of the board of supervisors and would give those representing the black community a hard time, "doing to [them] just what the Board does to the community." The play-acting and verbal sparring in a relatively informal setting "broke the tension" and "helped the community understand its own power."[34] When a large contingent of community members attended the actual board meetings, they arrived with standard school-issue composition notebooks which contained their notes and journal entries from the workshops. In those notebooks they had also recorded the same data about community demographics that previously was known only to the white supervisors. The earlier opportunity to practice their arguments made a huge difference when the interactions were now public. Their preparations allowed them to assume a new advocacy role.

One black resident who had attended the workshops stunned the board of supervisors with his aggressive questioning. Later, when the residents had a chance to caucus among themselves, they congratulated one another, saying: "That was just like in the workshops."[35] Southern Echo had done what Bob Moses said the civil rights movement did in the early 1960s: it gave black people in Mississippi a chance to meet. It provided a space for an organized constituency to practice democracy, to resist the power structure's meta-narrative, and to confront its own power.

Similarly, Marshall Ganz describes how the United Farm Workers (UFW) developed tactics in the 1960s and 70s that emboldened Mexican immigrants and Mexican Americans to define and pursue their collective concerns, despite their limited resources.[36] Targeting Mexican resident farmworker families who were the growing sector of the workforce, the UFW used the term "campesino" in the title of the worker association to evoke ideas of resistance and connection with the land that had been part of a longstanding movement of the Mexican peasantry. By tapping their historic lineage as campesinos, the UFW helped these farmworkers gain a dignity that mobilized them to action.[37] Ethnic identity as redefined through this social movement "transformed farmworkers into 'chavistas,' supporters into 'voluntarios,' the grape strike into 'La Causa.'"[38] The embrace was facilitated by the fact the movement was rooted in and expressed itself through traditional national, religious, and political symbols and practices.

At regular union board or planning meetings, processes of internal deliberation and the mechanisms of organizational accountability enabled the insiders (primarily Mexican Americans who were raised in the United States and no longer worked in the fields) and the outsiders (Mexican farmworkers, most of whom were immigrants) to generate the discipline and motivation to sustain difficult vertical relationships. The Roman Catholic masses celebrated by "huelga priests" affirmed values of sacrifice and solidarity even when the celebrants were not Catholic. The cultural traditions celebrated on Friday nights turned the gatherings into a combination ethnic labor association, mutual benefit society, and community action organization. New chapters in the collective account of the movement were told through reports of success and support, reenacted through theater and song.[39]

What gave the UFW "juice" was the fact that it was as much an "identity project" as a pursuit of interests. But this project was not identity politics as conventionally understood. In conventional interest-group politics, the conflict arises over institutionalized interests, and the identities of the actors are more or less defined. By contrast, this project was a social justice endeavor that sought to redefine the identities of its participants as members of a democratic polity. It drew on elements of racial and ethnic identity to shift participants' view of what it meant to be a Mexican immigrant or a Mexican-American citizen. It engaged the farmworkers in "a narrative reconstruction of who they were."[40]

Ganz used the phrase "charismatic communities" to describe the transitional space that this identity project occupied.[41] Fueled by moral fervor, these communities became crucibles within which new understandings of identity and commitment were forged and in which new democratic practices were learned. The intense level of commitment among participants became a source of power, not only by reconfiguring their understanding of themselves but also by motivating them to make morally persuasive claims on others (rendered credible by their own sacrifices). Charismatic communities are organized groups that in some way reconfigure existing power relations. The collective energy of the people forges a new condition of activism and self-awareness, a condition that involves experimentation, sacrifice, and struggle. Participants often sustain high levels of energy, take risks, and concentrate for an extended period of time because they are internally motivated by a commitment to change the lives of those they care about. Witnessing such communities in action allows us to imagine the real story of marginalized groups whose official history is shrouded in racism and fear.

Inspired in part by the example of the United Farm Workers, in the

1990s the Workplace Project on Long Island democratized the education courses they held for immigrant workers. Instead of the traditional know-your-rights workshops led by legal-aid lawyers, they conducted "workers courses" set up to provide "group opportunities for reflection that will lead to analysis and action."[42] Whereas a know-your-rights workshop on health and safety might begin by having an expert explain how to file a legal claim, the first class at the Workplace Project began with a videotape called "Uvas No" ("No Grapes") put out by the UFW. The video humanized the high rates of cancer and birth defects that had appeared among farmworkers and their children and linked them to the use of pesticides. Workers then collaborated on a drawing that portrayed the hazards at their own workplaces. It was only after lengthy group discussions about why such hazards were so prevalent that a representative of OSHA was invited to speak to a classroom full of people whose understanding of the issues did not depend on the expert's view of the law. When the health and safety official finally showed up, the immigrant workers asked well-informed questions and used the time to gather data that would help them prepare their own activist strategy. By the end of the course, participants had developed a plan for tackling the problems they had analyzed.[43]

In these spaces—classrooms, union halls, courtrooms, sidewalks—entrenched hierarchies and symbols of power become inverted. The contrasting images are there: a woman singing in court as if she was in church, ministers kneeling in front of a distribution plant as if they were in a prayer meeting, white laborers orchestrating a news conference, black students pulling their chairs around a table to master calculus, Latino workers teaching the experts about hazards in their workplace. In these settings, relationships transgress formal notions of "representation," in which the few speak while the many remain silent. These sites openly invite experimentation so that the silent speak and the less powerful participate. By rehearsing their capacity to resist oppressive forms of power-over, participants imagine alternatives to their own moral or material distress. They practice forms of resistance that enable them to speak out with greater self-confidence in more public settings.[44] Change occurs under the radar; people participate, deliberate, and emotionally engage. Not only do the low become high or the powerful weak but ideas of power and hierarchy themselves become destabilized.

Challenging Embedded Hierarchies

Nevertheless, many of these communities remain relatively alienated despite acts of collective engagement in semi-public or intermediate spaces. Informal pressure among peers ostensibly committed to working together can reproduce horizontal coercion.[45] And the renaming phenomenon to which we alluded in Chapter 4 can be reproduced through flattened hierarchies that do nothing to adjust fundamental power relationships. Reproducing power-over hierarchies in the name of power-with may simply encourage conflict-avoidance schemes that lead to alienation and individual forms of sabotage. For these reasons, a participatory framework needs to address internal, not just external, racial and political hierarchies and emphasize democratic practices and accountability from the inside out.

Such practices may appear messy and unstable. They can be incredibly time-consuming. But by continuously challenging internal racial hierarchy and meeting in advance in small groups to rehearse larger risk-taking ventures, participants make genuine democracy possible. The contribution of a variety of stakeholders creates opportunities for innovation and sustainability. In Richmond, Virginia, for example, community architects engaged in a "participatory design" process to build support for the construction of public buildings. The black community demanded that the architects hold multiple meetings with various neighborhood action groups, to address the needs of all stakeholders.[46] Although the initial public forums were chaotic, over time people began to feel that their concerns were being heard. They also learned to listen to what other people were saying, and sometimes they changed their minds, or at least altered their priorities. Once the buildings were under construction, the investment of energy the architects had made in working with neighborhood committees during the initial design-development phases was recovered. The public, engaged from the beginning, remained engaged. Long-term maintenance of the buildings was easier because community members saw the buildings as responsive to their needs. The architects benefited

from referrals and good will. By reframing the initial conflict as a source
of productive energy, what seemed pointless to some in the short term
had on-going benefits for everyone.

Within organizing efforts that emphasize hierarchy, opportunities for
vertical deliberation—between leaders and members—is especially important. Although the UFW functioned through a leadership hierarchy, it
used a dual kind of team organization. The "inner circle" combined leaders with strong ties to the Mexican-American constituency—who were
more likely to know where to find resources, whom to recruit, what tactics
to use, and how to encourage these constituencies to identify with the organization—with leaders who had weak ties to the constituency but who
were more likely to know how to access the diversity of people, ideas, and
routines that facilitate broad alliances. The UFW was effective, Marshall
Ganz concluded, because it organized a Mexican-American constituency,
engaged in deliberative meetings with members, and encouraged ongoing assessment of the organization's activities where differing points of
view were expressed. Linking access with commitment, and information
with influence, were key to the UFW's strategy because it enabled innovation, flexibility, and motivation for sustained struggle.[47]

By contrast, the much less successful Agricultural Workers Organizing
Committee (AWOC) of the AFL-CIO used a top-down strategy aimed at
recruiting mostly single white men—casual day laborers in very seasonal
crops who represented a rapidly disappearing remnant of dust-bowlers in
an increasingly Mexican workforce. AWOC targeted workers who gathered daily for early morning shape-ups because they were "easier to organize" for short-term mobilizations. Even when their tactics shifted to include nonwhites, they continued targeting workers based on short-term
political advantages, such as influencing sympathetic members of the
Democratic administration. Moreover, AWOC had no advisory councils
or farmworker committees. Staff meetings were irregular, lacked agendas, and were mostly venues for announcements, not for strategic reflection.[48]

The UFW's demonstration that power-with is a useful organizing tool
is a lesson labor unions are still learning. Ignoring the failed strategy of
AWOC in California, some union leaders are not ready to share power or

relate to workers as members of communities; instead, they rely on old techniques, educating members through newsletters rather than through interpersonal contact. But demographic shifts and the hiring of more Latino immigrants are forcing unions to employ Latino organizers, who then teach local unions how to organize the community and not just the workers. Recently, Latino union organizers for a carpenters union in Seattle held fiestas where the community danced and ate together. By combining union events with rallies for immigrant rights, they encouraged families to come out to the picket lines. Verlene Wilder, a black woman who is the lead organizer for the Seattle King County AFL-CIO Labor Council, reports on the difference this power-with orientation is having: "When I went to one of their meetings it was a culture shock. The meetings were conducted in Spanish; the white guys sat in the back. The [Latino] union leaders had educated the white carpenters to view the Latinos not as a threat but as a way to strengthen their union. The only way to protect their jobs and the union was to see the Latinos as brothers."[49]

That power-with can also co-exist with power-over was a lesson applied to good effect in the Workplace Project. Structures of accountability linked the executive director, Jennifer Gordon, to a board of directors composed entirely of immigrant workers. This framework constrained the informal power that Gordon had as the self-described "white, highly educated, English-speaking, connections-to-donors, much respected founder." While members were constantly encouraged to exercise their democratic imagination, "concrete mechanisms for member participation and governance [were] critical to keep leaders accountable and to make claims of democratic representation real." The Workplace Project was committed to ensuring that immigrant workers had real power, leadership, and control within the organization. There were clear lines of responsibility and an institutional structure that made explicit where the power to make particular decisions lay. According to Gordon, "The model of a membership-board with control over a director, who in turn supervised staff, who in turn supported worker committees with defined missions and their own leadership structures, all of which (board, staff, heads of committees) joined together in strategy retreats that set the course for the organization, worked well for us."[50]

In part it was important for efficiency reasons: everyone had input into key points of strategy and direction, but there was a division of labor between those who made the decisions and those who executed the plan. Gordon writes,

> For example, it allowed the board (all immigrant workers) to make and enforce its own decision about who would replace me, a decision that the staff would have made differently, without bowing to staff demands. And . . . it allowed the board to make decisions about goals and strategy from their perspective on the community's needs, which was different than my sense of where the organization should go, and have me carry their decisions out . . . I think it also made me more accountable as director to have to take responsibility for the decisions that I made, and to have limits on the decisions I could make . . . If we had operated by consensus, I feel like my power would have been amplified rather than restrained.[51]

Multiple forms of horizontal and vertical coercion can exist, even within progressive organizations. It is necessary to do more than just include people of color, whether as important decision makers or emboldened participants, within an existing hierarchy. Otherwise, even a progressive space is vulnerable to win/lose forms of coercion among peers as well as more subtle ideologies in which participation is merely another form of co-optation. Sharing power requires a commitment to democratizing horizontal as well as vertical hierarchies without necessarily denying all asymmetries of power.

Rotating leadership is one way to promote more democratic relationships between those "in charge" and those whom they represent or lead or facilitate—what we are calling vertical relationships. Another is to hold meetings to structure deliberations rather than just convey information. Meetings like those conducted by the UFW better prepare participants for collective decision-making. Experiments with role playing, as Southern Echo found, or interactive art projects, like a mural painted by members of the Workplace Project, can rehearse participants for external encounters with more formal power. Sometimes voting or other heavy-handed forms of decision-making are necessary, but even then it is important to resist up/down binary ways of framing the issue.[52] Sharing and rotating power can mediate the caustic effect of yes/no votes, which so often polarize communities by recreating and highlighting deeply embedded hierarchies.

There is often an unexpected advantage to working through the difficulty of maintaining a genuinely participatory multiracial collaboration. This process teaches its participants about a broader need to learn how to struggle with hierarchy, and not just in racially charged situations. Learning from the messiness of internal deliberation—and the power imbalances it often reveals—can inform the idea of structured deliberation more generally.[53] Reframing the idea of success itself can help change the structure of conflict from individual victories in open competition to problem-oriented approaches in which the rewards are internal and are not dependent on dominating others. It also can lead to new understandings of the problem and its solutions. Goals shift. The value of promoting collaborative free spaces within the institution itself becomes apparent. The hierarchy may still dominate, but it can encourage simultaneously open-ended spaces that invite experimentation and that ultimately may produce innovations from which others also learn or benefit.

The Relationship between Process and Outcome

The civil rights laws of the 1960s and their enforcement are a good illustration of the fact that centralized, top-down enforcement of norms is often necessary. Centralized enforcement may continue to seem preferable even after it has decayed into a mechanical bureaucracy untethered from a mobilized constituency. The conventional exercise of zero-sum power may also be required in crisis management or in purely administrative situations. Viewing power in win/lose terms may make sense within the private market of profit maximization. Indeed, the idea of power-with frequently operates in the shadow of more hierarchical power.

On the other hand, we are aware that a focus on short-term victories may promote a kind of unity that is enforced by repressing genuine differences. Liberal incrementalism enforced by centralized rules often promotes a rhetoric of civility, in which those who routinely win learn not to provoke instability and those who routinely lose are expected to value harmony over justice. The message is clear: the pie is already baked, and those who keep quiet and are patient may get a little slice.

While we recognize these flaws in the ways institutions distribute social goods, ours is a theory of democracy rather than equality. Our critique of hierarchy is not a disguised preference for equality of results as the appropriate measure of social change. We do not make a distributive argument, and our theory does not give priority to formal equality of outcome. We are arguing for a much more interactive and dynamic understanding of the relationship between process and outcome as well as the relationship between democracy and justice. We do not have ready answers or quick public policy formulas to propose. Just outcomes will emerge, we believe, from experiments in democratic process.

When the Reverend Johnson and the Pulpit Forum helped reformulate a labor dispute into a movement for "sustainable community," they could not anticipate that the white workers would in due course identify themselves as politically raced. Nor was the use to which Uri Treisman finally put the calculus peer workshop known or necessarily intended when he began his experiment. Their respective understandings of what was at stake were transformed in the pursuit of various short-term strategies; and that transformation, in turn, inspired them to redefine what they meant by success or justice.[54]

William Simon tells a story about a lawyer, Gary Bellow, who represented farmworker tenants in a dispute with their landlord. Bellow arranged to depose the landlord in a public place, so that the farmworkers could witness a role reversal. At the deposition they observed the otherwise powerful landlord in a less than all-knowing or all-powerful position. Bellow's strategy gave his clients an awareness of their collective power in a way that allowed them to imagine more. Bellow did not measure the "results" of the deposition by the specific information he was able to obtain from the landlord. Instead, he measured his results by the extent to which his clients expanded their understanding of the resources and responses available to them.[55] This lawyer endeavored to create clients who were capable of holding him accountable and making him responsive to their growing awareness of their own interests—an awareness that evolved along with their self-confidence and sense of collective power.

Like Bellow's decision to take a public deposition, a good process should expand the set of possible results rather than limit them; it should increase the total payoff available to all participants; and it should reveal how different participants value different resources. By sharing information and creating an atmosphere in which new ideas are not automatically discarded, participants may begin to imagine new forms of connection, with one another but also with novel outcomes. This is what happened in the police-beat meetings Archon Fung observed in Chicago. As a result of a deliberative process in which the views of the black residents on the East Side were finally solicited and heard, even the West Side neighbors eventually agreed that it made sense to concentrate police resources on the East Side.[56]

For us, power-with must involve more than instrumentally choosing the best means to achieve a predictable and desirable conclusion. It must prepare people to struggle against external challenges in ways they have not yet imagined, while also struggling with internal conflict. It should disrupt certain habits of individual thought or self-defeating rituals, while introducing new possibilities for reciprocity, collaboration, problem solving, networking, and innovation. To do this, a community needs the capacity to confront embedded internal hierarchies and to engage with the untidiness of conflict over time. It also needs to learn what it does not know and what it has difficulty learning. These capacities grow from a commitment not only to struggle but also to struggle toward a larger vision; the vision reframes the meta-narrative so that small wins are not translated into complete victories and devastating losses are not the end of the movement. Belief and faith also play important roles. If the process is open, transparent, joyful, and genuinely participatory, then more people are likely to have faith in and be part of the process. The results may differ from the ones originally imagined, but outcomes are still contingent on the input received. If, on the other hand, the process is simply a formal ritual with little connection between participation and outcome, then people withdraw, and with good reason. Participation in that kind of process merely legitimates the power that others hold.

Engagement, in the K-Mart struggle and in the UFW organizing effort, was linked to multiple outcomes—connection with others, a sense of belief in a just cause, a feeling of competence and dignity, as well as a particular policy decision or judgment. In none of these contexts was participation merely pro forma. Both the process and the outcome were continuously challenged and even changed by the dynamic interaction of the participants. Power-with is a process for interrogating both the means and the ends of power. If we are asking only if we can develop rules that optimize a fair distribution of chances to win, then we may be asking the wrong question. Imagine that after losing five times in a row, the boys in the golf ball relay race were still complaining that the game is unfair. What they should be asking is: Why are we still playing a game that only one team is good at?

Even if power-with forms of relationships and organization develop and endure, they must still take account of power-over hierarchy. Experiments in sharing and rotating power do not substitute for or supplant traditional power-over strategies. Our political race project does not anticipate the many constructive ways in which outsiders could actually become insiders who control the exercise of state or formal power. Given the historically contingent nature of our inquiry, things might be very different if racial outsiders become the dominant insiders who are in charge of the hierarchy itself. Our project's focus is on mobilizing resistance to hierarchies of power and has not yet explored ways of systematically restructuring those hierarchies. We have limited our discussion to implementing power-with in the shadow of such hierarchies, as independent and intermediate spaces or enclaves of resistance.

Gender and Power-With

We have cited with great enthusiasm some of the victories of the civil rights organizations operating in the South during the 1960s. The civil rights struggles, however, were also gendered. Many black women in the civil rights movement were denied positions of formal authority. They did not hold "titled" positions, yet they managed to build bridges between the personal lives of potential constituents and the political life of the movement itself.

By reaching out to local residents in their own homes and meeting places, they gave a human face to the movement and were able to persuade people that their participation was essential if the movement's goals were to be reached. Rather than focusing on their limited positions within the official hierarchy, women directed their leadership efforts toward involving members of the community. Some women, such as Ella Baker, helped create group-centered philosophies of leadership in which the executive committees and chairpersons rotated.[57] Women were "outside insiders" who used their gendered exclusion to establish different links between collective action and policy reform.

Indeed, many black women perceived themselves as integral and critical members of the movement.[58] Charles Payne concludes from his analysis of black women's activism in the Mississippi Delta that "men led, but women organized." One reading of Payne's construction suggests an impoverished view of women's leadership. Another interpretation, more sympathetic to our claims, is that for these women, organizing *was* leadership, based on an alternative view of power.[59]

This alternative and more generative view of power reflects Cryss Brunner and Paul Schumaker's model of power as social production rather than social control. Brunner and Schumaker associate this kind of power with women. They see a strong link between gender and power orientations: "Women in positions of authority are more likely than men to act on a social-production, rather than a social-control, conception of power."[60] They also hypothesize that fragmented communities that are more differentiated socially both need and are receptive to leaders who exercise collaborative power.[61]

In communities where citizens have experienced social fragmentation, they may become disillusioned with command-and-control arrangements and come to believe that widespread participation is necessary to accommodate the various stakeholders in their communities. They also may discover that collaborative leadership is simply more effective in achieving significant policy goals. Centralized command-and-control power systems may be relatively efficient and well suited to reaching goals for which there is a preexisting consensus.[62] But where the community has many citizens with diverse goals, a more collaborative and deliberative approach can help a heterogeneous community build the consensus necessary to address divisive problems effectively. Thus, Brunner and Schumaker conclude from their research that women play more critical roles in urban communities, where consensus building requires a transformative conception of power.

Carol Hardy-Fanta's research on Latino electoral campaigns in Massachusetts is consistent with the thesis that a commitment to power-sharing is often gendered. Over half of the Latinos to run for a state-level office or higher since 1970 have been women. Latinas have won 87 percent of their campaigns for school committee. Men have won 13 percent.[63] The women's robust links to their community helped explain their success rate, at both the state and local level. They were elected at higher rates, they were considered better campaigners, and they were more likely to transform the discourse of politics to include more active participation by their constituents.

Hardy-Fanta found that both Latina and Latino politicians sought elected office because they felt they were well-qualified and had long-standing ties to the community. But when male candidates were questioned about why they decided to run for office, they were more likely to cite a "need for Latino representation." Several then used a single word to answer the question of motivation: "ego."[64] The Latina candidates, by contrast, connected their motivation for running to their experience with church activities or community activism. They spent more time knocking on doors and connecting personally with the people in their community. They felt empowered to run for office based on their experiences working with others rather than their ambitions for themselves.[65] One respondent in a 1996 study of women municipal officeholders in Massachusetts said, "Women care more about community and less about personal aggrandizement."[66]

While both men and women said they spent "a lot" of time knocking on doors, the Latina candidates spent considerably more time talking to local groups, sitting and talking in peoples' homes, greeting and talking to people while walking through neighborhoods.[67] They had "stronger interpersonal skills."[68] Hardy-Fanta concludes that Latina candidates create a discourse about politics "that changes its meaning to include community and culture." The political backgrounds of Latina candidates found the connection between going out in a van to encourage parents to send their children to church and going out in a van to drive voters to the polls. Only the women questioned the meaning of conventional, candidate-centered politics or stressed the importance of getting the community to "start talking to each other." By contrast, the men had a fairly conventional set of assumptions about the meaning of politics. They stayed close to "the politics of voting and election campaigns" and, like the boys in the golf ball relay race, focused on outcome rather than process.[69]

Because some research suggests particular receptivity to concepts of power-with among women, it may be that the next step should be to study women of color. Just as black women were the bridge leaders in the civil rights era and Latinas are challenging conceptions of representation in contemporary Massachusetts, women of color could be a critical bridge connecting racial literacy, political mobilization, and collaborative power. Indeed, the Latina candidates in Hardy-Fanta's study gained political resources when they pushed through boundaries of gender, culture, and politics. Combining race and gender with collaborative forms of power may yield the most transformative model of all.[70]

We have chosen, however, not to stress the link between gender and power, although it is a potentially important site of struggle. We certainly invite others to explore it further. Indeed, we believe that a richer discussion of political race would incorporate more research on issues of gender. Gender is a strong lens for viewing manifestations of disempowerment or disengagement. But it needs to be linked to race or class if the perceived unfairness is to generate a public willingness to act collectively.

For example, even the so-called gender gap is actually a race, class, and gender gap. When white women were polled separately, they were split almost evenly in their preference for the two major parties. It was only when *all* women were polled that the views of women of color then created the much-publicized gender gap, according to which "most" women support Democrats and "most" men support Republicans.[71] Working women (both black and white) favored Democratic candidates by large margins, whereas women "at home" favored the GOP.[72]

In the United States, gender has always been both framed and fragmented by race and class. Gendered identity for black and white women, the historian Evelyn Brooks Higginbotham writes, "was reconstructed and represented in very different, indeed antagonistic, racialized contexts." Despite statutes that explicitly used the term "any woman," nonetheless slave women or "negroes" were excluded from protections offered to "white women's bodies," and the conflation of race, gender, and class evoked different "social perceptions of black and white women's work roles."[73] In response, black women often subordinated gender issues to a racial identity that defined and connected them "as a people" but also suppressed their internal differences. The inchoate sense of common destiny meant they could not acknowledge the way intragroup social relations functioned as relations of power.

Although the history of this country meant that black and white women had very different experiences, within the black community hierarchy did not disappear. For example, many people of color react to racism by engaging in psychological behaviors that are self-defeating. Internal hierarchies coalesce around skin color, hair texture, and other domains that reproduce the external subordination or reinforce negative stereotypes.[74] This is especially true around issues of gender. Although racial solidarity served blacks well in the struggle for civil rights, Higginbotham warns that blacks have not "sufficiently addressed the empirical reality of gender conflict within the black community or class differences among black women themselves."[75] However, as can be seen in the experience of women in the early civil rights movement, gender can be a source of fragmentation as well as innovation within the black community itself. Linking gender to race and class may therefore help reveal these embedded hierarchies while it also situates the experiences of men and women in sites for collective action and resistance rather than in individualistic notions of either success or failure.

Confronting this tension through the lens of race could affirm the value of power-with for white women, too. For example, research indicates that while many women have a collaborative view of power, this is often accompanied by a very individualistic view of failure.[76] Too often women internalize hardship or cultural expectations as their own fault or something they caused to happen. Janie Ward and Carla O'Connor's work suggests that black girls may be more resilient than white girls in the face of social stress and failure, because they tend to frame their situation within the larger issues of race and class. Struggling with these issues, rather than with gender, seemed to help most low-income black adolescent girls maintain high expectations for themselves. Their knowledge of the constraining effects of race and class and their interaction with significant others who exemplified a willingness to struggle contributed to their academic ambitions and sense of autonomy. Similarly, Ward found that black adolescents whose environment emphasized the necessity of fighting against oppression (psychologically and at times socially) were better prepared to withstand racism. Ward concludes that "resistance fosters resilience. It is a preventive psychosocial intervention that boosts hardiness and psychological resilience in black children."[77]

To serve as a progressive force, gender should be understood in the context of race and class. Otherwise, many middle- and upper-middle-class feminists may be inclined to promote gender-blind policies to allow individual women to make it in a man's world. They resent efforts that "celebrate as virtues all those aspects of the identity of the oppressed which are associated with strategic self-preservation in a condition of weakness: acuity of perception of the other's feelings; the masking of assertive and direct modes of leadership with indirect suggestion and persuasion; the assertion of power through good works, to occlude one's interest in power."[78] Feminists for whom these psychosocial accommodations are not virtues instead encourage women to explore their individual capacities and celebrate their individual success as though it were a transformative practice in itself. These women take exception to strategies claiming that what looks like a deficit can be in fact a source of solidarity and strength.

We do not detect quite the same degree of animosity among middle-class blacks toward self-preservation strategies that emanate initially from conditions of weakness. Racial solidarity is still seen as a source of strength, especially to the extent that it frames a critique of injustice that reminds each individual she is not alone. Moreover, external forces, such as racial profiling, reinforce cross-class convergence around strategies of resistance within the black community.

Unfortunately, despite the valuable lessons learned from linking race to gender and class, issues of gender have in this country, and certainly in the last half of the twentieth century, been most often associated with the claims and needs of middle- and upper-class white women.[79] Even more than race, gender equity has been a vehicle for infiltrating rather than challenging hierarchy, so that the girls can enjoy the privileges once held exclusively by the boys.[80] Although affirmative action has most often been cast as a race issue, it has in fact benefited white women far more than people of color. White women, as a result, have enjoyed unprecedented upward mobility.[81] Consciousness of gender inequity, unlike race, has also not seemed to construct a collective or oppositional consciousness about structures of power, although it apparently often yields more collaborative ideas about building relationships. Unless it is linked to race, therefore, gender may be less helpful as the primary engine of transformative political mobilization, although it offers much on which to build. The "personal is political" slogan originated with feminists as an effort to raise consciousness, and it is an effective way of suggesting that public actions have private consequences. But it is often less effective in identifying structures of public power.[82] As a result, Professor Mary Katzenstein admonishes white feminists to be ready to follow the leadership of women of color, if they intend to return to the question of what a just society requires.[83]

We have chosen in this book to focus on race; yet our analysis need not be limited to race. We encourage others to explore the ways in which gender and race intersect to produce synergies of social change. While focusing on race, we are simultaneously pushing for a more inclusive concept of power, so that whoever exercises it does so with different goals and more democratic practices.

Conclusion

Power-with is not a vanguard movement but a communal process of resistance that builds strength incrementally. It provides a foundation for hope in the face of more powerful foes and changes our understanding about what is success and what is failure. Since everything cannot and will not change at once, victories and defeats become data points that inform both the process and the vision. Nothing is ever complete or total. Not even the vision.

Starting with ideas of participation traditionally associated with the third dimension of power, power-with conceives of resistance as necessarily related to the generative capacity of collective struggle and interaction. Borrowing from Foucault's conception of power, it emphasizes the generativity of human agency and rejects the inevitability of domination. Our reconceptualization of power in service of resistance and struggle also builds on the feminist critique that ideas of power are not exclusively about zero-sum dominance. It contemplates the emergence of a collective energy that changes those involved in the struggle as well as altering their material conditions.[84]

We should re-emphasize, however, that our concept of power-with is not designed to accomplish a specific set of public policy reforms. Despite our belief in the need for a revived progressive agenda, our analysis is not dependent upon the more traditional definitions of social change that are bound up with elections, regulations, and litigation. Indeed, power-with might be employed by those who have a very different vision of social justice than our own.

The merits of rethinking power extend beyond changing the rules so that everyone can win something and feel good about himself or herself. They also go beyond generating more innovative solutions to complex problems or connecting with a magical collective energy that often has profound interior and external consequences. In our view, unless we begin to rethink power, we are going to witness the slow but steady evisceration of American democracy as fewer and fewer people participate, as government decision-making loses legitimacy, and as private power becomes more and more concentrated in the hands of a few winners, who will not hesitate to take all. Put simply, we need to rethink power in order to save democracy.

This story, which we learned from Martha Minow, is the old one about the walled city of Verona. Over time, the population inside the wall grew and the city became overcrowded. The problems from this circumstance mounted, until one day the Bishop decided something had to be done, and called a meeting with the Chief Rabbi. The Bishop said, "The overcrowding has become unbearable. The Jews must leave." The Chief Rabbi said, "Leave? But we have lived here for generations! Surely we should talk about so drastic a measure." The Bishop replied, "But who should talk? We could have a debate. But everyone in town cares about the subject." The Rabbi proposed, "We could hold it in the amphitheater; there is room for everyone." But the Bishop said, "No one could hear us there. It will have to be a silent debate."

They agreed, and the big day arrived. Everyone turned out and watched expectantly as the Bishop began. He raised his right hand up to the sky. The Rabbi brought his right hand down and pointed to his left palm. The Bishop held up three fingers. The Rabbi held up one. The Bishop reached under his chair and took out a wafer and ate it, and a glass of wine and sipped it. The Rabbi pulled out an apple and took a bite. At that moment, the Bishop leapt up and said, "You are right, the Jews can stay. We in Verona will have to find another way to solve our problem."

A crowd gathered around the Bishop, excited and perplexed. "We followed the debate very closely, but what exactly was said?" one person asked. "Ah, the man was brilliant," exclaimed the Bishop. "I said, 'The

Lord of All commands that the Jews leave Verona today.' He replied, 'But the Lord is here in Verona with the Jews, too.' I answered, 'The three aspects of the Trinity—the Father, the Son, and Holy Ghost—guide us on this matter.' And he answered, 'But there is just one Almighty, one King of the Universe.' I responded with the wafer and the wine to say, 'Jesus died for our sins so the Christians could be saved.' But he responded with the apple, noting 'We are all children of Adam and Eve.' And indeed we are. We are in this together; we will work it out together."

Meanwhile a crowd surrounded the Rabbi. "Rabbi, Rabbi, Rabbi, what happened?" they cried. "I have no idea," said the Rabbi. "The Bishop said, 'The Jews of Verona must leave here today.'" I answered, 'We are staying right here.' He returned, 'I will give you three days to pack.' I offered, 'We'll take a week.' Then he ate his lunch and I ate mine."

Many messages are embedded in this story. The one we focus on in this chapter is the way the Bishop and the Rabbi embody twenty-first-century American concepts of representation as defined by the United States Supreme Court. The clerics "represented" the citizens of Verona in a public conversation. But it was a conversation conducted exclusively through the use of publicly incomprehensible symbols. Although professing to seek a forum with room for all the citizens of the town, the Bishop and the Rabbi in fact communicated not at all with those seated in the amphitheater. Their authority attracted a rapt audience, but the citizens themselves were not engaged in the process of decision-making. This was representational synecdoche (sin-ek'-duk-key)—the part substituted for the whole. The Rabbi substituted for the Jews, the Bishop substituted for the Christians, and their silent interaction substituted for the conversation of democracy.

American democracy is today constituted by elites who are charged with policy deliberation and are presumably held accountable through elections. Those elections, however, often offer little real choice and thus fail to engender meaningful dialogue between voters and those who win election. Like the Bishop and the Rabbi, these elites operate at a disconnect from—indeed, often unintelligibly to—those they "represent." Big-money politics and the modern media have reduced American voters to spectators, like those earnest citizens who observed the silent dialogue in Verona's amphitheater.[1] The political parties are almost empty shells whose primary function is to raise money on a vast scale to finance costly media-based campaigns. Even party conventions, which once offered the possibility of rich democratic participation for some activists, are now carefully stage-managed events. Coded gestures and rhetorical winks stand in for complex ideas; dialogue and community participation are absent. Candidates are produced and packaged for a television audience, celebrated and orchestrated with elaborate story lines, a sales pitch, message discipline, and a showcase of ordinary people to symbolize "what the candidate wants you to believe he stands for," as President George W. Bush's chief of staff, Andy Card, pithily put it.[2] The entrenchment of the two major political parties has contributed to an institutional torpor that sucks the vigor out of political debates.[3]

These contemporary practices rest on a combination of peculiarly American ideas about democracy.[4] One such idea is that democracy is mainly about the right of individuals to choose individual candidates, and not about the value of groups that form around common concerns and participate in an ongoing democratic conversation. Another idea is that when groups must be formed in order to elect representatives, the best way to form them is through geographic districts created by politicians who choose which voters to represent. The notion here is that representatives should be elected by aggregations of individuals that may have nothing more in common than geographic proximity. Third, American-style elections give all the power to the candidate who emerges with the most votes, and then declares that winner the representative of "the whole district." This myth—that the majority stands in for the minority—tries to convince the electorate that something is present which is in fact absent, namely, true representation. Just as the flag stands in for the nation, candidate-centered winner-take-all elections, we are asked to believe, can somehow stand in for genuine participatory democracy.

These ideas are the central dogma of the Supreme Court's representational theology. Consistent with the elite-centered notions of some of the Constitution framers, the Court claims that whoever wins an election represents everyone, even those who voted against the winning candidate. This understanding of representation reflects the same synecdoche embodied by the Rabbi and the Bishop in Verona. Had the Bishop won a citywide election (primarily because there were more Gentiles in Verona than Jews), he would then have represented the Jews as well as the Gentiles, even though the Jews had not voted for him. He would have "represented" them even as he ordered them to leave the city. The Bishop would have been standing in for everyone in the city of Verona.

In short, the dominant approach to representation in the United States today seems to ignore the complexity of the representational relationship in a multiracial democracy. Democracy is supposed to bring the people into the arena of public decision-making as participants, not as spectators. However, our system of representation, based on winner-take-all elections, means that a majority of citizens in the nation at any given moment are not represented by people whom they chose to represent them and are thus alienated from meaningful democratic participation. Alienation is further exacerbated for people of color, who experience arbitrary constraints superimposed by a highly racialized political landscape. Our system erects barriers that dissuade many people of color from even attempting to engage in any sort of political activity. When we do vote, the candidate we support often loses or our votes are simply not counted. In Florida during the 2000 presidential election, for example, over half of the votes that were not counted were cast by black people, who made up only 11 percent of the electorate, according to findings of the Civil Rights Commission.[5] The system is no more legitimate in representing people of color than a similar system would have been in representing the Jews of Old Verona.

But the canary metaphor reminds us that experiences which converge around a racial minority are often a diagnostic tool. Starting with the experience of people of color, we can begin to identify the crucial missing elements of American democracy—missing elements that make the system fail not just for blacks or Latinos but for many other groups that are similarly situated. It is not preordained that democracy is best realized by creating a hierarchy in which an elected representative acts and the voters watch. The constitution does not mandate the aggregation of people into geographic election units. The choice we have made to create territorial districts does not reflect a particularly democratic sensibility, especially when such districts are used in conjunction with winner-take-all rules.

Winner-take-all territorial districting is fundamentally flawed because some minority—black, Republican, or Green—will always feel unrepresented. But equally important, a commitment to geographical districting pushes the legal system into inconsistency, as we will show in the discussion that follows. And not surprisingly, this zero-sum electoral system depresses voter turn-out, further eviscerating democracy. With only half of eligible voters participating even in presidential elections, the United States has one of the lowest levels of electoral participation in the democratic world; of the 172 countries that profess to be democracies, 81 percent have higher levels of voter turnout.[6] Ostensibly developed to protect the people from an unelected monarchy, our winner-take-all elections have recreated a political hierarchy that diminishes the people's role in determining their own destiny and privileges institutional order over widespread and ongoing public participation.

By starting this exploration with the experience of people of color, our project has a motivational goal as well as a diagnostic one—to imagine and inspire alternative and less hierarchical representational relationships that can evolve from the insights that the miner's canary provides. This political project uses the very vulnerability of the canary to suggest that the canary has more in common with the miner than the miner yet realizes. The canary is not disposable but is rather indispensable. By encouraging us to explore more dynamic ways of participation in civil society and governance, our political race project has a major role to play in revitalizing the way we conceive and practice democracy.

We begin this exploration of the role political race can play in democratic renewal by considering recent efforts to rectify the exclusion of people of color from public life. Since these remedies—namely, majority-minority districts—have operated within the context of geographic districts and winner-take-all elections, they remain mired in the flaws of representational synecdoche. Indeed, the shortcomings of thinking "the part is the whole" have prompted the Supreme Court to strike down a number of majority-minority districts over the past decade. The Court, however, has limited its critique to districts involving race; its jurisprudence is thus hopelessly confused, as we will see, because the problems the Court identifies in majority-minority districts are fundamentally about weaknesses inherent to *all* districts in our present electoral system. These problems are endemic to representational synecdoche itself. To reclaim the missing elements of representation, we consider alternative electoral systems that would encourage participation by more of the whole and would give all citizens a sense that their vote counts in our democracy.

But participation in public life, we believe, is not just about voting. The exercise of political imagination can foster democratic involvement from the bottom up. Even within the current flawed system, significant change is possible.

Majority-Minority Districting

The flaws in the present system of geographic districting are usually invisible even to the Court's legally trained eye. Invisible, that is, except in matters involving race. What seems perfectly normal and justifiable under theories of either adequate representation or virtual representation becomes appalling to a majority of the Supreme Court when white citizens complain about districts that have been drawn to enhance the voting power of a racial minority. These majority-minority districts have been successfully challenged in a line of race-conscious districting cases starting in 1993 with *Shaw v Reno.*[7]

Two kinds of anxiety arise when race-conscious districting comes before the Court. The first is the fear of "stigma." The Court majority equates an apportionment plan that uses race as a predominant criterion for drawing districts with "political apartheid" and rejects it as reinforcing impermissible racial stereotypes. Stereotypes reflect "the perception that members of the same racial group—regardless of their age, education, economic status, or the community in which they live—think alike, share the same political interests, and will prefer the same candidates at the polls."[8] Believing that a single black person can stand in for or share the same characteristics of the entire racial group and that others, on behalf of the racial group, can determine what the group thinks or wants is stigmatizing because it stereotypes blacks as being unable to think for themselves.

Besides stigma, the opposition to race-conscious districting also reflects a second concern of the Court's conservative members: "representational harm."[9] As Justice Sandra Day O'Connor wrote in *Shaw v Reno*, "The message that such districting sends to elected representatives is equally pernicious. When a district is created solely to effectuate the perceived common interests of one racial group, elected officials are more likely to believe that their primary obligation is to represent only the members of that group, rather than their constituency as a whole." At its center, the message of race-conscious districting is "pernicious" because it suggests that any black person elected will represent only the black community that elected him or her; the reverse, of course, is not true.

Justice Clarence Thomas expressed both of these concerns in his opinion in *Holder v Hall*.[10] According to Thomas, race-conscious districting is based on "the implicit assumption that members of racial and ethnic groups must all think alike on important matters of public policy." This is the stigma argument. Thomas also suggested it would be "politically unwise for a black official from a black majority district to be responsive at all to white citizens." This is the representational harm idea. Both stigma and representational harm have been characterized as "expressive harms." An expressive harm is one in which the message conveyed by a governmental action, rather than any concrete harm caused to individual voters, expresses a value structure that offends constitutional principles.[11]

Justices Thomas, Antonin Scalia, Anthony M. Kennedy, and William H. Rehnquist are the most conservative members of the Court; when joined by Justice O'Connor, they form the Court majority. These justices by and large have repudiated the idea that an individual who is not heterogeneous can somehow stand in for a heterogeneous whole, when that individual is elected from a district consciously drawn to include and possibly maximize the voting strength of black or Latino voters. In other words, a black person elected in a majority-black district is unlikely to represent the whites who also live in that district; nor will she represent all the blacks in the district.[12] In its essence, this position is a rejection of the concept of representational synecdoche—that an individual can stand in for a group. The "expressive harm" condemned by the Court's race-conscious districting cases is the related idea of racial synecdoche implicit in this form of racial-group representation. Indeed, in the same opinion first announcing the Court's concerns about race-conscious districting, Justice

O'Connor explained that the message conveyed by race-conscious districting runs against basic democratic norms. When elected officials believe that their primary obligation is to represent only the members of the group that elected them, "this is altogether antithetical to our system of representative democracy."

Yet the same Court that has insisted the part cannot legitimately represent the whole in the case of racial minorities has used—indeed, has celebrated—this very principle in all other electoral situations. What the Court sees as problematic in the case of race it celebrates in the case of politics. The concerns articulated so forcefully in the context of majority-minority districts do not seem to inform the Court's jurisprudence in the area of partisan gerrymandering or the one-person/one-vote principle, as we will see. The individual representatives of a political party or the elected candidates from a geographic district are deemed by the Court to be perfectly adequate and independent surrogates for the larger population. Using theories of "adequate" or "virtual" representation to justify geographic districting, the Court has opined that the winning candidate still "adequately" represents those in the district who vote for a losing candidate. While racial minority group members would ostensibly suffer stigma from being collected into a single district in which they hold the majority, political majority group members who are routinely collected into a single district by others acting with ulterior motives are said to experience no meaningful stigma.

The Court examined election districts in which race is alleged to be a predominant factor in their composition as if the districts exist in isolation. This microscopic investigation of each district revealed the practical improbability of genuine representation of a complex and dynamic community of interests when using a single winner to represent the whole. In a winner-take-all model, some group—the minority—inevitably loses. The identity of that minority, whether political or racial, *is chosen by others:* those who create the district boundaries. In the race-conscious districting cases the Court responded to the problem of the losing minority as being a special case—racial synecdoche—when in fact it is simply political synecdoche of a different color. Because race makes the problem so visible, race itself is misunderstood to be the problem. Like a neon sign, race glares so bright in the eyes of the Court that it becomes the only thing the Justices can see.

The Court has not been completely oblivious to the problems that inhere in its models of representational synecdoche, but it has diagnosed them on the wrong level. That is, a majority of the current Court condemned the practice of race-conscious districting because it perpetuates stigma and sends the wrong "representational message" that the elected official stands in for only a part of her district rather than her entire constituency. The black representative, elected by the majority black electorate, may fail to "represent" the whole and just focus on the needs of those who voted for her. Similarly, the black voters will be stigmatized by the choices of those drawing the election districts to lump or pack blacks as blacks into a single district.

The problems created by representational synecdoche, made visible in the context of majority-minority districts, are twofold. First, it is a representational challenge (if not an impossibility) for a single elected official to stand in for the whole district, especially if that single individual is accountable—in policy-making terms—primarily to those who voted for her.[13] Second, it is noxious to the voters' sense of autonomy to have their choice of representative essentially made on their behalf by those who draw the district lines so as to determine which majority, and which minority, will fall within those lines. Both of these are major problems, but neither of them is a tension caused by, or peculiar to, race. Instead, race-conscious districting becomes a kind of miner's canary that allows us to recognize synecdoche as a core problem within our political system as a whole.

Partisan Gerrymandering

What troubles the Court in the context of race-conscious districting happens routinely in any districting system that relies on winner-take-all elections. These elections reflect commitments shared by the majority of the Court to a particular version of democracy in which representative democracy is reduced to the successful election of a single person. At a macro level, this system can lead to outcomes that hardly reflect the will of the voters. For example, Democrats in Oklahoma won 37 percent of the vote in 1996, but of the six House seats and two Senate seats occupied by Oklahomans in Washington, not one was held by a Democrat.[14] To challenge this allocation, the Democrats would have had to file a case claiming partisan gerrymandering. In this kind of case, one of the two political parties challenges the districting decisions made by the competing party.

For example, after the 1980 census, Republicans in Indiana, wielding the reins of first-dimension power within the legislature, constructed the districts unfairly to diminish Democratic voting strength, according to their Democratic opponents. In the resulting case, *Davis v Bandemer,* the Court—acknowledging that citizens are also voters who affiliate with political groups—confronted the problem of how one group can be represented by a member chosen from another group.[15] The Democrats complained that a disproportionate number of Democratic voters were relegated to districts dominated by Republicans. How can Democrats living in Indiana have confidence that their Republican representatives will pay attention to their needs?

This is the same question Justice O'Connor and others ask regarding individual majority-black districts when they raised the question of representational harm. Just as the Court worried that the black elected official in a majority-black district may disregard the interests of white constituents, Democrats in Indiana worried that Republican elected officials in a majority-Republican district may disregard the interest of Democratic constituents. If, as was alleged, Republicans rigged the district lines in Indiana to assure control of a disproportionate number of legislative districts, then the issue of representational harm is joined with the issue of stigma. The majority-Republican districts were formed according to the belief that a single Republican can determine what the entire group of Republicans in his or her district thinks or wants. This is stigmatizing because it stereotypes Republicans as being unable to think for themselves, in the same way that majority-black districts supposedly stigmatize blacks.

The Court's standard answer when the question is raised about political partisanship rather than racial partisanship is twofold. First, the Court has refused to examine a single district in isolation. To do so would jeopardize the concept of winner-take-all elections. Second, the Court has employed a series of "virtual representation" assumptions to justify the way that winner-take-all elections over-represent the winning party.

Let us examine the Court's first response more fully. A look at any single district would reveal the fact that a sizeable minority is not represented by the election winner. That is the definition of "winner takes all"—whoever gets the most votes gets *all* the power, not just the lion's share of it. The unsuccessful minority loses, and its votes are effectively "transferred" to the majority winner, sort of like spoils of war. As Justice Byron White wrote for the Court in 1971, "As our system has it, one candidate wins, the others lose. Arguably the losing candidates' supporters are without representation since the men they voted for have been defeated; arguably they have been denied equal protection of the laws since they have no legislative voice of their own . . . But we have not yet deemed it a denial of equal protection to deny legislative seats to losing candidates, even in those so-called 'safe' districts where the same party wins year after year."[16]

The main goal of redistricting is for the party in power to gain control of as many districts as possible by fine-tuning the voter composition of each district. The incumbent party does this by drawing district lines and district shapes that have predictable political consequences. The majority party in each district should have enough votes to assure a win, but the minority party should also have a substantial number of votes, but not enough votes to win, in each district; otherwise, those minority votes might fall into a district where the minority would become the majority and win a seat. As Justice White notes, the district majority is a creature whose "political complexion" is usually predetermined by "the location and shape of district" lines.[17] The resulting district majority is "created" by those choosing which voters to put in that district. A district with a significant majority of Republican voters will predictably elect a Republican representative. This is why the parties fight so hard to control the shape of the district.

The essence of districting is to maximize the chances that your group is the district majority. This is its project. That it is increasingly successful can be seen in the small number of districts that actually change hands during the ten-year period between census enumerations. Swing districts are a vanishing breed. Only three congressional districts in the entire country changed hands as many as three times in the 1990s.[18] Justice O'Connor observed this phenomenon in *Bush v Vera*, identifying with specificity the role incumbents—as incumbents—play in this project: "For the sake of maintaining or winning seats in the House of Representatives, Congressmen or would-be Congressmen shed hostile groups and potential opponents by fencing them out of their districts. The Legislature obligingly carved out districts of apparent supporters of incumbents, as suggested by the incumbents, and then added appendages to connect their residences to those districts."[19]

Submergence of Democrats within majority-Republican districts, or the reverse, is routine.[20] The Court, therefore, has refused to scrutinize these politically motivated districts unless the party accused of gerrymandering has significantly underrepresented the voting strength of the complaining party *statewide*. Their focus has been on discrimination against Democratic voters "over the State as a whole, not Democratic voters in particular districts."[21] The Democratic plaintiffs must "prove both intentional discrimination against an identifiable political group and an actual discriminatory effect on that group," such that the gerrymandering consistently degraded the group of voter's "influence on the political process as a whole."

In its commitment to protecting the principle of winner-take-all districting, the Court has turned a blind eye to claims of the losing political minority within the context of an isolated district. In the context of these partisan gerrymandering cases—unlike the race-conscious districting cases—the Court shifted its focus from the representational harm or stigma involved in a single district. The Court concluded that the claim of partisan gerrymandering can be analyzed only on a statewide basis to assess whether the partisan minority is not just submerged in one district but is essentially shut out from political influence in the state as a whole.

The Court has put forward a virtual representation trilogy to justify its methodological choice not to examine individual districts in partisan gerrymandering cases. The concept of virtual representation has three dimensions: (1) Those in the minority party (those who voted against the winning candidate) are represented "virtually" by choices made by like-minded individuals who are more successful in other districts. (2) The district rather than the voters is represented. (3) The winning candidate will represent the winners and the losers because of the principle of reciprocity. All three parts of the trilogy operate to support the Court's decision to view the "political process as a whole" and not to examine the merits of individual districts.

The first virtual representation assumption is that the Democratic voters in Republican districts are virtually represented by choices made by Democratic voters in other districts with a Democratic majority. Democrats are best represented by like-minded candidates even "when that voter cannot vote for such candidate and is not represented by them in any direct sense."[22] As long as some Democrats are elected somewhere in the state, the Democrats in Republican-dominated districts are still represented.

But the Court has not rested solely on the primary idea of virtual representation. It has gone on to claim that to the extent the district "speaks" with one voice, it is the voice of the district "as a whole." Justice White said in *Davis v Bandemer*, "The power to influence the political process is not limited to winning elections. An individual or a group of individuals who votes for a losing candidate is usually judged to be adequately represented by the winning candidate and to have as much opportunity to influence that candidate as other voters in the district."[23] Justice White's "adequately represented" language suggests that all the people in a district can be serviced by the dutiful exercise of a single district caseworker who can bring home patronage. When the representative services the district, losing voters presumably have "as much opportunity to influence" that representative and as much access to patronage benefits as winning voters. So the second virtual representation hypothesis implies that all residents in the district have a common interest in gaining patronage or service. The role of the representative is not policy-making but patronage-dispensing. Essentially, the representative is treated like a caseworker for the district as a whole.[24]

The third part of the virtual representation trilogy depends upon a pragmatic application of the Golden Rule. The individual who votes for a losing candidate is "deemed to be adequately represented by the winning candidate" because of the prudent and realistic principle of reciprocity.

This pragmatic principle suggests that if you are the winning majority, you should represent the losing party adequately so that when you lose they will represent you adequately. The idea is that governing majorities are shifting rather than fixed; those in power need to worry about defectors. They also need to govern knowing they will one day be the losers. This concept also draws on eighteenth-century ideas that the representative is the natural leader of the community who is able to stand in for the whole because he or she can stand above the whole and take a long view.[25]

All three of these assumptions rest firmly on the foundation of representational synecdoche; to call that fundamental idea into question would destroy the concept of districting altogether. To assess the claims of political minorities within a single district would, as Justice White notes, not be "easily contained," especially if such minorities are numerous enough to "command at least one seat" were the district redrawn to favor their choices. If the Court began to investigate the claims of the losing minority, it "would make it difficult to reject claims of Democrats, Republicans, or members of any political organization" and it would make it difficult for many districts "to survive analysis" unless "combined with some voting arrangement such as proportional representation or cumulative voting aimed at providing representation for minority parties or interests."

Should the Court attempt to adjudicate those political consequences on behalf of the losing party within each district, it would be forced to invalidate the basic election rules that govern all districts. Justice O'Connor clearly recognized this dilemma when she took issue with Justice White's "virtual representation" approach in *Davis v Bandemer*. In that case, White determined that the Court would in fact intervene on behalf of the losing group but only if that group could show that its influence on the state's political process as a whole was unfairly diminished. O'Connor rejected White's use of a statewide baseline for assessing the voting influence of a political group. She remarked, "To treat the loss of candidates nominated by the party of a voter's choice as a harm to the individual voter, when that voter cannot vote for such candidate and is not represented by them in any direct sense, clearly exceeds the limits of the Equal Protection Clause."[26]

In her view, the first virtual representation idea—that the Court should act to ensure that Democrats in Republican districts are represented at least somewhere by Democrats in Democratic districts—does not make sense. Because districting is so essential to the democratic structure of American government, the Court should just stay out of it, she says, even in the most egregious cases of partisan gerrymandering. Instead, since the part must represent the whole, each person is represented. All residents can rely on the elected official to merge their interests into the interest of the of the district "as a whole."

Because of her confidence in the second and third virtual representation assumptions, representational synecdoche in this context has not troubled Justice O'Connor. The voting preferences of the individual voter can and should be ignored after the election because a conscientious representative will look out for all district constituents equally. To explore the political as opposed to patronage consequences of geographic districting would jeopardize districting as a means of allocating representation. Districting, in O'Connor's view, contributes to "a strong and stable two-party system," which preserves the health of "our political institutions, state and federal." Since we can rely on either party to dispense patronage to constituents who happen to be members of the opposing party, the political parties alone should conduct districting, without judicial intervention.

To do otherwise would destabilize the shared interests that all voters who occupy the same land mass necessarily have. After all, a stable governing coalition counts for more than meaningful representation and political accountability. O'Connor assured us that the Court need not worry about "the drawing of electoral boundaries through the legislative process of apportionment" because districting is a "critical and traditional part of politics in the United States, and one that plays no small role in fostering active participation in the political parties at every level."[27]

Although Justice O'Connor took issue with Justice White's reliance on the first virtual representation premise, both White and O'Connor essentially endorse winner-take-all districting and its inevitable dependence on the concept of representational synecdoche: the part substitutes for the whole. All voters should feel represented because the person elected by a district majority will somehow represent the interests of everyone in the district.[28] To understand this complex phenomenon of winner-takes all districting, it may help if we return to first principles—and back to Old Verona.

An Ancient Perspective on Geographic Districting

You are seated in the amphitheater many hundreds of years ago. Below you the Rabbi and the Bishop are in animated but mute discussion. "Surely," someone to your left says, "we must be allowed a say in this debate. After all they are deciding our future too. I know we cannot all talk at once. And some will question whether we have anything to add. But at the very least, we need someone to interpret what the Rabbi and the Bishop are doing. I cannot hear a thing!"

You are on a bench in the highest row in the outermost circle, at a great distance from the arena below. This is where women are permitted to sit, when they are invited into the stadium at all. "How shall we choose someone to help us understand what's going on down there?" you ask your neighbor. Running through your mind are the various ways your neighbor might respond to your question. You are especially intrigued because she has confided in you her ability to see the distant future. This gift is peculiar and limited, though, because the only future she can see is the struggle about democratic representation that would occupy the United States Supreme Court in the late twentieth and early twenty-first centuries. She has explained that democracy means rule by the people, and she has told you how these people are committed to democracy.

According to the U.S. Supreme Court opinions that your neighbor has divined, the only way to ensure adequate representation is to divide the amphitheater into districts. Everyone in the amphitheater must be represented, although that does not guarantee each person a vote. Each spectator takes his or her seat, and the seats are aggregated and then divided into districts. An election must be held to choose the representative of the occupied seats. If you have a seat, that means you are represented; it does not mean you can actively choose who represents you. Indeed, the representative serves without regard to the number of people who actually cast their lot. The person who is elected stands in for the district, acting as intermediary to, or translator for, the Rabbi and the Bishop.

"Why can't you choose who represents you in some way other than because of where you sit?" you wonder. It's because, your neighbor explains, "their Supreme Court seems hypnotized by this legacy of British rule." She seems genuinely perplexed that this idea of territorial representation is nowhere required in any of the founding documents of the country.[29] She scribbles some notes on a piece of slate and hands it to you. The note reads: "Territorial districting apparently comes from the idea that the district, like a town or a section in this amphitheater, represents the people in it. A representative can quiet the many voices of the town by raising his own, making the debate more orderly. The district—not the groups or people within it—is what is represented. Those who share the same seating section in an amphitheater are presumed to have enough in common to be represented legitimately by the same person."

"How close together do you have to be?" you ask. "Could a district be Rome or all of Sicily?" "Of course," she whispers. "Proximity is a flexible idea and as best I can tell it doesn't have anything to do with physical distance but just the number of seats, which have to be roughly the same from district to district." "But," you object, "what if I disagree with my neighbors? And what if the representative agrees with my neighbor and not me?" "Don't worry. If you have a seat in the district you are still represented." "But how can that be? I will not have voted for the representative. I can't even vote. I am a woman." "Do you have a seat?" she asks gently. "Yes," you reply weakly. "Then you have no worry. Because your seat is counted at the time they configure the districts, you, too, are represented."[30] In the twenty-first century in the United States, she explains, children, ex-felons who have served their time, current felons incarcerated in prisons within the district, non-citizen immigrants, and others who are unable to vote as well as those who choose not to vote are counted when the territorial districts are drawn up.

"Has it always been this way in America?" you ask, now tired. "No, not at all," she says. "For almost half of the twentieth century, from 1929 to 1967, a number of places—they call them states—including some of the largest ones, experimented with methods other than single-member districting for choosing their Congressional delegations. Americans use districts," she continued "because the U.S. Congress has chosen to do so."[31] "Who is the Congress?" you ask. "The representatives," she replies.

"Let us send a committee to represent us," you exclaim. "That is not possible," she chides. "Whoever wins a majority of the votes cast within the district, or close to a majority, wins the right to represent everyone." "But what of those of us who cannot vote or disagree with the choice?" She looks askance. "You just do not understand. The winner, enjoying the confidence of a majority or at least the greatest number of voters, enjoys the confidence of the district. In fact, he represents the minority even if those in the minority are his bitter opponents. Such is the magnanimity of the representative. And after all, this is necessary for 'stability and measured change.'"[32]

You glance at the senators' ornate, marble seats engraved with their names. Your eyes drift down to your plain stone bench permanently attached to the outer-edge of the highest reaches of the sloping balcony. Because you are a woman, you know you will never sit closer to the center. "Where are the natural districts in an amphitheater with fixed seating?"

"Well, there is a kind of natural district. We could draw concentric rings starting with the seats at the bottom where the senators and other important people sit. The rings would march up the stadium steps, capturing each row of seats as they went. The districts closer to the center would be fatter as they circled the amphitheater to ensure the same number of seats were in each district. By the time we got to the top row, the women would occupy their own district!" "But shouldn't each district have the same number of voters?" you ask. "Remember, we women cannot vote."

"Voters? Haven't I told you that we are counting seats, not the people who sit in them?" Your neighbor is becoming impatient with all your questions. "Okay," she says. "Let me explain one more time." She picks up the slate, wiping off her previous notes. "I am going to spell it out." Her note reads: "This task is compelled by the Supreme Court's one-person/ one-vote jurisprudence, which mandates that the districts do not divide the seats unevenly. In the one-person/one-vote line of cases, the Court focuses on equality of district population, reflecting its concern that constituent complaints about local service or requests for patronage will be equally attended to. In the name of equal representation, the Court seeks to assure all the people that they have equal access to the inbox of democracy. The number of persons counted in this effort is based purely on census figures; the election districts are drawn following the census and will, therefore, be equal in population (assuming the census to be accurate, which it often is not) but unequal in numbers of registered voters if registration rates vary by area."[33]

You are not sure this makes any sense, but you have another question. "Who gets to decide the shape of the district, anyway?" you ask. "Why, the senators of course," she answers, incredulous at your ignorance. This worries you since you have little confidence that the senators will draw districts with your interests in mind as opposed to theirs. You are sure that they want to retain their personally engraved marble seats. But you keep your concern to yourself. Instead, you decide to move on to see if another geometric form could work. "Instead of rings, is it possible to shape the district like a slice of pie?" you ask.

"This is not about shape. They can be any shape," but then your neighbor pauses as if in deep thought. "Well, let me be more careful. This is one area in which appearances *do* matter." She tries to explain. "If the district is not compact and if its ungainly shape suggests presumptions about the *race* (though not necessarily the religious affiliation or ethnicity) of the people in the district, that would reinforce stereotypes and send a pernicious message to the representative."[34] "Well then," you conclude, "we cannot draw a district that would track the seats occupied by the women. The last ring would not be funny shaped, but it might send the wrong representational message. Grouping the women might suggest that women have interests in common or think alike. It might prevent the representative from seeing his obligation to represent men too."

You are very proud of yourself for understanding this concept. Democracy is not so hard. It is about elementary calculations that can be done on one's fingers.[35] You realize that district shapes should be more like triangles radiating out from the center of the arena. That way, every district would be an equally populated pie slice arranged cheek by jowl around the arena, capturing a cross-section of the people, senators to women.

Your instinct is to treat the amphitheater as a giant pie to be subdivided in equal-size slices, based on the number of "seats" or potential pie-eaters who might occupy each seat.

But as the debate goes on and the sun beats down, you start to drift off, imagining other ways you could be represented. What if representation was configured as a horizontal as well as vertical relationship? It could be a relationship that anticipated communication between you and your neighbor not just between you and the single district representative who was center-stage. Your gaze would be drawn not only to the leading characters in the debate but expanded to include the other citizens in your district. If you deliberate horizontally as well as vertically, then through that interaction you could formulate collective views and generate citizen confidence in one another's capacity to think about public policy problems.

And what if you could move your seat to *choose* your conversation partners? What if people could go to a different part of the arena to join one of the animated conversations that were springing up around the amphitheater? If the seats in the amphitheater were not assigned according to your status or gender, and if the seats in the amphitheater were lightweight and portable, people could move their seats or choose their districts by where they chose to sit. It might even include a more active role for you, the citizen. It might encourage meetings with your neighbors before coming into the amphitheater. In these smaller groups, you might construct your own solutions to the problem of overcrowding in Verona. Or you might rehearse strategies for interrupting the dominant conversation in the main portion of the arena.

Unfortunately, portable seating was not a technology yet available in Old Verona. Nor did contemporary ideas about representation imagine a larger role for the people themselves other than ratifying the decisions made by their official representatives.[36] The pie-shaped districts that fanned out from the center at least guaranteed equal distribution of a fixed resource (the representative's attention) and, at minimum, guaranteed that those closest to power were in a position to translate what the more powerful were doing.

Given the subject of the debate, there was an additional concern, but you quickly discounted it. It wouldn't even matter if the pie-slice districts randomly distributed Christians and Jews. Surely the Jews of Verona would not have a basis for complaining of lack of representation. After all, the U.S. Supreme Court, with the benefit of centuries of wisdom to draw on, had determined that if a district has an individual to represent the district, everyone "seated" in the district is represented as well.

The One-Person/One-Vote Rule

With the divine intervention of your amphitheater neighbor, you read books not yet published, including some by critics of the winner-take-all districting project.[37] You have worn your brain out studying the decisions of the U.S. Supreme Court, but you have not been able to find a Court opinion that reflects what you learned from the critics—that districting disempowers voters because election outcomes are predetermined by the legislators who draw the district lines, not the voters who live inside them. This worries you. You have little confidence that the senators of Verona will in fact stand in for your interests. You conclude that the Court's uncritical embrace of districting has disabled it from having a consistent or clearly articulated idea of what representation means in a heterogeneous democratic state. You are not sure you want to consult the future, if the future is represented by the twenty-first-century American court. You are persistent, however, and try to reread the cases so as to have a recommendation to offer your neighbor, who seems deep in thought herself, while patiently sitting in the upper reaches of the amphitheater of Verona.

You learn that in a series of cases in the 1960s the Supreme Court tried to bring some order to what it had previously shunned as the "political thicket" of issues surrounding representation. These cases involved challenges brought by residents of suburban and urban areas who argued that the number of elected officials from their districts was not sufficient for their burgeoning populations. The incumbent elected officials in the state legislatures of Alabama and Tennessee had refused to redraw district lines despite massive changes in population because to do so would mean they would lose political clout and most likely their legislative seat.

These cases, starting with *Baker v Carr* in 1962 and *Reynolds v Sims* in 1964 and continuing into the twenty-first century, focused on remedying "rotten boroughs" or districts of wildly varying populations. The Supreme

Court, goaded by political scientists like Robert Dixon, invented a constitutional principle to deal with this problem. It was called the "one person, one vote" rule. But, surprisingly, the rule had little or nothing to do with voting. The Court ruled that each state had to divide its total state population by the number of congressional seats the state had been given to come up with an ideal district size, in terms of population. The Court then required that each district's population not vary too much from that ideal number.[38]

Despite the rhetoric that refers to voting, the relevant variable in these cases is equal population, not equal voting power. The legal doctrine requires equalizing the population among districts without regard to the number of registered or even potential voters. The only way to understand this doctrinal rule as a matter of representational theory is to imagine that the Court wants assurance "that constituents have more or less equal access to their elected officials, by assuring that no official has a disproportionately large number of constituents to satisfy." The Court is unconcerned with discrepancies in registration or turnout figures or even eligible voters between and within districts.[39]

This reflects the second virtual representation principle: that everyone within a given district is deemed represented by virtue of a single elected individual who stands in for the whole district. It is bodies that count, not voters. The irony of this approach is illustrated by prisoners serving time in one district although they consider another district their "home district." For example, felons imprisoned in rural districts are counted as "residents" living within those districts for the purpose of the census and therefore for the purpose of apportionment. The rural district is given additional representation to account for the population increase attributable to the prison. Yet in 48 states prisoners convicted of felonies cannot vote while serving their sentence.[40] And even if they could vote, they would probably want to vote (or at least would enjoy more potential policy influence) in the district in which their family and friends also reside or in which they resided prior to their incarceration. More than 80 percent of New York state's prisoners are black or Hispanic, and about 65 percent come from a few select areas of New York City. Yet 64 of the state's 71 prisons are located in Republican districts. The strategic placement of prisons in predominantly white rural districts often means that these districts gain more political representation based on the disenfranchised people in prison, while the inner-city communities these prisoners come from suffer a proportionate loss of political power and representation.[41]

The Court's numerical test—assuring good faith efforts to reach zero deviations in population when comparing one district within a state to another—is based solely on the number of people actually counted by the census on a fixed date, no matter who actually lives within the district.[42] It has nothing to do with voting at all. It has even less to do with effective, participatory democracy.

The Supreme Court's one-person/one-vote rule actually reflects a theory of service in which the representative functions not only as a waiter but as a megaphone and a mailbox.[43] Each representative should have the same chance of getting the same number of letters or complaints for service from constituents. We call this the mailbox or inbox view of representation; its purpose is to emphasize the patronage and caseworker role as distinguished from the public policy-making role of the representative.

As F. R. Ankersmit notes, this theory of political representation is "in fact, not a theory of representation at all, but a theory *against* representation." It is not an affirmative case for representation because it gives the representative no guidance on policy matters or legislative votes; political issues are often too complex to "be formulated in a clear question to the electorate."[44] It focuses instead on the representative's role as a dispenser of patronage or constituent service.

Majority Representation of Minority Interests

The core assumption within the existing districting paradigm is that the district winner represents the losers. This assumption is based on the idea that whoever is elected is a virtual representative of all the voters *and* nonvoters in the district, including those who voted against the winning candidate. The commitment to the notion that the majority can adequately represent the minority extends to racial minorities—elected officials who owe their election success exclusively to support from white voters nevertheless are deemed to represent voters of color. Even when voting is racially polarized over a long period of time (as in North Carolina in the

1980s, where more than 80 percent of whites chose not to vote rather than vote for a black candidate), the racial majority presumably enjoys "democratic legitimacy."

The Voting Rights Act was amended in 1982 to challenge this assumption. Congressional hearings showed that blacks were being shut out of the political process throughout the South and that Mexican Americans were similarly marginalized in the Southwest. The third virtual representation assumption of reciprocity apparently did not obtain. Because whites were assured victory as long as whites voted as a racial bloc, their majority status gave them total power. They never needed to watch out for dissident members of the white community joining with black or Hispanic voters to support a minority candidate.

The 1982 amendment to the Voting Rights Act gave blacks and other statutorily protected groups the right to challenge districting schemes in which the black minority could prove that white voters dominated election outcomes and failed to take their interests into account. The first case to interpret the 1982 amendments, *Thornburg v Gingles,* showed that in many election years no blacks anywhere in the state of North Carolina had been successful at being elected to the state legislature. Thus, the first virtual representation principle also went by the boards. Blacks who were a minority in one district could not be deemed "represented" by blacks who were a majority in another if there were in fact no majority-black districts in the North Carolina legislature.

Essentially, this and other cases showed that because whites controlled the instruments of second-dimension power (that is, the rules by which the voting game was played), whites comfortably enjoyed first-dimension dominance. Thus, the cases established a legal claim to the creation of majority-minority districts, to give blacks or Hispanics the same opportunity previously enjoyed exclusively by whites to be the racial majority and to control the outcome of some district elections.

But when the commitment to winner-take-all districting has the effect of creating majority-black districts, some whites object. In North Carolina in 1993, for example, whites who did not even live in the majority-black district successfully challenged the drawing of that district on the grounds that it denied them the right to participate in color-blind elections. When the case came to the Supreme Court, the justices in *Shaw v Reno* recognized the danger of synecdoche as an organizing principle, but only in one limited way. Preoccupied with the problem of racial classification as a per se constitutional violation, the Supreme Court focused not on the limitations of political synecdoche but of racial synecdoche. The Court, for the first time, apparently became aware of the inexorable consequences to unrepresented minorities in winner-take-all districts. It perceives two such minorities: (1) the blacks who are "trapped" in the racial category, and (2) the whites who are the district minority.

Focused on individual districts, the Court imagines their black majority representative to function exclusively as a public policy delegate of that majority and worries about the representative's self-interested partisan role. The fiction of the representative as the conscientious trustee who thinks only of the interest of the district as a whole—a keystone in the partisan gerrymandering jurisprudence—is tossed aside. Also abandoned is the idea that the Court can examine political influence only in the context of a statewide baseline rather than by reviewing individual districts. Contrary to its practice in the partisan gerrymandering case of focusing on the political process as a whole, the Court measures the constitutionality of each challenged district. Political "responsiveness" is no longer determined by aggregating all the districts to assess overall political fairness. Unlike the one-person/one-vote cases, where the only doctrinally relevant variable is the number of people living in the district, the Court moves in the direction of assessing or measuring the representative's behavior within the legislature.

The conservative Justices on the Court, in their interpretation of the Equal Protection Clause of the U.S. Constitution, also determine that legislatures should not place a single member of a racial group with other racial group members because of assumptions that their racial characteristics reflect any commonality. One cannot attribute characteristics associated with a group (the whole) to an individual member of that group (the part). Racial gerrymandering, Justice Thomas subsequently wrote, "offends the Constitution whether the motivation is malicious or benign." A legislature may not draw districts "based on the stereotype that blacks are reliable Democratic voters."[45] In Justice Thomas's view, a single member of the racial group cannot adequately represent the whole race; nor can a member of a racialized group elected in a majority-minority district represent the whole district.[46] The conservatives on the Court call it stigma, not politics, even when the evidence demonstrates that those in the racialized group actively choose to affiliate politically and seek, as does any political group, "to control the drawing of electoral boundaries through the legislative process" of districting. As Justice O'Connor recognized in the context of partisan gerrymandering claims, the opportunity to influence the drawing of district lines "plays no small role in fostering active participation in the political parties at every level."[47] Yet, according to Justice Thomas, blacks who affiliate in local political organizations to influence the districting process are to be denied that opportunity on the grounds that they are perpetuating racial stereotypes and representational harms.

But this dual set of concerns, voiced with great vehemence by Justice Thomas in particular, are misplaced when racial group surrogates are affirmatively chosen by the racial group members themselves, not by others. This is especially true where black voters prefer and even vote for the black candidate when given a choice between a black and a white candidate with similar views. Indeed, racial group members frequently and voluntarily choose to affiliate with the same political party. Especially for blacks, racial identity is a salient political cue.[48] Survey evidence and voting behavior show that blacks overwhelmingly share perceptions about their common interests. These perceptions extend beyond the race of the candidate to the ideology or party platform on which the candidate runs, and they help explain sharply divergent voting patterns across racial groups even among black and white individuals with common party affiliation. In North Carolina, for example, black Democrats are far more reliable Democratic voters than white Democrats. As a result, a fragile majority of the Supreme Court recently recognized that a legislature seeking to create a safe Democratic district can treat black Democrats and white Democrats differently.[49] Under such circumstances, racial synecdoche in the political arena is as much political as racial.

Yet, despite the way racial synecdoche converges with political synecdoche, there is a troubling paradox raised by the Supreme Court's jurisprudence in this area. That paradox is captured by the strange efforts of a three-judge federal court in Alabama to squeeze the legitimate political activity of several black grassroots organizations into the court's racial classification terminology. [50] The federal court failed to grasp the political nature of race, certainly in this part of Alabama, at least as experienced by many people of color.[51] In its effort to interpret the *Shaw v Reno* line of cases, the lower court disrupted the political process by intervening in a way that Justice O'Connor thought entirely inappropriate in the context of partisan gerrymandering.

The Alabama Circuit Court, in state litigation challenging the drawing of Alabama legislative districts after the 1990 census, had already found that race was not in fact used as a stereotyped proxy for political affiliation, as had been claimed by the opposition, but reflected the actual interests of black citizens expressed through the leaders of their own political organizations. The state court found that the black political organizations in question—the Alabama Democratic Conference, the Jefferson County Citizens' Coalition, and the Alabama New South Coalition—"represent the political interests of over 80% of the black voters in Alabama."[52]

These black political organizations in Alabama and many other parts of the country function exactly like those purposive and coherent associations of people that we often refer to as political parties. They are even more political than other groups in our political life, such as Dole voters, McCain voters, or even members of the Republican or Democratic Parties. Yet, in Alabama a three-judge federal court, eager to enforce *Shaw v Reno*, ruled in April 2000 that—contrary to the findings of the state court in Alabama—the voluntary political affiliation of those who, in part because of their race, joined together in real political action impermissibly tainted Alabama's 1993 state redistricting plan, the same plan that had been upheld by the state court.

Some argue that this just means "race is different." Unlike other group or party affiliations, racialized politics actually mobilizes its partisans. The energy and zeal of racial politics is potentially polarizing; its emotional content makes compromise difficult. Alternatively, race is a more remote proxy for interest than is political affiliation, the evidence of racial bloc voting notwithstanding. Moreover, even if race is a proxy for political affiliation, racial proxies do not give an individual black Republican a chance to opt-out of the racial constituency. And of course race is permanent rather than transitional. In these ways, race-conscious districting causes distinct harms that are not found even in the most partisan gerrymanders.

Relying on such arguments, the *Shaw v Reno* line of cases denies blacks an open opportunity to join in political association. In the views of the conservative justices, a majority-minority district, confected with race as a predominant consideration, is both stigmatizing to the racial minority and representationally harmful to those from the white racial majority who live in that district. Political gerrymandering may also deny power to a political minority, but, in the Court's view, it does so on grounds that are not permanent and not stigmatizing. The decision to waste the votes of a political minority, or pack them into a single district, is not permanent because new coalitions may form that contravene traditional partisan affiliations. The decision is not stigmatizing because it is not based on immutable physical characteristics; it is instead legitimately based on shared political values. In this reading, stigma is a proxy for stereotyping voters and aggregating them into units of representation only when applied to a racial group, even one that acts politically, votes cohesively, and shares common political values.

Yet none of these concerns actually explains why the Court should disapprove districts that put those politically raced as black in a district for that reason while vindicating districts that put those politically affiliated as a Democrat into a district for that reason. Especially since race is a better proxy for political behavior than party identification, why is it that only members of the former group are stigmatized by the districting decision? How is it that the majority of blacks become victims of stereotyping and political apartheid when they manifest by their voting behavior that they hold certain values and attitudes in common with other group members, that they desire to have ongoing relationships with individuals like themselves, and that, based on those relationships and a sense of linked fate, they choose to engage in sustained or coordinated efforts which have a goal broader than a single election? This is what the Alabama Democratic Conference, the New South Coalition, and the other black political organizations demonstrated through-out the 1990s.

Certainly some blacks may want to opt out of a majority-black district; some very liberal Democrats may want to opt out of a majority blue-dog Democratic district too. While majority-black districts may treat blacks as a monolith, so do majority-Republican districts that intentionally fragment the black minority so they can be consistently ignored. Indeed, this is the very problem inherent in winner-take-all districting. The solution, to which we return, requires, as Justice White recognized, that we draw districts "combined with some voting arrangement such as proportional representation or cumulative voting" if we want to honor the interests of dissenting individuals who seek exit or agency.

Yet because of the Court's preoccupation with stability over participation and its commitment to colorblindness as the necessary antidote to what the white majority has done in the past to stigmatize the racial minority, a majority of black voters—even where they manifest ongoing political relationships and consistently similar political choices—are not given the option of coalescing politically *as black voters*.[53] They may be collected in one safe Democratic district if the legislature exercises its discretion to protect incumbents or to protect one of the two major political parties. But the experience of blacks, as blacks, simply disappears. As Justice Scalia declares in another, though related, context, "We are just one race here. It is American."[54]

This interpretation is certainly perplexing to those of us committed to participatory democracy. For us, the stigma of being collected into a single district based on assumptions made by others in power extends beyond race to politics. All voters should district *themselves* by the way they cast their ballots; the incumbent politicians should not limit that choice by the way they draw the districts. To limit the stigma argument to racial minorities denies those group members any hint of autonomy, especially where there is genuine and documented across-the-board political cohesion within communities of color showing that blacks or Hispanics are in fact a political constituency, that is, they function as if they are part of at

least the first stage of the political race project. Indeed, advocates and political theorists have made strong arguments that aggregating blacks or
Hispanics into racially identifiable districts is a form of political fairness
rather than an instrument of racial stereotyping.[55]

Imagine a thought experiment in which blacks in Alabama form a political party, the Progressive Party, and through that party gain control of
enough legislative seats to draw districts to protect their party's legislative
proportion. This party welcomes the membership of persons of any race,
but it originated to speak to the interests of previously unrepresented
blacks and thus is comprised, almost exclusively, of black members.[56] The
Progressive Party's constituents—black voters—demonstrate political cohesion; they function as a voluntary political association; they seek to influence district-drawers to concentrate power in the hands of their partisans. At the next round of redistricting the party achieves, in effect, the
same ends as racial redistricting, but it achieves them through political gerrymandering. Should the Progressive Party's success in the redistricting context (including the use of some funny-shaped districts) be
measured by the more relaxed criteria applied to partisan gerrymandering rather than the intense scrutiny given racial redistricting? More to
the point, would the Court uphold such a plan, under the deferential
Bandemer review normally applied in political gerrymandering cases, or
would it invalidate such districts as race-based, invoking *Shaw*?[57]

The purpose of the thought exercise is to demonstrate that, in our view,
the Court's jurisprudence in this area is conceptually chaotic. As long as
race correlates so highly with political preference, efforts to distinguish
between racial and political gerrymandering will remain hopelessly inco-
herent.[58] There are several ways to explain how the Court got into such a
quandary. One is that members of the Court do not care about voting as a
means of giving citizens a meaningful voice in their democracy. This
might seem at first preposterous; but it is plausible if one believes that the
Court does in fact realize the limits of winner-take-all districting, but its
good judgment is overtaken by its passionate commitment to a laissez-
faire role in the political thicket of representation.[59] A second explanation
is that the Court simply does not see the limits of representational synec-

doche except when race makes them visible. In this explanation, race-conscious districting is no different from any other line-drawing effort involving the allocation of a single representative to speak for or stand for a collection of voters who happen to live within the artifice of an election district. Yet, because it is a case in which racial and political synecdoche converge, the Court finds the arrangement suspect. To the extent this is correct, the Court confuses its own view that race is only about racial classification with the actual act of classification that dominates the entire project of districting. Such confusion is a natural by-product of the Court's moral accounting of race, in which race is a single, fixed, and invariably stigmatic category

Yet another interpretation is that the limitations of representational synecdoche are acceptable to a Court more concerned with stability than participation. That someone external to the voters is making choices on their behalf might not offend the Court, because the delegation of voter choices to elected officials does not threaten the Court's narrow view of political stability itself. This view borrows heavily from Justice O'Connor's conclusion that democracy is about "stability and measured change." In this understanding, race is stigmatizing because it is polarizing; but here the Court confuses polarization and paternalism.

While the act of classifying people by race may in many instances polarize, the Court offers no evidence to support that conclusion when legislatures draw majority-minority districts. Meanwhile, the Court simply overlooks what districting does to enable others to restrict the range of choices available to all the voters. It ignores, in other words, the paternalism by which key decisions about democratic representation are delegated to the representatives rather than to the represented. In fact, paternalism that leads to feelings of alienation or exclusion can polarize; in any event, it certainly paralyzes. But the Court fails to detect the challenge to fundamental democratic legitimacy that is ongoing when—by virtue of this pattern of paternalism—half of the eligible voters do not participate in acts of self-governance. Rather than confronting our failure to give the voter an opportunity to exercise an unfettered choice, the Court finds comfort instead in the avoidance of conflict and in the ostensibly "race neutral" symbols of synecdoche—the selection of a part that can speak for the entire group. It values rituals of stability over genuine acts of participation.[60]

But conflict per se within the political arena is not what causes voters to withdraw in alienation or disgust. It is rather the sense that others are manufacturing the conflict for the purpose of winning rather than governing. The real harm, which the Court fails to recognize in its zeal to stamp out race-consciousness, is the harm perpetuated by a system that gives incumbent legislators the power to choose their next round of voters. This diminishes competition, wastes votes, and contributes to the view that your vote does not count, that what is being discussed does not affect your life, and that discussion of the "greater good" does not include you.[61] The harm is in not getting services to your part of town and, most important, in not having a voice in a government that is accountable to you or to those to whom you believe your fate is linked.

In these ways, race-conscious districting is no different from other forms of first- and second-dimension power. Race-conscious districting accepts the idea that districting is the process of allocating zero-sum power to one group and taking it away from another. It does not challenge the power of incumbents—all incumbents—to hold the *real* election during the legislative session at which the districts are confected. It allows the second, agenda-setting dimension of power to proceed for the most part undisturbed as long as some black majority districts are also created. But the underlying rules of the game remain intact, and elections remain merely periodic opportunities for the people simply to ratify the choices already made by incumbents, who, though now a more integrated and diverse group, seek to hold onto power.

In this interpretation, race-conscious districting retains and legitimates the existing hierarchy of representative democracy by creating, for visible inspection, a more "integrated" legislature. Yet, as we have seen, although it mirrors all the assumptions of partisan gerrymandering, it alone is vulnerable to judicial focus at the individual district level. Perhaps this is because race-conscious districting, like all districting, accedes to the principle that power is zero-sum. Those who argue for race-conscious districting claim that those who have been denied power "deserve" a chance for some of what has already been distributed to others. Race-conscious districting merely gives new people the chance to exercise some conventional power.

But the same premise that is used to justify giving new people power in a zero-sum scarcity model contains the seeds of its own demise. The very representational message that the Court fears is realized if the newly empowered black majority seeks power in order to exercise it on its own behalf rather than in the interest of the whole district. Race-conscious districting is vulnerable as a principle because it does not challenge the idea that a single representative can effectively stand in for a complex whole, nor does it challenge the idea that elected officials, rather than the voters themselves, should be choosing the units of electoral control.[62]

In its zeal to stamp out race-consciousness, however, the *Shaw* line of cases, for the most part, has ignored the political nature of race-conscious districting as an expression of the conscious and voluntary will of a majority of black voters. What is more, the Court inexplicably, but temporarily, has suspended its understanding of the second-dimension rules that govern all redistricting. It considered legislatures' use of race to create majority-minority districts an unacceptable exception to "neutral" districting principles. Yet those who seek to influence the legislature's decision as to where to place the district lines are never acting neutrally; they always act politically, governed by the same second-dimension rules, whether they are members of a single racial group or a single political party.

The experience of racially marginalized groups both opens a window through which we can see the larger failings of a geographically based representational system and provides an entryway for more systemic reforms. If the goal is merely formal equality within a flawed system, then race-conscious districting is the remedy. This is certainly a plausible alternative when plaintiffs demonstrate that race is a political category, as they did in Alabama, where 80 percent of blacks affiliated with one of three local organizations. It is just as appropriate, however, to use the insights of the canary to rethink the atmosphere in the political mines in which we all labor.

Race-conscious districting highlights the importance of interrogating the relationships between first- and second-dimension power. Race reveals relationships of power that transcend conventional and individualistic notions of racial essentialism or moral stigma. It does this by showcasing the limits of the representational model that the Court has used to justify a flawed set of election rules. This model constrains the definition and function of the representative role and suggests an impoverished view of how to engage more people in the political process.

Each of the Court's doctrinal interventions has been responsive to deficiencies in the prevailing system of representation. But none of the Court's opinions or jurisprudential approaches has contained a normative vision of what representation should look like.[63] Nor does the U.S. Constitution have much to say on the subject. As a result, the case-by-case development of a "theory" of representation, whether in the one-person/one-vote cases, the partisan gerrymandering cases, or the race-conscious districting cases, is actually not a theory at all. It is an ad hoc defense of a system of winner-take-all geographic districting that we inherited from the British, without an effort to articulate a consistent vision of representation itself. A general incoherence lies just beneath the surface of every decision the Court has made.

Coherence would be desirable, but for our political race project, it is not enough just to reconcile the inconsistency in approaches with some meta-narrative of race-blindness and representation. Better to challenge as well the narrow, winner-take-all paradigm out of which the Supreme Court decides all of the voting cases that come before it. This means ultimately confronting the need for a more complex vision of representation and, at the very least, struggling to expand the concept of representation itself to ensure that legitimate options are not left off the table. This more transformative option seeks to enrich the democratic participation of all voters by involving previously ignored elements of interactive representation and power-sharing between the represented and the representative; it seeks horizontal as well as vertical interaction, meaning democratic engagement among the voters and between the voters and their representatives. It is not content with a theory of representation that merely justifies the substitution of different winners based on who prevails in seizing first-dimension power. Instead, as we show toward the end of this chapter, it would rely on the interplay between ideas of political race and ideas of dynamic citizen involvement to help reveal and then reinforce these missing elements.

The Missing Element of Representation

It was a hot Saturday in May 1996. About fifty women, many of them poor, some of them welfare recipients, boarded a bus in South Georgia and traveled for several hours until they reached a suburban Atlanta congressional district. There they spent the day handing out literature, making telephone calls, and doing whatever they could to reelect Cynthia McKinney, a Democratic congresswoman who was fighting a slew of well-funded contenders in a primary election battle. The women on the bus were not from McKinney's district, but they still viewed her as their standard bearer. The women on the bus knew they had a representative in Congress, though not in the traditional, regionally defined sense of the term. Theirs was representation based on demography, not geography. Asked about the women on the bus, McKinney, the first African-American woman elected to Congress from Georgia, explained: "They've never been able to vote for me, but they feel represented by me. These are poor people who are coming from rural South Georgia because they don't want to lose their voice in Congress."[64]

The passion of these women for a representative voice echoed the motivation of many black people throughout the South. Growing up in North Carolina in the 1950s, State Senator Frank Ballance testified in a voting rights case in 1983 that he used to think of Adam Clayton Powell as his representative even though Powell was elected to represent a black majority district in Harlem. Senator Ballance was saying that many blacks in North Carolina felt more represented by blacks outside the state than by whites elected from their own district. Echoing Ballance's testimony was Arkansas state representative Ben McGee's statement in *Whitfield v Democratic Party of Arkansas* that he willingly traveled long distances through the eastern delta region to help raise funds for black candidates running in Phillips County, in a local race in which McGee would not be able to vote.

Q: Now, why would you come from Crittendon County to participate in a fundraiser for a county race that was basically a local race to Phillips County?

A: Well, the reason I would come, first of all, there are no blacks elected to a county position in eastern Arkansas and no blacks serving in the House of Representatives in eastern Arkansas and no blacks elected to anything other than school boards in districts that are predominantly black. And I feel like blacks should be elected to public office because they should have the chance to serve.

McGee had explained in his trial testimony in the case why he cared so much about electing more black representatives: "I want to help get blacks elected so little black children can see them serving and I want to dispel the myth that some white kids might have that blacks can't serve or shouldn't be serving at the courthouse. And when my little girl goes to the courthouse or when other little girls go to the courthouse, I want them to be able to see black people working up there." Many blacks shared McGee's desire to see black people "working up there" in the courthouse. Albert Turner acted like a proud father showing off his newborn infant when he escorted a visitor through the courthouse in Perry County, Alabama. He pointed out the sheriff, the tax assessor, the many black people working up there on behalf of their community. Like Ben McGee, Frank Ballance, and Albert Turner, the women on the bus interrupted their daily routine, got on a bus, and traveled a long distance to do something they thought was even more important than simply taking the short walk to the ballot box on election day.

For the fifty or so rural black women in Georgia, the collective experience of racial discrimination forged both a racial and a political identity. Race for them was a reason to get on the bus, even if they had to rely on a form of virtual representation. They were motivated to get on the bus because they saw their chance for representation in this one black woman. She was carrying the expectations of these nonvoters as well as the voters in her district. She was somehow standing in for them as if she represented them too. *Their* community—defined initially by race—was real. It existed and it mattered, no matter how a court or a legislature drew election district lines.

Back in the old city of Verona, we discover that the women there, too, have become actively involved with the issue of representation. These women, sitting in the outer ring of the amphitheater, have now canvassed the twentieth-century literature on political theory and concluded that democracy is fundamentally a concept of collective action. They have read, for example, Hannah Pitkin, who says, "What distinguishes politics . . . is the possibility of a shared, collective, deliberate, active intervention in our fate, in what would otherwise be the byproduct of private decisions. Only in public life can we jointly, as a community, exercise the human capacity to 'think what we are doing,' and take charge of the history in which we are all constantly engaged by drift and inadvertence . . . The distinctive promise of political freedom remains the possibility of genuine collective action, an entire community consciously and jointly shaping its policy, its way of life."[65]

Yet, the women of Verona discover, with prodding from the United States Supreme Court, that twenty-first-century Americans pursue a formulaic and individualistic approach to democracy that unsettles their potential as a force for collective decision-making. The Court apparently seeks comfort in the assumption that electoral accountability assures "responsiveness." If the elected official casts a legislative vote against the actual preference of his or her constituents, they can vote him or her out at the next election. But given the construction of districts in which only one winner represents the whole, electoral accountability assures responsiveness only because of what Ankersmit calls "the spongy nature" of the word responsive: a great deal can be absorbed by this concept without it visibly changing shape. It is basically a device for hiding the complexity involved in providing representation by a single person to an increasingly diverse and shifting population. Left unexplored are the many difficult theoretical questions lurking in the meaning of the term "to represent"— literally, to make present those who are not literally there, to re-*present*.

Justice John Paul Stevens has articulated the prevailing view that "the word 'representative' describes the winners of representative popular elections."[66] In his dissent to Justice Stevens's opinion, Justice Scalia gave a slightly different account, in which "surely the word 'representative' connotes one who is not only elected by the people, but who also, at a minimum, acts on behalf of the people."[67] In either account, the concept of representation is uncoupled from ongoing and interactive citizen participation. People in a district vote and give power to someone to represent them and, thus, to wield power-over in their name. Representation occurs from the one-time delegation of the power of a community. Through voting, or other rituals, a community hands over its power to a representative.

Representational power is figured as something finite, something that can be given and received, as a package might be conveyed. In this way, the delegation of power is zero-sum. Through voting, or through more implicit mechanisms of delegating power to a representative, power is relinquished on one side and gained on another. The representative gains the power of a majority of his or her constituents and can then exercise that power within the deliberations of the legislative body. But the transfer of power is a discrete act that occurs in an election and is not revisited until the next election cycle.

That the voter's role is confined to a single discrete act combines with other aspects of the game to discourage most Americans at this point from even participating in the ritual exercise of voting, which is usually, inconveniently, held on a working day.[68] Many studies of the American electorate have found a troubling pattern in which more and more people do not vote. In the 1996 presidential election, for example, less than half the voting-age population went to the polls, and in intervening congressional elections turnout typically hovers around a mere 30 percent.[69] Of young people between the ages of 18 and 26, historically declining rates of participation correlate with surveys of this cohort complaining that they do not feel represented.

Most explanations for this withdrawal from elections emphasize the fact that politics is now dominated by elites who offer broadly similar programs, thus discouraging interest and participation by the public-at-large.[70] This elite control over politics has a lot to do with media access; the absence of virtually any public control over broadcast television means that candidates must purchase airtime in order to reach viewers.[71] Even where there is public control, however, the Supreme Court has said that access to publicly broadcast debates may be limited to the two major party candidates, thereby perpetuating their stranglehold on the bounds of political debate. In addition, the winner-take-all system gives strategists powerful incentives to try to depress voter turnout among supporters of the opposition, which further contributes to low turn-out. As a result, candidates aim their appeals at a narrow and not particularly representative slice of the electorate that is considered most likely to vote. This strategy purposefully discourages others without power from actively participating in public life, whether as voters or, even more, as citizens.

Except for the affluent and well-educated segments of the population, including retired people and senior citizens, few people even attend to or notice what passes for politics in our culture.[72] The candidates respond by developing a personal narrative that others will find compelling—a Vietnam hero; a successful, pragmatic businessman; a "compassionate conservative"; the "man from Hope"—rather than developing programmatic ideas and mobilizing grassroots involvement that is sustained between election cycles. The political parties are umbrellas carried by whoever has built up relationships within the party establishment and its funders, rather than by organized groups of citizens who seek to identify and resolve the challenges facing the American people. Thus, individual voters increasingly see a disconnection between the act of voting and a meaningful voice in governance.[73]

Not surprisingly, then, between elections and even during the campaign season, the tissue connecting candidates with their constituency is thin.[74] In the absence of local, on-the-ground organizations and issue-oriented political parties, there is little room for an interactive relationship or intermediary forms of communication with the people. As one Democrat said in a recent survey of voter attitudes toward the electoral process, "I didn't feel I had much of a say. It just seems whomever the party sent out, we were expected to accept. It wasn't as if there were a variety of people to choose from. It just seems like the candidate was prepackaged, endorsed by the party and that's the way it is, take it or leave it."[75]

A vibrant democracy needs more intermediate spaces for individuals to participate beyond just voting. Although voting is not, literally, a passive act, it is rendered perfunctory by the structures of representational synecdoche. The right to vote has become both important and empty. It is important in that it signals formal membership within the political community. It grants dignity and status to its bearers. Certainly, the experiences of black Americans in the South in the 1960s, through the struggles at Selma, Alabama, and elsewhere, vividly highlight the important dignitary aspects of the right to vote.

But voting is also a meaningless ritual when it is not tied to power in any substantial way, when it simply signifies assent to choices others have engineered or arranged. Even assuming voting's efficacy as a means of civic engagement, it is rendered empty by voters' inability to have a voice in how their votes are allocated, or by any assurance that their vote will make a difference. Hollow promises that "every vote counts," incantations of "count every vote," and stories of extraordinary elections decided by a handful of votes merely function as exceptions that prove the rule in the face of the overwhelming and lopsided reelection rates of state and federal legislatures.[76] Moreover, in a winner-take-all system, only votes cast for the winner "count" in the sense that only the people who cast those votes have a true representative in the legislature after election day.

A focus on individual candidates winning individual elections ignores the evidence that democratic collective action usually begins on the ground. It is most likely to be sustained and meaningful when it is chosen by the people themselves rather than imposed on them by others acting on their behalf. Although people might be inspired from top-down leadership, and they may acquiesce in the choices made by politicians as to which voting district they are assigned, the hard work of democracy is really found in mobilizing the interactive and engaged participation of ordinary people at the grassroots level. And that is where political race comes into play.

Creating Places to Regenerate Democracy

Attacks on race-conscious districting demonstrate the limitations of strategies that function exclusively within the modern conventions of power. Examining our current regimes of voting rights in light of the elements of power-over, we see even more clearly how race and voting serve as the miner's canary alerting us to the underlying problems in our modern embrace of representational synecdoche. The women who traveled several hours by bus to support Cynthia McKinney did so because of their political commitment. Their activity not only joined them to the first stage of the political race project; in mobilizing around their political commitment, they represented the essence of democracy. Institutions of democracy should recognize and respect such political commitments. Yet under current arrangements, the commitments of the women on the bus were only virtually represented. Their involvement was solicited for the purposes of an election campaign, but once the election was over their activity also waned. They were making the best of their situation because our political system does not yet honor more democratic practices.

Unlike race-conscious districting, which is a necessary and pragmatic reform in a system committed to winner-take-all districting, we might imagine forms of representation that are not tied to geographic districting. Such representational models envision a more fluid idea of both racial and political representation based on cross-racial political action in pursuit of an encompassing democratic vision.

Intermediate groups, including those forged by a political race commitment, offer conditions for democratic participation that have largely been ignored or disregarded. Essential to the concept of political race is a kind of contingency—that a politically raced group might coalesce at a specific time, in response to a specific issue—as in the case of Greensboro's Pulpit Forum and the organizing against K-Mart's labor practices. It might well be that in a particular context minority groups would be most aligned with the canary's view. Not all groups, in other words, function as a nucleus for political race. Yet racial minorities are neither monolithic nor homogeneous. To conceive of them too rigidly is both to perpetuate the synecdoche we criticize and to risk succumbing to the perils of essentialism.

Our focus here is on those who, because of their membership in marginalized, weak-we groups, when given the opportunity will tell us a story about American democracy that will challenge the stock story of radical individualism. We believe that members of those racialized groups who choose to affiliate can develop a narrative that others outside the group might subscribe to as well. In using political race to tell a different story about the missing element in conventional concepts of representation we also return to the alternative idea of power-with. In order to revivify the democratic space, we need to move away from rigid zero-sum conceptions of power as primarily an instrument of control over others.

The missing element of representation is the creation of participatory as well as merely instrumental interactions between citizens and representatives.[77] This absent element will not suddenly appear even if we were to reform what representatives do in the halls of power, where there may already be more collaborative, persuasion-based politics than either political scientists or laypeople realize. Nonpartisan interest groups, which could conceivably foster closer ties between representatives and those they represent, are often nonparticipatory. Many people who "belong" to Common Cause or the ACLU have never attended a meeting. Faith-based groups have been suggested to reconnect citizens to politics in a meaningful way because they are anchored in the community and they value relationships over time. But this is still an evolving idea with many progressive critics.[78] National political parties, as presently constituted, seem far less promising. Even as they offer the chance to tap the energy of those who have been ignored in contemporary politics, unregulated local parties could become exclusionary, just like the white primary and other practices of the Democratic Party in Texas during the first half of the last century.[79] So what institutional structures might be necessary to create a more participatory democracy for all Americans?

One approach to reviving a more dynamic view of the representational relationship would be to honor the political commitment so necessary to the political race project. In order to permit voters to choose how they link their fate, organizers might encourage local governments and state legislatures to adopt forms of proportional representation. While these reforms still emphasize an electoral orientation, they provide incentives for the development of intermediate political organizations. Because proportional representation systems lower the threshold of exclusion, smaller minority parties—which are often closely tied to bottom-up citizens' movements—can gain a voice within collective decision-making bodies. Power is distributed consistent with the proportion of votes cast for the candidate or the party within the electorate. Whether based on cumulative voting, single transferable voting, or party list systems, these second-

dimension election rules promote different kinds of first-dimension outcomes. They open up the electoral process in ways that enable local grassroots organizations to flourish and thus begin the process of restoring
some of the missing elements in present practice.[80]

Not only would proportional representation help foster the development of grassroots political organizations, it would also ensure that representative bodies more accurately and fairly represent voters. In a proportional representational system, the winner gains a proportion of the
power but not all of the power. This ensures minority representation of
organized constituencies and thus leads to more diversity within collective
decision-making bodies. The voter is actually represented by the person
for whom she votes rather than by the person who gains the most votes
and thus represents "everyone."

Each voter's vote counts when it is cast. In a party-list system of proportional representation, the party runs a slate of candidates who are
committed to a legislative platform, who are held accountable to the
party's vision, and who have an organic relationship to the party's base of
voters rather than to its funders. Depending upon the percentage of votes
cast for the party, a certain number of candidates on the party list are
elected. Assume a ten-member city council. If the party wins 30 percent of
the vote, then the party gets 30 percent of the seats, or three of ten seats in
the city council. Those council seats are then filled with the first three
names on the party list. If the party gets 40 percent of the vote then it gets
four seats, filled by the first four names on the party list, and so on. The
order in which names are listed is an internal party issue, around which
different constituencies can mobilize and negotiate. These internal struggles enable issue-oriented constituencies to advocate effectively for real
power within the party itself. As a result, women do much better with
party list systems than they do in winner-take-all candidate-centered elections like the ones we have in the United States.

June Zeitlin, executive director of the Women's Environment and Development Organization, knows that proportional representation systems
benefit women. In a letter that *The New York Times* declined to publish,
Zeitlin wrote: "Women are grossly underrepresented at all levels of gov-

ernment worldwide. However, women fare significantly better in proportional representation electoral systems . . . The ten countries with the highest percentage of women in Parliament have systems that include proportional representation." Zeitlin, who spearheads a campaign called 50-50: Get the Balance Right, aimed at increasing women's participation in government, has noticed that proportional representation mechanisms work in many countries in tandem with the deliberate political goals of progressive parties.[81]

It is also plausible that these reforms would resonate within communities of color. Indeed, the political scientist Katherine Tate finds that some blacks have articulated a quiet unease with present strategies for majority-minority districting and have expressed a willingness to change the rules to make them more fair. Within the black community, and including some black members of Congress, the survey data Tate examined suggests there is "ready-made" support for reforms to the election rules, including moving from a winner-take-all district system to proportional representation or cumulative voting.[82]

Some courts are beginning to recognize the dynamic and energizing potential of these alternatives. They are permitting local governments to remedy voting rights violations, for example, using cumulative and limited voting, which are modified forms of proportional representation.[83] Such local reform efforts are consistent with a political race strategy even if, alone, they are insufficient to transform the representational relationship. At least proportional election rules would reduce issues of stigma for all voters, since voters would choose to "district" themselves by the way they cast their votes and not based on decisions made for them by self-interested incumbents. Moreover, the representational message would reinforce ideas of political accountability and encourage more voters to turn out on election day, since their votes not only would be tabulated but will lead to the election of someone or some party they support.

Proportional representation would also be a reasonable option to restore a greater role for local political organizations within the representational relationship. It gives local political organizations incentives to mobilize and educate voters to participate in the political process because such organizations are rewarded with "seats" consistent with the number of voters who support the organizations' candidates or platforms. It measures voting, not breathing.

Finally, proportional representation values legitimacy of the democratic process beyond just voting. Indeed, it does so in ways that might alter outcomes by virtue of the infusion of new ideas and new political organizations. It also may permit greater lateral and vertical interdependence between voters from different parties and between voters and their elected representatives. The representative is chosen to reflect a political mandate on the issues and is in this sense a delegate of his or her constituents. But the representative, informed by his or her constituents' interests, is also empowered to exercise judgment and discretion. By virtue of this dual role, there is more likely to be an ongoing relationship around issues of concern, especially if the representative is held accountable by multiple local party organizations. These local groups could become quite effective at generating citizen engagement and meaningful participation on election day but also between elections.

Of course, as with every formal set of election rules, there are trade-offs. Higher rates of participation, more robust forms of debate, and greater minority representation can themselves become barriers to efficient decision-making. Proportional representation would lower the bar to successful cross-constituency and multiracial coalition organizing, but even with proportional representation it would still be essential to fight fragmentation and to aggregate, rotate, and share power among progressive interests in a lasting and sustainable way in order to realize a fully democratic movement. Moreover, while proportional representation may lead to a more diverse set of legislators and the ability of virtually every voter to point to someone as her true representative, the compromises necessary to pass laws takes place through coalition-building within the legislature. For all of its flaws, the one strength of a territorial-based scheme is that a significant amount of compromise among voters has to take place when they choose a candidate.[84]

Perhaps the German system, which combines both winner-take-all districts *and* a party list system can resolve some of these issues, especially if it were adopted in the context of bicameral U.S. state legislatures in which the lower house would be based on geographic districts and population and the upper house would use a party list system. In addition, there are interventions that could ease the transition under proportional representation to power-sharing within the legislature itself.[85] In any event, proportional representation at least moves toward experimentation with forms of representation that are more interactive.

In some areas, districts and notions of representative democracy might be abandoned altogether in favor of a shift to direct democracy, in which individuals speak without being represented.[86] Or changes could involve referenda and initiatives to institute nondistricted elections that enable and indeed encourage multiple and locally organized political parties to begin to play the role of intermediary between the people and their formally designated representative.[87]

Alternatively, as discussed in Chapter 3, city councils and school boards could re-emphasize voluntary engagement of citizens in local collective decision-making. Archon Fung's street-level democracy describes the local school councils and police/community boards in which he observed participatory democracy in action. He describes richly dynamic relationships of contiguity in which the elected official or the bureaucrat does not stand in for the people but stands by or with the people. He and other researchers noticed higher participation rates in high-crime Chicago neighborhoods with lower aggregate levels of education and wealth, spurred in part by the "realization by beat-meeting participants that their own participation mattered."[88] In these relationships, interaction involves a meaningful exchange of ideas about the policymaking of the official and is dynamic, deliberative, and complex rather than static and fixed.

All of these options meet different needs for reform and might work under different circumstances. The key point is to encourage localities to design democratic experiments that promote political relationships that are interactive, sustained over time, and exist horizontally among voters as well as vertically between the representative and his or her constituents.

Vivid and Dynamic Representation

Most of the work of those who would reform our democracy focuses either on the construction of intermediate institutions or on restructuring electoral rules. These are both important sites for engagement and reform. For all their virtues, however, proportional representation and other temporary installations of a citizen voice within a winner-take-all election arrangement are not likely to deliver more substantive justice. Social change strategies cannot simply be propped up by more participatory views of formal, election-based politics. Even if progressive officials succeed at expanding their democratic base, they may lose more than they gain unless they are prepared to push beyond an election-centered focus for ratifying the distribution of power as if it were a fixed commodity.

On the other hand, surprising reforms can occur in the interstices of existing institutions. Even in the context of the delegation of authority, a progressive actor can use power in ways that challenge conventional understandings and reveal the generative force of power-with. Our political system might heed the lessons of the canary to create intermediate space for political organizations to proliferate at the local level. Were that to happen, more people might feel, as the vast majority of blacks do, "that their fate as an individual is tied to the fate of the group as a whole."[89] It is this sense of common fate or common destiny that a political system premised on radical individualism destroys. While the choice and definition of the group will and should vary, a greater sense of common fate could revive politics to become more of what Hannah Pitkin reminds us it is supposed to be: "the possibility of a shared, collective, deliberate, active intervention in our fate, in what would otherwise be the byproduct of private decisions." We here offer some examples.

First, imagine a group of stage actors who decide to run one of their members for city council in a large city in South America. Upon election, the troupe's nominee hires members of his theater troupe as legislative aides. Rather than acting as traditional aides, however, these actors use their knowledge of the theater to facilitate constituency groups within the electorate. They engage the community by teaching theater techniques to the people, who then role-play as a way of exploring current public policy problems. The spectators rise out of the audience and actively participate in the creation of a very different kind of aesthetic space. The elected official and his fellow dramatists join with their constituents in theater festivals to share their work and to engage the problems facing their community. Local residents, organized as theater groups, rehearse for future action, reflecting on their reality by re-living "the past to create the future." By experiencing solutions to real problems as embodied ways of acting together, they collaborate to create new laws and to change the circumstances of their material reality.

Our city councilman is not imaginary. This "invented reality" is based on the actual experiences of a dramatist-legislator running for city council (as Vereador) in Rio. Though his approach might seem rooted in the magical, his actions in service of democracy are realistic to their core. His name is Augusto Boal, and he ran on the platform, "Vote for me, Elect my Theater Company." He won two terms as a city councilman. Rather than hire a campaign staff, or run a traditional campaign, Boal hired members of his theater group to function as "jokers" who facilitated the development of seventeen constituency groups.[90]

The engagement that Boal as city councilman sought was between the "represented" and policy creation. The place of the artist and the audience was destabilized, producing an interactive kind of engagement, the very antithesis of synecdoche and standing in.[91] Representation became a dynamic process involving a variety of relationships that were constantly being negotiated. Especially in poor communities, the constituency groups created aesthetic spaces with special properties: they exercised "a power of enchantment" and simultaneously recreated "an inaccessible area"—a theater of conventional power that would later be transgressed by the audience. Yet the spectator-actor did not make this transgression *in place* of the other spectators *but with them*. They transgressed a space that in traditional theater may be cordoned off with the help of curtains or a stage. In "legislative theater" the space represents the "power" or concentrated energy of people working together. They used theater techniques to transform the images in the play and, by extension, transform themselves. "Each member of the audience can decide whether she feels represented by this intervention or not, and, if she doesn't she can go on stage and give her own version of things."[92]

During his two terms in office, Boal introduced successfully thirteen laws that were drafted by constituency groups. Yet because Boal in his magical pragmatism played his formal role with a more transitive understanding of the representative relationship between him and his constituents, he never once introduced a bill of his own. His friends worried that others would question his ability if he did not initiate legislation, and so on one occasion Boal did try to compose a law from his own head rather than just passing laws that came out of the "people's desires." Boal recalled that in Sweden red and green traffic lights are accompanied by different noises to alert blind people when it is safe to cross the street. Inspired by this example, he wrote out the text of the law without consulting anyone. When the blind people in one of his theater groups heard about his law they were furious: "Swedish drivers stop at red lights! Here they don't," they yelled at him. "Do you want to get us killed?" Boal pulled the bill.

Chagrined by this encounter, Boal responded by limiting his legislative autonomy. But citizen participation along the lines Boal intended need not destroy the role played by the representative. It could, in the long run, strengthen the ability of representatives to make decisions on behalf of constituents when lengthy deliberations are not practical. When citizens interact in an ongoing way with their elected representatives, they may be willing to trust those representatives to make such decisions on occasion. And those representatives may be in a better position, informed by a range of perspectives, to exercise their discretion. Most importantly, voters will have a basis for trusting their representatives to know when not to make such decisions before returning to the electorate.

In this light, one could re-interpret the story of Boal and his proposal for making the crosswalks safe by arguing that his only mistake was not realizing that this was an area in which he did not know enough about those affected and interested to act independently. By virtue of the numerous meetings and interactions he had had with his constituents, he had already given the voters confidence that they *could* affect the decision-making process. In addition the voters would have come to trust Boal's knowledge of their needs and his judgment if he had come to them first with his proposal. Boal, in other words, could have effectively represented his constituents, even within more conventional forms of representation, had he known more precisely when he needed their input before exercising his authority. In these ways a dynamic view of the concept of representation strengthens even the more conventional notion of representation by urging representatives to share more of the labor of making decisions with their constituents.[93]

The second example is less fantastic but equally surprising. It also used role-play training for constituents of conservative Republican legislative districts in New York to rehearse effective lobbying visits. What is unusual is that these constituents were Latino immigrants and nonvoters. They were also non-English speakers. They included, in fact, undocumented workers who organized a campaign to adopt stricter penalties for home-owners and small businesses that failed to pay their workers. They successfully recruited ten Republican state senators, five from suburban Long Island, to co-sponsor their legislation. Even though they could not vote, they believed they had a right to inform the senators of their views, and they believed the senators would be interested in hearing their ideas about solutions. The language problem was resolved through simultaneous translation through radio transmitters. "Upon entering, we would hand the senator or his staff-person a translating receiver that looks something like a radio-only Walkman and ask him to put on the headset. As the team leader began to speak in Spanish, the senator would hear the words in English. All of our members could communicate directly with the senator and his staff, and vice versa, as the entire conversation was being simultaneously translated by one of our staff-people."[94]

What is significant for our purposes is that the immigrants themselves "ran the meeting, explained the problem, outlined their proposed solution, and fielded the senator's questions." This is a very different dynamic than is possible where the Rabbi and the Bishop gesture in the amphitheater to a silent audience. Here the solution is not one that rests with, or is initiated by, the representative. Like the constituents in Boal's legislative theater experiment, the immigrant workers generated ideas; they then took the process one step further and actively worked to implement their solutions. Nonvoting constituents came forward, worked together, proposed and then lobbied for new legislation. The Unpaid Wages Prohibition Act was signed into law in 1997 by Republican Governor George Pataki.[95] The law dramatically increased the penalties against employers who do not pay their workers, from a 25 percent civil fine to a 200 percent civil fine, and from a misdemeanor with a maximum $10,000 penalty to a felony with a maximum $20,000 penalty. No state or federal law about wage payment has ever been this strong.

An organizing strategy from Coalition L.A. also reminds us of the potential for reimagining the meaning of representation within the current winner-take-all frame. It shows that representation can become an activity that constitutes and transforms the actors and the system in which they act; it implicates each person's sense of responsibility and political commitment. In 1997 Coalition L.A. united behind three candidates challenging the re-election of an incumbent council member who seemed more conservative than, and out of touch with, his district. A year earlier, the coalition had searched for local candidates who would reflect the district demographics, allowing organizers within each community to develop their own criteria for candidates. "There was not a search to find a person to run but rather to find a [group of] effective spokesperson[s] for the platform."[96] Each of the candidates came from a different community within the diverse district; each shared a platform advanced by the district coalition. A short-term goal was to force the incumbent into a runoff, but the coalition's real aim was to organize the district's diverse communities, not just replace an incumbent with a new officeholder. "In our mind, it is a good thing that there are multiple candidates. It is only when the community feels like they can organize around one of their own [that] they get involved. So we would say that the coalition of candidates is not a transitory strategy" for winning a council seat. "It is a new way of elections for communities to get involved."[97] Their focus was less on elections and more on the development of an ongoing relationship among members of the community.

Each of these examples helps us to explore the ways that the represented and the representative can stand with one another, communicating and interacting back and forth. Those who represent act in conjunction with others; they do not simply act alone. Representatives occupy a special position within a community, but this position does not necessarily entail monopolizing all the power of a community. It entails, rather, being the person who is most responsible for facilitating the dynamic forces of a community, for bringing people together, for maintaining the energy of a community. Representing people entails building a working relationship with them that is, in effect, a cooperative enterprise. Representation is not a one-time handing over of a commodity that bundles the power that the people would otherwise conserve for themselves. People do not surrender their power when they go to the voting booth or cooperate in collective struggle.

Getting communities involved in imagining their future is the problem that democracy is supposed to solve. But the challenge of involving people in the decisions that affect their lives is not solved when traditional electoral politics overemphasizes candidate-centered relationships. As should be evident from these stories, there are already ways, within our existing frameworks of district elections, to push for a more interactive accounting of the representative relationship. While these examples work within the current model of representational synecdoche, they also emphasize ideas of contiguity and association rather than substitution or disconnection.

Ours is not so much a theory of representation as it is an effort to describe missing elements in conventional ideas about representation.[98] We recognize the value of expertise and do not seek to efface the representative's role as a thought-leader, synthesizer, or originator of ideas. Nor do we suggest that the experimental approaches we have proposed should be imposed top-down or at the national level. We are simply emphasizing the importance of pragmatic experimentalism at the local level that questions the view that experts should be the primary or exclusive decision-makers. Expertise is valuable in the traditional sense, but it is important also to acknowledge the value of the viewpoints of those whom in principle the representative is meant to support and particularly the opinions of those with the most to lose. This involves taking the third step of political race, imagining power-with experiments in political deliberation and organization that are engaging for, and transformative of, both the individual and the group.

One of the most important of the missing elements in the current static concept of representation is the sharing of expertise in a way that enhances the capacity of the group to solve problems or to think innovatively about public policy issues. Such sharing must reflect long-term interdependent or interactive relationships (both horizontally between citizens and vertically between citizens and their representatives) and sys-

temic approaches to solving problems that permit collective experimentation and opportunities for self-correction. These elements are at the heart
of what we call self-governance.

Conclusion

F. R. Ankersmit writes that "metaphor is the heart that pumps the lifeblood of political philosophy."[99] But there is an important difference between the *literary* use of a metaphor, such as the miner's canary, to make a
political point more vivid and the *literal* use of synecdoche to structure a
political system. If metaphor is the heart that pumps the lifeblood of political philosophy, representational synecdoche is a piece of fossilized bone
that, at best, holds clues about a creature that once lived, but no longer.
Representational synecdoche is not, like a metaphor, an image that highlights an important aspect of a larger idea. In fact, it works in just the opposite way—to minimize the complexity of the entity being represented.
Representational synecdoche offers merely the petrified remains of a system that once promised to evolve into a complex, organic whole.

We embrace metaphors, such as the miner's canary, as literary devices
that enable critique and action. We reject racial and political synecdoche
in representation, because the substitution of the part for the whole disables progressive social change. Political race stands in opposition to this
approach by reclaiming race in order to resist hierarchies, engage in collective struggle, and practice democracy. Formal election opportunities
within winner-take-all hierarchies and highly charged public discourse
arenas do not generate citizen participation except in episodic bursts. The
story of the Rabbi and the Bishop captures the way such politics typically
accomplishes just the opposite: by devaluing citizen understanding and
diminishing citizen engagement.

For the current Supreme Court, the measure of our democratic health
seems to depend on merely holding elections within equipopulous districts, counting votes that are cast, and declaring a winner. The Court fails
to understand that its arguments against majority-minority districts apply
to all districts in our current electoral system because the fundamental
problem is not race-based districting but representational synecdoche itself. The fact that fewer than half of those eligible to vote take advantage

of the opportunity is discounted or ignored. Just recently the Supreme Court, in invalidating California's open-primary law, dismissed the state's argument that it had a compelling interest in advancing voter turnout and instead prioritized the "associational rights" of the two major political parties.[100] We are offering a way to interrogate those kinds of associational rights from the perspective of an engaged democracy.

Traditional views of power, because they explore only a rigid zero-sum first-dimensional interpretation, reinforce the Court's impoverished theory of both race and democracy. These views of power ignore the feedback loop between racial and political literacy that we have attempted to identify. Similarly, current approaches to race and politics do not encourage local, grassroots organizing or develop strategies of progressive critique out of the experience of political activism. None of the dominant ideas about race considers the ways in which representational synecdoche is more dangerous to genuine democracy than the abstract fears of racial essentialism with which the Court is preoccupied. Instead, each embraces a set of top-down decrees that disable genuine and critical participation at the local level and lock our political system into a hierarchical conception of power.

Through the distortion of time in the extended parable of Verona, then by use of several real-world examples, we have tried to invigorate the definition of representation. We have explored more dynamic forms of representation in light of what we have learned about political race, including the importance of participation, the crucial role of individual agency, the way power frames relationships, and the value of power-with. We do not invoke our political race project because we believe race represents or stands in for all aspects of power relations in the society. Instead, we seek to use political race to create a dialogue about interactive forms of representation and more inclusive practices of democracy. Political representation becomes less about relinquishing power or seizing power or surrendering power. Instead, it becomes more about facilitating a dynamic engagement that begins to tell new stories about democracy. These stories involve organizing at the grassroots level, sharing power, and engaging the people themselves in actions that dissipate fear and build confidence.

Each story takes a path outside the range of currently acceptable accounts in order to assign radically different meanings to "representation." By subverting the assumed structure, we have attempted to suggest the possibility of an intermediate "free space" where the opportunity to question, reframe, and experiment with heterogeneous models of representation is not structured by the crabbed ideas of democratic representation that seem to hold the Supreme Court in thrall. Examples abound; we have but to find them, connect them one to the other, and then understand the challenge they provide.

WHITENESS OF A
DIFFERENT COLOR?

A series in the *New York Times* entitled "How Race Is Lived in America" focused on two Cubans, one white and one black. They were best friends as boys in Cuba, but their lives took a disconcerting turn when they each emigrated separately to the United States.[1] Their experience illustrates the difficulty of "living on the hyphen" in this country and the powerful pressures to conform to the black-white imperative of racial management. For Latinos, it also points toward a less visible but potentially more viable path over this racialized terrain—through a pan-ethnic Hispanic/Latino identity which would challenge not just the racial borders themselves but the underlying systems of wealth and power that the racial "border patrol" currently protects.[2]

Joel Ruiz and Achmed Valdez grew up together in Cuba. Though Joel was black and Achmed white, neither thought much about this difference when they were young. Racism was a feature of pre-revolutionary life in Cuba, and it had not been totally stamped out; but it did not seem to determine one's life chances there, and it did not stand in the way of friendship between the two boys. Their common identity as Cubans trumped divisions of race.

When Joel and Achmed grew up, they made independent decisions to leave their homeland. Each was apprehended by the U.S. Coast Guard and sent to Guantanamo before being allowed to enter Miami. Joel's experience in Cuba had not prepared him for the way race matters in the United States. In Miami, Joel found a segregated city. Whereas Achmed went initially to Hialeah, the first stop for white Cubans, Joel went to the black ghetto of Liberty City. As the reporter, Mirta Ojito, put it: "This was Miami, and in Miami, as the roughly 7 percent of the area's Cubans who are black quickly learn, skin color easily trumps nationalism."

This point was driven home to Joel one night when a white Cuban-American policeman stopped and frisked him. Joel had been celebrating Valentine's Day in a popular Cuban restaurant with his uncle and three women friends. The policeman said to him, "I've been keeping an eye on you for a while. Since you were in the restaurant. I saw you leave and I saw so many blacks in the car, I figured I would check you out." Though the officer used Spanish to communicate with Joel, the actual words he spoke drew a racial line between them that denied their common nationality. After that incident, Joel felt trapped. Though he still identified himself as Cuban, whites saw him as black, and blacks saw him as Cuban. "They tell me I'm Hispanic. I tell them to look at my face, my hair, my skin. I'm black, too. I may speak different, but we all come from the same place."

Joel's experience of being named black by white Americans in a way that subordinated his Cuban-ness shows how the black-white boundary in the United States disciplines those who would challenge its impermeability. The white Cuban-American police officer disconnected Joel from his national identity and placed him firmly on the black side of America's principal divide, between whiteness and blackness. What Joel's fellow Cubans had already discovered, and what was expressed most clearly by this officer's conduct, is that "whiteness" in the United States is a measure not just of the melanin content in one's skin but of one's social distance from blackness. The Cuban-American policeman asserted his own shaky claim to whiteness by harassing Joel for being black. But native-born black people rejected him, too; as a dark-skinned Cuban-American, he was too Cuban to be black, and too black to be white. Joel Ruiz, like many other nonblack nonwhite immigrants, found himself squarely on the hyphen of America's racial divide.[3]

The Racial Bribe

The toughest border patrol in this country may be the one that polices the racial boundaries between black and white. And no group has played a more important role, historically, in the way whites have policed these borders than the group known today as Hispanics or Latinos. Whereas dark-skinned Hispanics like Joel have been pushed into the black category, lighter skinned (or richer) Hispanics like Achmed have been offered a chance to become white, so long as they maintain their social distance from blackness. This offer is part of what we call the racial bribe.

The racial bribe is a strategy that invites specific racial or ethnic groups to advance within the existing black-white racial hierarchy by becoming "white." The strategy expands the range of physical characteristics that can fall within the definition of "white," in order to pursue four goals: (1) to defuse the previously marginalized group's oppositional agenda, (2) to offer incentives that discourage the group from affiliating with black people, (3) to secure high status for individual group members within existing hierarchies, and (4) to make the social position of "whiteness" appear more racially or ethnically diverse.

The official U.S. census has been instrumental in managing the racial bribe by assigning the many types of Hispanics to the category of white, although the racial make-up of the various Latino groups was indeterminate by conventional analysis. In 1930 the sociologist Max Handman noted: "The American community has no social technique for handling partly colored races. We have a place for the Negro and a place for the white man: the Mexican is not a Negro, and the white man refuses him equal status."[4] The problem of what to do with "partly colored races" represented by Mexicans and other Latinos can be seen clearly in the 1930 census. The basic racial categories that year, in the eyes of census officials, were "White," "Negro," and "Other race." But "Mexican" was also included on the census questionnaire in an attempt to keep track of the nation's growing Spanish-origin population.[5] In prior years the majority of Mexicans, who considered themselves white, had answered accordingly on the census. This had so skewed the numbers on Spanish origin as to make that population seem invisible, and this invisibility led to the addition of "Mexican" as a racial category in the 1930 census. Yet, when many Mexicans switched their identification from "White" to "Mexican" in that year's census, the white population appeared to suffer a significant decrease.[6] In order to protect the numerical supremacy of whites, the Census Bureau never again used "Mexican" under the race category. In future censuses, it subsumed the entire Mexican category directly into the white category, reinforcing the Mexican racial ideology that had long denied the presence of Africans in the Mexican cultural mix. This denial was important to Mexican-Americans because, as Professor John G. Mencke put it, "America's racial system recognizes only the dichotomy of white and black, and the mixed blood is invariably classified as black if his ancestry is known."[7]

Despite inconsistencies within the census groupings, the management of relations between Hispanics and whites has always contained the peculiar promise to some Hispanics that they could become white.[8] Implicit in this promise was the assumption that Mexicans would not be treated like black people and locked into a permanent condition of racial inferiority. And in California in the early twentieth century, it contained the implicit assumption that Mexicans would not be treated like Asians, either. Prior to the large black migration during World War II, the big distinction in California was among whites, Mexicans, and Asians, and virulent anti-Asian racism made Mexicans "whiter."[9]

The promise of assimilation has also been extended to some elite groups among Hispanics, such as Argentines or Chileans, in distinction to other ethnic subgroups, such as Guatemalans, Hondurans, or Panamanians, whose members are the least European and the poorest and as such do not qualify for whiteness.[10] Conventional conceptions of race construct different kinds of relationships among Hispanics themselves and between Hispanics and others, including non-Hispanic whites or non-Hispanic blacks, in order to control access to power within the Hispanic community itself.

The racial bribe is not unique to Hispanics. At various times in U.S. history, a similar offer of racial assimilation has been made to Jewish, Irish, Italian, and other non-Anglo European groups, who were allowed to move out of their ethnic enclaves and assume the mantle of whiteness. In most regions of the United States, the only group to whom it has not been available is blacks (though in California, as we have noted, Asians were also denied the option of becoming white for most of the nineteenth and twentieth centuries).[11] Although individual light-skinned blacks may be racially ambiguous in certain contexts and wealthier blacks may be granted certain privileges, as a group blacks traditionally have been the anchor of an oppositional identity. This is what the political scientist Jennifer Hochschild calls "black exceptionalism" because it defines the "real" racial divide as lying between "blacks and all other Americans, of whatever hue or background."[12] Or as Professor Pedro Noguera concludes, black people function as "the negative referent group."[13] By offering this option of whiteness over time to selected nonblack nonwhites, the racial binary of black and white is preserved and race in the United States is made more manageable for those seeking to hold onto zero-sum power.

But offering the racial bribe to the group known today as Hispanics or Latinos has proved difficult.[14] The groups that make up this general category range from Europeans to Africans to Asians and comprise a variety of racial types, skin colors, and names—think of Pelé from Brazil or Alberto Fujimori from Peru.[15] Moreover, each Latin nation has both a racialized and an ethnic identity that preceded the entry of its emigrants into this country, and these designations were rarely drawn precisely on the black-white binary. Because Latinos are neither a uniform "race" nor a uniform ethnic group but still occupy a nonwhite political space in this country, they necessarily complicate the task of racial management for those in power. The prominence of non-Europeans inhibits the assimilation of Latinos on the white ethnic model that more easily accommodated Italians, Irish, Jews, and others.

Simon Bolívar himself, at the dawn of the national period in Latin America, understood that the emerging Latin American identity was an amalgam of peoples.[16] Today, each ethnic or national identity has a specific racial discourse rooted in both its colonial history and its immigrant experience.[17] Mexicans, Cubans, and Puerto Ricans have had different interactions with the white/Anglo majority in their country of origin, and those interactions have colored immigrants' encounters with the white majority in the United States. Also, critical differences in conceptions of race come into play from one Latin American nation to the next. While no Latin American country has escaped the use of racial categories to manage and discipline various populations, the techniques employed contrast sharply with those of the United States.[18] Unlike the pressure to reduce race to either black or white, the dominant ideological response within Latin America has been to celebrate, to a lesser or greater extent depending on the country, the idea of the *mestizaje*.[19]

The concept of mestizaje does not necessarily produce the kinds of racial categories constructed by the concept of miscegenation in the United States. According to the mestizaje ideology, the mixture of Indians, Europeans, and Africans created a distinctly new type in Latin America, a kind of cultural suspension within which each element continues to exist but with emphasis on two principle types, the Indian and the European.[20] In Mexico, the mestizaje represses the presence of blacks within Mexican (and by extension Spanish) culture and society. And in its manifestation among Mexican elites, it also represses the diversity of Indian cultures.[21]

In Brazil, by contrast, elites had to figure out a way to acknowledge that Brazil was fundamentally a country of blacks, without succumbing to the dominant racialist ideas about superior and inferior races. The Brazilian response was to create an ideology of whitening, as we saw in Chapter 2. The whitening thesis, tied as it is to social class, permits even the darkest of Brazilians to be considered white—provided they have enough money to distance themselves socially from the poor black majority. This is a fundamentally different system from that of other Latin American countries, which, while celebrating racial mixing in theory, continue to privilege whiteness as an expression of European-ness.

Once these various national groups moved into American society, they had to come to grips with their own internal racial politics. Their specific discourses on race, molded by local history in Latin America, had to adapt, somehow, to the dominant American racial framework. Among the different accommodations available, three stand out. One entails creating an identity based on cultural nationalism: Cuban culture would be celebrated as distinct from Mexican culture, and so on. A second alternative is for select groups to accept the offer to become white. This option draws the internal racial divisions within each nationality into bold relief and highlights the color line. This is what has happened in the case of Cuba. Our nation's official antipathy toward Fidel Castro in fact masks a long relationship between Cuban elites and the United States.[22] As a consequence of this relationship, combined with Cold War iconography, Cubans in the

United States have enjoyed the status of preferred immigrants among all the major Latin American nationalities.[23] Light-skinned immigrants like Achmed and the Cuban police officer have been offered, and most have accepted, the racial bribe of whiteness.

A third approach, closely linked to the project of political race, is to construct a pan-ethnic Hispanic/Latino political identity that adapts to the structure of America's racial hierarchy but does not reproduce that structure internally.

In the context of U.S. ethnic history, each of these approaches has made sense at one time or another.[24] The assimilationist model is predicated on option two: the assumption that national identities can be suppressed only through the imposition of a more encompassing identity, like race, or a new national identity, such as "American."[25] But in the case of groups whose members take pride in a nonwhite identity, assimilation is not as likely as it was for European ethnic groups, for reasons that originate both inside and outside the group itself. Some survey research suggests, for example, that Hispanics, more so than either blacks or whites, agreed that groups should "maintain their distinct culture" rather than "adapt and blend into the larger society"—that is, they favored option one.[26] But for those who reject the racial bribe offered by option two, or to whom such an offer has never been made, the third approach of creating a social space between the individual national identities and the wholesale adoption of a new national identity might make more sense. Were the Hispanic community to occupy this unique social space, this emerging pan-ethnic identity would have the potential to become a site for progressive political mobilization as part of a political race project.

Mexican Americans

The value, indeed necessity, of this intermediate step can be illustrated through the experiences of Mexican Americans. Mexicans in the Southwest came under American jurisdiction at the close of the Mexican-American War. For most of the twentieth century, when the term "American" was used in the Southwest, it generally referred only to white Europeans, not to Mexicans. The term "Mexican" was likewise associated with racial background, not with the presence or absence of citizenship.[27] Mexicans were subject to the same kinds of Jim Crow laws that were used to discipline blacks. Discrimination was *de jure*.[28]

Though early white settlers brought slaves with them to Texas, the importation of African slaves from Mexico ended early in the state's history because slavery, though legal in Texas, was illegal in Mexico. What Texans imported from Mexico instead of slaves was a system of peonage similar in some ways to medieval serfdom. The workers were "free," but they were tied to the land through a complex economic and semi-kinship system of sharecropping.[29] When disenfranchised poor whites drifted in from other parts of the South and began competing for resources, for a time cultural inhibitions prohibited landowners from treating these white men and women like Mexicans or recently freed slaves.[30] They were seen as both competitors for land ownership and, as laborers, a source of wage inflation because they could not be paid as poorly as blacks or Mexicans.

In this context, an interesting social discourse emerged.[31] Poor whites came to be considered essentially black by virtue of "scientific" eugenic theory. Their economic failures were, in the eyes of bankers and other suppliers, Darwinian proof of their "unfitness," and thus they could be handled by these white elites in the same way as Mexicans and blacks, who were also "inferiors."[32] In the meantime, Mexicans who had become prosperous began stressing their "Spanish" (that is, European) roots and denying their black heritage. Consequently, in the eyes of white power brokers, these Mexican elites became, socially, honorary whites.[33]

What this tells us is that there was a point in Texas history at which poor whites, blacks, and Mexicans were structurally situated in essentially the same social position.[34] The forces that prevented an alliance from forming were many, but in some cases poor whites and Mexicans in South Texas and poor whites and blacks in East Texas created coalitions that formed the roots of modern Texas populism.[35]

The ambiguous relationship between blacks and Mexicans sometimes destabilized the political alliance built out of resistance to an oppressive economic regime. Although shared economic deprivations might have strengthened cross-racial alliances, the color line proved a powerful barrier. Although Mexicans were, as a group, clearly viewed by both whites and blacks as nonwhite, there was internal pressure especially from Mexican elites to situate themselves as white.[36] This meant, of course, defining the group against blackness.

We see this strategy in action when Texas, in order to keep its schools segregated and to avoid spending money on any but the traditionally white schools, used the line between blacks and Mexicans to support white privilege. An unreported 1948 federal court decision, *Delgado v Bastrop Independent School District,* clearly declared the illegality of segregating Mexican Americans; nevertheless, state education authorities collaborated with local districts to evade the force of that decision.[37] They simply eliminated the existing category of Mexican schools and declared that Mexican Americans had always been Caucasian. Since there is no obligation to distinguish among Caucasian students, the quality of the Mexican schools did not change; the fact that Mexican children were in substandard schools now became just a matter of bad luck, not discrimination. The Mexican children continued to be treated unfairly. They received none of the material privileges or resources given to the white schools. But they received the psychological boost that came from the state's telling them they were no longer like black people.

Despite disastrous consequences such as the *Bastrop* case, the racial identity of Mexican Americans was fiercely contested within the Mexican-American community. In the early years of the Mexican-American variant of the civil rights movement, the operating premise of the elites was that Mexicans are "racially white" and thus have to be careful about forming alliances with blacks. Although Mexican mobilization clearly emulated black mobilization in the civil rights movement, some Mexican-American leaders went to great pains to distinguish themselves from blacks. As Neil Foley puts it: "In pursuing White rights, Mexican Americans combined Latin American racialism with Anglo racism, and in the process separated themselves and their political agenda from the black civil rights struggles."[38]

The complicity of Mexican Americans in reinforcing the color line did more than support black disenfranchisement. This strategy undermined potential relationships with other similarly situated people. It fueled the nativist impulse within black communities and contributed to political and social isolation from both blacks and whites. To many whites, some Mexicans might have been white, but as a general matter they were colored and, worse, a debased and mongrelized amalgam of races. To many blacks, Mexicans were racialized by their alien status as outside the black-white binary and in some important sense outside the polity.[39] To the extent that this encouraged blacks to see all Hispanic/Latinos as foreign and a threat to their tenuous grip on social resources, it has continuing implications. In California, for example, conservative Republicans like Governor Pete Wilson have garnered black support by successfully promoting anti-immigrant laws. And in Los Angeles, older blacks joined moderate and conservative whites to defeat a progressive Mexican-American candidate in the 2001 mayor's race.

As this short sketch of Mexican Americans in Texas suggests, race would be a central issue within the formation of any emerging Hispanic identity in the United States. It could not be avoided, either internally or externally. The key question is how it would be negotiated.[40] Would Latinos find an "official" space outside the black-white binary, or would they be pushed into one racial category or the other? Because the unity of the Hispanic community depends on successfully negotiating internal racial differences without succumbing to conventional designations or hierarchies, the hope is that through this process of negotiation Hispanic communities can produce something like what we have called political race. We turn to Chicago in order to illustrate this hopeful possibility.

A Chicago Story

The neighborhoods of Pilsen and Little Village in Chicago are, today, primarily Mexican American, with a significant population of Puerto Ricans and other Latinos. Neighborhood activism dates back to the 1950s, when Mexican Americans became the primary leaders of an organization called the Pilsen Neighbors. This group's first act was to establish a buying collective, but then their focus widened to health care, local schools, job training, and the provision of other social services, including bilingual and bicultural programs. Eventually, Mexican-American activists, building on this and similar neighborhood organizations in the city, formed the Independent Political Organization (IPO) in an attempt to fashion an electoral strategy that would allow them to challenge the dominance of Chicago's political machine.

In the twenty years between 1960 and 1980 Chicago's population of Mexicans, Puerto Ricans, and other Latin American ethnics grew from 3 percent to over 14 percent. To discipline community activists and prevent this emerging numerical concentration from translating into electoral clout, the leaders of Chicago's political machine split the Mexican-American community into discontinuous aldermanic districts. Citywide, the Mexican-American community still had the numbers to deliver a meaningful bloc of votes, but they did not have the votes that counted in individual districts. Realizing that they could not succeed by simply organizing around their Mexican-ness, activists began to focus on organizing within the Puerto Rican community and forming alliances with the progressive black community.

The Mexican-American and Puerto Rican communities had in fact been cooperating since the early 1970s, when they organized the Spanish Coalition for Jobs, as well as a conference called Latino Strategies for the 70s. This conference was crucial because it put citywide solidarity among Latinos squarely on the agenda. The neighborhood leaders who participated in that meeting stressed their belief that the future of the two communities was linked, both by a shared linguistic heritage and by a political opposition to their treatment by City Hall. Because these neighborhood activists were convinced that electoral politics would be the key, much of their activity centered on voter registration.

The critical moment for the coalition came in the 1983 election campaign of Harold Washington, the first black candidate for mayor. Washington premised his campaign on opposition to the machine's domination of city affairs. To prevail, he would have to galvanize and hold all of the disparate aggrieved groups. The Mexican-American and Puerto Rican neighborhoods delivered big for Washington. Of the 48,000 votes that separated Washington from his Republican rival, close to 28,000 of them were cast in the four wards that had been drawn by the machine to disaggregate Mexicans and Puerto Ricans and prevent them from mobilizing resistance to an incumbent machine politician.

One of Mayor Washington's pledges was to reform the patronage system. This meant he would have to dismantle the bureaucracy and replace commission members and committee chairs. He had defined his challenge for City Hall specifically in terms of opposition to the machine and its paternalistic politics that had the net effect of neglecting black and Latino neighborhoods. Besides a more efficient bureaucracy, Mayor Washington wanted to get resources to the neighborhoods, especially those that had historically been low on the distribution list.

Although many Mexican and Puerto Rican activists worked for the election of Washington and his progressive vision, the new mayor and his supporters soon learned that winning is different from governing. Washington found his initiatives strangled by the internal politics of the Board of Aldermen, whose majority was still under machine control. In order to break this lock on the board, Washington's supporters needed a strategy for getting their people elected to these key positions. A legal challenge for fair representation under the Voting Rights Act, if successful, might give the progressive activists the majority they needed.

The plaintiffs, led by the Mexican American Legal Defense and Education Fund (MALDEF), claimed that the minority vote had been diluted through the familiar stratagems of packing, fracturing, and boundary manipulation. Though they lost in district court, the Seventh Circuit Court of Appeals ordered the creation of districts that would guarantee nineteen black wards and four mixed Mexican and Puerto Rican wards.

There was an irony to the Voting Rights Act decree and the districts that were created in satisfaction of the court order. Although the Mexican and Puerto Rican activists "won" four wards, in many ways these wards built on what the machine politicians had already done to fragment the existing ethnic Mexican communities. Rather than construct a ward primarily to reconnect the detached pieces of the Mexican community, the court joined these fragments to severed remnants of the Puerto Rican neighborhoods. The new wards maintained the basic footprint of the original wards that had split up the Mexican-American community in the first place but simply expanded the total Latino population within each district, by reconnecting more Mexican Americans with Puerto Ricans. The irony was that the remedial choices of a federal court—an external government actor—engineered "pan-ethnic" Latino, rather than Mexican or Puerto Rican, election districts. Those choices then helped fabricate a unique political space from the earlier mischief of machine politicians.

The creation of these four wards pursuant to the Voting Rights Act sped up the electoral coalition between Mexicans and Puerto Ricans. The activists now chose to organize around their self-identification as "Latino." Though the official term used by the Census Bureau is "Hispanic," in Chicago the term people use on the street is Latino: "When we call ourselves Latino we name ourselves; it is other people who call us Hispanic."[41] But the point is not the specific terminology; the point is that a powerful coalition emerged between groups that had previously identified primarily with their nation of origin.

This Latino alliance added persistently high unemployment, gang violence, decaying commercial districts, and high dropout rates to their electoral agenda. These issues went beyond the old patronage litany that promised to fix potholes and clean up vacant lots. Latino activists linked reorganization of the bureaucracy to issues of access to city resources and commercial reinvestment in the community. The progressive politicians who used Latinismo to join the interests of Puerto Ricans and Mexican Americans focused on structural changes that would bring long-term improvements to each community.

The new crop of Latino candidates challenged the few incumbent aldermen who were Puerto Rican and Mexican American, by making an issue of the incumbents' dependence on and loyalty to the machine and their distance from the neighborhoods. The hardest fought struggle was for the election of Luis Gutiérrez, a Puerto Rican, to the Board of Aldermen. Gutiérrez had to defeat not just a white machine candidate from the old district but also a Mexican-American machine politician, Manuel Torres. The district, while now a majority Latino district, was more Mexican than Puerto Rican, and the machine ran an old-fashioned campaign to encourage Mexicans to vote for Torres because he was Mexican. But the Mexican and Puerto Rican communities stuck together to vote for Gutiérrez, a candidate of their choice who was also Latino but who had an organic link to the community. Latino identity won out over Mexican identity in this neighborhood that had been so ill-served by the machine in the past, and Gutiérrez, a Puerto Rican, prevailed.[42]

This Chicago example synthesizes in a few easy strokes the very difficult work of creating a new political identity out of the diverse elements that constitute the geographic districts of Pilsen, Little Village, Humboldt, and the near West Side. Gutiérrez's victory would not have been possible if the old model of cultural nationalism had driven the electorate. Nonetheless, there will still be specific and local efforts that look like the traditional interest-group or cultural-nationalist model. Reaching a broader conception of Latinismo that is tied to the concrete needs of both communities in Chicago did not just happen overnight. Real differences continue to exist. Yet, the emergence of a Latino political identity in Chicago inspires hope that unity across Latin groups will not reduce to just old-fashioned ethnic or identity politics.[43]

Mexicans and Puerto Ricans in Chicago had to confront the contradictions and discomfort within their own communities in order to make Latino politics work. Because they were in a majority-rule winner-take-all political system, there was a tremendous incentive to make the community they represented as large as was consistent with cohesiveness in order to ground their claims to a share of political power. But they had to do this without allowing their effort to collapse into identity politics, because there was more at stake than just short-term electoral politics.

Moreover, agreement on a single issue does not suggest that community exists or that Latinos can be mobilized around a shared identity to become a significant political force. The leading opinion research on the Hispanic/Latino political community nationwide concluded that in "only one policy area, bilingual education, are Mexican, Puerto Rican, and Cuban views sufficiently coherent and distinct to constitute a distinct public policy."[44] Yet despite this finding, the study also concluded that these groups share similar views on government spending for health care, crime, drug control, education, the environment, and child care. But the groups diverge strikingly on welfare policy and affirmative action.[45] Interestingly, Puerto Ricans were highest in their estimation of the amount of discrimination experienced by blacks, whereas Cuban Americans were behind even whites in their estimation of discrimination experienced by blacks. This, of course, might be explained by the phenotypic types that predominate among the elite in those communities, as well as local competition for social goods.

Indeed, these differences should be expected and should not obscure the fundamental point, which is that local political action—built through community institutions of churches, unions, or neighborhood associations—is a precondition to a national pan-ethnic identity. That point is summed up by Henry Trueba: "Latinos, in fact, are creating a new identity on the basis of common cultural values and the increasing advantages of political alliances for action presumed to benefit the diverse Latino ethnic subgroups. In some real sense, political action seems to play an instrumental role in forming a new ethnic identity with new cultural ties and values among Latinos who have been marginalized and isolated."[46]

That was certainly the case in Chicago, where political action anticipated and took advantage of external interventions by government actors to forge the local pan-ethnic coalition. What the experience of Chicago teaches is that we must be wary of generalizations from national data. Political race is created on the ground. It finds a space for organizing that is rooted in ethnicity but expands beyond parochial concerns. Latinos in Chicago had to organize outside conventional racial and ethnic paradigms. Furthermore, while the story of pan-Latino unity in Chicago had its climax in the electoral victories of Washington and Gutiérrez, this Chicago story is not really about electoral politics. The seeds of unity were sown long before there was an election to attend to. As has so often been the case in the black community, intergroup unity came about because the mistreatment these groups suffered was meted out not according to their specific ethnicity but because they were seen as Spanish-speaking foreigners, despite their citizenship. They were shoved into barrios in the same way that blacks were pushed into ghettos. The brutal beating of two Puerto Ricans by the Chicago police in 1965 galvanized not just the Puerto Rican community but all Latinos, since the beating was emblematic of the treatment of barrio residents. A shooting of a young Puerto Rican man in 1966 caused these resentments to boil over into a riot and pushed progressive Puerto Rican and Mexican-American political activists together to oppose a hardening urban inequality.[47]

Electoral politics was one strategy for this opposition, but it was not the engine driving pan-Latino mobilization. In a more general sense the real engine was a fear of permanent outsider and subordinate status. What the Mexican-American and Puerto Rican activists understood was that their sense of their own cultural distinctiveness could only translate into marginality, whereas a consolidation of efforts and interests could translate into real social gains. As one activist put it: "Individually, we are not going anywhere. So respect for differences could represent a way for us to unite. The idea of Latinismo is a very good strategy . . . I feel pity for those leaders that stand up in meetings and say 'We must fight and struggle for the rights of the Puerto Ricans, the Mexicans, or the Cubans separately.' I feel pity for these leaders because they do not understand Latinismo. They do not know that we basically have the same culture and needs. And the only way to alleviate those problems and gain political respect is to work together as one group."[48] Or as Rosa Clemente, a Puerto Rican youth organizer in New York proclaims, "Being Latino/a is not a cultural identity but rather a political one."

A Los Angeles Story

The story of the Figueroa Corridor Coalition for Economic Justice in L.A. is about the way a working-class community stood up to forces of the government and large land developers, to demand a share of the local prosperity and a seat at the table when decisions affecting their neighborhood were being made. Yet, what makes this story different from hundreds of tales of working-class resistance is that the coalition had to create a form of politics that would negotiate the changing racial make-up of the community from predominantly black to predominantly Latino. In addition to that general change, community leaders had to transform the resistance from a Mexican-inspired effort to a Latino-based initiative that could encompass what had become primarily Central American neighborhoods. A united Latino community was essential to forging a coalition with neighboring Asian and black communities. If this had been strictly a nationalist effort or a class-based effort, it would have failed. Like the protest led by the Pulpit Forum in Greensboro, North Carolina, it had to give cultural resonance to democratic working-class-based resistance. And it found this in churches, unions, and decades-long street-level organizing.

In 1994 Governor Pete Wilson was in a tight race for reelection in California. He found himself trailing Kathleen Brown, sister of former governor Jerry Brown and daughter of the still-beloved governor who built modern California, Edmund G. "Pat" Brown. In a tactical decision with long-term strategic consequences, Governor Wilson tied his hopes for reelection to his fervent advocacy of Proposition 187. This proposition was designed to protect the public coffers by denying medical and educational services to undocumented immigrants and their children. While his support of Prop 187 secured his reelection, Governor Wilson's deal—like every deal with the devil—came at a heavy cost, this time to the Republican Party in California.

While the majority of voters believed that the proposition was aimed at undocumented Mexicans, in practice it hit a much larger target, including Asians and Central Americans. These immigrants eventually became citizens and they registered to vote. And in every election since 1994 they have punished the Republican Party. Democrats now control the statehouse, both houses of the legislature, and both Senate seats. Even arch-conservative Robert Dornan from legendarily conservative Orange County lost his seat to a Latina and then cemented his defeat by challenging her election with an extended complaint about "illegal" voting by immigrants.

By galvanizing the Latino and Asian communities, Proposition 187 laid the foundation for cross-racial coalition-building around issues like those that lay at the heart of the Figueroa Corridor Coalition for Economic Justice. The strength these immigrants found in responding to Prop 187 has been translated into increased labor activity and has led to additional coalitions among Asian, Latino, and African-American communities that have a specific political content apart from "rent-seeking" by each faction of the coalition.

In a dramatic example of this political cooperation, the bus riders' strike joined primarily Latino bus riders with predominantly black bus drivers in an effort to secure better service and fare stabilization.

Though originally opposed by environmental groups because the settlement would take money away from the subway system then under construction, the environmentalists were brought around, and part of the settlement resulted in the creation of Environmental Justice Los Angeles (EJLA).

This coalition, along with Robert Garcia of the Center for Law in the Public Interest, next organized a civil rights challenge that was instrumental in stopping the conversion of a fifty-acre field in Los Angeles known as the Cornfield into an industrial complex. Instead of more factories, this working-class Asian community got a park and a lesson in building democracy from the street level up.

The bitterness sown by Proposition 187 yielded political fruits that were not limited to cultural nationalism. Community activists took the lesson of defeat and used it to organize the communities that were the target of Prop 187. Central to their organizing was to make common cause with labor and progressive activists across racial lines in order to create a community base that could defend itself and turn its issues into policy. Efforts to drive a wedge between the historically antagonistic black and Latino communities spurred more creative community organizing that dates back to Governor Wilson's 1994 campaign. As Karen Bass, Executive Director of the predominantly black Community Coalition based in South Central Los Angeles, says, "Latinos and African-Americans have more issues in common than ones that divide them. Ninety percent of the kids in the criminal justice system and in foster care are African-American and Latino," she says. "The most important factor here is that we're neighbors."[49]

Part of this new cooperation comes from the expansion of the Latino community beyond the traditional Mexican-American base. While Latinos of Mexican descent still predominate, there has been a steady influx of people from Guatemala and El Salvador. The civil wars in each country during the past thirty years have greatly accelerated the stream of refugees and immigrants. Like the circumstances in Chicago, where interaction between Puerto Ricans and Mexican Americans led to the articulation of a Latino identity through which to conduct politics, the existing category of Hispanic/Latino in Los Angeles provided a means to mediate the interaction of these new immigrants with established Mexican-American communities as well as with immigrant Mexican communities. The coincidence of this migration pattern with the politics of Proposition 187 gave added immediacy to the need to join these disparate groups into a cohesive whole that could develop a new politics of resistance.

Because of organizing across racial lines and creating a meaningful Latino identity, Los Angeles came close to getting its first Latino mayor in over a hundred years. Yet if Antonio Villaraigosa, a Mexican American, had succeeded in being elected mayor, he would not have been just a Latino mayor; his candidacy was the product of the progressive coalition-building that produced the bus riders' strike, EJLA, the Cornfield Park, and the Figueroa Corridor Coalition. But he faced a formidable challenge. He had to unite the various Latino subgroups as well as progressive whites, Asians, and blacks. Having a Spanish surname was not enough; he had to speak directly to the needs of each group in a way that could join them together to a common vision of progressive change.

The Challenges of an Electoral Strategy

Although an impressive coalition between progressive younger elements of the Latino and black communities emerged around the candidacy of Villaraigosa, what is important to remember is that this was not just a coalition cobbled together for an election. In Los Angeles and in California generally there has been historic antipathy between the Mexican-American and black communities, born of racism on one side and nativism on the other. While they might not always stand together behind a single candidate, the ground work for a more enduring unity was being laid in the labor struggles that united bus drivers and bus riders, that sought to bring "Justice for Janitors" and to translate the hopes and democratic aspirations of working people of all races.

The leadership came from the dishwashers, chambermaids, janitors, and bellhops who spent their days off going "door-to-door canvassing in the barrio neighborhoods of Los Angeles, confronting their neighbors with a forceful warning that unless they vote, they can forget their dreams of a living wage, health insurance protection, and better schools for their children."[50] It was the Latino working-poor and immigrant families of Los

Angeles who took the insult and threat of Proposition 187 and turned it into a force for remaking democracy from the street up. When this united Latino effort moved citywide, it had to find a way to include the black community. This proved to be its greatest challenge.

Although Villaraigosa was the candidate who spoke the language of a broad coalition of Latinos and progressive blacks, he had difficulty putting together the kind of black-Latino power base that is often discussed but has proved hard to assemble in many regions of the country. Villaraigosa came in first in a crowded field during the nonpartisan primary, but then lost in the head-to-head general election run-off with a white Democratic candidate. Twenty-five percent of the voters for the successful white candidate, James K. Hahn, were black, while only 7 percent of Mr. Villaraigosa's were. Roughly 80 percent of blacks voted for Hahn, whereas the Latino turnout, which was unusually high, went overwhelmingly for Villaraigosa.[51] Hahn's support tended to be older and, in the black community, tied to his father's solid political legacy as the representative of a majority-black district for forty years. Nevertheless, the failure of a black/Latino coalition to emerge in L.A. and elsewhere has prompted Jennifer Hochschild to conclude that a big part of the problem is identity politics.[52]

We offer an alternative explanation to tie Hochschild's analysis to its proper context: that a progressive strategy is flawed if its primary focus is to win within the zero-sum world of elections. It is electoral politics that makes identity politics a high-stakes enterprise. By focusing on the descriptive elements of community and reducing a candidacy to those elements, electoral politics feeds interracial competition because it offers the appearance of racial symbols but does not encourage genuine cross-racial political engagement over time. Even the groundwork of groups like Environmental Justice Los Angeles, the Figueroa Corridor Coalition, the Cornfield Coalition, the Community Coalition, and the Organization of Los Angeles Workers did not give Villaraigosa enough of a cross-racial foundation to stand on in the heat of an election. In addition, Villaraigosa's vulnerabilities were exploited in the waning days of the campaign by an ominous attack-ad broadcast by his opponent, who was willing to do whatever was necessary to win this head-to-head contest.[53]

Similar challenges faced blacks and Latinos in New York. In his bid for mayor, Fernando Ferrer invoked the coalition that in 1989 had elected David Dinkins, New York's first black mayor. Ferrer publicly sought to join the black and Puerto Rican communities in reviving this winning electoral base, but no sooner had Ferrer sought the endorsement of civil rights activist Al Sharpton, "arguing that blacks should support [his] bid to become the city's first Puerto Rican mayor, as part of an effort to ease historical rifts between the two groups," than Sharpton demanded that Ferrer endorse two black candidates in return for that support.[54] Ferrer refused. Sharpton immediately retorted, "If there's going to be a real coalition, we want a real coalition . . . I am telling you on the record that without those two issues resolved, there will be no endorsement. I do want to heal the rift, but healing means that everybody must be a part . . . They're talking about a black-Latino coalition," Sharpton said. "I mean, where is it?"[55]

While the temporary estrangement from Sharpton threatened to undo his efforts to win black support, Ferrer struggled to consolidate Latino support behind his candidacy. Harking back to the Dinkins coalition, a confident Ferrer remarked, "David Dinkins got 70 percent of the Latino vote in 1989. Does anyone seriously believe I'd receive less than that?" Yet even his Latino support seemed to be rooted in a marginally thicker version of old-fashioned identity politics. As the journalist Mireya Navarro reported, "In interviews around the city, some Latino voters showed enthusiasm for Mr. Ferrer, but many others said they had not yet tuned in to the primary race, and some were not even sure who Mr. Ferrer was." A Dominican-American City Councilman, Guillermo Linares, said that for Ferrer to attract Dominican voters he "needed to address issues critical to them, like immigration." And community activists started asking questions even as they reflected the kind of racial or ethnic pride that Ferrer was counting on. One community organizer said of Ferrer, "All of these years, what has he done for the city of New York?" Although she supports one of Ferrer's opponents, she still hoped that "he does enough numbers that he doesn't embarrass the community."[56]

The conflict between Ferrer and Sharpton was not only about identity politics. It reflected the problem with trying to construct a candidate-based coalition in which issues of identity dominate. It is in this context—of media-driven, candidate-centered, winner-take-all election contests—

that Hochschild is correct. At least as reported in, and fed by, the media, leaders seeking points of influence within a zero-sum hierarchy conduct negotiations. They proceed on the assumption that an electoral strategy based on a shared descriptive identity may be a powerful motivator to inspire supporters when an individual candidate tries to break the glass ceiling for his or her racial or ethnic group.[57] They also assume that a shared identity also means a shared political outlook. Building from the top-down, they may even trumpet the candidate's racial-group authenticity as a qualification for election.

Villaraigosa's candidacy was plagued by similar conflict, even though he had qualms running as the "Latino" candidate. He ran a campaign that suggested this was not just about Antonio Villaraigosa but about speaking to the needs of the people who lifted him up.[58] Nevertheless, he had to run in an electoral climate in Los Angeles that turns out to have more in common with the atmosphere in New York City than was initially noted. In both cities, the black/Latino coalition is fragile.[59]

One reason for this seeming deadlock is the lingering effect of identity politics, in which electoral coalitions are mobilized around ethnic or racial identity, a source of pride and energy that yields high voter turnout but may then exacerbate friction between competing ethnic or racial groups. A second is the residue of Hispanic whiteness. Because the promise of the racial bribe invites some Hispanics to turn their back on their indigenous roots, many blacks do not trust Latinos to fight alongside them over the long haul. Blacks fear that new immigrants will monopolize the good jobs but, more important, will displace them as the racial group with the strongest moral claim on existing resources. The Hahn coalition successfully exploited blacks' resentment of emerging demographic shifts and their fear of what Latino power might mean.[60]

Immigrants bring new energy and pride to progressive struggles. But they also bring their ignorance of the history of U.S. slavery and its enduring legacy.[61] Latinos and other nonwhite groups may need to do more to convince the black leadership and the black community that they share their fate and are willing to join forces directly rather than compete for a small sliver of elite recognition. This is not to say that blacks are innocent by-standers. Indeed there is mutual suspicion, reinforced by black anti-immigrant sentiment. But these sources of inter-group friction could be worked out were there a political party or political space that built on neighborhood organizing efforts and was accountable to local, democratically rooted institutions. Or if, as with the farmworkers movement described in Chapter 5, electoral politics was simply one option among a complex set of progressive strategies.

When electoral politics dominates, relationships become frayed. Incumbents from both communities still try to protect prior deals, often using racial or ethnic advancement to camouflage bargains for patronage and position.[62] In Los Angeles, for example, it was evident that some black leaders supported Hahn to protect their own prerogatives; they held on to their individual access in the world of existing arrangements rather than play a less visible role in a more progressive coalition. This is not surprising. After all, dog-eat-dog competition measured in traditional zero-sum terms is all that can comfortably fit within the narrow opening of electoral politics.

This, then, is the third and perhaps more important explanation for the current instability of black-Latino alliances. It is simply not enough to concentrate on electoral politics in a winner-take-all contest if the goal is to develop and sustain cross-racial coalitions. The chance of electing a person of color does not create the conditions for sustained mobilization beyond election day, even when that person is a racial-group pioneer. Indeed, it would take an extraordinary candidate to produce a vital coalition without the experience of working together in a nonelectoral setting. Even the example of Harold Washington, despite his importance in galvanizing community groups, would have come to nothing if the communities themselves had not begun cross-ethnic and cross-racial organizing decades before.

A preoccupation with electoral politics can distract from the hard work of organizing a base of community participation. Especially if electoral strategies are founded primarily on shared identity without ever anticipating the second or third stages of political race, the potential for long-term cooperation growing out of an understanding of shared interests is less likely. The focus is on winning an election, and the challenges of governing are often neglected. The community is disengaged once victory is theirs.

In the long run, a social movement will not evolve consistent with the idea of political race if its efforts are constrained by either simple identity politics or liberal interest-group politics. As we saw in Chapter 5, successful social movements draw on the courage, faith, and commitment of participants, rooted precisely in the fact that their endeavor is about broader themes of social justice and not simply about narrow self-interest. Their energy to continue comes from the struggle to redefine what their identity means—in economic, political, and moral terms.

To remain animated beyond a single electoral victory, the energy of racial identity has to be summoned as a moral force with social justice commitments. Otherwise it just devolves into patronage and the special pleading that typified the Chicago machine. Gerald Torres made this point forcefully in 1994, when, as a minor appointed functionary in the first Clinton administration, he was summoned to a meeting in the Old Executive Office Building. The meeting was called to discuss ways to get out the message about the various good things the administration had done for the Hispanic community. After some discussion, the person leading the meeting suggested that those present construct a list of all the Clinton appointees who are Hispanic. This list, when publicized, would demonstrate the administration's noble intentions and good will toward the Hispanic community. The discussion continued until Gerald slammed his hand on the table. He said that if the administration wanted to earn the support of the Hispanic community, it would have to demonstrate that desire through an enumeration of the various *policy initiatives* that have actually improved the lives of significant numbers of the Hispanic population. "Except for my mother," he explained, "no one voted for Bill Clinton so I could have a job."

Yet, policy initiatives to improve the lives of Hispanics alone are also not enough to sustain a social movement. Even when ethnic politics seems to work, as in Chicago, it is critical to keep the racialized position in mind, but not as an end in itself. It is a means to diagnose and respond to deeper structural infirmities. As the sociologist Cathy Schneider describes in reference to Puerto Ricans in New York City:

> I saw this very clearly in . . . Brooklyn. For decades the Hasidic Jews and Puerto Ricans competed for public housing and other community resources. The positive consequence for the Puerto Rican community was that it became one of the most organized Puerto Rican communities in the city. Through this organization they took control of the local area policy board, won several lawsuits around public housing, helped design a new Latino district, and elect[ed] Nydia Velazquez to the House. The negative was that when the Republicans in the congress, Governor and Mayoral offices began major cuts, the activist I interviewed observed "Nationalism still mobilizes—300 people showed up at the last town hall meeting, but there was no follow up. Everyone screamed fight, fight, fight. After that, nothing." There was no effort to organize residents against the privatization of social services, the cuts in basic health care and welfare, the scarcity of or current assault on low-income housing.[63]

In Schneider's description of Brooklyn politics, the progressive content of an organized Puerto Rican community was blunted when activists failed to move beyond the nationalist impulse. Their initial organizing took race into account but then failed to push through the isolating structure of identity-based interest-group politics. Instead of recognizing that the community needed the resources for both poor Jews and Puerto Ricans, activists attempted to oppose the outside attacks by defining their political community narrowly and electorally, thus weakening both the potential impact of their efforts and their capacity to resist.

By contrast, the political race coalition in Chicago was based on an articulation of social and economic justice issues that drew its energy from coalitions that predated the electoral strategy and that bubbled up from the bottom to bring the community together. A political race coalition might choose to support a specific candidate as one means among many of reinvigorating democratic institutions. But it requires the kind of street-level democracy evidenced in Chicago and emerging in Los Angeles.

Though our mostly preliminary assessments of the mayors' races in Los Angeles and New York seem to suggest that real street-level cross-racial and cross-ethnic mobilization is a precondition for building the kind of cooperation that we have characterized as political race, we want to be clear that we are also saying the battle never ends. Even the longevity of coalitions does not eliminate the obligation to continually attend to the roots of cooperation and to be vigilant about challenging the reproduction of both racial categories and racial hierarchies. Democracy, we would argue, is about finding spaces for power *with* the community, not simply power *for* the candidate.

The Persistence of Racial Hierarchy and Racial Privilege

We cannot be totally sanguine about the natural possibilities of a transition from a Hispanic/Latino identity to political race because the pressures to conform to the conventional system of racial management are great. As the historian Noel Ignatiev recounts in his book *How the Irish Became White*: "It was a passage in *Boston's Immigrants* that first drew me to my own question: it recounts the complaints of Boston Irish 'that colored people did not know their place.' How, I wondered, did an Irish immigrant, perhaps fresh off the boat, learn 'the place' of the Negro."[64]

Andrew Hacker takes Ignatiev's discovery to make the claim that the pressures of racial management in the United States will compel Latinos to choose between being white or black. As it stands now, Asians are gradually becoming honorary whites, according to Hacker's view, while Latinos are, at minimum, nonwhite and still have a choice to make.[65] It is precisely against this view that we have been writing. We argue, rather, that there is a third way which draws on the concept of political race. But the social pressures Hacker and other scholars describe cannot be discounted.

Many people today view Asians (a complex pan-ethnic term in itself) as lying on the white end of the racial spectrum.[66] As Hochschild writes, "Asian Americans frequently resemble whites (so far as we can tell from very scanty survey data)." While there are important analogs between the Latino and the Asian experience with race in this country, there are also important differences. Nonetheless, as the experiences in the Cornfield Park and the Figueroa Coalition illustrated, a similarity in outlook toward many issues can permit a coalition to be built across Latino and Asian communities. As Hochschild points out, "A survey in Los Angeles shows the pattern clearly. Latinos and Asian Americans are consistently more likely to give the response sympathetic to immigrants than are whites and African Americans."[67] This similarity of attitude helps explain the ready affinity between the Asian and Latino communities in response to Proposition 187.

But immigrant issues are not the only ones that unite Asians and Latinos. Even on the question of Asian assimilation, Hacker may be wrong. Hochschild notes that "in every one of the dozens of survey questions on the point [of racial and ethnic separation] Anglos see much less racial discrimination than do African Americans, even though they are more likely to express racial or ethnic stereotypes; Hispanics and Asians typically fall somewhere in between, but closer to blacks in their perceptions."[68]

This reality is reflected in local politics, where Asians have sufficient numbers to form a constituency to which aspirants for political office must respond. In Monterey Park, California, Latinos and Asians joined together to stop the city from declaring English the official language. Out of that struggle a Latino-Asian coalition was formed that propelled Judy Chu into the California State Assembly. Significantly, Chu did this by beating a Latino candidate in a district where Latinos outnumbered Asians by close to 20 percent. Although her opponent was a respected Latino mayor of a neighboring city, Chu secured the backing of the outgoing assemblywoman, Gloria Romero, as well as progressive, pro-labor Latina Congresswoman Hilda Solis.[69] Chu neither rejected her racial identity nor merely embraced the symbolic nationalism of a candidate-centered campaign. Instead, Chu forged an alliance that used the outsider status of both Asians and Latinos to create a progressive political identity.

Despite the important examples of cross-racial coalition-building in California and Chicago, political race requires that we exercise constant vigilance in renegotiating the black-white binary. The internal dynamics of race within each national subgroup are complex. And like any historical moment, the contingencies admit of many possible futures. There are, however, reasons to believe that political race may ultimately prevail over the alternative approaches of simple cultural nationalism or cooperation with the racial bribe. The maintenance of a large and cohesive political group means that even the elite, at whom the racial bribe has been historically aimed, would have to reject it as corrosive to the political strength of the Hispanic/Latino population. Division of the potential political base along conventional black-white lines would dissipate the numerical strength that the political elite is counting on. It needs to have the numbers even as its relationship to blackness continues to evolve. By choosing to become white on the European ethnic model, each of the component groups within the pan-ethnic Hispanic/Latino identity would either have to repress the black content of their own national identity or rewrite the meaning of their culture consistent with the black-white binary that governs race in America. There are political costs to either strategy. Those costs are inconsistent with the national political ambitions of the Hispanic/Latino elite.

This is because the construction of a national platform through the development of a pan-Hispanic/Latino identity requires the maintenance of as large a grouping as possible that can come together across a range of issues. One key is to organize according to interest, within a larger social justice frame, rather than any essential characteristic. Such an approach promises to reduce the friction between the major ethnic groups within the Hispanic/Latino grouping. This is one of the lessons from the coalition between Puerto Ricans, Mexican Americans, other Latin Americans, blacks, and progressive whites in Chicago. From the perspective of the imperatives of liberal interest-group politics, success with that vision would rupture bipolar racial hierarchies and build from a Hispanic/Latino identity into a cross-racial affiliation with blacks and whites.[70]

A related pressure that might prevent groups who in the past would have taken the racial bribe from doing so is fundamentally political. By political we mean a growing awareness of the energy within the Hispanic/Latino community for mobilizing around a social justice agenda that starts with race but does not end there. To succeed as a national strategy, creation of a Hispanic/Latino identity must accommodate the wide "racial" and color variation within each of the component groups without reproducing domestic racial hierarchy. This issue will not be worked out once but must be dealt with self-consciously and over time.

If this happens, pressure at the local and national level to develop a Hispanic/Latino identity as well as the racially indeterminate, though nonwhite, content of that identity will create new possibilities that illustrate two foundational ideas of political race. First, this pan-ethnic identity will remind us that political race is not about membership in an externally defined racial group; instead, it is about commitment. Second, it will help teach those outside the community important lessons about building progressive alliances on the ground.

These lessons are reflected in the emerging black-consciousness movement in Brazil. Yet we need not look all the way to Brazil to see leadership of color using race to generate progressive alternatives that benefit more than their own careers or their immediate constituents. The Latino leadership who designed and fought for the Texas 10 Percent Plan could safely have done nothing and most would not have suffered electoral repercussions. They could have saved their relationships with their legislative colleagues for conventional gains for their constituents. Instead, they understood their constituents not just as the people in their districts but as the black, Latino, and poor white rural students who had traditionally been excluded from the flagship campuses.

Those committed to the political race project understand this as well. For example, the progressive coalition that emerged in the aftermath of Proposition 187 has helped move the political debate and the grounds for political action from race to class without pretending that race does not have a role. The coalition has enabled labor to join forces and to link Asians, Mexicans, and black people. It has experienced set-backs as well as victories. But when it succeeds, it is because it continues to work through issues of race internal to the coalition as well as in the larger society. Because whiteness is measured in social distance from blackness, the coalition has had to have leaders who actively oppose the efforts of conservatives to exploit both the racism of Mexicans and the nativism of blacks.[71] By using racial identity and immigrant status to energize a movement for social and economic justice, it moves beyond interest-group pleading to confront the question Hochschild and others have posed: "whether African Americans, other people of color, and like-minded whites can surmount their partly outdated assumptions, mutual mistrust, and substantive disagreements enough to pursue their shared material and philosophical goals."[72]

The lessons from Chicago, Los Angeles, and Texas demonstrate that the political space opened up by the Hispanic/Latino identity may initially be defined externally by government census categories or electoral districts. It may be driven by national elites interested in maximizing their numerical constituency. But it will be occupied by local communities of interest, and its content will not be determined in advance. These communities will then have an impact on the construction of issues that will inform the elite's conception of the meaning of the category.

Conclusion

Our discussion of Hispanics/Latinos and others who find themselves on the hyphen of the black-white binary is situated within a peculiar local racial history. But it foreshadows the danger that a multiracial movement which simply succeeds in repopulating a racial hierarchy may nevertheless simultaneously reproduce or fortify the hierarchy itself. The many stories collected in this chapter indicate the promise of a cross-racial and democratically committed alliance whose leaders are people of color but who struggle together against hierarchies of power at the right historical time. Some of these stories also illustrate the difficulty of maintaining transformative political commitments in an era of scarcity when the promise is not greater democracy but the acquisition of more material resources for some. Our discussion of Mexican Americans highlights both of these points, but it also illustrates our central claim that race is connected to power and that the Hispanic/Latino identity has within it a promising and powerful role to play in destabilizing the black-white binary.

We take two lessons from interpreting the Hispanic/Latino identity in the United States in light of the pressures to conform to the black-white binary and other conventional racial management techniques.

First, the use of race as a political category gains its legitimacy from its promise to increase the quantum of democracy in society and to resist unfair concentrations of wealth and power. As we have already argued, merely acquiring power for one's self or one's own group without challenging the very nature of that power does not constitute political transformation. We cannot assume that, once confronted and negotiated, the impact of race fades as a fundamental political issue.

Second, the use of political race makes sense only when some of the political efforts aim to change the nature of power away from zero-sum competition for resources. Power constructs the self; and in a hierarchical capitalist society that is not shaped by democratic pressures, it will eventually construct selves in the shapes of winners and losers. The contests in New York, Chicago, and Los Angeles, aimed at least partially at the acquisition of state power, must not only attend to the existing distributions of power and resources but must reflect experiments with internal forms of democratic participation that reconstruct the concept of power itself.

One of the critical issues raised in the context of the emerging Hispanic/Latino identity in the United States is how to value racial difference within the context of political unity. We have not been describing new racial categories. We have not been talking about doing away with race. Instead, we think that the lessons of the development of a Hispanic/Latino identity point to the possibility of using race and politics to create an identity that resists conventional categories and supports democratic renewal. That, we think, is at the heart of the concept of political race.

"To my friends, I look like a black boy. To white people who don't know me I look like a wanna-be punk. To the cops I look like a criminal." Niko, now fourteen years old, is reflecting on the larger implications of his daily journey, trudging alone down Pearl Street, backpack heavy with books, on his way home from school. As his upper lip darkens with the first signs of a moustache, he is still a sweet, sometimes kind, unfailingly polite upper-middle-class black boy. To his mom and dad he looks innocent, even boyish. Yet his race, his gender, and his baggy pants shout out a different, more alarming message to those who do not know him. At thirteen, Niko was aware that many white people crossed the street as he approached. Now at fourteen, he is more worried about how he looks to the police. After all, he is walking while black.

One week after Niko made these comments to his mom, the subject of racial profiling was raised by a group of Cambridge eighth graders who were invited to speak in a seminar at Harvard Law School. Accompanied by their parents, teachers, and the school principal, the students read essays they had written in reaction to a statement of a black Harvard Law School student whose own arrest the year before in New York City had prompted him to write about racial profiling.[1] One student drew upon theories of John Locke to argue that "the same mindset as slavery provokes police officers to control black people today." Another explained a picture he had drawn showing a black police officer hassling a black woman because the officer assumed she was a prostitute. Black cops harass black people too, he said aloud. "It just seems like all the police are angry and have a lot of aggression coming out." A third boy concluded that when the cops see a black person they see "the image of a thug." Proud that he knew the *American Heritage Dictionary*'s definition of a thug—a "cut-throat or ruffian"—he concluded that the cops are not the key to understanding racial profiling. Nor did he blame the white people who routinely crossed the street as he approached. If what these white people see is a thug, "they would normally want to pull their purse away." He blamed the media for this "psychological enslavement," as well as those blacks who allowed themselves to be used to "taint our image."

One boy spoke for 15 minutes in a detached voice, showing little emotion; but he often strayed from his prepared text to describe in great detail the story of relatives who had been stopped by the police or to editorialize about what he had written. Only after all the students left did the professor discover why the boy had talked so long—and why so many adults had shown up for this impromptu class.

Several of the boys, including the one who had spoken at length, had already had personal encounters with the police. Just the week before, two of the boys had been arrested and had spent six hours locked in separate cells. In retrospect, their essays, and even the ad libbed insertions, both masked and revealed the real pain of their own experience. Perhaps reading the essays built up their confidence, because the details of their story came out in a subsequent email one of the boys, Rashid, sent to the professor:

> It all started when I asked Jonathan if he wanted to go back behind the Professional Ambulance Center and look at a mural. We stopped in the corner store before entering the walkway that led to the P.A.C. In the store I purchased a Sprite and Jonathan got a Slice, then we were on our way. On the walk way there were no signs implying that there were to be no people in that area (no trespassing). Because of this Jonathan and I kept on walking, not because we did not see any signs but because we had no idea that we were not supposed to be in that area. It was around 5:10 p.m. when we started down the road, it wasn't cold but not hot either. It was Spring and still daylight.
>
> When the two police officers started walking towards us I did not

even see them. It was only because of Jonathan saying "Oh gosh we're about to get in mad trouble" that is what drew my attention to the two cops advancing up the train tracks. I could tell Jonathan was worried and frightened of the possible outcome of the whole situation. At this time I did not know we were going to get in trouble for being back there because we saw two white kids walk right past them. The two kids looked like they were a little bit older than us, like 15. The only two things different about them were their dress style and skin color. There were also more children of European descent further up the tracks. I could not really see any details except they were making a lot of noise and one person had a blue shirt. When the police got up to us they emptily asked if we had any "knives, guns, or drugs" and started patting us down. They fished out everything in my pockets and told me to put my soda on the floor. The officers took our book bags and proceeded to search them. One cop started looking through my drawing book. At this time I felt like I had no rights. My soda was almost half way done. The only thing running through my mind was Amadou Diallo. The officers put us in handcuffs that were purposely too tight and they took us past the place we entered to where they entered. On the way to their car the police made countless smart remarks, like all your little graffiti is about to come to an end.

In the MBTA Police car the officers said many inappropriate terms. One referred to Jonathan as a jackass. I could not identify what the cop said after I told him where I was originally from but he looked at his partner with a look that could only mean that we were lucky we got the right one. He continued to say inappropriate things to his partner and other drivers when he stuck his head out the window. After arriving at the station I could tell that we weren't suppose to be there. There were a bunch of officers there all looking at me about to laugh, basically with smirks on their faces.

They took us in separate rooms that had plastered benches with handcuffs attached to them. I was put in one set. I was asked to empty out all my pockets and everything on me into a small plastic bag. This was hard, only having one hand and leaning over. I was also asked to take off my belt with one hand. One called my mother and Jonathan's father. After that drama he took me and Jonathan's picture and finger-prints. The man with my bag said that this was the end to all my little

Bible tagging stuff with a wicked smile on his face. I had two shirts on at this time. Then the officer doing the prints asked me to take off my shoes and my extra shirt, all the same with Jonathan. He then got on the phone and asked somebody if he could put 14-year-olds in cells. They chatted for a little while then the one on my side said "we're not really supposed to but just do it anyway. OK bye." He took the lead with Jonathan behind him and me behind Jonathan. Jonathan was put in cell 9 and I was escorted to cell 11. I asked the officer if we could be put in the same cell for conversational purposes. To this he replied with a strong no.

The officer stated that we would be released to Jonathan's Dad when he got there. I might add that we were in the cell till 11:00 and Jonathan's Dad came at around 7:00. Their excuse was that there were a lot of arrests and the computer was slow and it was still processing our identity. We still remained without our stuff even with a court order. For a while I will remain without a book bag or my drawing book but in a world of racism after you purchase something you never know if it is truly yours.

His friend also emailed his version of the incident.

The day was Wednesday, and I had just come from the basketball court. My friend and I were walking down Rindge Ave. and decided to go into Food Town. After we came out of the store, we then decided we wanted to go look at a graffiti mural. We entered through the driveway of the pro-ambulance company. We walked down a few more meters until we got to where the ambulances park. The mural that my friend and I wanted to look at was on the other side of the pro-ambulance building.

My friend and I walked down a little hill to get to the mural. When we got to exactly where the mural was, we observed for about 20 min. before noticing two police officers approaching us on the left-hand side. One of the police officers says, "What are you guys doing?" And my friend responds, "Just analyzing this mural." Then one of the police officers asks, "Are you guys taggers?" And I say no. And one of the police officers says to his partner, "Just arrest them." Both police officers searched us before putting us under arrest. They walked us back to their cars before taking our belongings. My friend asked the question, "Why are we being arrested?" And the officers responded, "Because you're trespassing M.B.T.A. property." My friend asked, "This is M.B.T.A property?" And the police officer responded, "You know it is" with an attitude.

As we were walking back to the police car, my friend noticed other white kids walking on the tracks, so my friend asks, "Why don't you arrest them?" And the police officers respond, "We only have two sets of cuffs." While we were riding in the car, one of the police officers was using very vulgar language, such as the f- word at times. The officer was also giving people bad gestures. I asked the officer, "Are you guys Cambridge police?" And he responded, "Why are you so worried about it?" Then I asked him where we were going, and the passenger officer responded, "Roxbury" with an attitude. When we got to the M.B.T.A headquarters, the police officers took our backpacks and began to rifle through them. They took out my markers, Bible, a sticker, and my drill bit, which was to be used for a school project. I asked the police what they were going to do with our belongings. And they responded, "We are going to keep it because it is graffiti material, and we are going to see if any of the stuff in your book matches up with stuff on the streets." Then the officer said, "Your graffiti is forever gone."

After the booking officer gathered all of my personal information, he brought us over to a computer where we were fingerprinted and photographed. Then he told us to take off our shoes and shirts. And I said, "What's going on?" And he said, "You got to go in a cell." Then I asked him when we could come out, and he said, "When your father comes." After about three hours, my friend and I yelled for the officer to come. When he came, I asked him if we could leave yet, and he said, "Once the computer processes your identity." Then I asked him if my father had come. And he responded, "Your father has been here for two hours." Then he left.

Three hours later the officer comes back in and releases us. I asked him, "Has the computer processed our identity yet." And he said, "No. The only reason why I am releasing you is because your father works for the M.B.T.A." And he said it with a smirk.

Watching the Canary

Rashid and Jonathan (not their real names) are the sons of a lawyer and a transit employee, respectively. "Why don't you arrest *them*?" one of the boys asked the officer, referring to the white kids walking in the same area. "We only have two sets of cuffs," the officer replied. These cops knew whom to take in: the white kids were innocent; the black boys were guilty.

In the words of one of their classmates, black boys like Rashid and Jonathan are viewed as thugs, despite their class status. Aided by the dictionary and the media, our eighth-grade informant says this is racial profiling. Racial profiling, he believes, is a form of "psychological enslavement." Others might say the police are simply arresting people suspected of violating society's norms. We have called this process interpellation—the prerogative of those with power or privilege to name status relationships. By hailing these powerless boys as "the right ones," the police officers participated in and reinforced racial hierarchy. Few object because the boys fit both the cops' profile as well as the one harbored by most Americans.

But these black boys are not merely victims of racial profiling. They are canaries. And our political-race project asks people to pay attention to the canary. The canary is a source of information for all who care about the atmosphere in the mines—and a source of motivation for changing the mines to make them safer. The canary serves both a diagnostic and an innovative function. It offers us more than a critique of the way social goods are distributed. What the canary lets us see are the hierarchical arrangements of power and privilege that have naturalized this unequal distribution.

Throughout this book we have urged those committed to progressive social change to watch the canary—and to assure the most vulnerable among us a space to experiment with democratic practice and discover their own power. Even though the canary is in a cage, it continues to have agency and voice. If the miners were watching the canary, they would not wait for it to fall off its perch, legs up. They would notice that it is talking to them. "I can't breathe, but you know what? You are being poisoned too. If you save me, you will save yourself. Why is that mine owner sending all of us down here to be poisoned anyway?" The miners might then realize that they cannot escape this life-threatening social arrangement without a strategy that disrupts the way things are.

What would we learn if we watched these particular two black boys?

First, we would discover that from the moment they were born, each had a 30 percent chance of spending some portion of his life in prison or jail or under the supervision of the criminal justice system. Compare this statistical chance of being incarcerated to that of Niko's white classmates at his private school. White adolescent boys' chances of being incarcerated are close to 4 percent.[2] Niko, Jonathan, and Rashid are academically motivated students; black boys who do not have access to the kind of parental resources these three boys enjoy are unlikely to attend college. Among black men between the ages of 18 and 30 who drop out of high school, more become incarcerated than either go on to attend college or hold a job.[3] According to data from 1999, of black men aged 22 to 30 who dropped out of high school, 41 percent were incarcerated, 30 percent were in the workforce, and 29 percent were unemployed, were not actively seeking employment, or had gone on to college. By contrast, only 6 percent of white male high school drop-outs aged 22 to 30 were incarcerated that year, whereas almost 78 percent were in the labor force and 17 percent were unemployed, were not actively seeking employment, or had gone on to college.[4]

Why are so many young black men not attending college or working? Edward Luttwak, a foreign policy analyst, tells about an experience at a gas station in Japan in the early 1990s that caused him to seek an answer to that question.[5] As he drove up to the pump, four young men rushed to service his car, check the tires, wash the windows, and pump the gas. Luttwak realized he was paying for this service through the inflated price of gas in Japan, a price kept high by the government to subsidize the temporary employment of those who need help with the transition from high school to work. When Luttwak returned to the United States, the price of gas was much cheaper, and four young men were still hanging out at the gas station. Though they offered him no service, Luttwak realized he was paying for them anyway—through tax dollars that went to finance the criminal justice and welfare systems, through the high rates of car insurance, and, if he were really unlucky, through his own blood. In the United States, if young men are not tracked to college and they are black or brown, we wait for their boredom, desperation, or sense of uselessness to catch up with them.[6] We wait, in other words, for them to give us an excuse to send them to prison. The criminal justice system has thus become our major instrument of urban social policy.

David Garland explains that imprisonment has ceased to be the incarceration of individual offenders and has instead become "the systematic imprisonment of whole groups of the population"—in this case, young black and Latino males in large urban municipalities. Or as the political scientist Mary Katzenstein observes, "Policies of incarceration in this country are fundamentally about poverty, about race, about addiction, about mental illness, about norms of masculinity and female accommodation among men and women who have been economically, socially, and politically demeaned and denied." In the powerful words of Loïc Wacquant, prisons are the latest in the "historical sequence of 'peculiar institutions' that have shouldered the task of defining and confining African Americans, alongside slavery, the Jim Crow regime, and the ghetto."[7]

But how does this "race to incarcerate" happen disproportionately to young black and Latino boys? Why is it that increasingly the nation's prisons and jails have become temporary or permanent cages for our canaries? One reason is that white working-class youth enjoy greater opportunities in the labor market than do black and Latino boys, owing in part to lingering prejudice.[8] According to survey data, 54 percent of whites still think blacks are not as intelligent as whites; 62 percent think blacks are lazier; 56 percent think blacks are more violent than whites; and 78 percent think blacks prefer welfare over work.[9] While many whites' attitudes have softened in recent times, latent prejudice among over half the white population helps explain high unemployment rates among black and brown young men, as well as the absence of a huge public outcry and massive protests when the police routinely arrest fourteen-year-old boys such as Rashid and Jonathan.

A second reason for the disproportionate impact of incarceration on the black and brown communities is the increased discretion given to prosecutors and police officers and the decreased discretion given to judges, whose decisions are exposed to public scrutiny in open court, unlike the deals made by prosecutors and police.[10] Media sensationalism and political manipulation around several high profile cases (notably Willy

Horton and Polly Klaas) led to mandatory minimum sentences in many states. Meanwhile, laws such as "three strikes and you're out" channeled unreviewable discretion to prosecutors, who decide which strikes to call and which to ignore. Many prosecutors are elected in winner-take-all races that do not give minorities a voice. Others, including well-intentioned white prosecutors as well as increasing numbers of people of color who hold this position, have been hamstrung by legislatures, whose laws are often passed without hearings and certainly without the involvement and support of the communities most directly affected.[11]

A third and, according to some commentators, the most important explanation for the disproportionate incarceration of black and Latino young men is the war on drugs. In this federal campaign—one of the most volatile issues in contemporary politics—drug users and dealers are routinely painted as black or Latino, deviant and criminal. This war metaphorically names drugs as the enemy, but it is carried out in practice as a massive incarceration policy focused on black, Latino, and poor white young men. It has also swept increasing numbers of black and Latina women into prison.[12] The number of women incarcerated for drug offenses rose by 888 percent from 1986 to 1996, in contrast to a rise of 129 percent for all non-drug offenses; black and Hispanic women represent a disproportionate share of the women sentenced to prison for a drug offense.

In the Reagan administration, ideologues were looking for a federal policy they could support, while simultaneously slashing most federal social programs.[13] Presidents Ronald Reagan and George Bush had a distinct agenda, according to Marc Mauer: "to reduce the powers of the federal government," to "scale back the rights of those accused of crime," and to "diminish privacy rights."[14] Their goal was to shrink one branch of government (support for education and job training), while enlarging another (administration of criminal justice). Mauer concludes that the political and fiscal agendas of both the Reagan and first Bush administrations were quite successful. They reduced the social safety net and government's role in helping the least well off. Their success stemmed, in part, from their willingness to "polarize the debate" on a variety of issues, including drugs and prison. "We must not seek 'consensus,' we must confront," wrote Deputy Attorney General William B. Reynolds in the final year of the Reagan presidency.[15]

Their tough-on-crime policies shifted resources dramatically: between 1980 and 1993 federal spending on employment and training programs was cut nearly in half, while corrections spending increased by 521 percent.[16] At the federal level, 75 percent of the total increase in incarceration resulted from an increase in drug offenders serving federal sentences. Continued by the Clinton administration, this war has quintupled our prison population in 25 years, earning for the United States the dubious distinction of incarcerating the largest percentage of a country's population outside of Russia.[17] Indeed, we now incarcerate a higher percentage of black men, by a factor of six, than did the Botha government of South Africa, which was deliberately and legally racist. During the height of apartheid, 729 out of every 100,000 black men in South Africa were in prison; thanks primarily to the war on drugs, 4,617 out of every 100,000 black men in the United States are incarcerated.[18] The 458,000 people now imprisoned for drug offenses in the United States outnumber those incarcerated for all offenses in the entire European Union, whose total population exceeds ours by 100 million.

Although blacks represent 15 percent of all drug users, they make up 33 percent of those arrested for drug possession.[19] In New York State, blacks and Latinos constitute 25 percent of the state's residents, 83 percent of people in state prison, and 94 percent of people incarcerated for drug offenses.[20] From 1985 to 1995 drug offenders constituted 42 percent of the rise in the black state prison population. In Massachusetts, where Rashid, Jonathan, and Niko live, blacks were 39 times more likely to be incarcerated for a drug offense than whites.[21]

Racial targeting by police (racial profiling) works in conjunction with the drug war to criminalize black and Latino men.[22] Looking for drug couriers, state highway patrols use a profile, developed ostensibly at the behest of federal drug officials, that suggests blacks and Latinos are more likely to be carrying drugs.[23] The disproportionate stops of cars driven by blacks or Latinos as well as the street sweeps of pedestrians certainly helps account for some of the racial disparity in sentencing and conviction rates.[24] And because much of the drug activity in the black and Latino communities takes place in public, it is easier to target.

Open-air drug markets and the trafficking of drugs have wreaked havoc on communities of color, without question. Some link the higher incarceration rate of blacks and Latinos to higher rates of crime within those communities. Likewise, some suggest tougher law enforcement measures that disproportionately affect blacks may be necessary to maintain the security of law-abiding blacks and to improve the reputation of black people in the eyes of others, especially whites.[25] But in the context of drug interdiction, "these defenses of racial profiling do not withstand empirical and legal scrutiny," according to one commentator.[26] For example, in Illinois, the state police initiated Operation Valkyrie, an aggressive program to enforce traffic laws on interstates as part of drug interdiction efforts. While Latinos were less than 8 percent of the Illinois population and took fewer than 3 percent of the personal vehicle trips in the state, they constituted 30 percent of the motorists stopped as part of the enforcement of discretionary offenses such as failure to signal a lane change or driving one to four miles per hour over the speed limit. Those troopers working with Operation Valkyrie stopped Latinos two or three times more frequently than regular troopers patrolling the same highways and enforcing the same laws. In three counties in northern Illinois, Latinos made up 25 percent of the persons stopped by Valkyrie officers, compared with 8 percent of those stopped by non-Valkyrie officers.[27] In other words, the racial disparity in arrests—even if explained by greater use of drugs in public— is only a symptom of a larger problem.[28]

While being arrested is a critical initial step in one's interactions with the criminal justice system, at each subsequent stage of contact blacks and Latinos fare worse than whites. How else can one understand the fact that while blacks represent only 15 percent of all drug users and 33 percent of those arrested for drug possession, they make up 55 percent of those *convicted* for drug possession and 74 percent of those sentenced to prison for nonviolent drug offenses?[29] This lopsided impact of the war on drugs on black and brown communities introduces a new disciplinary force in the lives of people raced black. It has a real impact on the lives of those pulled over or stopped. But it also contributes to the interpellation effect on the entire community, including the psychological enslavement of an upper-middle-class fourteen-year-old black boy each day as he walks home from school. The disciplinary force of the state impacts the lives of black people much more severely than it impacts the lives of white people.[30] If a criminal suspect looks like a black person, then a black person looks like a suspect in the eyes of the state. Thus did Diallo's wallet become a gun.

A fourth explanation for the high rates of incarceration of black and brown young men is the economic boon that prison-building has brought to depressed rural areas. Prison construction has become—next to the military—our society's major public works program. And as prison construction has increased, money spent on higher education has declined, in direct proportion. Moreover, federal funds that used to go to economic or job training programs now go exclusively to building prisons. In the 1990s, corrections was the fastest growing budget category in states such as New York and California, while higher education experienced the greatest reduction.

Since 1982 New York State has opened 38 new prisons, all in rural, mainly white areas represented by Republican state senators. The state has added more than 46,000 prison beds, at a capital cost of $4.5 billion, not including debt service. Although two thirds of black and Latino prisoners come from New York City, 74 percent are housed in rural prisons at least three hours' drive from the city. At the beginning of 2000, 93 percent of New York State inmates were confined in Republican senate districts.[31] Not only do federal funds now go to communities that once shunned prisons, but political clout travels in that direction as well. Although they cannot vote, the bodies of these black and Latino inmates are counted in the redistricting process, which is based solely on census enumeration, to enhance the political power of these districts.

A fifth explanation is the need for a public enemy after the Cold War. Illegal drugs conveniently fit that role. President Nixon started this effort, calling drugs "public enemy number one." George Bush continued to escalate the rhetoric, declaring that drugs are "the greatest domestic threat facing our nation" and are turning our cities "into battlegrounds." By contrast, the use and abuse of alcohol and prescription drugs, which are legal, rarely result in incarceration. Yet drunken drivers kill about 22,000 people a year—more than the number of annual deaths from the entire web of underground drug trafficking and drug addiction.[32] Less than 9,000 people a year die in drug-related suicides or accidents; an additional 11,000 drug-related deaths are due to violence associated with the drug trade.[33] Over-all alcohol-related deaths, including alcoholism, by contrast, total 94,000 annually.

Most people (78 percent) arrested for drunk driving are white males, and they are generally treated as misdemeanants. They receive sentences involving fines, license suspensions, or community service. Few of these drivers are given jail time.[34] George W. Bush, President of the United States, was stopped for driving while intoxicated and, even after he was arrested, was fined but got no jail time. He may have received leniency simply because he was a son of privilege; or he may have received such treatment simply because he is a white man with family and community supports.

When drunk drivers do serve jail time, they are typically treated with a one- or two-day sentence for a first offense. For a second offense they may face a mandatory sentence of two to ten days. Compare that with a person arrested and convicted for *possession* of illegal drugs. Typical state penalties for a first-time offender are up to five years in prison and one to ten years for a second offense. Unlike drunken drivers—including those engaged in criminally negligent homicide—it is often the nonviolent drug offenders who are harshly punished, and this practice disproportionately affects blacks and Latinos.[35]

Even when using the *same* drugs, drugs users are treated unequally. In a private drug treatment facility such as the Betty Ford Center, most residents are white and well-to-do. In the public jails and prisons, most of those incarcerated for drug possession and other nonviolent drug offenses are black or Latino. Drug use for whites is medicalized; for blacks, it is criminalized. While we certainly do not dismiss the harm that drug abuse and drug addiction can do to addicts, to victims of crime, and to the communities where they live, the research we have seen suggests that, like alcohol, illegal drugs and drug dependency are more appropriately treated as a public health crisis than as a criminal justice crisis.

We do not, by any means, claim to have exhaustively researched the criminal justice implications of racial profiling, the war on drugs, or our nation's mass incarceration policies. What we do claim is that canary watchers should pay attention to these issues if they want to understand what is happening in the United States. The cost of these policies is being subsidized by all taxpayers; one immediate result is that government support for other social programs has become an increasingly scarce resource.

Books, Not Bars

The most hard-hit state budget priority has been higher education. In 1984 California spent more than 2.5 times as much money on higher education as it spent on prisons.[36] Eleven years later, California, which once had the premier system of higher education in the country, was spending more on prisons than on higher education. For the cost of imprisoning one person for one year, California could educate ten community college students, five California state university students, or two University of California students. But instead, California decided to pass a "three strikes and you're out" imprisonment policy.[37] The decision to incarcerate a third-strike burglar for forty years meant that the state was foregoing the opportunity to educate 200 community college students for two years.[38] A similar shift in budget priorities has affected many other states, including New York, Connecticut, Mississippi, and North Carolina.[39]

In 1996 Californians voted on Proposition 209 to ban affirmative action in public universities. For those who had been watching the canary, this was not surprising. They understood the significance of the fact that the issue of affirmative action was put on the ballot in California at the same time funding priorities were dramatically shifting. When higher education becomes a scarce resource, conflicts naturally arise about who "deserves" admission. Regrettably, those who are not admitted are encouraged to point fingers at the canary rather than to observe it for larger lessons. Instead of questioning why there are not enough high-quality schools to meet the statewide demand, they question the admission of people of color to the schools that exist.

They start by saying, "Look, black and Chicano students can't even do well on the SATs." Then they conclude that unqualified black and brown students are taking the place of more qualified white applicants. No one apparently looks at the real reason more working-class whites with lower SAT scores in California are denied access to elite public universities. Instead, they identify the problem as located solely within the most vulnerable population.

Thus, lost in the debate over affirmative action were two relevant and problematic policy developments. The first was the choice to invest in incarceration rather than education. The second was the decision, initially made in the 1950s, to distribute access to the highly selective and most prestigious state universities using high-stakes aptitude tests.[40] We have already discussed the dramatic rise in incarceration and its immediate effects on young blacks and Latinos. We now turn to the less dramatic but no less significant long-term consequences of using high-stakes aptitude tests for admission to public colleges and universities, whose mission is to serve the nation's democracy and economy by developing critical skills in citizens and future leaders.[41]

It turns out that conventional test-based admission policies both mask and sustain deep flaws in the way our society allocates opportunity and privilege to *all* students. The discrepancy between the standardized aptitude test scores of black and Chicano students against those of their white counterparts is actually a miner's canary warning that these tests are the wrong instrument to measure likelihood of success—not just the success of minority students but everyone's success. As explained in Chapter 3, standardized tests like the SATs correlate far better with socioeconomic status than with students' future performance in school or, more importantly, in life. They systematically disadvantage not only people of color but working-class whites as well. Like the Hispanic and black Texas professors who joined the coalition around the *Hopwood* case in 1996, those scholars watching the canary in California explored these deeper structural inequities in academic journals; but at that time very few canary watchers in California were given access to the popular media to explain what was happening.

The initial decision to employ aptitude tests was motivated, at least in part, by a desire to distribute educational opportunity more broadly throughout the society; it was thought that high test scores would allow students from working-class and middle-class backgrounds, who otherwise might not be noticed by highly selective institutions, to demonstrate their innate ability. Establishing a uniform measure of natural aptitude would be a great equalizer, an independent measure of individual ability that was not dependent upon the quality of schooling or the level of family resources. But what began as an effort to widen the net has, in practice, constricted it. These tests, as currently used, have become increasingly removed from their original and highly egalitarian animating vision. The relationship between SAT scores and the public mission of higher education has become quite tenuous, to say the least.

The first problem is the demonstrable and direct relationship between high scores and parental income. Reliance on the tests skews access in favor of the most privileged members of society. Among those black and Chicano students at UC Berkeley who did not do as well as others on the SAT, 36 percent of them came from households with incomes of less than $15,000 a year. On the other hand, 60 percent of the white students whose SAT scores got them into Berkeley came from households with incomes of more than $60,000 a year.[42] The correlation between high family income and high SAT scores is especially important because higher education has become a gateway to democratic citizenship. It is difficult to get a secure job without a college degree, and without a job, a person is not treated like a contributing member of this society.[43]

Second, students with lower scores who were admitted through affirmative action seemed nevertheless to go on to have productive careers, often surpassing their white colleagues whose entry test scores were higher.[44] Their lower scores on the entry level tests did not predict their eventual success as citizens, workers, or educated human beings. A study of the careers of three generations of students of color admitted to the University of Michigan Law School supports the argument that these tests have often failed to identify those who in fact have much to give in service of the legal profession and its larger goals.[45] The study shows that what the University of Michigan aimed for in lawyers and what it selected for in most law students were not the same things. According to the University of Michigan Law School mission statement, the school "looks for students

likely to become esteemed practitioners, leaders of the American bar, significant contributors to legal scholarship and/or selfless contributors to
the public interest." The school also expects that all those it admits will
"have a strong likelihood of succeeding in the practice of law and contributing in diverse ways to the well-being of others."[46] Yet this study found
that the criteria the Law School has routinely employed to admit most of
its applicants have little if any predictive value for success at achieving
these goals. The authors could not even find a relationship between admission indices and income as an attorney, though they did find a correlation between high admission indices and career *dissatisfaction.*

Third, the study shows that over-reliance on test scores in admissions
policies also often rewarded people who gave little back to society.[47] The
Michigan researchers found a negative correlation between high admission test scores and community service after graduation.[48] In other words,
those with high index scores—those deemed by conventional measures
the most "qualified"—nevertheless tended to contribute less to society
in the long run than those with lower scores.[49] While years since graduation is the most important factor in a law graduate's likelihood of doing
pro bono work, serving on community boards, or providing leadership
more generally, minority status is the most important of the other relevant variables.

Black and Latino graduates used the opportunity offered by their education to provide service to under-represented segments of the population
and to supply community leadership more generally at higher rates than
their white counterparts. Among those Michigan graduates who entered
the private practice of law, "minority alumni tend to do more pro bono
work, sit on the boards of more community organizations and do more
mentoring of younger attorneys than white alumni."[50] Alumni of color
also provided, on average, considerably more service to clients of color
than do white alumni; this was in part because all Michigan alumni, including white alumni, were disproportionately likely to serve clients of the
same race. If fewer blacks and Latinos graduate from law school, legal services to the black and Latino communities are likely to decrease significantly.

When the lens is widened to include performance after graduation, graduates of color succeed in ways that elude many of their white counterparts. Black and Latino graduates also realize the expectations of the admissions committee that chose them as students, in part because the committee actually looked at what they had accomplished in the multiple domains of their life prior to admission.[51] These candidates were evaluated based on criteria such as leadership ability, community service, motivation (as evidenced in their ability to overcome obstacles), and unusual evidence of accomplishment that suggested the ability to follow through on goals. Evidently, those who were leaders in their community before law school also did more relevant community and public service after they graduated.[52]

Harvard University also sponsored a study of three different classes of undergraduate alumni over a thirty-year period to learn what correlates with success. Similar to Michigan's criteria, the researchers measured success as financial satisfaction, career satisfaction, and contribution to the community. Two things correlated with success in these three categories: low SAT scores and a blue-collar background. Apparently, high SAT scores are not the critical ingredient for measuring long-term achievement. What matters is one's ambition, drive, and opportunity to succeed. Other variables that correlate with success, such as intense involvement in extracurricular activities, willingness to ask for help, the tendency to reflect on one's work and revise it, and the ability to prioritize and juggle tasks, are not measured by the SAT.[53]

Finally, as Richard Atkinson, President of the University of California, began to realize, the emphasis on test performance has distorted educational practices in junior and senior high school. Many teachers now emphasize test-taking techniques rather than the skills of critical inquiry and reflection that are more generally associated with the qualities valued in an educated person and citizen. For example, Atkinson became skeptical of SAT testing after he realized that test preparation for the SAT begins in sixth or seventh grade in affluent school systems. He observed 12-year-olds being grilled on analogies. For example: "Melodian is to organist as (choose one) reveille is to bugler, solo is to accompanist, crescendo is to pianist, anthem is to choir master, kettle drum is to timpanist."[54] Lani Guinier presented that analogy to Professor Lino Graglia of the University of Texas Law School, who was defending the SATs, and he said, "Are you asking me if that question is on the SAT?" Guinier said, "No. We're telling you it's on the SAT and we want to know the answer." Graglia didn't know the answer. But so what? Unless, perhaps, a high school senior is planning to be a music educator, why does he or she need to be able to answer this question?

Admissions officers and others nevertheless defend these tests by saying that they are efficient, and in any event they are designed only to predict successful first-year performance in college or, for the LSAT or GRE, first year grades in graduate school. Yet the average correlation between SAT scores and first-year college grades is about 30 percent.[55] Correlation simply means some relationship. It does not mean that SAT scores actually predict first-year college grades 30 percent of the time. In a study examining the LSATs and first-year grades of all students at the University of Pennsylvania Law School, the LSAT predicted only 14 percent of the variance in first year law school grades, and a few of the students with perfect LSAT scores ended up with some of the lowest course grades in the first-year class.[56]

As did the black and Hispanic activists in Texas, Atkinson and others in California eventually began to question what is represented by performance on a single paper-and-pencil high-stakes test, in which a large part of what is measured is quick strategic guessing. For Atkinson, aptitude testing of this kind does not represent excellence. For other researchers, such aptitude testing, especially given the extensive test-preparation industry that is mobilized by high-income parents to prepare their children to improve their test scores, in fact simply represents wealth.[57] This may explain why standardized aptitude tests correlate far better with parental wealth than with future academic success.

Some point out that these tests may select for people who are good only at taking tests and lack other social skills that make people effective lawyers or good citizens. Those who do well on tests and exams may have qualities of mind and habits of work that ultimately deny them a "full" life (for example, they may have an ability to tune out all other distractions, including family and friends). Even if the tests do correlate modestly with college or law school grades, the Michigan study found that students who get high grades in law school do less community service after they graduate, perhaps because they prioritize grades or their jobs over everything else.[58] Equally damaging, the tests often have a deleterious effect on those who do not score well. These students may internalize their performance as a lack of ability when it reflects a multitude of other variables, including what Claude Steele calls "stereotype threat."[59]

These hypotheses are especially significant in light of the original meaning of the term "meritocracy." In 1958 the British sociologist Michael Young coined this term to satirize the rise of a new elite that valorized its own mental aptitude. According to Young, a meritocracy is a system of rules put in place by those with power, which leaves existing distributions of privilege intact while convincing both the winners and the losers that they deserve their lot in life.[60] That the "winners" of a test-centered meritocracy seem to take their privileged position for granted may explain why those who should succeed according to conventional predictors do not make more effort to do so.[61] It may also explain why the whole-person, particularized selection criteria used to admit many candidates of color actually correlate with the career paths and service attributes of minority graduates.[62]

Young's insight—that those who succeed in a self-described meritocracy begin to take their success for granted—deserves further investigation. It may be, for example, that a test-centered approach socializes successful students to believe they have "earned" their success and have no obligation to give back. The skew toward personal entitlement and away from public service is arguably related to the way the tests "select in" those who are highly competitive within the established rules of the game, which include a narrow, individualistic version of achievement. Simultaneously, the tests "select out" those who need more time to reflect, who see nuances even in standard answers, who are more likely to seek imaginative solutions to complex problems, or who seek to pursue their ideals rather than advance their material interests.

Timed testing using questions for which there is ostensibly only one right answer may also train successful candidates not to question authority, not to look for innovative ways to solve problems, not to do sustained research or to engage in team efforts at brainstorming, but instead to try to answer questions quickly and in ways that anticipate the desires or predilections of those asking the questions. The tests alone, however, are not the problem. It is the message conveyed by the exaggerated claim that test performance equates with "merit." Students quickly learn that individual achievement within narrow parameters is more valuable than leadership, public service, or self-sacrifice for the larger good.

Canary watchers might find that alternative admission approaches, including weighted lotteries, the Texas 10 Percent Plan, or whole-person portfolio assessments, should be tried as experiments to help us rethink how these schools admit *everyone*.[63] It would be useful to consider alternative indices that reconnect qualifications at the admission stage with competence after graduation or with values that the school and others proclaim as measures of long-term success. Rather than attacking the canary, we should learn from it in order to reconnect a school's mission with its admissions criteria for *all* incoming students.

From Canary Watching to Political Race

Even if public universities were to learn from the long-term success of affirmative action to relink their admissions practices to their democratic mission, there is still a larger question that looms. Why is higher education such a scarce resource that it has to be meted out by choosing among eager candidates, all of whom could be trained to do the work? The answer to this question, at least partially, gets us back to the federal government's war on drugs.[64]

For every person jailed in the prosecution of the drug war, some person is being denied educational, health, or other public resources. For all poor people, social resources are being diverted from those institutions that ameliorate the harsh impacts of the private economy. But middle-class people are also losing out on access to educational resources they value. Between 1984 and 1994 California built 16 new prisons; during the same decade, the state built only one new campus of the California State University System. The Department of Corrections increased its personnel by 25,864 while higher education personnel dropped by 8,082. In California, prison guards have become a more powerful political constituency than teachers. This is borne out by an analysis of recent spending on schools compared with prisons. In 1995 a first-year college professor in California made $41,000 a year. A prison guard made $51,000 a year.[65]

The ancillary costs of this war go beyond the specific and isolated effects on the people caught up in it. The market forces set in motion by the commitment to this internal war produce a demand for raw materials to feed the incarceration industry. Extensive new prison systems need a steady supply of prisoners. In Texas, the Department of Corrections has resorted to importing prisoners, because the jail-building enterprise (especially those that are privately run but publicly funded) continues to produce more beds than the state can fill with its internal prosecutions alone. Prisoners have become "captive consumers" (in the words of the criminologist Nils Christie), "prized for the services they require, the money they attract and the jobs they create."[66] Needless to say, these developments have created enormous pressure to continue high incarceration rates, an objective largely accomplished through the disproportionate imprisonment of black and Latino drug offenders.

What might happen if the metaphor of the miner's canary in conjunction with the concept of political race were used to mobilize local constituencies around this issue of mass incarceration? In the first step of political race, the miner's canary metaphor would highlight the racial nature of the way that criminal behavior is defined. It might locate the discourse of drugs within the discourse of race, in the same way that in Chapter 2 we located the discourse of poverty and welfare within the discourse of race. It would show how the war on drugs treats blacks and Latinos more harshly than whites arrested for the same behavior.

Crime-plagued communities might seem an unlikely place to mobilize against the use of prison as an instrument of social control. After all, these communities seek measures that hold the promise of safer streets. Yet these same residents are likely to applaud alternatives, such as drug treatment, because they recognize that "the criminal justice system is a repository for many unaddressed social problems," including poverty, addiction, and mental illness.[67] Mary Katzenstein, a professor at Cornell University, reported that in her large lecture course on prisons the first four rows of the hall were filled almost entirely with black and Latina women, each of whom knew someone caught up in the vortex of the drug war. She predicted that these women would lead a movement to fight the use of the criminal justice system to control and incapacitate black and brown men.[68]

On the other hand, unless the issue of drug enforcement is simultaneously put into a larger context, its racial dimension will overshadow all else. Therefore, in the second step of political race, local activists of color would move from focusing on the racialized character of the war on drugs to formulating a more expansive interpretation. They would show that although the war on drugs has a real impact on the lives of convicted offenders, a disproportionate number of whom are black and Latino, it also uses up social wealth that could be more effectively spent in other ways. Activists could show that this policy is arbitrary for those swept up in the criminal justice system, and it is not a cost-effective use of law-abiding taxpayers' dollars. For example, 50 percent of those sent to prison in Brooklyn, New York, for drug crimes were re-arrested after three years, while the recidivism rate of those who entered a treatment program was only 23 percent during the same time period.[69] The benefits of treating drug use as a public health rather than a criminal justice problem are high both to the drug offender and to the taxpayer. Harm reduction and treatment diversion programs could save millions of dollars in taxpayer money.[70] According to Anne Swern, it costs $69,500 a year to house an inmate with a drug habit on Riker's Island, New York City's largest jail. It costs $82,000 a year to hold a criminal in New York City before his trial and then imprison him in an upstate cell. It is much more cost-effective to treat a person for his drug problem than to imprison him; even in New York State—which has the highest such costs—residential drug treatment at $21,000 a year is still one-fourth the cost of prison.[71] The estimated annual cost to society of incarcerating drug offenders is $6.1 billion.[72]

Thus, in this second step of political race, activists would move beyond the diagnostic tool of canary watching to organize black and brown communities around the issue of over-incarceration, and would do so in ways that invited new allies from outside these communities. The critical move is to expose the moral peril as well as the inefficiencies of this dynamic to the body politic generally. The use of prisons to target and incapacitate specific populations within the black and brown community is undoubtedly a moral issue. But opposition to the prison-building industry and the war on drugs could also be advanced in a way that makes the convergence of interests between black and brown communities and rural or poor whites obvious. The narrow ideology of doing only for one's own group could be challenged by focusing, as did the Multi-Cultural Community Association in the Alhambra School District, on short-term tactical alliances that can identify long-term strategic goals for systemic and institutional change. These activists near Los Angeles, as well as those in Texas who crafted the Texas 10 Percent Plan, built their coalition around efforts to identify the structural foundations of inter-ethnic conflict.[73]

Political race would allow these activists to point out, first, that the animosity fueling Proposition 209 (which opposed affirmative action in admissions) actually arose, in part, because California was in that year beginning to spend more money building prisons than colleges. They could show that for every black person in a state college, five black people were in prison. For every one Hispanic male in a four-year state college, three were in prison. For every one black male who graduated from college, 100 black males were arrested.[74] And the costs of incarceration were three to six times the cost of educating the same person. It is no wonder people were rebelling at the pinch in finding a place for their children in good, affordable public colleges.[75]

Activists could next point out that spending for prisons not only burdens state and federal budgets, but it does not in fact provide the economic boon to rural areas its promoters promise. In Delano, California, a city of 35,000, residents had lobbied over a decade ago for construction of nearby North Kern State Prison, hoping it would lower the town's 26 percent unemployment rate. Delano, also known as the birthplace of the United Farm Workers, had staked its hopes on the promise of an increase in local businesses and jobs. But the unemployment rate today is the same as it was in 1990 and the county is now paying jobless residents to leave town.[76] Although a third of the 23 new prisons built in California since 1980 are in the Central Valley where Delano is located, the unemployment rate in the valley remains five times the state average. Only 7 to 9 percent of prison jobs go to local residents, and these are the low-paying service jobs. Because of this, the attitude in the town toward the prospect of building still another prison is now mixed. According to Napoleon Madrid, Mayor of Delano, of the 1,600 jobs projected for the new prison, the Department of Corrections estimated only 72 would go to the residents of Delano. Other rural communities are discovering reasons not to support new prison construction. Aware that prisons discourage more attractive forms of investment while triggering damaging environmental consequences, a group of Wayne County, Pennsylvania, rural residents joined with urban dwellers from across the country to protest the construction of a new federal prison in their community.[77]

An important aspect of this second step in political race includes moving beyond a simple monetary analysis of costs and benefits. Activists could demonstrate that the costs of the war on drugs accrue not just to the black and brown community in the form of lost wages and lost opportunities, nor just to the white community in the form of budgetary shifts. There is also a cost in terms of lost civil liberties and the expansion of police intrusions into citizens' daily lives. The policy agenda of the federal government, going back to the Reagan administration, to shift resources away from the federal government while simultaneously reducing privacy rights threatens to infringe on the physical mobility of more than racial minorities.

Gail Atwater, a white woman in Texas, discovered just how aggressive law enforcement has become when the U.S. Supreme Court upheld the constitutionality of her arrest *and* incarceration for failing to make her children wear seat belts. The maximum fine for this infraction is $50. As Emily Whitfield, a spokeswoman for the New York office of the ACLU, said, "Now we have a situation where the government, even if they can't put you in jail after you're convicted, can put you in jail before you're tried." Justice David H. Souter, writing for the Court majority, concluded that although Ms. Atwater had been subjected to "gratuitous humiliations" and "pointless indignity," what happened to her did not violate the Fourth Amendment.[78]

What exactly *did* happen to her? Ms. Atwater, a middle-class self-described soccer mom who had just picked up her two young children at practice, was driving her pickup truck 15 miles per hour on the streets near her home. She and her children were looking for a rubber vampire bat that had been attached to the truck's window by a suction cup. She had allowed her children to unbuckle their seatbelts to help her look out the window for the lost toy. When an officer came along and ordered her out of her car, she expected to get a ticket, but instead the officer informed her that she was under arrest. When her children became upset, the officer refused to let her take them to a neighbor's house and threatened to take them into custody as well. Fortunately, a neighbor came along in time to take the children. Ms. Atwater was jailed, fingerprinted, required to post bond, and charged a $150 fine.

About the same time that the Supreme Court upheld the officer's right to subject Gail Atwater to "gratuitous humiliations," another white woman and her child were killed by CIA contract employees when their small plane—suspected of transporting drugs—was gunned down in Peru.[79] Peru's Air Force issued a statement confirming that the missionaries' plane was shot down after it was detected at 10:05 a.m. local time by "an airspace surveillance and control system" run jointly by Peru and the United States.[80] No drugs were found.

Within the same month, the national press reported that California forcibly tried to remove a white man from his home in Oregon to serve the remaining portion of a sentence in California for a crime he had committed fifty years earlier. The man, a seventy-year-old father of five children who was suffering from cancer and heart disease, was a model citizen in Oregon, by all accounts.[81] "Bob's been the rock of so many people's lives here," said Tammy Ferguson, his ex-wife's sister. "If there were ever a man truly devoted to being rehabilitated, it's Bob Burns." Yet California demanded he pay them the time he owes for driving the get-away car in a robbery in which one of his accomplices fired a gun and killed a young state patrolman.

We might be inclined to see each of these three incidents as a matter of local discretion or simply aberrational. The White House specifically called the shooting in Peru of the Baptist missionary as she held her six-month-old daughter on her lap "an isolated incident."[82] Justice Souter concluded that full custodial arrests for trivial offenses did not violate the constitution because, he said, "there simply is no evidence of widespread

abuse of minor-offense arrest authority."[83] But the experiences of our canaries—black and Latino young men—have taught us otherwise. By linking back to their experience, we begin to see that the language of the war
on drugs, the target of its violence, and the punitive and retributive atmosphere it creates are not limited to young men of color. They may be its
shock troops, but they are not the only ones in the line of fire. The Bill of
Rights itself, as well as the right to vote, is at stake.[84] Bob Burns has never
been accused of using or selling illegal drugs, but the punitive approach to
the way he might spend his remaining years has certainly been reinforced
by the drug war's zero-tolerance policies. And when a disproportionate
number of blacks and Latinos, even after discharging their debt to society
and completing their prison terms, are nevertheless permanently disenfranchised as a result of the war on drugs, their inability to vote adversely
affects Democrats more generally, and not just black Democrats.[85]

The war on drugs not only criminalizes black and brown drug users
but has begun to have a spillover effect on working-class whites as well. To
take one example the Bush administration has begun enforcing a "dual"
sentence for drug offenders, including those convicted merely of drug
possession. Poor and working-class students who are able to attend college only through financial aid will now become ineligible for assistance if
they are convicted of drug possession. "I was amazed," said a student from
Cincinnati when he discovered he was no longer eligible for low-interest
federal college loans and grants. "It's like two penalties for one crime."[86]
The story Luttwak told contrasting young men at gas stations in the
United States and Japan becomes even more compelling in this context.
The war metaphors in our drug policy sanction a punitive approach that
interferes with efforts at treatment as well as rehabilitation through education. And the penalties exacerbate the vulnerability of poor students
generally—disproportionately those who are black and Latino but not exclusively so.

To move beyond critique to action, political race requires progressives
to take a third step. Their strategies would not be just to destroy the legislative will to build new prisons. Like Jennifer Gordon's Workplace Project,
they would instead seek to involve those directly affected in helping to formulate different legislative priorities. Activists would have to imagine ex-

periments in political deliberation and organization that are engaging for, and transformative of, both the individual and the group. They might look at Boal's theater of the oppressed or other innovative forms of political and popular education to enable rural whites to begin to develop the collective consciousness that is more often found in communities of color. Like Coalition L.A., they might invite each community to run candidates from the community as part of a commitment to a shared program rather than a single-election victory. Those trying to organize unions to support a social movement against mass incarceration would tie the issue to larger struggles and use engaging forms of internal democracy that encourage participation among individuals who are often less comfortable within traditional arenas of power. Like the Latino organizers in Seattle who held family fiestas at which issues of immigration policy were linked to the need to build a union, they would also use cultural material and familiar rituals to inspire confidence in their goals. They would experiment with organizational forms that enable workers and union leaders to practice democracy together, building on the moral energy participants bring to the task of solving the problems at hand.

Such strategies would seek to invite greater participation by constituencies of color, by those who are functionally black as well as by those who share the goals of the political race project. To encourage more interaction, it would sometimes be necessary to allow separate meetings in which each group worked through its own internal issues before rejoining the larger community. This approach was used successfully in the Alhambra Coalition that brought together the Asian and Latino communities around the issue of disproportionate school suspensions of Latino youth. Within this coalition, rotating and accountable leadership enabled interactive and co-active participation. Or like Archon Fung's street-level democracy described in Chapter 3, when voting or other heavy-handed forms of decision-making were necessary, participants would resist up/ down and binary ways of framing issues.[87] Even when yes/no votes ultimately are adopted, it is important to reassure participants who lose that decisions can be revisited in light of new information.

Major reform projects could grow out of intermediate free spaces that encourage meaningful participation of those who are often discouraged or excluded by traditional political institutions. We have seen such spaces created by transgressive singing of spirituals in a courtroom, by the nonviolent civil disobedience of ministers who assume leadership of a labor-management dispute, and by novel dramatic forums that enable legislative constituencies of quite ordinary people to create and enact "laws." Within these alternative theaters of power, people's shared commitments dominate and reconfigure their relationships.

We imagine that people of color, like the black workers in the K-Mart union who first invited Reverend Johnson and the Pulpit Forum into their organizing effort, will develop and occupy such free spaces early on. They may gain confidence to resist by gathering first in the black church. But they may eventually be joined by whites whose solidarity is built perhaps on their union affiliation or membership in the larger community and not on their race or religious culture. Or they might be inspired by white college students who occupy a college administration building, in conjunction with students of color, to spark the moral conscience of a university community—who speak out on behalf of the lowest paid workers, and then vacuum up when they leave.[88] Or they might find inspiration in the "social sculpture" of students like Andrew Epstein, a 22-year-old Amherst College student who convinced the college administration to place signs for one day on all coffee urns signaling that the sale and distribution of caffeine on campus would no longer be permitted. This was part of his final project for an art class, to draw attention to what he regards as the hypocrisy of drug laws. A painting is easily ignored, he said, but remove part of a person's daily routine and notice will be taken.[89]

We are intrigued by models of community building that seem to excite sustained involvement by people for whom the more common rituals of public life have lost their meaning. We believe that new social movements may need to be more playful, experimental, and even theatrical in order to garner the active and continuing support of those most likely to take the risk of social change. It is in this experimental space that alliances once thought impossible become conceivable, or even probable.

For instance, a new activism emerging in communities of color involves young people who recognize that the current boom in prison building is connected to cuts in social spending.[90] Van Jones, director of the Ella

Baker Center for Human Rights, describes "the first hip-hop generation sit-in," when 175 young people organized by the Third Eye Movement were arrested at the San Francisco Hilton as part of a campaign against Proposition 21, which lowered the age when children can be tried as adults to fourteen.[91] Another organization, formerly known as the Overseas Development Network and now named JustAct: Youth Action for Global Justice, hired "working class youth of color who were very engaged in survival struggles in their communities." JustAct now has twin concerns: organizing both global youth and the more than 70 percent of American young people who do not attend four-year colleges. The infusion of new leadership by people of color resulted in a metamorphosis that affected more than the organization name. By linking local and global struggles, they witnessed a convergence between the energy of young people of color and the vocabulary of those concerned about the global corporate agenda.[92]

The Role of Allies

We use the term political race to describe several kinds of functionally black allies. We include those whose material interests are similar, such as the poor white high school kids in rural Texas who, because of the class bias of the state's testocracy, had no access to the flagship public universities. The term race in this sense can be used to describe the material interests of people who are "black" in many more senses than they realize. We also include those whose political sympathies cause them to identify with the struggles of racialized groups regardless of whether they fall within the same diagnostic category. In this way, political race connotes those who have made a concrete choice to engage in transformative political struggle. Sometimes both elements are present. For this reason we emphasize the surprising role of the white workers at the K-Mart plant, who acted in response to a lawsuit that named only the black workers and ministers as trespassers. These white workers agreed to call a press conference, demanding to know why "they" had not been sued by K-Mart. After all, they were part of this struggle, too.

But not all efforts by whites to support or join movements initiated by people of color constitute political race. Let us return for a moment to the white students at Niko's former private school. We earlier mentioned that white boys among Niko's classmates had a 4 percent chance of being jailed or imprisoned during their lifetimes, compared with a 30 percent chance for their black male counterparts. These statistics suddenly assumed real-time proportions in February 2001 when a beloved math teacher was stopped by police twice within a two-week period. Rob Howard, Jr., who is black, had taught Niko and his classmates in sixth and seventh grade. In November 2000 he began teaching at Young Achievers, a public school in Jamaica Plain, a racially mixed neighborhood in Boston. One day as Howard approached the Young Achievers school, a white policeman, who was searching for a peeping Tom, stopped him and demanded to see identification. Two weeks later, the same police officer was on the prowl for an armed robbery suspect. Again, he stopped and patted down Rob Howard, just steps from the same red-brick school. At this point, Howard's students at Young Achievers wanted to take action. "I thought it was wrong when they did it the first time because they didn't really know Mr. Howard," Joseph Brazzo, a seventh grader at the Boston public school with an 83 percent nonwhite student body, said. "But to do it the second time when they had already checked him was also wrong."[93]

The Young Achievers students, teachers, and staff planned to march around their school's neighborhood and to launch a letter-writing campaign—activities designed to draw attention to their view that Howard was being harassed for "walking while black." Outrage over the incidents prompted intense discussions at all grade levels about racism and sparked the plan to walk around the school's neighborhood to rally for "safe spaces." "What we want is children to understand what happened and develop the skills needed to react in ways that are constructive for them," Young Achievers principal Virginia Chalmers said. "It's not just seeing something. It's not just feeling something. It's doing something about it."

A *Boston Globe* article about the planned march alerted several parents and students at Niko's private school. One parent called Chalmers to ask if the private school kids could join the rally; she was told that their support was welcome. About thirteen kids from the private school and several parents showed up the next day for the rally. A large contingent of the private school students arrived late to the assembly, carrying their own posters.

They joined the march as students headed out and found themselves at the front of the line. Niko also attended the rally, but because he went with another black family and arrived on time, he was able to blend into the march without much fanfare. The cameras and news reporters focused on the group leading the procession—mostly white private schools kids and their parents. The private school students reportedly told the media that they were marching because "Rob is our teacher."

Some might see this as political race in action. The white privileged students were supporting black people's rights to walk freely down the street. Also it was great, these observers might note, to have the media showcase white people and privileged private school students supporting black people and fighting racial profiling. But many who lived in Jamaica Plain and who taught at the Young Achievers school saw it differently. They did not trust the private school kids, who departed as quickly as they had arrived, while the predominantly black and brown Young Achievers were left to confront the issue of racial profiling every day on the streets of their city. The private school kids did not function as respectful visitors, in the view of the Young Achievers, and should have been more careful to march with the community rather than in front of it. They fretted that the media had manipulated its coverage to showcase the private school kids and to ignore the students who had worked all week to prepare for the rally.

At Niko's school the next day, a black teacher and administrator tried to bring awareness of the danger of media manipulation to the attention of all the kids at the school. The teacher walked into the assembly and read aloud a strongly worded and quite negative letter written in anger by a third party who also worked at the private school, lived in the Jamaica Plain neighborhood, and was embarrassed by the positioning of the private school kids. The letter said the private school kids "were not marching for Rob. They were marching for themselves. They were not marching with the Young Achievers community but they were marching alone and for their own glory. They took away the moment that belonged to the community of Young Achievers."

After reading the letter, and warning the private school children that they had put their own good deeds in jeopardy because they allowed themselves to be used by the media, the black teacher left the room. She did not stay to answer questions or to deepen the critique in any way. The private school kids were offended both by the letter and the manner in which it was presented to them. The tone of the letter and the teacher's failure to stay to discuss its message left the private school kids dispirited. One white student who did not attend the rally but who was present when the letter was read circulated an email on behalf of his classmates, defending their participation in the march. "I personally did a report at the end of last year about police brutality and racial profiling, and care very much about the issues expressed at the march . . . About the fact that Rob is, or was, our teacher, I know this statement has an imbedded possessive meaning. I suppose that it would be more proper to say Rob once taught us, or Rob is a friend of ours, but I do not consider the difference profound, and I do not believe that this opinion should be counted against me. In sixth grade, Rob was my excellent teacher and he is still my good friend. Rob has been a very influential person to me, and I know he has been much more influential to some of my peers. I have never thought of him as less than a person, and I have certainly never, to my knowledge, used him."

When the private school parents heard from their confused children, they vehemently defended the eighth graders. These young people should not be held responsible if the media failed to cover fairly the larger role played by teachers and students at the Young Achievers School; while a small private school contingent may have hogged the spotlight, those were unfortunate consequences that they neither chose nor intended. That their kids took time from school to attend the rally and make a public statement of support was the more important message, and it was in danger of being lost in the venting being done at their expense. For many, this was the first public protest they had attended. To draw negative conclusions from such a formative moment would likely discourage impressionable young adolescents from protest activity in support of worthy causes in the future. Their kids now just felt "powerless and discouraged."

In the midst of all the hand-wringing about the damage being done to innocent children, a white parent named Carlene emerged to say that she, too, had been doing a lot of hand-wringing. But Carlene's focus was on watching the canary. She sent the following email:

Dear 8th Grade Parents,

For the past few days, I have been doing a lot of hard thinking and talking about the march at Young Achievers. In doing this work around issues of race, I have learned that things are rarely "either/or" but often "both/and." I know that our intentions, to support Rob and the students at Young Achievers in their protest against racial profiling, came from a place of true commitment and caring.

Another thing I have learned, however, is that intentions and outcome sometimes don't match, and that those who are "targeted"—be it because of race, gender, sexual orientation—often focus on the outcome, while those who are not "targeted" (i.e., white, male, straight) focus on their own intentions. I know that I have used the phrase, "But I didn't mean to . . . " more often than I care to admit when I have screwed up.

And I screwed up . . . again. As a friend of mine said, "I was quite disappointed when I heard (and then saw on the news) that [the private school] contingent was at the front of the line. It was a throw back to what White people did in the civil rights movement. People at Young Achievers appreciated your coming, but felt that it was inappropriate to get in front of the YA community who worked on this for a week. I felt disappointed that people didn't do whatever it took to let this be a moment for the YA community with [private school] support." I know that I should have thought about this more carefully at the time.

But all the wishing that I would have, should have, could have thought about all this at the time doesn't change the outcome . . . I didn't. I don't want to mire myself in guilt and blame, but I am accountable and need to take responsibility for my thoughtlessness. And when you are white, as I am, thoughtlessness has far-reaching implications. As my friend says, many of the children at YA "have experienced this themselves or have had family members treated as Rob was. The opportunity to stand up was truly significant for them. I believe that all of this should have been considered by the parents. It would have been an opportunity for children to learn how to support without taking center stage."

This will still be an opportunity for my child to learn. I deeply regret, however, it will come at the expense of/on the backs of the children at

YA. My son and I will talk about the chant that the YA students taught us, "We have the power. You have the power. I have the power." What does this mean if you are a person of color? How does it change, even if used in support, if you are a white person? What is support without taking center stage? What will we think of the next time, including how the media plays into the scenario? It would be easy, because of our family's privilege as whites, to say this is too hard and drop out. Why is it critical to our lives to keep acting and learning?

One thing that I am scared of is that the "hardness" of this learning will diminish my son's willingness to go public with his support of social justice—whether it be in conversations with peers who don't agree with him or in public demonstrations of activism. Although my son has been concerned with the issue of racial profiling and has friends that have experienced it, he was reluctant to join the march since he had never been involved in a public display of activism and he didn't know what to expect. I, on the other hand, wanted him to experience what it felt like to be part of the power of group commitment. In order for him to learn from this and be willing to go forward, I need to help both of us to see and act on the lessons learned while still celebrating our intentions and the joy of the commitment and action. I am going to share this email with him and continue talking.

Although I was, at first, angry at [the black administrator] for reading the letter and then leaving without discussion, I have found it useful to "sit with the feelings" and "live with the discomfort." I have probably done more self examination and talking with my own son and other parents than I might have done otherwise. My heart is saddened . . . and I need to, as a friend says, "keep on keepin' on." I think we need to respond to YA in some way and I look forward to us learning together how to be better allies. Thanks for learning with me.

Carlene wanted her son to "experience what it felt like to be part of the power of group commitment." But she also wanted him to understand that chanting "We have the power" means something different to young students of color who do not ordinarily feel entitled to say those words and mean them. Not only will some of them be stopped by the police, but many, like Jonathan and Rashid, have already been stopped by the police, questioned, even arrested, and all of them know someone in their family who has been in a situation similar to Rob Howard's. These kids are often criticized or even threatened when they disagree with the powers that be. The magnitude of the challenge facing the Young Achievers included the need to learn how to confront wrongdoing by those in authority and to speak in their own collective voice, especially when criticized or threatened. For the private school kids, the rally served an entirely different purpose. It was a one-time effort to support a beloved teacher.

Subsequently, Carlene and a few others convened with the eighth graders to discuss what had happened. Many of the eighth graders at the private school had stood up for their beliefs for the first time at the Young Achievers rally. They were at various stages of finding their own voices. But some eighth graders spoke with the voice of experience. A black girl, Jamila, eloquently pleaded for the private school parents and kids not to make activism a once-in-a-lifetime event. Please, she said with heartfelt emotion, do not let your concern with racial profiling become a "one-act play" simply because this time you happened to know the subject of the incident. Although they engaged with race in their choice of topics to study or write about in school, they did not explicitly interrogate the way their own actions helped perpetuate hierarchies of power in the wider society.

Jamila's message was both simple and complex. More people need to be vigilant and watch the canary. But observation and analysis alone are not enough. Sustained actions should follow. Our fates are bound up with the fate of the canary. Without a sense of linked fate, allies or coalition partners are merely temporary associates who function on a parallel track and who can opt to leave at any moment. The goal of marches against racial profiling should not simply be to liberate people like Rob Howard so he can escape the stigma of externally imposed and state-enforced stereotypes. The ultimate goal has to include as well a desire to liberate *everyone* who is ensnared within hierarchies of power that ostensibly name them as individuals yet trap them within fixed social locations.

That goal will be realized only when more privileged whites, as well as middle- and upper-class people of color, join their fate with those less fortunate and make personal sacrifices in the short-run to struggle together for larger social justice ideals. Like the white workers at K-Mart, they will need to transform their own understanding of power and their relation-ship to it. Only by embracing racial solidarity and understanding that they, too, were, in fact, functionally black could those white workers em-brace labor solidarity. To be respectful allies whose support is not only needed but welcome over time, white progressives may have to learn the same lesson—that through the agency of political race, they need to yoke their fate to those with a long history of struggling for justice, a struggle lived in the exigencies of daily life and not just in the risks taken on a sin-gle day of activism. Resistance, in Jamila's words, cannot be a "one-act play." It eventually needs to become a drama of transformation, as the participants struggle to envision more democratic forms of relationships and of power itself.

Jamila's articulate plea moved a few parents to action. In response, one parent, Sherry, wrote an email to the whole class that began, "Thank you, Jamila," for forcing parents and kids to confront the fact that it was "easy to attend a rally in support of someone I knew," or to protest "a stranger being harassed by the police in my own town." But "it's not enough to wait until events occur where our presence makes sense, and to do nothing in between." The parent's email included a link to the American Civil Lib-erties Union web site as a place to begin to get involved.

Eventually Carlene, whose canary-watching moved her to convene the subsequent meeting, or Sherry, who was moved "to action" by Jamila's heartfelt words, may join the political race project. Shared ethnicity is not a precondition for this project, but in its absence these white parents will need to make concerted and ongoing efforts to build the trust and create the context for solidarity that is necessary for the project to be effective and sustainable. They can write letters, join rallies, and take action to af-fect public policy. But they also need to find communities of color who are mobilizing and to build sustained relationships with those communi-ties to support their local efforts.[94] Similarly, middle- or upper-class peo-ple of color should support indigenous leadership of those who are poor or working-class within their communities. All those who enjoy racial or class or gender privilege should conscientiously work to develop the lead-ership of those who do not. Unless allies challenge their own embedded privilege, they face the real danger of reproducing the very hierarchies of power they seek to topple.

This does not mean there is no role for white leadership in political race. Some examples that we have cited with sympathy included whites in key leadership roles. The UFW included in its inner circle several white ministers and white community organizers. Their participation was key to the success of the organizing effort because they had access to different leadership skills, technical resources, and networks of support. Jennifer Gordon, formerly the executive director of the Workplace Project, is a highly educated white woman. But both the Workplace Project and the UFW are examples of organizations that situated themselves within a community of color. They built on the counter-intuitive "epistemic privilege" of the canary and the solidarity or sense of linked fate that perspective often breeds. Situating a political race project within a community of color does not mean that every person of color has the capacity to do his or her own analysis but that, as a group, they are often on the brink of an immanent social critique. It is the potential in coming together as a group that builds—through degrees—on the receptivity to critique that political race seeks to recover.[95]

This is not an easy challenge. The parents of children at Niko's private school found themselves confronted with the way they had inadvertently occupied more than their share of "space" in a multiracial rally. As they discovered the unintended consequences of their own good intentions, some asked: Why should I fight for you and not for me? Why should I fight at all?

There are two interrelated questions here. One is the question whites often ask: *Who do you know who gives up power voluntarily?* The other question is one we hear more often from people of color: *Why should people of color join with others to fight for change when these "others" have proven themselves in the past to be unreliable or self-interested allies at best?* These questions state a version of Derrick Bell's interest-convergence thesis. Bell argues that blacks do not gain rights unless whites determine it is in their own self-interest to provide such rights. Since racism is in the self-interest of many whites, Bell cannot imagine a future without racism. If racism is pervasive and inevitable, then how can political race possibly challenge it? And how can blacks trust such undependable allies?[96]

Part of our response lies in our definition of racism. We are not focused on the bigotry of individuals in power. We recognize the moral framework that dramatized that bigotry in order to eradicate the formal, legal, and highly visible scaffolding on which Jim Crow and other racist hierarchies were built. Those structures had encouraged irrational prejudice to rationalize the distribution of resources and the corruption of civil and legal rights. But our current racial discourse has moved too far in the single direction of fighting irrational prejudice. It deploys the language of morality and blame to target individuals whose offensive views become the exclusive focus of discussion. It ignores the powerful inequities that feed and are nurtured in turn by those individual views. In this context, we are compelled to supplement what is now a purely moral framework by which to judge individual bigotry. Our strategy has been to develop a new language to understand the many ways racism is deeply imbedded within, and constituted by, relationships of power and society as a whole. We are less interested in measuring blame and more concerned with developing a political framework that spurs us to respond and act. We define racism, therefore, as acquiescence in and accommodation to racialized hierarchies governing resource distribution and resource generation.[97] Racism treats the inequitable distribution, generation, and transfer of resources as normal, natural, and fair. Thus, our definition of racism relies on whether people *naturalize* racialized hierarchies.[98]

In terms of our guiding metaphor, racism is a condition that unquestioningly pathologizes the canary. Racism explains the canary's condition as its own problem, without further investigating or even questioning the conditions in the mines. Racism locates the dominant explanation for the depressed socioeconomic, health, and educational condition of people of color and their over-representation in the criminal justice system in the character of the people themselves, rather than in the structures of power that create the conditions of their lives. The content and experience of racism varies depending on local conditions, but like the air we breathe or the economic system we share, it affects us all.[99] As with second-hand smoke, the closer to the source you are, the more toxins you breathe, but even at the periphery the smoke is still toxic. We all could see the smoke in the room, but we allowed ourselves to believe that if we were not smoking ourselves, we were not at risk. What seems like common knowledge to-day—that second-hand smoke entails a significant peril to health—took years to establish. The political meaning of this analogy is fairly obvious: there is no such thing as a naked individual who exists outside of a cultural, social, or institutional context.

We see the challenge of political race as acting in ways that disrupt racialized hierarchies by changing the background stories we tell one another about race, wealth, and power. But as Derrick Bell reminds us, one of the pernicious effects of racism is that it often disables those whose interests do converge with people of color from fighting the structure that disempowers them, too. White working-class people in particular have embraced a story about their place in America that has historically been rooted in their distance from blackness. As a result, they have failed to recognize the many ways in which the inequitable distribution of social resources in our society reduces their own well-being. If poor and working-class whites would link their fate with people of color who have been raced as losers in a winner-take-all society, whites, too, would benefit. Our conception of political race both foregrounds and builds on Dr. King's insight that by freeing black people from the injustices that circumscribe their lives, America will be freeing itself as well.[100]

This applies to those white people who now hold power as well as those who do not. By joining the political race movement, those enjoying power now do not necessarily lose it altogether; they retain a measure of it and hold that power with greater security because the losers' energy will be used constructively to innovate rather than self-destructively to manipulate the system. This is related to what students of corporate management call the dispersion paradox—that by giving up power you gain power, because control that is too tight and power that is too concentrated demoralize workers and undermine innovation.

All people will regain some of what they have lost in the name of liberal individualism if they link their fate with others and begin to reimagine themselves as part of a community and not just as atomized, self-interested individuals. Indeed, one of the grounding premises of our political race project is that we can no longer afford to overlook the importance of a different set of public values and approaches to collective, as opposed to private, decision-making. Instead, political race tries to refocus our attention on building public relationships and tapping into the power to create rather than simply to control by encouraging joyful interactions with many others.

The Limitations of Political Race

Although most progressives share our view that race is central to an understanding of the American condition, some are skeptical of our formulation of political race and reject the call for a coalition that starts with race. They agree with part of our argument—that people of color, and women, are often the most committed organizers and the ones most amenable to a root-cause analysis of the forces shaping their unsatisfactory condition. Yet their progressive organizing efforts do not begin with a group defined racially (according to standard criteria) and then try to move that group to a more systemic analysis of social and institutional change through education or internal discussion. They simply resolve to bury those categories without destroying or resolving them.[101] Exercising the first and second dimensions of zero-sum power, these progressives start with a race-neutral set of issues and then choose among these issues in a racially sensitive way. In organizing their institutional leadership structure to address those issues, they are willing to assure that a few people of color will always fill leadership positions.[102] But they are unwilling to give up or interrupt their own power in the process. Consequently, the hierarchies of race and gender often simply re-emerge internally within the dynamics of these groups. Also, the failure to keep the canary front and center undermines the psychological resources of people of color whom the group counts as members.

The political scientist Jennifer Hochschild, for example, offers the "left wing version of a color blind ideal." "America is raced," she says, but progressives should "willfully choose to ignore color in the name of eradicating racially based inequalities."[103] Hochschild observes the structure of racial hierarchy and concedes that once in place, it continues.[104] But focusing on racial discrimination, in her view, only encourages an oppression sweepstakes between Latinos and blacks. Bald racial demands simply alienate white and Asian voters, who feel that this is not their fight.

Like Derrick Bell, Hochschild notes that whites are willing to challenge racial bias but only where it does not adversely affect their self-interest. As a result, "Anti-discrimination goals are no longer the most stable arena for making common cause across racial and ethnic groups."[105] To avoid fragmentation of short-term cross-racial coalitions, Hochschild is clear: blacks should change their focus away from race, meaning away from anti-discrimination agendas. Instead, progressives should all focus on forming race-neutral coalitions, to create a "we" that will immediately deliver progressive public policy outcomes.[106]

Hochschild sees race through the conventional lens of identity and discrimination, and she sees power through the lens of conventional electoral and public policy access. In our view, this perspective undervalues the assets of a racialized community that was initially forged from stigma but subsequently nurtured through resistance and struggle. Appeals like Hochschild's that focus on public policy makers implementing, from the top down, a host of universal programs are limited because they fail to confront the benefits to whites of racism and fail to mobilize the primary stakeholders to organize for change.[107] Even more, solutions that make no mention of race or gender and instead appeal to the greater good are often understood by many blacks (especially black women) as excluding them.[108] When the barriers that racism poses for people of color are not directly confronted, their sense of isolation is only reinforced. Finally, universal appeals sometimes mask appeals to the status quo, in which commitments to rules trump commitments to justice.[109]

Hochschild demurs to existing racial polarization in the hope that, over time, when people interact and build trust, attitudes will soften.[110] But as Dr. King forcefully stated in his "Letter from a Birmingham Jail," substituting racial peace for racial justice is a recipe for delaying racial justice.[111] Sometimes those in moral distress must destabilize the current situation so that mere racial peace is not a realistic option.[112] As Dr. King said: "No social advance rolls in on the wheels of inevitability. Every step toward the goal of justice requires sacrifice, suffering, and struggle; the tireless exertions and passionate concern of dedicated individuals."[113]

Still, Hochschild's focus on electoral coalitions offers useful reminders of the limitations of our methodology. Ours is not an approach by which to galvanize routine candidate-centered political expression. We, too, share her view that excessive preoccupation with racial symbolism in the electoral arena, in an increasingly diverse society, leads to divisive intergroup competition. Our energy, however, is not directed toward acting within conventional electoral coalitions. We do not argue that if more black or Latino candidates would run for office, the political race project would be achieved. We have tried to highlight both the realistic nature of our critique and our commitment to transforming the received wisdom that change is driven either from the top through electoral politics or public policy pronouncements or through an apolitical commitment to individual advancement. We have criticized both the vanguard models of change and the now-popular idea that the way to eliminate poverty is to eliminate, one by one, people who are poor.[114]

We offer an alternative methodology based on an understanding that genuine change will come only when an activated grassroots base initiates it. The losers of society stand to gain the most, and risk the least, from mobilizing for change, and they already have the tools for analysis at their disposal.

We do not mean to suggest that racialized communities are already functioning models of political race, or that all members of a racialized community are poised to join, or inclined to support, a political race project. We recognize that outsiders may be consumed with basic survival, or less articulate in the stylized art form of conventional political speech and argumentation. Even when they experiment with art as a form of guerilla theater, unless they are already enjoying some class privilege, their creative impulses may not be welcome. That certainly is one of the lessons Rashid and Jonathan learned when viewing the mural already painted on the wall behind the Pro-Ambulance Center in North Cambridge. Those whose artistic inclinations are quickly stamped out may resent the prospect of having to struggle along with others who seem more privileged or less invested in progressive change. They may be particularly skeptical of the offer to join, in the name of political race, with others whose commitments or credentials are not based on a common racial phenotype or shared class or culture. Moreover, on the frontlines, they may be the most vulnerable to retaliation or discipline against those who resist conventional authority.

Indeed, those in authority commonly exercise power to punish and isolate the canaries. Perhaps even worse, for those with a structural view of power, resistance is futile, since those who do resist will, especially if successful, eventually become like those they replace. We acknowledge these limitations. Any such intervention, therefore, depends upon an ability to situate the political race strategy within a more complex view of power. We recognize that power, especially when summoned for social change, is often zero-sum, top-down, externalized, or coercive. But while we recognize this dominant form, we conclude it is necessary to explore alternative forms of power in an effort to open up public space to those who have felt left out for so long.

In these alternative forums, those most vulnerable need allies they can trust not only to fight with them when they feel strong but to push them to resist internal hierarchies, which are dysfunctional even as they provide the illusion of strength to some because they undermine the confidence of others. Within these spaces the participants will all need the psychological equivalent of their own personal board of directors: a group of people who share their vision and who hold one another accountable to that shared vision.

These alternative spaces are not substitutes for the more traditional theaters of power. We envision these aesthetic spaces as "in-between" places that provide venues for novel forms of interaction. They can be found within traditional hierarchy, completely outside that hierarchy, or overlapping and moving inside and outside simultaneously. Bob Moses, a civil rights hero in Mississippi, described these institutional interstices as the "crawl spaces of democracy." It is within the crawl spaces of democracy that the political race project will find a home.

On the other hand, Hochschild is right in identifying a tendency among people of color to start and end every conversation with race, while ignoring its linkages with class, gender, and sexuality. Many organizations of color, concerned about police brutality and inequities in the criminal justice system, focus exclusively on racial profiling and the disparity between sentencing for crack cocaine (used more often in the black and brown communities) and powdered cocaine (used more often among whites) without realizing that these are symptoms, not the real problem. The traditional civil rights paradigm encourages this single-minded focus. It works to compensate victims of discrimination and often overlooks the possibility that those victims are potential agents of a form of social change that is both more structural and transformative.

The conventional and compensatory mindset does not position its adherents to take maximum advantage of the way race offers a language and a motivation for challenging larger systems and patterns of injustice.[115] It fails to show those who otherwise feel privileged that their own rights and liberties are also ultimately at stake.[116] To ignore race is to ignore a critical tool for understanding systems of power in this society. Without race as the miner's canary, institutional hierarchies of power that threaten the well-being of everyone remain invisible.

Class, which in this country has not been a source of pride, critique, or collective consciousness, has failed to serve in that role.[117] In contemporary American politics, class is as individuated as any other variable. We have come to see that, in general, it is easier to teach black people about class than to teach white people about race. Unless one has a community orientation toward structural rather than individual pathologies, it is difficult to understand either race or class.

For this reason gender is also an interesting but problematic variable. Like race, and unlike class, gender is a familiar and visible aggregation or grouping that, however imperfect, can help us see or name systems or relationships of power. Yet few progressive activists have pursued our mostly preliminary effort to reintroduce gender into the discussion of racial literacy and political action.[118] Nevertheless, we continue to believe that political race must assert its linkages to class, gender, and sexuality or else risk fragmentation.

Participants in the political race project may encourage these linkages to emerge because of what joint participation does *to* us, not just *for* us. Participation is not solely a means to gain a specific benefit; it is also a valuable means of understanding our own position. Different ideas energize the process and challenge us to rethink our own truths. On the other hand, political race is an inherently unstable activity. What it means to belong must be constantly renegotiated. Similarly, our political race project may need to be reconfigured once it is no longer a project of transformation; moving from an oppositional stance to the exercise of traditional forms of state power is beyond our current imaginings.

What we do know, however, is that if it succeeds, political race will stand in sharp contrast to the "one-way libertarianism" that Nicholas Lemann decries. In the emerging selfishness that Lemann observes, middle-class voters believe that government owes individual resources to support individual opportunity but the individual owes nothing back to society. What is missing is the case for a broader, shared vision that goes beyond market values; what we get instead is an invitation to participate simply as voters, not citizens. According to Lemann, the only groups who have not signed on to this worldview are African Americans and Latinos.[119]

Building on their weak-we community orientation, political race tries to initiate a process that involves blacks and Latinos first as citizens. That process is inconsistent with a bureaucracy that protects the powerless as clients; it is a process, rather, that respects and indeed learns from their participation. It tries to create a politics, with values that permit collective decision-making that is more than simply an aggregation of individual interests. It is a politics that fosters interdependence between people and between persons and their community, the ability to work through conflict rather than to avoid it, and a willingness to share power as a force for innovation and not just control. It is through such a process that the political race project can liberate the future by creating a space for political action to occur in the present.

The Role of Faith

The concept of political race requires trust and faith in the belief: (1) that people who are white will voluntarily support the leadership of people of color to fight for social justice; (2) that the social movement they construct from race will be democratic and visionary; and (3) that it will be democratic and visionary in part because of the way that political race reconceives structures of representation and power.

We have found an inspiration for these leaps of faith in the subversive techniques of the literary movement called magical realism. The magical realist leads readers into a new place and then shocks them into a different sensibility by transforming, without warning, the realistic into the fantastic. Similarly, the concept of political race shocks us out of traditional ways of reading race. Blackness becomes disconnected—within this context—from biology, ancestry, and the prejudice of individuals. It becomes transformed into a political and social signifier, not just of those who may be descriptively black but of all who are vulnerable under current hierarchies of power. We use blackness as a metaphor for social position vis-à-vis material privileges and resources within this society. Political race helps us understand who is functionally black, whether that person identifies with blackness or not.

In magical realism, the initial emphasis is on the insights of realism. The magic comes in rejecting conventional explanations for the reality observed, and then taking the leap to ask new, startling questions. Similarly, the canary metaphor helps us initially to see the reality of the mines, and then the concept of political race scrambles that reality like a kaleidoscope, in order to achieve a new clarity about the possibilities immanent in social life. With each new twist or turn, the image changes, as communities embark on local experiments and redefine their goals and desires.

Like every act of faith, political race is fragile unless the insights that ground it are renewed through practice. People do not assume it. They *choose* it by their actions. Our faith arises from what we have observed, that people join with one another in part because they believe in a vision of social justice and are committed to a cause larger than themselves. Believing in a community of any size, from neighborhood to nation, requires faith in others and compels us to cross the threshold of hope. Democratic faith connects a mature oppositional consciousness with the building of coalitions, collective identities, and cooperative efforts to overcome limited material resources.[120] It is not satisfied by relationships in which the majority defines the goals and coerces or cajoles the minority into accepting them, or encourages the minority to integrate into the majority and leave behind community for the promise of the individual free-

dom to consume.[121] We do not seek common cause behind a false or arti-
ficial consensus in which we paper over dissent or diversity. We do not
encourage the tyranny of fragmented majorities but rather seek openings
for resistance in the interstices of power.

We seek to find these openings by renewing the faith that once animated the civil rights movement. We see this faith among opponents of
the death penalty who labor diligently in defiance of what seem to be un-
beatable odds. We see this faith in Rose Sanders, a civil rights attorney in
Selma, Alabama, who said, when asked why she continues to struggle,
"You have to believe that the mighty river is filled drop by drop. You just
have to put your drop in the river, and somebody else will put in their
drop, and then eventually one day those drops will make a river. And then
faith—that's what keeps us going."[122] We see it also in Ella Baker, who said
in 1970: "Every time I see a young person who has come through the system to a stage where he could profit from the system and identify with it,
but who identifies more with the struggle of black people who have not
had his chance, every time I find such a person I take new hope. I feel new
life as a result." We feel it in the photograph of Carrie Mae Weems, in an
exhibit of African American Photographers at the Museum of Arts and
Technology in Washington, D.C. Under her portrait are the words, "I
knew, not from memory, but from hope, that there were other models by
which to live."

It is upon the foundation of this emancipatory faith in the unseen and
the unlikely that we try to build. We are not satisfied with irony, hedo-
nism, or futility as present-tense options for progressive social change.
We are brimming with optimism about the capacity of the presumed losers to question the rules as well as to challenge the very basis on which
those rules have been formulated. We believe in the willingness of people to struggle when they have a clarity and sense of mission about the
challenges they face. We are convinced that in the long run the losers
gain more by spearheading a movement for social change than by special
pleading or special interest. Indeed, we believe that new forms of social
change will emerge if more people are aware of those ways in which power
subtly shapes the rules of the game and the ways in which we tacitly accept

those rules without question. Knowledge is power; being connected to others with knowledge, and then acting based on that knowledge and that connection, is more powerful still.

We credit the civil rights movement and the liberal legal model to the extent that each created a space for progressive politics and reduced racism as conventionally defined. This tolerance model has made alliances possible that were once unthinkable.[123] But the civil rights movement too often seems to measure progress by looking backward; we want to shift the focus to where we are going, not how far we have come. In the past, conventional ideas of race were deliberately tied to issues of social policy in order to make programs of general concern sound like special pleading. Our response is to reclaim race in order to "complete" democracy.[124]

And here we return to where we began. Through the metaphor of the miner's canary, the methodological apparatus of political race, and the narrative strategy of magical realism, we invoke ideas of spontaneity, resiliency, and creativity, and harness them to our belief that what is real is in part a function of what we allow ourselves to dream.

NOTES   ACKNOWLEDGMENTS   INDEX

NOTES

Prologue

1. *Miller v Johnson,* 515 U.S. 900 (1995); *Shaw v Reno,* 509 U.S. 630 (1993); *Rice v Cayetano,* 528 U.S. 495 (2000) (invalidating under the Fifteenth Amendment a Hawaii constitutional provision under which only descendants of the original Hawaiians may vote for the leadership of a state agency that administers programs and millions of dollars in public money on their behalf). This decision was "consistent with the trend of the Rehnquist court seeing discrimination and reverse discrimination as the same thing." Linda Greenhouse, "Justices Void Hawaii Setup That Limits a Vote by Race," *New York Times,* February 24, 2000, at A14.

2. This "do not offend" approach is a form of one-way regulation—only subordinated groups require boundaries. It plays into the problem of specialized and victimized treatment. On the other hand, the race matters approach is controversial. Greater genetic variation exists within populations typically labeled black and white than between these populations. As Anthony Appiah writes there are no real "races" in the United States; there are only social groups that have been constructed for purposes that cannot be defended on biological or scientific grounds. Consequently, no one can persuasively claim that all blacks think alike or want the same things. See K. Anthony Appiah and Amy Gutmann, *Color Conscious: The Political Morality of Race* (1996).

3. Jerome G. Miller writes, for example, that three of every four (76 percent of) African-American 18-year-old males living in urban areas can now anticipate being arrested and jailed before age 36. In the process, each young man will acquire a "criminal record." By the late 1990s, federal statisticians were predicting that nearly one of every three adult black men in the nation could anticipate being sentenced to a federal or state prison at some time during his life. *Search and Destroy: African Americans in the Criminal Justice System* (1997).

4. I wanted to help prepare my son for what MacArthur fellow and documentary filmmaker Louis Massiah witnessed when he embarked daily on a walking tour of his North Philadelphia neighborhood, a ritual made necessary by the many changes since his childhood. He still lived in the imposing brownstone in which he had grown up, a house

whose mighty ceilings and elegant beveled glass panes were reminders of a different time, in which middle-class black people walked the streets proudly with their heads high. Now, when he walked outside his own front door, he saw scenes of devastation and disrepair. The middle-class black people had moved away. Many of the blacks still living in the inner city neighborhood, nevertheless, walked quietly and without fear. The old black women lugged their shopping bags and never looked back. The young black women strutted with nary an eye over their shoulder. But the young black men, the teenage boys in his neighborhood, walked with a heavy burden of race and gender. They walked with fear of the cops, whose response to the combination of poverty and machismo is to be prepared for confrontation and never let down your guard. They also walked with wary eyes, potential prey for other young black males. They were afraid of others just like them, whose race and gender roles required that they be on the lookout. They were prepared to respond to potential acts of disrespect; they were prepared for confrontation. They never let down their guard.

5. See Z. N. Hurston, "How It Feels to Be Colored Me," in *The Norton Anthology of African-American Literature* at 1009 (Henry Louis Gates, Jr., and Nellie McKay, eds., 1997).

6. So, what does "race" mean? Law Professor Angela Harris suggests that the answer depends on several questions: Compared to what? As of when? Who is asking? In what context? For what purpose? With what interests and presuppositions? Harris concludes, "Questions of difference and identity are always functions of a specific interlocutionary situation and the answers, matters of strategy rather than truth." Any "essential self" Harris tells us is always an invention; the evil is in "denying its artificiality." Context, in other words, matters. See also Michael Banton, "The Idiom of Race: A Critique of Presentism," in *Research in Race and Ethnic Relations* at 21 (Cora Bagley Marret and Cheryl Leggon, eds., 1980).

7. There are important analogs between the Hispanic and the Asian experience with race in this country. However, it is important to note that the effort to create either a pan-Hispanic or a pan-Asian identity has important similarities, but also important differences. Not the least of the differences is the experience with race both in the various national subgroups as well as during the colonial confrontation with Europe. Those differences are then refracted through the lens of American conceptions of race. See for example the treatment of Chinese and other Asians in Ian Haney-Lopez, *White by Law* (1996); Yen Le Espiritu, *Asian American Panethnicity: Bridging Institutions and Identity* (1992), and Robert Chang, *Disoriented* (1999).

8. See Edward Lucas White, *El Supremo: A Romance of the Great Dictator of Paraguay* (1916), discussing the racial and social policies of Jose Gaspar Rodriguez Francia. One of Francia's insights was that the social problems of Latin America in general, but his country in particular, would not be solved until the question of color distinctions was eliminated. Toward that end he mandated policies that essentially required miscegenation.

9. In a conversation one day when I was home during a semester break from college, my mother remarked to me, "Gerald, you are white in ways you don't even know."

10. We are indebted to Neil Foley for bringing this phrase to our attention, although it makes its appearance in the title of the book by Mathew Frye Jacobs, *Whiteness of a Different Color: European Immigrants and the Alchemy of Race* (1998). In Foley's usage it suggests the racial bribe that is at the core of the ambiguous relationship in the Hispanic community (at least among Mexicans and Mexican-Americans) between their Americanized racial identity and their historical racial identity. As he puts it in an interesting paper that is

due to be published by Texas A&M Press as part of the Webb Lecture Series: "The category of Hispanic has thus removed the racial notion of Mexicans on the border between blackness and whiteness; as a census category and ethnoracial identity, it has come to signify a whiteness of a different color, a darker shade of pale, a preference for salsa over ketchup. Those identifying themselves as white and Hispanic, whether consciously or not, are implicated in the government's erasure of the Indian and African heritage of Mexicans. The journey of mixed-race Mexicans thus ends at the doorstep of Hispanic whiteness where no blacks or Indians are free to enter." Neil Foley, "Beyond Black and White: Mexican Americans, Civil Rights, and their Problem with the Color Line" at 20–21 (unpublished manuscript, May 2000, on file with authors).

1. Political Race and Magical Realism

1. See Felix S. Cohen, "The Erosion of Indian Rights, 1950–1953: A Case Study in Bureaucracy," 62 *Yale Law Journal* 348, 390 (1953), where Cohen writes, "like the miner's canary, the Indian marks the shift from fresh air to poison gas in our political atmosphere, and our treatment of the Indian . . . marks the rise and fall in our democratic faith."

2. Martin Luther King, Jr., *Where Do We Go From Here: Chaos or Community?* at 138 (1967).

3. Diana Jean Schemo, "Despite Options on Census, Many to Check 'Black' Only," *New York Times,* February 12, 2000, at A1, A10. See also Eric Schmitt, "Blacks Split on Disclosing Multiracial Roots," *New York Times,* March 31, 2001, at A1, A12: "When Milton Heard was filling out the census form for his family last year, he hesitated where it asked the race of his two sons, Jacob and David. Mr. Heard, who owns a women's apparel and cosmetics store [in Mississippi], is black. His wife, Chong Suk, is Korean. His sons, ages 21 and 17, are black with distinct Asian features. For the first time, the 2000 census allowed Americans to check more than one category to identify their race. But after talking with his sons, Mr. Heard said he marked only black for them, not black and Asian. 'I thought about it and thought about it, but in the end I didn't feel there was enough information about what the government was trying to do,' said Mr. Heard, who is 76."

4. Michael Dawson, *Behind the Mule: Race and Class in African-American Politics* (1994).

5. We are not, in other words, supporters of Rossi's Law, named after the sociologist Peter Rossi: "the expected value for any measured effect of a social program is zero." See Jacob Weisberg, "For the Sake of Argument," *New York Times Magazine,* November 5, 2000, at 48, 51.

6. Sharon Groch, "Free Spaces: Creating Oppositional Consciousness in the Disability Rights Movement," in *Oppositional Consciousness* at 1 (Jane Mansbridge, ed., forthcoming), citing Pamela Allen, *Free Space: A Perspective on the Small Group in Women's Liberation* (1970), and Sara M. Evans, *Free Spaces: The Sources of Democratic Change in America* (1986).

7. Tomiko Brown-Nagin, "The Transformation of a Social Movement into Law? The SCLC and NAACP's Campaigns for Civil Rights Reconsidered in Light of the Educational Activism of Septima Clark," 8 *Women's History Review* 81, 83, 90 (1999). This is what some call "resource mobilization theory." See, for example, John N. McCarthy, "The Trend of Social Movements in America: Professionalization and Resource Mobilization" (CRS Working Paper, no. 164, 1973); Anthony Oberschall, *Social Conflict and Social Movements* (1973); and Charles Tilly, *From Mobilization to Revolution* (1978).

8. *Plessey v Ferguson,* 163 U.S. 537 (1896). This rule was commonly "enforced" through the 1970s and 80s and is still, for many people of color, especially blacks, self-defining.

9. Philip Weinstein, *What Else But Love? The Ordeal of Race in Faulkner and Morrison* at 72 (1996).

10. Toni Morrison, *Beloved* at 200 (1987).

11. Kendall Thomas, "Racial Justice: Moral or Political?" unpublished draft forthcoming in Austin Sarat's *Law's Conception* at 6, 8–9, 11 (2001). "The moral concept of racial justice tries to capture and control the explosive, agonistic conflicts that characterize American racial politics . . . Against the moral vision of racial justice, the political model places primary accent and emphasis on who controls decisionmaking about the distribution of state or state-sanctioned burdens and benefits, and, more importantly, on who is in a position to make those decisions stick, by force if necessary."

12. See Mary C. Waters, "Explaining the Comfort Factor: West Indian immigrants Confront American Race Relations," in *The Cultural Territories of Race: Black and White Boundaries* at 63, 69 (Michele Lamont, ed., 1999).

13. Don Terry, "Getting Under My Skin," *New York Times Magazine,* July 16, 2000, at 32, 35.

14. Groch, "Free Spaces," at 1, 2–3, 7–8.

2. A Critique of Colorblindness

1. David Plotke, "Racial Politics and the Clinton–Guinier Episode," 42 *Dissent* 221 (Spring 1995).

2. Plotke seemed to suggest that rendering differences unspeakable renders them meaningless. The solution is universal social programs to address the needs of racialized groups without ever mentioning race. David Plotke, *Building a Democratic Political Order: Reshaping American Liberalism in the 1930s and 1940s* (1996).

3. We concede, as W. E. B. Dubois stated so eloquently, "the problem of the 20th century" was the problem of the colorline. Indeed, the issue of race and racism has plagued this country from its founding. But we take Dubois's admonition to mean that the problem is the way in which American society has dealt with race. The problem is not inevitable from the fact of race itself as a social construction.

4. This is not to say we are endorsing racism, whether practiced by individuals, groups, or social structures of any denomination. But we are redefining racism so that it does not encompass all discussion of race. We certainly do not go so far as R. Emmett Tyrell, for example, the conservative editor of *American Spectator,* who stated in an interview on C-SPAN that "whoever mentions race first is the racist in the room." Rhonda M. Williams, "Unfinished Business: African-American Political Economy During the Age of 'Color-blind' Politics," in *The State of Black America 1999* at 137 (Hugh Price, ed. 1999). We are also trying to create a space for a more frank engagement with race, independent of its manifestation as individual racism.

5. To these legal scholars of color, much of the popular as well as juridical debate about race, racism, and equality seemed to lack a real social, historical, or structural dimension. The empirical reality that they observed within communities of color belied the claims made by neoliberal and neoconservative legal commentators that the problem of race had largely been solved. But they also witnessed a vacuum in the theoretical debate.

6. See generally Ian Haney-Lopez, *White by Law* at 203–207 (1996), for a list of cases dealing with race as a pre-requisite for citizenship and their dispositions.

7. Melissa Nobles, *Shades of Citizenship* at 58–75 (2000).

8. Alexander Bickel, *The Least Dangerous Branch* (1962); Herbert Wechsler, "Toward Neutral Principles of Constitutional Law," 73 *Harvard Law Review* 1 (1959); Herbert Wechsler, *The Courts and the Constitution* (1965); Herbert Wechsler, *The Federal Courts and the Federal System* (1959); Herbert Wechsler, *Principles, Politics, and Fundamental Law* (1961).

9. *Loving v Virginia* 381 U.S. 1 (1967). That, of course, was the winning argument in *Plessy v Ferguson,* 163 U.S. 537 (1896). See also Bickel, *Least Dangerous Branch;* Wechsler, "Toward Neutral Principles of Constitutional Law"; but cf. Charles Lund Black, *A New Birth of Freedom: Human Rights, Named and Unnamed* (1997); Charles Lund Black, *People and the Court* (1960); Charles Lund Black, *Perspectives in Constitutional Law* (1970); Charles Lund Black, *The Unfinished Business of the Warren Court* (1970).

10. See Neil Gotanda, "A Critique of 'Our Constitution Is Colorblind,'" in *Critical Race Theory* at 260 (Kimberlé Crenshaw et al., eds., 1995).

11. See Jerome Bruner, *The Culture of Education* (1996).

12. See Gerald Torres and Kathryn Milum, "Translating Yonnondio by Precedent and Evidence: The Mashpee Indian Case," 1990 *Duke Law Journal* 625 (1990).

13. Gerald Lopez, "Lay Lawyering" 32 *UCLA Law Review* 1, 3 (1984).

14. See Derrick A. Bell, Jr., "Serving Two Masters: Integration Ideals and Client Interests in School Desegregation Litigation," 85 *Yale Law Journal* 470 (1976).

15. See Dirk Johnson, "Then, the Color of Classmates, Now the Color of Money: Busing Revisited," *New York Times,* September 26, 1999, at 3.

16. We think it is important to note that there are both "modernist" and "post-modernist" strains within critical race theory. In fact, some CRT writing that claims a post-modernist pedigree relies on the modernist notion of a single validating norm or emancipation and with it commitments that strongly parallel the liberal commitment to rights. See Angela Harris, "Forward: The Jurisprudence of Reconstruction," 82 *California Law Review* 741 (1994).

17. This should not be interpreted as failure to appreciate the work that commitments to liberalism did. As Paul Sniderman and Edward G. Carmines note, "It is liberalism's lasting honor to have been in the vanguard of a crusade to achieve racial equality in America. Liberalism has by no means been the only force at work, nor always the most important, particularly in the early years when black leaders and black communities, acting on their own initiative and drawing on their own resources, launched the modern civil rights movement. But absent liberalism's commitment, the revolution in the legal and political standing of American blacks since the mid-century would have been inconceivable." Paul Sniderman and Edward G. Carmines, *Reaching beyond Race* at 141 (1997).

18. Lino Graglia, "A Misguided Statement," *Austin American Statesman,* December 19, 1998. See also Lino Graglia, "Still Hope for a Society Where Race is Irrelevant," *Austin American Statesman,* December 18, 1998.

19. Clark Freshman, "What Ever Happened to 'Anti-Semitism'?" at 9–10 (manuscript, July 2, 1999). See also Patricia J. Williams, *The Alchemy of Race and Rights* at 8 (1991).

20. This is of course a version of the Aristotelian virtue of treating likes alike. See Aristotle, *Ethics* (John Warrington, ed., 1963); Catherine MacKinnon, *Toward a Feminist Theory of the State* (1989).

21. See Reva B. Siegal, "Discrimination in the Eyes of the Law: How 'Color Blindness' Discourse Disrupts and Rationalizes Social Stratification," 88 *California Law Review* 77, 88,

91 (2000). Recently, philosophers such as K. Anthony Appiah and Amy Gutmann have used both analytic philosophy and contemporary human biology to dismiss "scientifically" based theories of race. See K. Anthony Appiah and Amy Gutmann, *Color Conscious: The Political Morality of Race* (1996).

22. Interestingly, unlike the first governing rule, the second rule is asymmetric in its application. Although rules that rely on race to protect the racial minority are suspect, public officials who may be influenced by racial bias against the racial minority are given the benefit of the doubt. When those who claim that covert racial bias has influenced the way public officials or public agencies treat them, they must establish discriminatory intent. A pattern of bias is often not enough to establish proof that these officials harbor actual bad purpose. The courts assume that individual public officials are neutral and require those challenging their good faith to prove otherwise. By contrast, the courts now assume a stigmatizing effect with no requirement of proof of purpose when the public acts affirmatively to remedy racial discrimination.

23. Kimberlé Crenshaw, "Colorblind Dreams and Racial Nightmares: Reconfiguring Racism in the Post Civil Rights Era," in *Birth of Nation 'hood* at 101 (Toni Morrison and Claudia Lacour, eds., 1997).

24. Plotke, *Building a Democratic Political Order.*

25. Lani Guinier, "The Miner's Canary: Race and the Democratic Process," 42 *Dissent* 521 (Fall 1995) (illustrating this point with David Plotke's admonition to avoid talking candidly about race because those who do speak in the language of racial identity tend to overstate the role of race and emphasize racial exclusion instead of simple political weakness).

26. Gotanda, "Critique of 'Our Constitution Is Colorblind.'"

27. See Thomas Byrne Edsall and Mary D. Edsall, *Chain Reaction: The Impact of Race, Rights, and Taxes on American Politics* (1991).

28. See Linda Hamilton Krieger, "Civil Rights Perestroika: Intergroup Relations after Affirmative Action," 86 *California Law Review* 1251 (1998).

29. David Plotke, "Racial Politics."

30. See Theda Skocpol, quoted in J. Phillip Thompson III, "Universalism and Deconcentration: Why Race Still Matters in Poverty and Economic Development," 26 *Politics and Society* 181, 183 (1998).

31. Mark A. Graber, "Conflicting Representations: Lani Guinier and James Madison on Electoral Systems," 13 (3) *Constitutional Commentary* 291 (Winter 1996).

32. "[T]he normative logic of the [Court's] moral view" of race attempts "to exclude politics from its discursive domain . . . This paper asks whether the governing grammar of contemporary American debates about the conditions and content of racial justice will be adequate." Kendall Thomas, "Racial Justice: Moral or Political?" at 1, 9, 23 (unpublished draft forthcoming in Austin Sarat's *Law's Conception,* 2001).

33. See Haney-Lopez, *White by Law.*

34. See Gerald Torres, "Local Knowledge, Local Color: Critical Legal Studies and the Law of Race Relations," 25 *San Diego Law Review* 1043 (1988). Arthur Schlessinger captured this well in *The Disuniting of America* (1992).

35. See Emily Eakin, "Bigotry as Mental Illness or Just Another Norm," *New York Times,* January 15, 2000, at B9.

36. See, e.g., James Traub, "Schools Are Not the Answer," *Sunday Times Magazine,* Jan-

uary 16, 2000, at 52, quoting Lawrence Katz and Christopher Jencks, *The Black–White Test Score Gap* (1998).

37. Edsall and Edsall, *Chain Reaction* at 23 (discussing the change during the decade of the 1980s). Jennifer Hochschild, "Madison's Constitution and Identity Politics," in *Defining the Conditions of Democracy* (Theodore Rabb and Ezra Suleiman, eds., forthcoming).

38. Thomas Dye, *Who's Running America?* (1979).

39. See Beverly I. Moran and William Whitford, "A Black Critique of the Internal Revenue Code," 1996 *Wisconsin Law Review* 751 (1996).

40. Oliver and Shapiro, *Black Wealth/White Wealth.*

41. See Michael Sherrad, *Assets for the Poor* (1991), and Robert E. Friedman, *The Safety Net as Ladder* (1988). See also Hochschild, "Madison's Constitution" at 21–22.

42. Dalton Conley, *Being Black, Living in the Red: Race, Wealth, and Social Policy in America* at 1 (1999). On median net worth, the figures Conley cites are $43,800 versus $3,700.

43. Ibid. at 38, citing the Harvard Joint Center for Housing Studies. See also Raymond S. Franklin, *Shadows of Race and Class* (1991).

44. William P. O'Hare, *Wealth and Economic Status: A Perspective on Racial Inequality* at 2, 14 (1983). Henry S. Terrell, "Wealth Accumulation of Black and White Families: The Empirical Evidence," 26 *Journal of Finance* 363, 366 (1971). See Beverly I. Moran and William Whitford, "A Black Critique of the Internal Revenue Code," at 765, reproducing a table "Distribution of Financial Assets, 1979" from O'Hare, *Wealth and Economic Status* at 2, 12.

45. See Gerald Torres, "Taking and Giving: Police Power, Public Values, and Private Right," 26 *Environmental Law* 1 (1996). See also Robert Nozick, *Anarchy, State, and Utopia* (1974); Richard Allen Epstein, *Takings: Private Property and the Power of Eminent Domain* (1985).

46. See Oliver and Shapiro, *Black Wealth/White Wealth* at 131, 134–136.

47. Marcellus Andrews, *The Political Economy of Hope and Fear: Capitalism and the Black Condition in America* at 20, 22, 167–168 (1999). See also Deborah C. Malmud, "Affirmative Action, Diversity, and the Black Middle Class," 68 *University of Colorado Law Review* 939, 983–984 (1997).

48. See DeNeen L. Brown, "Her Sisters' Keeper: She May Have Escaped Poverty, But She Can Never Escape the Ties that Bind Her to Her Family," *Washington Post Magazine,* January 23, 2000, at W14.

49. See Oliver and Shapiro, *Black Wealth/White Wealth* at 167, 168, 170.

50. Hochschild, "Madison's Constitution" at 21–22. Hochschild notes that "even controlling for factors that influence whether a person is likely to be employed, blacks in the labor force are twice as likely to be jobless as similar non-Hispanic whites, and are less likely to have jobs than Hispanics and Asians. Earnings show the same pattern of considerable, and even growing, racial and ethnic inequality. One can tell the same story with regard to disparities in bank loans for homes, differential treatment by real estate agents, residential segregation, inconsistencies in medical treatment, and a dozen other practices. Blacks have drastically lower wealth holdings than whites with similar incomes, and there is little evidence to suggest that this critical disparity is lessening."

51. Oliver and Shapiro, *Black Wealth/White Wealth* at 81–82.

52. Conley, *Being Black, Living in the Red* at 60.

53. Ibid. at 70.

54. Oliver and Shapiro, *Black Wealth/White Wealth* at 133.

55. Conley, *Being Black, Living in the Red* at 72.

56. See Andrews, *The Political Economy of Hope and Fear* at 31. See also Rhonda Williams, "Accumulation as Evisceration: Urban Rebellion and the New Growth Dynamics," in *Reading Rodney King* at 84–85 (1993).

57. John Langbein, "The Twentieth-Century Revolution in Family Wealth Transmission," 86 *Michigan Law Review* 722 (1988). See also Derek Bok and William Bowen's, *The Shape of the River* (1998).

58. See Max Weber, *Essays in Sociology* 181–182 (Hans Gerth and C. Wright Mills, eds., 1946). See also Tomiko Brown-Nagin, "The Effect of Class Stratification on the NAACP LDF's Institutional Reform Litigation" (manuscript, Fall 2000).

59. Hugh Price, "Foreword" in *State of Black America 1999* at 12, 13 (1999).

60. Jodi Dean, *Solidarity of Strangers: Feminism after Identity Politics* at 2–3 (1996).

61. See discussion of social citizenship below citing Kenneth Karst, *Law's Promise, Law's Expression: Visions of Power in the Politics of Race, Gender, and Religion* (1993); Kenneth Karst, Leonard W. Levy, and Dennis J. Mahoney eds., *American Constitutional History: Selections from the Encyclopedia of the American Constitution* (1989); Kenneth Karst, *Equal Citizenship and the Constitution* (1989); Harold W. Horowitz and Kenneth L. Karst, *Law, Lawyers, and Social Change: Cases and Materials on the Abolition of Slavery, Racial Segregation, and Inequality of Educational Opportunity* (1969). See also William Forbath, "Caste, Class, and Equal Citizenship," 98 *Michigan Law Review* 1 (1999).

62. *Jones v Alfred H. Mayer Co.,* 392 U.S. 409, 443 (1968).

63. *Kelley v Bennett,* 96 F.Supp. 2d 1301, (M.D. Ala. 2000), rev'd on other grounds, *Sinkfield v Kelley,* 531 U.S. 28 (2000). A state court had earlier found that the black organization had the support of 80 percent of blacks in Alabama. This and related cases are discussed at greater length in Chapter 6.

64. *Holder v Hall,* 512 U.S. 874, 893 (1994) (Thomas, J. concurring in the result).

65. *Shaw v Reno,* 509 U.S. 630, 647 (1993) (O'Connor, J.).

66. Beth Roy, *Bitters in the Honey: Tales of Hope and Disappointment across Divides of Race and Time* at 334, 337, 368 (1999).

67. See Paul M. Sniderman and Edward G. Carmines, *Reaching Beyond Race* (1997), esp. ch. 5.

68. Anne Phillips, *The Politics of Presence* (1995); Clint Bolick, *The Affirmative Action Fraud* (1996) at 128–129.

69. Sniderman and Carmines, *Reaching Beyond Race* at 141.

70. J. Phillip Thompson, "Universalism and Deconcentration" at 181, 191, 201–209.

71. Edsall and Edsall, *Chain Reaction.*

72. See *Kelley v Bennett.*

73. Manthia Diawara, *Englishness and Blackness: Cricket as Discourse on Colonialism* (1990).

74. This occurs in one of two ways. In one case racialized grievances are used to showcase the ways in which those who are "raced" carry with them a liability without similarly converting that liability into a political asset. In the other instance, racialized grievances are used to surface discontent within many marginalized communities without providing a basis for common cause. Instead, each community mobilizes around its "special" in-

terests and becomes vulnerable to divide and conquer strategies based on the sweepstakes of competing oppressions. In this later way, even those who promote entrepreneurship within communities of color may stoke the flames of racial division as each racialized group competes to "own" or control their "share" of the pie.

75. Nicholas Lemann, "The New American Consensus: Government of, by and for the Comfortable," *New York Times Magazine*, November 1, 1998, at 37.

76. Gary Wills, *Necessary Evil* (1999).

77. See Crenshaw, "Colorblind Dreams and Racial Nightmares."

78. Luis Fraga, "Racial and Ethnic Politics in a Multicultural Society" (lecture presented at the Metropolitan Research and Policy Institute, University of Texas at San Antonio, April 7, 1999, rpt. in Edsall and Edsall, *Chain Reaction*).

79. R. Emmett Tyrell, as quoted by Rhonda M. Williams, "Unfinished Business" at 137.

80. Andrews, *The Political Economy of Hope and Fear* at 3.

81. See Charles A. Murray, *Losing Ground: American Social Policy, 1950–1980* (1984).

82. Daniel P. Moynihan, *Beyond the Melting Pot: The Negroes, Puerto Ricans, Jews, Italians, and Irish of New York City* (2d ed., 1970).

83. See Roy, *Bitters in the Honey.*

84. See Andrews, *The Political Economy of Hope and Fear* at 4.

85. See Thomas F. Pettigrew, *Racial Discrimination in the United States* (1975).

86. See Dinesh D'Souza, *The End of Racism: Principles for a Multiracial Society* (1995); Dinesh D'Souza, *Illiberal Education: The Politics of Race and Sex on Campus* (1991); Richard J. Herrnstein and Charles Murray, *The Bell Curve* (1994); Lino Graglia, "Professor Loewy's 'Diversity' Defense of Racial Preference: Defining Discrimination Away," 77 *North Carolina Law Review* 1505 (1999).

87. Roy, *Bitters in the Honey.*

88. The enslaved conditions of blacks, for example, was not an issue in Brazil the way it was for the United States at the very founding of the republic in crafting the representation clauses of the federal constitution. See U.S. Const. Art. I, Sec. 2, cl. 3 (granting southern states additional representatives by counting their non-voting slaves as three-fifths of a person); Art. I, Sec. 9, cl. 1 (permitting the importation of African slaves until 1808); Art. IV, Sec. 2, cl. 3 (requiring states to enforce fugitive slave laws). See Thomas E. Skidmore, "Racial Ideas and Social Policy in Brazil, 1870–1940," in *The Idea of Race in Latin America, 1870–1940,* 8 (Richard Graham, ed., 1990).

89. Nobles, *Shades of Citizenship* at 117. Compare this to Jose Vasconcelos, *The Cosmic Race* (1979).

90. Nobles, *Shades of Citizenship* at 87.

91. Ibid. at 108, 109.

92. Skidmore, "Racial Ideas and Social Policy," at 18.

93. João Batista de Lacerda, the Director of the National Museum of Brazil, delivered his paper with the "whitening thesis" embedded in a "scientific assessment of the races" at the First Universal Races Congress in London in 1911. Thomas Skidmore, *Black into White* at 65–66 (1974). When he delivered this paper, Lacerda noted that W. E. B. Dubois, "a mestiço," praised it. Ibid. at 67. See also Nobles, *Shades of Citizenship* at 85–128; Rebecca Reichmann, ed., *Race in Contemporary Brazil* (1999).

94. Skidmore, *Black into White* at 64–66.

95. Reichmann, ed., *Race in Contemporary Brazil.*

96. Skidmore, *Black into White* at 68.

97. Carl Degler, *Neither Black nor White: Slavery and Race Relations in Brazil and the United States* at 183 (1986). Edison Carneiro, *Ladinos e crioulos* at 116 (1964). Skidmore illustrates this problem when he writes, "The publication of my *Black into White* (*Preto no Branco* [Rio de Janeiro: Ed. Paz e Terra, 1976]) led a columnist for the leading Rio daily to denounce American professors who try to introduce 'an irrelevant discussion of the racial problem.' (João Luiz Faria Netto, "Importaço supérflua," Jornal do Brasil, July 17, 1976)." Skidmore, "Racial Ideas and Social Policy" at 36. Reichmann, ed., *Race in Contemporary Brazil* at 14–20. Melissa Nobles *Shades of Citizenship.*

98. See Nelson do Valle Silva and Carlos Hasenbalg, "Race and Educational Opportunity in Brazil," in Reichmann, ed., *Race in Contemporary Brazil* at 58.

99. Charles Wagley, as cited in Degler, *Neither Black nor White* at 104–105.

100. Ibid. at 105. (We have here adopted the North American language of racial categories, rather than using the Portuguese categories used by the Brazilians.)

101. Kathleen Bond, "Racism: Black Movement Searches for Justice in Brazil," in *News from Brazil*, no. 374, November 12, 1999 at internal footnote 1 (emphasis in the original).

102. Degler, *Neither Black nor White* at 179. See, e.g., Bond, "Racism." See also Nobles, *Shades of Citizenship* at 85, and Luiz Claudio Barcelos, "Struggling in Paradise: Racial Mobilization and the Contemporary Black Movement in Brazil," in Reichmann, ed., *Race in Contemporary Brazil* at 155–166.

103. See Nobles, *Shades of Citizenship,* chs. 3 and 4.

104. See Donna Lee Van Cott, *The Friendly Liquidation of the Past: The Politics of Diversity in Latin America* (2000).

105. Degler, *Neither Black nor White* at 184.

106. Reichmann, ed., *Race in Contemporary Brazil.*

107. Nobles, *Shades of Citizenship.*

108. See Bond, "Racism."

3. Race as a Political Space

1. *Hopwood v Texas* 78 F.3d 932 (5th Cir. 1996).

2. Sturm and Guinier, "The Future of Affirmative Action: Reclaiming the Innovative Ideal," 84 *California Law Review* 953 (July 1996); Lani Guinier, "Confirmative Action in a Multiracial Democracy," in *State of Black America 2000* (Hugh Price, ed., 2000).

3. Linda Wightman, quoted in Lani Guinier, Michelle Fine, and Jane Balin, *Becoming Gentlemen: Women, Law, And Institutional Change,* at 104n11 (1997).

4. Sturm and Guinier, "Future of Affirmative Action."

5. For example, Jorge Chapa, then a professor at the Lyndon Baines Johnson School of Public Affairs at the university, had crucial demographic information.

6. Sturm and Guinier, "Future of Affirmative Action."

7. Ibid. at 979, 989.

8. H.B. 588, 75th Leg. (Tex. 1997); William Forbath and Gerald Torres, "Merit and Diversity after Hopwood," 10 *Stanford Law and Policy Review* 185 (1999).

9. Compare the impact of the changes in higher education admission plans in Texas and Florida. The Texas plan was formulated by the communities that were hurt the most by the elimination of affirmative action. The process, once initiated by those who knew they were being left out, also revealed structural inequalities in the admissions process that hurt communities that were like communities of color. In Florida, by contrast, Governor Jeb Bush unveiled his 20 percent plan without consulting the affected communities and

without guaranteeing access to the flagship campuses that were historically the routes to social power. Instead, his One Florida Plan was concocted to head off the threatened anti-affirmative action referendum that Ward Connerly, a conservative black California businessman, was trying to put on the Florida ballot. At least one commentator attributes the high black voter turnout in the 2000 presidential elections to these misguided efforts to undo affirmative action. See Dick Polman, "Florida Blacks Mobilized against a Bush Named Jeb," *Philadelphia Inquirer,* November 20, 2000.

10. See Bruce Walker, "Report on Admissions," forthcoming. See also the reports on current progress at the website: http://www.utexas.edu/student/research/reports/reports.html.

11. Jane Mansbridge and Aldon Morris, eds., "Oppositional Consciousness" (manuscript, August 2000). See also Gary Alan Fine, "Public Narration and Group Culture: Discerning Discourse in Social Movements," in *Social Movements and Culture* at 128–129, 134 (1995) (describing system of shared knowledge, beliefs, behaviors, and customs to which group members can refer and which they can employ as the basis of further interaction; a social movement is a "bundle of stories"); Oscar Gandy, Jr., *Communication and Race: A Structural Perspective* at 48 (1998); Anthony Pratkanis and Marlene Turner, "Persuasion and Democracy: Strategies for Increasing Deliberative Participation and Enacting Social Change," 5 *Journal of Social Issues* 187, 195–196 (Spring 1996).

12. *New York Times,* June 16, 2000, at A1, A24.

13. Martha Mahoney, "The Anti-Transformation Cases," September 16, 1999 (draft, on file with authors), citing Robin D. G. Kelley, *Hammer and Hoe: Alabama Communists during the Great Depression* at 136, 139–140, 154–156, 218–220 (1990). For example, the organizing drive of rubber workers at Firestone reflected mobilized black support while confronting, with difficulty, white racism and insecurity. Blacks apparently formed the majority of militant organizers among both workers and farmers in Alabama at that time. See also, for example, the story of Crystal Lee Sutton in Victoria Byerly, *Hard Times Cotton Mill Girls: Personal Histories of Womanhood and Poverty in the South* at 201, 206 (1986): "We were real strong with the blacks but we were weak with the whites."

14. Martin Luther King, Jr., told his SCLC staff that "we're going to take this movement and we're going to reach out to the poor people in all directions in this country. We're going into the Southwest after the Indians, in the West after the Chicanos, into Appalachia after the poor whites, and into the ghettos after Negroes and Puerto Ricans. And we are going to bring them together and enlarge this campaign into something bigger than just a civil rights movement for Negroes." Martin Luther King, Jr., Remarks, Southern Christian Leadership Conference's Staff Retreat, Frogmore, South Carolina, November 1967, Center for Nonviolent Social Change, Atlanta, Georgia; quoted in Stephen B. Oates, *Let The Trumpet Sound: The Life of Martin Luther King, Jr.,* at 449–450 (1982).

15. David Roediger, *Towards the Abolition of Whiteness: Essays on Race, Politics, and Working Class History* (1994).

16. Mahoney, "The Anti-Transformation Cases" at 56–57. The union, which was 90 percent black, energetically pursued grievances for nonmembers as well as members, did outreach to white workers, and fought against favoritism in ways that helped proportionately more blacks but also helped some whites. The union also became increasingly active in the local community on civil rights issues. Whites rejoined the union and a few whites who were not politicians even joined the Martin Luther King Day parade organized by the union. See also Kim Moody, *Workers in a Lean World: Unions in the International Economy*

at 178 (1999) (quoting a national organizer from Teamsters for a Democratic Union: "Smart white activists don't just tolerate this diversity, they seek it out. The union context brings out the best in people"). Of course, many unions had to be sued before they would admit black workers.

17. Immigrants from El Salvador and other countries with strong popular movements can be especially active participants in organizing efforts in the United States. See Jennifer Gordon, "We Make the Road by Walking: Immigrant Workers, the Workplace Project, and the Struggle for Social Change," 30 Harvard Civil Rights–Civil Liberties Law Review 407, 439n94 (1995). (Among the Workplace Projects' board members and the members of the workers committee are veterans of an agricultural cooperative in Honduras, the teachers' union ANDES in El Salvador, and the Salvadoran and Guatemalan student movements.)

18. Steven Greenhouse, "Los Angeles Warms to Labor Unions as Immigrants Look to Escape Poverty," New York Times, April 9, 2001, at 14.

19. See Gordon, "We Make the Road by Walking" at 428, 447, 444–450n72. "The long-term plan of the Project is to build individual workplace committees in each industry—one at each restaurant, each street corner, and each cleaning company where workers are interested in organizing . . . To . . . succeed in our ultimate goal, we must build a member-ship in which workers in one industry recognize that the problems of workers in other in-dustries are their problems as well . . . Our goal [is to organize] a broad-based movement of workers from different industries and communities in struggle against the vast array of social, economic, and political injustices that they face."

20. Cornel West, Prophesy Deliverance! An Afro-American Revolutionary Christianity at 71 (1982).

21. Fine, "Public Narration and Group Culture: Discerning Discourse in Social Move-ments" at 132.

22. Fredrick C. Harris, Something Within: Religion in African-American Political Activ-ism at 40, 28, 30–31 (1999). The faith-based bonds and shared rituals provide blacks with the material resources and oppositional dispositions through which to articulate griev-ances and forge collective identities. They foster "collective action frames" that "inspire and legitimize social movement activities and campaigns." Ibid. at 36, citing David Snow and Robert D. Benford, "Master Frames and Cycles of Protest," in Frontiers in Social Move-ment Theory (Aldon D. Morris and Carol McClurg Mueller, eds., 1992). See also, Sidney Verba, Kay Lehman Scholzman and Henry Brady, Voice and Equality: Civic Voluntarism in American Politics (1995).

23. Harris, Something Within at 139, quoting Andy Young as cited by Charles V. Hamil-ton, The Black Preacher in America at 132–133 (1972).

24. Harris, Something Within at 35, citing David Alan Corbin, Life, Work, and Rebellion in the Coal Fields: The Southern West Virginia Miners, 1880–1922 at 169 (1981). Christian-ity, for these insurgents, "promoted collective thought and action, gave cohesion and strength to a social class, and permitted the miners to resist the servility and feelings of in-feriority that class oppression often breeds in the oppressed."

25. Harris, Something Within at 35, citing Daniel Levine's analysis of communities in Colombia and Venezuela where community organizers used biblical scriptures as a means to "link faith to action" and to express "solidarity, sharing and sacrifice in the community." Daniel Levine, Popular Voices in Latin American Catholicism at 139 (1992). Marshall Ganz, "Resources and Resourcefulness: Strategic Capacity in the Unionization of California Ag-riculture, 1959–1966," 105 American Journal of Sociology 1034–1036 (January 2000).

26. Peggy McIntosh, "White Privilege and Male Privilege: A Personal Account of Coming to See Correspondences through Work in Women's Studies," Center for Research on Women, Wellesley College, Working Papers Series, no. 189 (1988).

27. They experienced the outcome of what Louis Massiah observed on the walking tours we described in the Prologue (note 4): black male alienation and constant confrontation rendered them more likely to go to prison than to college; thus, they became less available or "attractive" mates. This phenomenon is discussed in greater detail in Chapter 8. See also text accompanying notes 38–40 at pages 87–88.

28. Her reaction could be read as a critique of the social and regulatory regime of marriage associated with some queer theorists. See Janet Halley, "Recognition, Rights, Regulation, Normalization Rhetorics of Justification in the Same-Sex Marriage Debate," July 2, 2001 (unpublished manuscript). Or it could be seen to parallel the experience of young Japanese women who shun marriage and its idealization of family life because they have lost hope that they can bridge the inequity in gender roles in current Japanese marriages. As a result young Japanese women have created their own ways of having fun, and they don't feel excluded if they are not involved with someone. Peggy Orenstein, "Parasites in Prêt-à-Porter," *New York Times Magazine*, July 1, 2001, at 31, 34–35.

29. Julio Finn, *The Bluesman: The Musical Heritage of Black Men and Women in the Americas* (1992).

30. See Sara Rimer, "Joined at the Stoop: Neighbors Till The End," *New York Times*, November 7, 1999, at 1, 32.

31. This story was related to Lani Guinier in a personal conversation with Professor Randy Stakeman whose son, Jackson, is now in college.

32. Janie Victoria Ward, *The Skin We're In: Teaching Our Children to Be Psychologically Strong, Socially Smart, and Spiritually Connected* (2000). This is consistent, in many ways, with the more developed form of oppositional consciousness that Mansbridge and Morris articulate: "A more full-fledged oppositional consciousness includes identifying a specific dominant group as causing and in some way benefiting from those injustices. It also includes seeing certain actions of the dominant group as forming a 'system' of some kind that advances the interests of the dominant group. Finally, it can include a host of other insurgent ideas, beliefs and feelings that provide coherence, explanation and moral condemnation." "Oppositional Consciousness" at 6.

33. Evelyn Brooks Higginbotham, "African-American Women's History and the Metalanguage of Race," in *We Specialize in the Wholly Impossible: A Reader in Black Women's History* at 13 (Darlene Clark Hine, Wilma King, and Linda Reed, eds., 1995). "Race signified a cultural identity that defined and connected [blacks] as a people, even as a nation."

34. Beverly Daniels Tatum, *Why Are All the Black Kids Sitting Together in the Cafeteria? And Other Conversations about Race* at 72–74 (1997).

35. Comments at the Fifth Annual Derrick Bell Lecture, New York University Law School, November 10, 2000.

36. "Problems deemed too far astray of respectability are subsumed within a culture of dissemblance." Evelyn Brooks Higginbotham, "African-American Women's History and the Metalanguage of Race" at 17 (describing failure of black community to tackle the AIDS crisis because of historic association of disease and racial/sexual stereotypes).

37. See Janet Halley, "Gay Rights and Identity Imitation: Issues in the Ethics of Representation," in *The Politics of Law: A Progressive Critique* at 118 (David Kairys, ed., 1998).

38. The complex relationships between power, ideology, and interpellation as devel-

oped by Marxist social and political theorists are tangential to our argument; rather, we are relying on the more fundamental conclusion that through this process of interpellation power acts to construct certain subjectivities. Michel Foucault makes a similar argument in his theoretical construction of power and, importantly, locates power in many of the small events of everyday life. Power in his view is constructive as well as disciplinary: that is, it constructs the subject both through the process of interpellation described by Althusser as well as through the resistance that the exercise of power entails. See Chapter 5.

39. Francis X. Clines, "Appeals for Peace in Ohio after Two Days of Protests," *New York Times,* April 16, 2001, at A16 (describing how a black 19-year-old in Cincinnati, Ohio, ran when confronted by the police). "They keep asking me why did my son run," his mother, Angela Leisure said. "If you are an African male, you will run." Her view was supported "emphatically" in interviews conducted by the reporter in the predominantly black neighborhood known as Over-the-Rhine, where protests against the shooting originated and where merchants in the historic Finlay Market suffered the brunt of the vandalism and looting. A coalition of black civil rights groups and the American Civil Liberties Union of Ohio filed suit in federal court in Cleveland accusing Cincinnati of a "30-year pattern of racial profiling." The suit says that blacks are routinely singled out by the police for minor offenses far more than whites are and that police officers "tend to use excessive and deadly force against African-Americans more readily than against whites." The suit said that from 1995 to 2000, the Cincinnati police killed 13 suspects, all of them black. Timothy Thomas, a 19-year-old, was killed on April 7, 2001, the fourth black killed by the police since November. See also Colin Hay, "Mobilization through Interpellation," 4 *Social and Legal Studies* 208 (1995).

40. *Brown v City of Oneonta,* 195 F.3d 111 (1999).

41. Charles C. Lemert, *French Sociology: Rupture and Renewal since 1968* at 104 (1981). "The usage clearly exaggerates the importance of what we now recognize to be a very narrow zone of social viability" and unreflexively identifies "a local experience with the universal human condition." By contrast, the "we" of the weak-we member "refers to occasional, but deeply understood, groupings of individuals sharing similar or same historical experiences, usually below, or marginally outside, the world to which the first group's [strong] 'we' refers." The differences between the two groups is not simply one of degree; thus, we should avoid the temptation to "deride the strong-we position as 'essentialist,' the weak-we as 'tribalist.'" Rather, Lemert locates the important distinction between those who seek universal truths based on their individual experience (strong-we) and those who seek remediation of felt injustice based on concrete historical relations between the individual and local groups (weak-we). Strong-we individuals can thus be read as having "independent construals of self." See also Hazel Rose Markus and Shinobu Kitayama, "Culture and the Self: Implications for Cognition, Emotion, and Motivation," *The Culture and Psychology Reader* at 159–216 (Nancy Rule Goldberger and Jody Veroff, eds., 1995). We do not mean that all whites or all blacks are named by power in exactly the same way. But we do mean that in a society with as explicit a historical racial hierarchy as ours, such generalizations are nevertheless probative at the meta-level.

42. Michele Lamont, "Colliding Moralities between Black and White Workers," in *From Sociology to Cultural Studies: New Perspectives* at 263, 265, 266–267 (Elizabeth Long, ed., 1997).

43. We acknowledge our debt here to Troy Duster, who first suggested the analogy of

race to water, although he presented it as a way of reconciling the postmodern and the modern views of the left toward race. We, however, use the analogy to tell a particular story about racial agency, linking the concepts of action and identity to this specific historical period in the United States.

44. "To be white in America is not to have to think about it. Except for hard-core racial supremacists, the meaning of being White is having the choice of attending to or ignoring one's own Whiteness." R. W. Terry, "The Negative Impact on White Values," in *Impact of Racism on White Americans* at 120 (B. P. Bowser and R. G. Hunt, eds., 1981), cited in Janet Helms, *Black and White Racial Identity* at 50 (1990).

45. For a sample of this liberal theory of self, see Jeremy Bentham, *An Introduction to the Principles and Morals of Legislation* at 66–69 (1824; Alan Ryan, ed., 1987) (stating that communities are "fictitious bodies" and that only interpersonal comparisons of individual benefit are relevant for determining the utility of a given action); John Rawls, *A Theory of Justice* at 12 (1971) (describing the ideal decision-makers as a people who have no idea of their individual identities, and thus have perfect symmetrical relations to one another in order to reach a decision as to what constitutes a fair distribution in society); Robert Nozick, *Anarchy, State, and Utopia* at 32 (1974) (arguing that individual rights should be viewed as "side-constraints" on state action so as to preserve the autonomy of an individual).

46. It is a more public version of the self than the independent construal, but it is a modestly less other-directed version of the interdependent model.

47. See Jennifer Crocker, Brenda Major, and Claude Steele, "Social Stigma," in *The Handbook of Social Psychology* (Daniel Gilbert et al., eds., 1998); Claude M. Steele et al., "The Mentor's Dilemma: Providing Critical Feedback across the Racial Divide," 25 *Personality and Social Psychology Bulletin* 1302 (1999); Claude M. Steele et al., "Stereotype Threat and the Test Performance of Academically Successful African Americans," in *The Black-White Test Score Gap* (Christopher Jencks et al., eds., 1998); Claude M. Steele, "Stereotyping and Its Threat Are Real," 53 *American Psychologist* 680 (1998); Claude M. Steele, "Race and the Schooling of Black Americans," in *Sociocultural Perspectives in Social Psychology: Current Readings* (Letitia Anne et al., eds., 1997).

48. See Paulette M. Caldwell, "A Hair Piece: Perspectives on the Intersection of Race and Gender," 1991 *Duke Law Journal* 365.

49. See *www.census.gov/prod/3/98pubs/p20–504u.pdf* (visited 5/23/00). See Lani Guinier, *The Tyranny of the Majority: Fundamental Fairness in Representative Democracy* (1994); Michael Dawson, *Behind the Mule: Race and Class in African American Politics* (1994); Cheryl D. Mills, "Talking to Oprah Isn't Enough," *New York Times*, September 30, 2000, at A15, A27. Thirty percent of black women surveyed said they were "very interested" in politics and 43 percent agreed with the statement, "I have a moral responsibility to be involved in politics." For all women in the survey, the comparable figures were 25 percent and 38 percent. Black women turned out at the rate of 42 percent in 1998 while the overall turnout was closer to 38 percent, despite the fact that those making less than $20,000 a year are the least likely to vote. According to the Census Bureau, "Black voters were the only demographic group to defy the trend of declining turnout from 1994 to 1998. The black turnout increased in the same period." Indeed, many of the complaints about disenfranchisement of black voters that arose in conjunction with the presidential election in Florida in 2000 can be tied to a dramatic and unexpected surge in black voter

turnout. Harold Meyerson, "A House Divided," *L.A. Weekly,* June 15–21, 2001 (among registered voters Latinos outperformed all others in the city, voting at a rate of 41 percent compared with an overall citywide total of 36 percent).

50. Lani Guinier, "Confirmative Action," 25 *Law & Social Inquiry* 565, 570n18 (Spring 2000), interpreting the findings linking race to public service after graduation in David L. Chambers, Richard O. Lempert, and Terry K. Adams, "From the Trenches and Towers," "Michigan's Minority Graduates in Practice: The River Runs through Law School," 25 *Law and Social Inquiry* 395 (Spring 2000) (study of 30 years of affirmative action at the University of Michigan Law School).

51. Scholars of "narrative identity," for example, argue that experience is constituted through race-, gender-, or culture-specific stories, which help construe and consolidate identity and then guide action. Such stories connect individuals to a social network of relationships and allow them to discern the meaning of any single event in temporal and specific historic terms. See Margaret R. Somers, "The Narrative Constitution of Identity: A Relational and Network Approach," 23 *Theory and Society* 605, 613–616 (1994). See also Theodore M. Singelis, "The Measurement of Independent and Interdependent Self-Construals," 20 *Personality and Social Psychology Bulletin* 580–582, 588 (1994). See generally Ian Haney-Lopez, *White by Law: The Legal Construction of Race* (1996); Yen Le Espiritu, *Asian American Panethnicity* (1992; Markus and Kitayama, "Culture and the Self" at 159–216 (examining recent research on both American and Asian views of personhood). See also Ladd Wheeler, Harry T. Reis, and Michael Harris Bond, "Collectivism-Individualism in Everyday Social Life: The Middle Kingdom and the Melting Pot" in *The Culture and Psychology Reader* at 297–312 (defining Americans as individualist and Chinese as more collectivist).

52. Evelyn Brooks Higginbotham, "African-American Women's History and the Metalanguage of Race" at 3.

53. Will Kymlicka, *Citizenship in Diverse Societies* (2000); Kymlicka, *Contemporary Political Philosophy: An Introduction* (1990); Kymlicka, *Ethnicity and Group Rights* (1997); Kymlicka, *Liberalism, Community, and Culture* (1989); Kymlicka, *Multicultural Citizenship: A Liberal Theory of Minority Rights* (1995); Kymlicka, *The Rights of Minority Cultures* (1995).

54. M. L. King, *Where Do We Go from Here: Chaos or Community?* at 159 (1967).

55. While conceptualizing the weak-we group in terms of self-construal expands "construal of self" from its roots in social psychology's traditional studies of small groups, recent trends in social psychology have "embrace[d] larger, more abstract collectives such as racial and ethnic categories." Dale T. Miller and Deborah A. Prentice, "The Self and the Collective," 20 *Personality and Social Psychology Bulletin* 452 (1994). See also Somers, "The Narrative Constitution of Identity."

56. Nancy Rosenblum's study in *Membership and Morals* (1998) of groups like homeowner associations also illuminates the benefits of group membership. She notes that homeowner associations provide the opportunity for rule-following, collective self-government, and proprietary self-concern. While our project seeks to explore the dynamics of political and not just civic associations, participating in political race groups may cultivate both these important "old-fashioned" virtues as well as perhaps new conceptions of political strategy.

57. Michael Walzer, "Multiculturalism and Individualism," 41 *Dissent* 185 (Spring

1994)(comparing fears of grossly atomized and alienated individuals to fears of balkanized and self-involved groups; finding the latter less dangerous to democratic practices because of the socializing effect of group membership).

58. Judith Shklar, *American Citizenship* (1991). See also Orlando Patterson, *Slavery and Social Death* (1982); Clifford Geertz, "On the Nature of Anthropological Understanding," 63 *American Scientist* 48 (1975), cited in Markus and Kitayama, *Culture and the Self: Implications for Cognition, Emotion, and Motivation* at 163.

59. Oscar Gandy, *Communication and Race: A Structural* Perspective (1998); Natalie Angier, "Do Races Differ? Not Really, DNA Shows," *New York Times,* August 22, 2000, at F1, F6. Scientists say that while it may be easy to tell at a glance whether a person is Asian, African, or Caucasian, the differences dissolve when one looks beyond surface features and scans the human genome for DNA hallmarks of "race."

60. We want to stress here that we are using the peculiar meaning of race within the American context as a foundation for these claims.

61. One example of this alienation in our civic culture is low voter turnout. In 1996, 48.9 percent of the voting age population voted in the presidential election. In 1994, 36.6 percent voted in the congressional elections. In 1992, 55.1 percent voted. See http://www.census.gov/prod/3/98pubs/p25-1132.pdf. The 60.9 percent turnout in 1968 was the last time over 60 percent of the eligible population voted. See www.census.gov/population/www/socdemo/voting.html (visited 5/23/00).

62. Archon Fung, "Street Level Democracy," ch. 7 at 1 (Ph.D. diss., Massachusetts Institute of Technology, 2000).

63. Ibid., ch. 7 at 4–5: the goal is to find solutions to common problems rather than to aggregate opposing views. Deliberation seems appropriate "not only to decide the best course, but also to gain the allegiance necessary to implement it." Voting, however, is described as a "best guess" as to a working hypothesis, rather than a firmly arrived at view.

64. Ibid. ch. 11 at 39–40, 44, citing *Chicago Community Policing Evaluation Consortium* at 95–132 (1997).

65. Ibid., ch. 11 at 25: "City-wide evidence that compares neighborhood participation rates in Chicago's community policing program weigh against strong egalitarian predictions." Indeed, the effect of college education on the attendance at neighborhood beat meetings is the opposite of the expected direction—it weakly reduces beat meeting attendance. Ibid. at 18–21, 24.

66. Ibid., ch. 11 at 51. Forty-two percent of LSC members are black; 14 percent are Hispanic; 40 percent are white. Chicago's population, at the time of this study, was 38 percent black, 20 percent Hispanic, and 38 percent white. The authors of the study conclude that "the racial and ethnic composition of individual councils tend to resemble the race and ethnicity of the students in the schools." See Anthony S. Bryk et al., *Charting Chicago School Reform: Democratic Localism as a Lever for Change* at 11 (1998), cited by Fung, "Street Level Democracy," ch. 11 at 51.

67. Fung, "Street Level Democracy," ch. 11 at 30–32. Part of the reason that studies find lower rates of voting by race is that they often fail to control for class. See, for example, the work of Dianne Pinderhughes and Michael Dawson, both of whom find comparatively high levels of black voting.

68. Ibid., ch. 11 at 32. This is also consistent with studies finding high levels of black turnout when the first black runs for office in a previously all-white legislative body. See

Guinier, *The Tyranny of the Majority*, ch. 3. Although turnout often then recedes after the election of the "first black," this is not inconsistent with Fung's findings. Indeed, our claim, developed in Chapter 6, is that the synecdoche of using racial symbolism as a form of ascriptive as well as descriptive representation is a thin view of democracy that political race challenges.

69. Fung, "Street Level Democracy," ch. 11, citing evidence that counters the imagined criticism of strong egalitarians, like Jack Nagel, who assume that the more intensive "the form of participation, the greater the tendency of participants to over-represent high-status members of the population." Jack Nagel, *Participation* at 58 (1987). But see Jack Nagel, *The Descriptive Analysis of Power* (1975) at 51–52: in mixed ethnicity schools where the student body averages 50 percent white, an average of 85 percent of the LSC members are white.

70. Fung, "Street Level Democracy," ch. 11 at 52, citing the *Chicago Community Policing Evaluation Consortium* at 35 (1996).

71. Jennifer Gordon observed that the commonality of language and culture did not necessarily lead to consensus on strategy. Email to Lani Guinier, October 24, 2000.

72. Because race is a sociopolitical category and not a biological category, it must be analyzed with full awareness of the specific historical features of the category. Instances of white racial nationalism have to be understood within the context of those periods in American history when white racelessness was destabilized. Those periods can be characterized by insecurity in the boundaries of the dominant community. See Michael Omi and Howard Winant, *Racial Formation in the United States from the 1960s to the 1980s* at 20 (1994); Neil Foley, *The White Scourge: Mexicans, Blacks, and Poor Whites in Texas Cotton Culture* (1997).

73. Instead, the experience of blacks and other weak-we groups is important to understanding conditions for participatory democracy. To attack the biological essentialist theories of race does not, in our analysis, require that racial identity be abandoned as a basis for political organization and mobilization.

74. The role that white race-consciousness plays in contemporary America is not only a result of social and economic dislocation but of anxiety about experiencing loss of control in the absence of cultural or ethnic roots. In this sense, some whites resent in blacks what they have lost: a sense of ethnic pride or a sense of place. Lani Guinier, conversation with Phil Thompson, June 6, 1995.

75. One of our student research assistants offered the following contemporary illustration of the challenge of using the concept of race in a political way, but not essentializing it, and not using it as a term to exclude progressive minded people. Steig Olson writes: "I have seen this phenomenon happen, wherein race is an organizing, but not excluding term, with[in] the hip-hop community. Hip-hop . . . is a movement . . . that . . . organized around a form of black music (rap music) that is often a self-conscious attempt to address political, social and personal issues. There is certainly no attempt to be 'color-blind' in this music; in fact, issues of race are dominant. But the 'hip-hop movement' has become something broader than this music, and instead understands itself to be a certain kind of consciousness—aesthetic and political—that is centrally attuned to minority issues. To make this point, let me give you a run-down on the articles that are in the latest issue of *The Source*, which . . . calls itself 'the magazine of hip-hop music, culture and politics,' and [while it] concentrates on music (mainly black artists, but more and more Latinos, and a

few white artists), roughly the first third of the (long) magazine has . . . informative political articles. This month's included: (1) Ain't a Damn Thing Changed!: A History of Police Brutality in New York. (2) A short discussion of the four presidential candidate's positions on and plans for 'reducing juvenile crime.' (3) A short discussion of recent developments in the Assata Shakur case, as compared to Elian Gonzalez. (4) Positively Negative: Why some TV news stories about 'good' black folk have a detrimental effect. (5) The Bullets and the Ballot—about the hypocrisy of people who protest the Diallo verdict, but don't vote. (6) Stakes is High: about the Pechanga Native American tribe in California, and their experience with casinos. The definite consciousness that this magazine is addressing is concerned with race, particularly the black-American experience, but does not exclude other racial groups from that consciousness. It is hard to say what links all of those articles together, other than a certain 'canary' consciousness, a consciousness attuned to the presence of the poison gas, and the condition of those most vulnerable to it. Moreover, there is always the sense that looking at the experience of these minority groups gives an insight into broader issues, much like the miner's canary mentality that you are cultivating." Email from Steig Olson to Lani Guinier, April 9, 2000.

76. See Robert C. Smith, *We Have No Leaders: African Americans in the Post Civil Rights Era* at 258, 259 (1996) (describing the "new orthodoxy" in the post-civil rights era that the Democratic Party's "embrace of the cause of civil rights and racial justice has resulted in the disaffection of white southerners and the urban white lower-middle class, with the result that it is extraordinarily difficult to forge a majority presidential coalition"). See also Thomas Edsall and Mary Edsall, *Chain Reaction: The Impact of Race, Rights, and Taxes on American Politics* (1992).

77. As Martha Mahoney writes, "Emphasizing only race or only class has the effect of placing white workers in a more conservative position than when both are considered together. Every time either of these aspects—whiteness or class interest in solidarity—is made invisible by being pretended or assumed away, the other interests shift in response. If white dominance and privilege remain invisible and only class interests are emphasized, the fact that society is already constructed by race will cause some inevitable collision, as race (the 'Other' to white workers) shapes demands for inclusion and transformation." Mahoney, "The Anti-Transformation Cases" at 52. We agree with Mahoney, although we develop this argument in slightly different directions.

78. Michael Goldfield, *The Color of Politics: Race and the Mainsprings of American Politics* at 245 (1997). Statewide Operation Dixie leaders even sent back national CIO literature with interracial pictures. Their racial orientation at times caused them to lose textile elections where the percentages of blacks were high, because they failed to get sufficient support from African-American workers, an almost unheard of problem for CIO unions in the mid- and late 1940s.

79. Mahoney, "The Anti-Transformation Cases" at 55, citing an interview with Monica Russo, District Manager, Amalgamated Clothing and Textile Workers, Miami, Florida, October 1994. After the union lost the election they came back a few years later, consciously bringing both blacks and whites into leadership. In 1995 ACTWU merged with the ILGWU into UNITE. The second campaign, now led by UNITE, became the largest victory for the union in twenty years. See also David Firestone, "Union Victory at Plant in South Is Labor Milestone," *New York Times,* June 25, 1999, at A15: "Workers at the nation's largest textile plant—a huge brick fortress of resistance to labor organizing in the South—

apparently ended a 93-year epoch on Wednesday night and voted to allow a textile workers union inside the walls to represent them." Labor experts said the turnabout may be the result, in part, of "growing numbers of immigrants in the work force who tend to be more likely to support unionization."

80. Mahoney, "The Anti-Transformation Cases" at 60.

81. Eric Mann, *Taking on General Motors: A Case Study of the UAW Campaign to Keep GM Van Nuys Open* at 172, 151–184 (1987). Marshall Ganz's case study of the effectiveness of the United Farm Workers organizing efforts among Mexican Americans reflects a similar assessment.

82. Mahoney, "The Anti-Transformation Cases" at 46–47, citing Robert Zellner, "Labor and Civil Rights," Presentaion at Law and Society Association, Philadelphia, May 1992. The GROW project also apparently had a continuing impact on local politics after Mississippi civil rights organizations backed what was nevertheless a failed strike and Charles Evers "won political support during his gubernatorial campaign in Mississippi from striking white woodhaulers who had never before considered even shaking hands with an African-American." Ibid. at 48, citing Jason Berry, *Amazing Grace: With Charles Evers in Mississippi* at 219–250 (1978).

83. Beverley Skeggs, *Formations of Class and Gender* at 95, 74 (1997). See also Miriam Fraser, "Classing Queer: Politics in Competition," 16(2) *Theory, Culture and Society* 107 (April 1999). Fraser identifies a tension between an activism that requires a willingness to be visible and the refusal of many white working-class women to claim, even privately, a working-class identity or to be visibly identifiable as a member of the working class. Ibid. at 123–125.

84. Beth Roy explains the interaction beautifully in her analysis of interviews with white and black adults who attended Central High School in Little Rock, Arkansas, in 1957. *Bitters in the Honey* (1999) at 321–325. She is not surprised, therefore, that we do not really know who we are in class terms, that we have only the vaguest of class identities and tend to collapse all classes into one.

85. See Charles Tilly, *Durable Inequality* (1999) (race-based mobilization can draw attention to the systematic use of paired asymmetrical categories in exploitation, what class-based mobilization ordinarily overlooks).

86. Roy, *Bitters in the Honey* at 325–326.

87. Martha Mahoney, "The Anti-Transformation Cases" at 5 (draft manuscript September 16, 1999). For these reasons, in part, this nation has never developed a labor party, and union membership is down to around 12 percent. Any attempt to pursue class-based mobilization for comprehensive social policy reform almost always brings the cry of class warfare, which is the death knell for any serious debate within those lines of analysis.

88. The Reverend Bernice A. King, daughter of the late MLK, cautioned that "we must do more than honor a man of this magnitude with just a holiday; we must honor him with action. We must honor him by bringing into reality what he merely dreamed about. Until we are willing to honor Dr. King with consistent, liberating actions, then we dishonor him with our mere words, and he is a prophet without honor." "A Prophet without Honor," sermon delivered at Ebenezer Baptist Church to commemorate the twenty-fifth anniversary of the death of Martin Luther King, Jr., January 18, 1993, in *Hard Questions, Heart Answers: Sermons and Speeches* at 4 (1996).

89. Todd Gitlin, "Racial Obsession Taking a Toll," in *Chicano Politics and Society in the*

Late Twentieth Century (David Montejano, ed., 1999) at xi: "We think race, act race, tabulate race, celebrate race, fear race."

4. Rethinking Conventions of Zero-Sum Power

1. This aspect of "connectedness" as gendered is illustrated in a wonderful anecdote reported in *Reflections on Gender and Science* at 115 (1995) by Evelyn Fox Keller: "In a class after a reading of Genesis, my colleague had asked his students to think about why it was that the word knowledge was used in that text simultaneously in the sexual and the epistemological sense. One student, a young man, responded, "That's obvious. Both are about power!" "Oh no," retorted another student, a young woman. "It's because both are about being in touch."

2. Indeed, Jean Baker Miller, in *Toward a New Psychology of Women* at 116, 117 (1976), argues that the very meaning of power is "distorted" or "skewed" by the fact that power has traditionally been associated with men. Miller says, "Power so far has at least two components: power for oneself and power over others . . . The power of another person, or group of people, was generally seen as dangerous. You had to control them or they would control you." Miller sees power in what she calls "agency-in-community," which is very different from the more male-oriented perception of "self-separate-from-community" in which power is a win/lose situation by definition. But cf Catharine A. MacKinnon's position that women's way of exercising power is a function of and insight into their powerlessness. *Feminism Unmodified: Discourses on Life and Law* (1987).

3. The grandmother was asking, "What were the real rules?" See Elmer Eric Schattschneider, *The Semisovereign People: A Realist's View of Democracy in America* at 105 (1960): "Whoever decides what the game is about also decides who gets in the game."

4. This has elements of the second dimension in that, according to Michael Parenti, "One of the most important aspects of power is not to prevail in a struggle but to predetermine the agenda of struggle—to determine whether certain questions ever reach the competition stage." "Power and Pluralism: A View from the Bottom," 32 *Journal of Politics* 501 (1970).

5. Peter Bachrach and Morton S. Baratz, "The Two Faces of Power," 56 *American Political Science Review* 947 (1962); Peter Bachrach and Morton S. Baratz, *Power and Poverty: Theory and Practice* at 43 (1970): "Those who benefit are placed in a preferred position to defend and promote their vested interests."

6. The lessons that flow from the treatment of "victory" by the girls suggest that they reverted to the dominant gender construction of what it means to prevail. It means to divide and cements a power to exclude. It also suggests that, as Anna Yeatman argues, feminism conflated the very idea of freedom with established models of self-governance, effectively working for women to become like men. "Feminism and Power," in *Reconstructing Political Theory: Feminist Perspectives* at 144, 148, 152 (Mary Lyndon Shanley and Uma Narayan, eds., 1997).

7. That the girls were in the majority merely added an additional overlay by reference to an unconscious but generally accepted criterion to legitimate their decision (as the guest of honor picked up). Importantly, this vignette speaks to the ways in which conceptions of legitimate power are transmitted. How are lessons learned? How are they actualized? Where does power come from?

8. See, for example, Nancy Hartsock, "Political Change: Two Perspectives on Power," 1

Quest 10, 12, 20 (Summer 1974): "Most social scientists have based their discussions of power on definitions of power as the ability to compel obedience, or as control and domination. They . . . add that power must be power over someone—something possessed, a property of an actor that he can alter the will or actions of others in a way which produces results in conformity with his own will." Hartsock's view links concepts of power to conceptions of isolated and competitive individuals who exist without community.

9. John Gaventa, "Power and Participation," in *Power and Powerlessness: Quiescence and Rebellion in an Appalachian Valley* (1980). Gaventa borrows extensively from Steven Lukes, *Power: A Radical View* (1974). Both theorists build on conventional pluralists' understanding that power is something we "have" or "lack," something we "use" to create "a political effect on another actor." Clarissa Rile Hayward, "De-Facing Power," 31 *Polity* 1 (Fall 1998). The idea that power has three faces developed in response to Robert Dahl's classic formulation: "A has power over B to the extent that he can get B to do something that B would not otherwise do." Robert Dahl, "The Concept of Power," *Behavioral Science* 201, 202–203 (July 1957). See also Robert Dahl, "The Concept of Power," in *Political Power: A Reader in Theory and Research* at 80 (Roderick Bell, David M. Edwards, R. Harrison Wagner, eds., 1969); Nelson W. Polsby, *Community Power and Political Theory* at 55 (1963) (the study of power is a study of who participates, who gains and loses, and who prevails in decision making). Social theorists in the 1960s and 1970s objected to Dahl's preoccupation with power as exercised in formal institutions. Gaventa and Lukes drew attention to the way power was exercised more subtly both to set agendas and to shape preferences and interests.

10. Peggy McIntosh, "Interactive Phases of Curricular Re-vision: A Feminist Perspective," Center for Research on Women, Wellesley College, Working Papers Series, No. 124 (1983), uses five interactive phases on a broken pyramid to symbolize curricular reform development. Although her approach does not neatly fit the dimensions of power, it is nonetheless a useful synthesis.

11. In the first-dimensional view associated with the classic pluralists like Dahl and Polsby, the processes are assumed to be accessible to all and the absence of conflict in an "open society" simply reflects social cohesion. The pluralist assumptions are that grievances are recognized and acted upon consistent with participation and influence; participation is assumed to occur within open decision-making arenas and "because of the openness of the decision-making process, leaders may be studied, not as elites, but as representative spokesmen for a mass." See, for example, Gaventa, "Power and Participation" at 30.

12. The second dimension accepts the idea of power as zero-sum but adds a second "face" that may not be directly observable in open conflict. The second-dimensional approach suggests that the mechanisms of power are not always straightforward. Nor do they merely involve well-understood political resources, such as votes, jobs, or influence that can "be brought by political actors to the bargaining game" and can be wielded through "personal efficacy, political experience, organizational strength." Gaventa, "Power and Participation" at 14. Instead, the second face of power adds to these resources the ability to "mobilize bias," to create "a set of predominant values, beliefs, rituals and institutional procedures ('rules of the game') that operate systematically and consistently to the benefit of certain persons and groups at the expense of others." Bachrach and Baratz, *Power and Poverty* at 43.

13. Lukes, *Power* at 24, 34. The third-dimension approach emphasizes the way the powerful influence the less powerful's conception of the issues. Unlike the first dimension in which A exercises power over B by directly coercing or controlling or even—in the second dimension—indirectly influencing the rules so that B does what A wants, in the third dimension A may exercise power over B by constructing or structuring B's reality: by mobilizing myths and symbols to convince B that challenging A's power is fruitless. Thus, the analysis of power should also "consider the many ways in which potential issues are kept out of politics, whether through the operation of social forces and institutional practices or through individual decisions." The third dimension of power occurs even in the absence of observable conflict by influencing, shaping, or determining "conceptions of the necessities, possibilities and strategies of challenge in situations of latent conflict." See Gaventa, "Power and Participation" at 15. Martha Minow, *Making All the Difference: Inclusion, Exclusion and American Law* at 111, 237–238 (1990): "Power may be at its peak when it is least visible: when it shapes preferences, arranges agendas, and excludes serious challenges from either discussion or imagination."

14. Bill Readings, *Introducing Lyotard: Art and Politics* at 63 (1991).

15. This formulation of the interrelationship of the three dimensions of conventional political or social power borrows directly from John Gaventa's model. See Gaventa "Power and Participation" at 22. Gaventa explores the interaction of these dimensions in his effort to explain the silence and nonparticipation of powerless groups who might be able to change the relative inequity of their position if they were to mobilize.

16. In some interpretations, the third dimension seems to devolve simply into a claim of false consciousness. We thank Marshall Ganz and Orly Lobel for the reminder that the third dimension can also refer to structures that demobilize or discourage participation.

17. The first understanding of the "I am a power person" reply in the adult version reminds us of the power of terminology. By calling the game a "relay race"—the girls convinced the boys to play. This was not only a game but a game the boys thought they could win. Similarly, by using the term power instead of process, Martha believed she was gaining legitimacy in the eyes of authority at the meeting. See, for example, Ronald A. Heifetz, *Leadership without Easy Answers* at 101–102 (1994).

18. See, for example, Steven Winter, "The 'Power' Thing," 82 *Virginia Law Review* 721, 725 (August 1996): "The close interweaving of questions of power and agency is not fortuitous, of course. Power connotes potency, capacity, control and, for many, is virtually unthinkable without agency . . . [W]hat could 'power' possibly mean if A cannot even control his or her own choices?"

19. Jean Bethke Elshtain, *Power Trips and Other Journeys: Essays in Feminism as Civic Discourse* at 136 (1990) (power is of, by, and for elites). The third dimension is simply an architectural device to disguise the exercise of official power.

20. See Lukes, *Power* (power operates in the third dimension most effectively through the creation of hegemony).

21. Seth Kreisberg, *Transforming Power* at 55 (1992).

22. See, for example, Gail Collins, "Why the Women Are Fading Away," *New York Times Magazine*, October 25, 1998, at 54. On the other hand, Peggy McIntosh and others have challenged the "add women and stir" approach. See, for example, McIntosh, "Interactive Phases of Curricular Re-vision."

23. Louis Uchitelle, "Lonely Bowlers, Unite: Mend the Social Fabric," *New York Times*,

May 6, 2000, at A15, A16 (quoting the sociologist Theda Skocpol that advocacy groups are run by "elite people more than ever," while the millions of members mail in their dues and contributions).

24. See Melissa Harris-Lacewell, "Barbershops, Bibles, and B.E.T.: Everyday Black Talk and the Development of Black Political Thought" (unpublished manuscript, 2000)(describing the claim, supported by empirical and quantitative research, that blacks use community dialogue to jointly develop understandings of their collective political interests).

25. William Bowen and Derek Bok in their comprehensive study of affirmative action at elite institutions, *The Shape of the River* (1998), suggest that society benefits from opening opportunity to previously excluded groups, in this case, African Americans. The benefits they depict include development of a leadership cadre that better reflects American demographics, that enhances the ability of all Americans to work and play well with people who are different, and that promotes individuals who, despite weaker test scores and college grades, pursue career opportunities in business, law, and medicine at higher rates and are more likely to be civic minded.

26. Ibid.; Mari Matsuda and Charles Lawrence, *We Won't Go Back: Making the Case for Affirmative Action* (1997).

27. *Quiet Revolution in the South: The Impact of the Voting Rights Act, 1965–1990* (Chandler Davidson and Bernard Grofman, eds., 1994); Frank Parker, *Black Votes Count* (1990).

28. See, for example, Susan Sturm and Lani Guinier, "The Future of Affirmative Action: Reclaiming the Innovative Ideal," 84 *California Law Review* 953 (July 1996); Lani Guinier, Michelle Fine, and Jane Balin, *Becoming Gentlemen: Women, Law Schools and Institutional Change* (1997); Lani Guinier, *Tyranny of the Majority* (1994).

29. See Lani Guinier, "Confirmative Action," 25 *Journal of Law and Social Inquiry* 565 (2000), discussing David L. Chambers, Richard O. Lempert, and Terry K. Adams's study of Michigan Law School graduates since 1970: "Michigan's Minority Graduates in Practice: The River Runs Through Law School" 25 *Journal of Law and Social Inquiry* 395 (2000). See also David Wilkins, "Rolling on the River: Race, Elite Schools and the Equality Paradox," 25 *Journal of Law and Social Inquiry* 527 (2000).

30. James Carroll, "Black Caucus Sends a Message about Justice," *Boston Globe*, January 9, 2001, at A19: "It was the Black Caucus, and the Black Caucus alone, that showed itself sensitive to that gap (between what rules require and what is clearly true about the recent presidential election in Florida) . . . perhaps the Black Caucus registered its protest (when the electoral college votes were counted and when they could not get a single Senator to join in their written objection) as a way of bringing forward an ancient epiphany . . .: those who sit atop the social and economic pyramid always speak of love, while those at the bottom always speak of justice."

31. For example, affirmative action compensates for the inadequacy of conventional criteria to assess true merit. The problem with affirmative action, however, is that it fails to demonstrate that the conventional criteria are in fact inadequate to predict true merit not only for women or people of color but for almost all applicants. Sturm and Guinier, "Future of Affirmative Action." See also Lani Guinier, "Reframing the Affirmative Action Debate", 86 *Kentucky Law Review* 505 (1998).

32. To some extent this makes sense, in the psychosocial dimension of "confidence" or expectation of success. But it does not seem persuasive when made in response to hostility from working-class whites who resent their own failure to succeed.

33. Very little attention is paid to which racial group members benefit. At some elite colleges, for example, admissions officials no longer even recruit in urban public schools but limit their applicant pool to students of color from suburban or private schools.

34. "We naturally tend to be more aware of the power that limits us than we are of ourselves as limits to the power of others." Amelie Oksenberg Rorty, "Power and Powers: A Dialogue between Buff and Rebuff," in *Rethinking Power* at 5 (Thomas Wartenberg, ed., 1992). See also ibid. at 4: "Power is a mote in the eye of the perceiver. Like freedom, power is most acutely seen and most perceptively understood by those who lack it."

35. See, for example, Ellen Nakashima and David Maraniss, "13 Ways of Looking at Al Gore and Race," *Washington Post*, April 23, 2000 at W6 (describing a recent meeting with then Vice President Al Gore and black leaders, set up by Bob Johnson, founder of Black Entertainment Television).

36. For example, George Bush appointed several blacks to key White House and Cabinet posts. While this outreach is admirable, it is not at all clear that Bush's policy positions, even if enforced by people of color, would transform the social or economic position of those who are not already in the middle income bracket. Even with Colin Powell as secretary of state, there is no accountability mechanism in place other than the good will or conscience of the new insider. Moreover, penetrating one hierarchy does not assure that larger hierarchies in which they remain as outsiders are affected. For example, in South Africa black elected officials are "political insiders" but economic outsiders.

37. Sheryl Gay Stolberg, "Skin Deep: Shouldn't a Pill Be Colorblind?" *New York Times*, May 13, 2001, at 1, 3 (citing research at Yale University finding black doctors also offer common heart procedures more frequently to whites than blacks). "Doctors have been socialized to view patients who are poor, or black, or both, as inappropriate candidates for certain high-tech procedures." By participating within elite hierarchies, even black doctors internalize elite assumptions. In this sense, "there is something about going through medical school that creates, or reinforces, stereotypes, like some people's not wanting certain kinds of care or being less able to comply with doctors' instructions." Sheryl Gay Stolberg, "Blacks Found on Short End of Heart Attack Procedure," *New York Times*, May 10, 2001, at A20.

38. Raymond L. Hogler and Guillermo J. Grenier, *Employee Participation and Labor Law in the American Workplace* at 109 (1992). See also Orly Lobel, *Coercion and Agency in Labor and Employment Relations* (2000).

39. Lobel, *Coercion and Agency* at 77, citing James R. Lincoln and Arne L. Kalleberg, "Commitment, Quits and Work Organization in Japanese and U.S. Plants," 50 *Industrial and Labor Relations Review* 39, 56 (1996).

40. Gerald E. Frug, "The Ideology of Bureaucracy in American Law," 97 *Harvard Law Review* 1276, 1286–1287 (1984).

41. Susan Sturm, "Race, Gender and the Law in the Twenty-first Century Workplace: Some Preliminary Observations" at 2 (September 10, 1998, draft, on file with author).

42. Lobel, "Agency and Coercion" at 61. In addition to the idea of encoded hierarchy, a psychological ensemble is developed to cope with a culture that is essentially organized in a pyramid of power-over. Without emphasizing exit and voice to minimize the illegitimate use of horizontal coercion, the risk of replicating power-over relations is always present.

43. See Dana Milbank, "Harold Ford Jr. Storms His Father's House," *New York Times Magazine*, October 25, 1998, at 40. Milbank examines the political calculations of a young black congressman representing a politically safe (that is, majority black) district in Ten-

nessee that his father had once represented. But while the father was more oriented to the concerns of his black constituents, identifying with their poverty because of his own origins, the son is more oriented to his own ambitions, eyeing a possible Senate seat which requires that he moderate his political philosophy to appeal beyond the black majority in his district to the white majority in the state of Tennessee. Ford was then only 26 years old and yet was already networking with his eye on a larger prize.

44. J. L. Chestnut, Jr., and Julia Cass, *Black in Selma: The Uncommon Life of J. L. Chestnut, Jr./Politics and Power in a Small American Town* at 212 (1990). J. L. Chestnut states succinctly the danger of delegating to a charismatic leader, whether black or white, too much authority to frame the issues.

45. Ronald Heifetz, *Leadership without Easy Answers* at 73: "Authority relationships are critical to doing work in many routine situations and, applied properly, can be used invaluably in more challenging times; yet misapplied they serve to avoid work." Ibid. at 57 (arguing that authority can be given and taken away; it is "conferred power to perform a service."). See also Mano Singham, "Canary in the Mine: The Achievement Gap between Black and White Students," 80 *Phi Beta Kappan* 9, 14 (September 1998) (citing researcher Signithia Fordham's studies—"Racelessness as a Factor in Black Students' School Success," 58 *Harvard Educational Review* 54 (February 1988)—of black high school students in Washington, D.C. Fordham found a marked difference in attitudes toward academic success between generations of blacks attending school in the 1980s and those who participated in the civil rights movement. The civil rights movement generation pursued a temporary strategy of promoting trailblazers who would yield long-term benefits for their community. Young blacks observe that the success of the pioneers did not breed widespread success: "A few more blacks made it into the professions but nowhere near the numbers necessary to lift up the whole community." Singham, "Canary in the Mine" at 11. Thus Fordham reports that "young black people see the strategy of using individual success to lead to community success as a fatally flawed one.").

46. Nor is it limited to bureaucratic forms of organization. See Sturm, "Race, Gender and the Law" at 48. As Sturm observes, even egalitarian teams experience complaints of discrimination from women and people of color. Those newly included as "insiders" are unable to exercise influence, nor command respect of their peers.

47. Jean L. Cohen and Andrew Arato, *Civil Society and Political Theory* at 560 (1992): "The politics of identity constitutes the actors of civil society; the politics of inclusion, after the necessary transformations in the organization and orientation of these actors, establishes them as members of political society. The politics of reform, finally, involves the strategic activity of political organizations and parties in the generation of state policy."

48. John S. Dryzek, "Political Inclusion and the Dynamics of Democratization," 90 *American Political Science Review* 475 (September 1996).

49. Ibid. at 480.

50. David Ost, "Solidarity and Public Space in Poland: From Civil Society to Bourgeois Society" (paper prepared for Annenberg School for Communication Scholars Conference on Public Space, March 1–4, 1995).

51. Harris-Lacewell, *Barbershops, Bibles and B.E.T.* at 2, 7.

52. Social psychology studies find that "political learning is dependent at least to some degree" on political participation within and mastery upon one's environment. Ibid. at 17–18. See also Allesandro Pizzorno, "An Introduction to the Theory of Political Participation," 9 *Social Science Information* 45 (1970). This has certainly been the experience of Su-

san Sturm and Lani Guinier in co-teaching "Critical Perspectives: Issues of Race and Gender," a seminar that involved students sharing responsibility for planning and facilitation at the University of Pennsylvania Law School. See Susan Sturm and Lani Guinier, "A Failure Theory of Success: The Role of Multiracial Learning Communities" (manuscript, 1998).

53. Heifetz's thesis is that true leadership gives the power back to the people to do "adaptive work." See also Richard L. Berke, "The Good Leader: In Presidents, Virtues Can Be Flaws (and Vice Versa)," *New York Times*, September 27, 1999, at Week in Review 1: the moral leader (for some) is "the one who seizes upon the power of high office to enact policies that clarify national ideas and to inspire the people, summoning society to greatness."

54. Jose Calderon, "Multi-Ethnic Coalition Building in a Diverse School District," 21 *Critical Sociology* 101 (1995).

55. Ibid. at 105.

56. "Live Now Poll," *New York Times Magazine*, May 7, 2000 (cover data) at 56, 58.

5. Enlisting Race to Resist Hierarchy

1. "When someone is fired, there's someone at home depending on that paycheck. You're not just firing that individual, you're firing their wife, you're firing their husband, whatever." Governor Spencer, a K-Mart worker quoted in Kennedy School Case Study, part 1 at 3.

2. This was an interestingly personalized view of the union struggle because, as epitomized by a Greensboro *News & Record* editorial, April 16, 1994, at A8, the predominant view outside of the union and the Pulpit Forum was that the "union's problems with K-Mart are simply that: problems with the company. Wage complaints have nothing to do with the Jaycees or the GGO (Greater Greensboro Open)." Two interesting things to notice here: first, the view of the unionization effort as an isolated individualized struggle and the view that it was only about wages.

3. Kennedy School Case Study, part 1 at 16.

4. Ibid., part 2 at 5.

5. Ibid., part 2 at 6, quoting Reverend Johnson.

6. Lani Guinier, *Lift Every Voice: Turning a Civil Rights Setback into a New Vision of Social Justice* at 240 (1998).

7. "'A college professor at Guilford College, his whole class went with him to jail. He went, and they went with him.' Reverend Johnson laughed. 'And they were discussing their grades in jail.'" Interview with Reverend Johnson, as reported in Guinier, *Lift Every Voice*.

8. Guinier, *Lift Every Voice* at 242–243.

9. Ibid. at 243.

10. Michel Foucault developed these ideas during the course of writing several historical studies, or "archaeologies" as he referred to them, including *Discipline and Punish: The Birth of the Prison* (1975), *Madness and Civilization: A History of Insanity in the Age of Reason* (1964), *The Birth of the Clinic: An Archaeology of Medical Perception* (1963), and the first volume of *The History of Sexuality* (1976). In these meticulously researched studies Foucault argued that understandings of these fundamental concepts were a product of material, social, and economic forces. In the process, he developed a new conception of power that was radically different from the modern conception. See J.-F. Lyotard, *The Post-Modern Condition: A Report on Knowledge* (1984).

11. Foucault, *Discipline and Punish*.

12. In Foucault's analysis: "The real transactions of power are not in the relationships of citizens to the state, but in the relationships of people to teachers, doctors, therapists, social workers, and psychiatrists. These are not the benign and ameliatory aides of the welfare state but rather moral agents whose disciplinary power is based on their membership in the credentialed knowledge elite." James Farganis, "Post-Modernism," in *Readings in Social Theory: The Classic Tradition to Post-Modernism* at 420 (James Farganis, ed., 1996, 2nd ed.).

13. Patricia Williams, *The Alchemy of Race and Rights* (1991) (arguing against the postmodern view in support of a more emancipatory strategy that may be futile but is still critical); Harlon Dalton, "The Clouded Prism," 22 *Harvard Civil Rights Civil Liberties Law Review* 435 (1987).

14. Nancy Hartsock, "Political Change: Two Perspectives on Power," 1 *Quest* 14 (Summer 1974). Hartsock credits Berenice Carroll in an unpublished paper, "Peace Research," for pointing out that in *Webster's International Dictionary* (1933) power is first defined as "ability, whether physical, mental or moral, to act; the faculty of doing or performing something" and is synonymous with "strength, vigor, energy, force and ability." The words "control" and "domination" do not appear as synonyms. See Hartsock, "Political Change" at 15. In fact, Foucault was moving toward that conclusion in his later work. See *History of Sexuality*, Vol. 1: *An Introduction* (1976), Michel Foucault, *The Uses of Pleasure* (1984), and *The Care of the Self* (1984). We use realization here in the sense of achievement, accomplishment, and insight: knowing and doing.

15. But cf. Ronald A. Heifetz, *Leadership without Easy Answers* (1994) (suggesting the importance of uncoupling authority and leadership in order to explore fully the possibilities of leadership in new situations; Heifetz points out that power, especially the power to lead in complex or new situations, does not necessarily accrue to those in authority).

16. *Rethinking Power* (Thomas E. Wartenberg, ed., 1992); *Power in Modern Societies* (Marvin E. Olsen and Martin N. Marger, eds., 1993); Steven Lukes, *Power: A Radical View* (1994).

17. See Austin Sarat's piece on the death penalty lawyers in *Cause Lawyering* (Austin Sarat and Stuart Scheingold, eds., 1998); also see Derrick Bell, *Faces at the Bottom of the Well* (1992) (arguing that racism is inexorable and it is futile to resist it although necessary nonetheless).

18. Seth Kreisberg, *Transforming Power: Domination, Empowerment and Education* at 57 (1992), citing Dorothy Emmet, "The Concept of Power," in *Power* at 89–90 (1971).

19. David Shields, "The Good Father," *New York Times Magazine*, April 23, 2000, at 58, 61 (describing Phil Jackson's "emancipated" style of coaching and quoting his view of the most effective way to forge a winning team).

20. We know, for example, Bachrach says, "that as persons from lower classes become active within organizations, they become more active in politics . . . Persons who in their everyday life—in their clubs, professional organizations, and social activity—have the opportunity of formulating and honing their opinions are in a position to determine where their interests lie . . . It is not until socially disadvantaged groups become involved in structuring their own channels of communication and their own decision-making forums that they will begin to gain self-awareness." Peter Bachrach, "Interest, Participation and Democratic Theory," in *Participation in Politics* (J. Roland Pennock and John W. Chapman, eds., 1975). See also Michael Walzer, "Multiculturalism and Individualism," 41 *Dissent* 185

(Spring 1994) (arguing that participation in social conflict socializes individuals to increase their capacity and appetite for further social involvement).

21. Others, including the feminist Nancy Hartsock, have identified this alternative concept of power, although they do not develop it in precisely the way we do here. See Hartsock, "Political Change" at 23: "At bottom, political change is a process of changing power relationships so that the meaning of power itself is transformed." Janet Surrey, as cited by Kreisberg in *Transforming Power* at 64, describes "power with" as "truly a creative process, as each person is changed through the interaction."

22. John Gaventa also develops this concept based on Paulo Freire's idea that a "critical consciousness" grows out of democratic experience, and the denial of this opportunity has the additional cost of reducing the capacity of people to critically engage social institutions. See John Gaventa, "Power and Participation," in *Power and Powerlessness: Quiescence and Rebellion in an Appalachian Valley* at 18 (1980).

23. See Treisman, "Studying Students Studying Calculus: A Look at the Lives of Minority Mathematics Students in College," 23(5) *College Mathematics Journal* 362 (1992).

24. There are many bases on which to critique conventional educational approaches, from the preoccupation with testing (on the assumption that the role of education is to teach those who are smart and the tests are necessary to determine who in fact is "teachable") to the passive nature of much of our curriculum. See Mano Singham, "The Canary in the Mine: The Achievement Gap between Black and White Students," 80 *Phi Delta Kappan* 8 (September 1998) (describing the traditional model of education).

25. Jennifer Steinhauer, "So the Tumor Is on the Left, Right?" *New York Times*, April 1, 2001, citing study published in 2000 in the *British Medical Journal* comparing attitudes among pilots to those of surgeons, despite the spotlight now on medical error. While 64 percent of surgeons surveyed felt that high levels of teamwork occurred in their operating room, their view was shared by only 28 percent of surgical nurses and 39 percent of anesthesiologists, underscoring a strong disconnect between the different members whose functions are critical to successful surgery.

26. Anthony Pratkanis and Marlene Turner, "Persuasion and Democracy: Strategies for Increasing Deliberative Participation and Enacting Social Change," 5 *Journal of Social Issues* 187, 189–190 (Spring 1996).

27. Hartsock, "Political Change" at 10, 16. In many ways Nancy Hartsock describes our effort to reconceptualize power-with in conjunction with efforts to promote social change. In 1974 she wrote: "Thus, creating political change involves setting up organizations based on power as energy and strength, groups which are structured and not tied to the personality of one individual, groups whose structures do not permit the use of power as a tool for domination of others in the group. At the same time, our organizations must deal with the society in which we live on its own terms—that is, terms of power as control, power as a means of making others do what they do not wish to do."

28. Kendall Thomas, "Racial Justice: Moral or Political?" at 12 (unpublished draft, forthcoming in Austin Sarat's *Law's Conception*, 2001) (crediting Jane Mansbridge's terminology).

29. "One of the successes of Septima Clark as a bridge leader was her ability to connect the politics of the movement to the needs of the people." Belinda Robnett, "African-American Women in the Civil Rights Movement, 1954–1965: Gender, Leadership and Micromobilization," 101 *American Journal of Sociology* 1681 (May 1996). "She found that by lis-

tening to the problems of the potential rural constituents, they then became willing to listen to the teachers."

30. Guinier, *Lift Every Voice* at 197–198. Spencer Hogue and his wife Jane turned their living room in Perry County, Alabama, into one such school. As Spencer later explained, "We ran a school in our home to teach people how to read and write. People would come sit in the living room or we would move everything from the dining room into the kitchen and people would sit there. And a lot of people came to love us from that." Neither Spencer nor Jane Hogue had finished high school, but they discovered that people learn best from their peers.

31. Robnett, "African-American Women in the Civil Rights Movement" at 1682–1683.

32. SNCC (pronounced "snick") was the Student Nonviolent Coordinating Committee, founded by black students at Shaw University in Raleigh, North Carolina, in 1960 to coordinate sit-ins and fight white oppression. Eventually SNCC's membership extended to college campuses throughout the country.

33. Guinier, *Lift Every Voice* at 303. See also Pat Watters and Reese Cleghorn, *Climbing Jacob's Ladder: The Arrival of Negroes in Southern Politics* (1967).

34. Penda Hair, "Louder than Words: Lawyers, Communities and the Struggle for Justice," *A Report to the Rockefeller Foundation* at 75 (March 2001).

35. Ibid.

36. Marshall Ganz, "Resources and Resourcefulness: Strategic Capacity in the Unionization of California Agriculture, 1959–1966," 105 *American Journal of Sociology* 1004 (January 2000). Nationally driven AFL-CIO efforts to organize farmworkers in California had always failed, but just four years after the UFW had begun organizing and six months after calling its first strike the UFW signed its first multiyear contract, in 1966. The UFW also played a major role in the emergence of a Chicano movement in the Southwest, recruited and trained hundreds of community activists, and became a significant player in California.

37. Marshall Ganz refers to both these concepts in his defense of his Ph.D. dissertation, "Five Smooth Stones: Strategic Capacity in the Unionization of California Agriculture" (final draft) (June 7, 2000).

38. Ganz, "Resources and Resourcefulness" at 1036.

39. Ibid. at 1030, 1034: "Traditions of mutuality among extended families modeled the mutuality at the core of the striker community, and Mexican history came alive as slogans appeared on walls that read: Viva Juarez! Viva Zapata! Viva Chavez!" See also Peter Matthiessen, *Sal Si Puedes* (1969) (describing the uneasiness of some of the UFW workers and volunteers with the Catholic symbolism). Despite the dominant presence of Mexican Americans in the UFW, it organized all farmworkers, especially the Filipinos who would converse in Tagalog while others spoke in Spanish and English.

40. Marshall Ganz email to Lani Guinier, May 30, 2001.

41. Ganz, "Five Smooth Stones." The term "charismatic communities" was inspired by Durkheim's "collective effervescence," although Durkheim used it to describe religious communities and Ganz means to broaden its usage to include forms of commitment and connection that create an energy which makes people willing to sacrifice, experiment, and struggle toward noble social purposes. Email from Marshall Ganz to Lani Guinier, May 30, 2001: The idea builds on Victor Turner's idea *(The Ritual Process)* of "communitas," a liminal, solidaristic, egalitarian relationship into which people enter in moments of transi-

tion from one status to another, linking it with the intense moral communities at the core of most social movements.

42. Jennifer Gordon, "We Make the Road by Walking: Immigrant Workers, the Workplace Project, and the Struggle for Social Change," 30 *Harvard Civil Rights Civil Liberties Law Review* 407, 435–436 (1995).

43. The oppositional consciousness nurtured by the Workplace Project or Southern Echo should not, however, be confused with rituals of inclusion that openly celebrate diversity in some multiracial communities. For example, Cultural Sharing Day at PS19 in Elmhurst-Corona, Queens, which celebrated Chinese New Year, Dominican Republic Independence Day, and Brotherhood Week, was, according to Roger Sanjek, a "symbol of ethnic diversity" and an "exhortation of racial harmony" that acknowledges "the changing composition of the community" the school now serves. Roger Sanjek, *The Future of Us All: Race and Neighborhood Politics in New York City* at 333 (1998). Cultural Sharing Days signal openness to different perspectives, but they do not seek to inspire participants to continue to engage in disruptive or transformative collective actions to further social change. They do not rest on the idea of an oppositional civic culture but aim to incorporate a richer civic culture within traditional zero-sum politics. We are not disparaging these efforts to promote civic engagement; but we do distinguish them from the rituals of solidarity that seek to transform, rather than merely repopulate, fundamental I-win/you-lose hierarchies.

44. Lois Parkinson Zamora and Wendy B. Faris, eds., Introduction, in *Magical Realism: Theory, History, Community* at 10 (1995).

45. See, for example, the work of Orly Lobel, *Coercion and Agency in Labor and Employment Relations* (2000).

46. See email to Lani Guinier from Hazel Edney, October 5, 1998, who covered these meetings for the black press.

47. Ganz, "Resources and Resourcefulness" at 1015–1017. The energy and commitment of the UFW can be traced in part to biography. The AFL-affiliated union organizing campaign was led by middle-aged white men whose organizing experience was primarily in insider politics. In the UFW, the leadership was Mexican and Mexican-American men and women mostly under 34 whose lives were rooted in the farmworker community but extended well beyond it. Their experience in and local knowledge of the farmworker community combined with white clergymen who had come to share a vocation to improve the lives of farmworkers. Thus, they enjoyed multiple sociocultural networks and tactical repertoires learned by organizing people like themselves.

48. AWOC led more than 150 strikes, some of which yielded temporary wage increases, but they failed to produce stable membership or a union contract. Ibid. at 1022, 1027.

49. Grace Lee Boggs, "Unions Are Doing It Backwards," *Michigan Citizen*, July 1–7, 2001. See also David Moberg, "Organization Man," *The Nation*, July 16, 2001, at 23, 28 (John Wilhelm, head of the Hotel and Restaurant Employees Union, says locals in L.A. and Las Vegas must develop their identity as immigrant unions; in the dynamic energy among new immigrant workers lies great potential for union organizing and progressive politics).

50. Email from Jennifer Gordon to Lani Guinier, October 25, 2000.

51. Ibid.

52. The techniques for deciding without resorting to the crude dynamics of binaries are well known within the literature of group process.

53. See Susan Sturm, "Second Generation Employment Discrimination: A Structural Approach," 101 *Columbia Law Review* 458 (April 2001). See also our discussion of Archon Fung's observations about the monthly police beat meetings in Chicago in Chapter 3. Our own experience with participation on university appointment committees has been valuable in helping us (1) to develop relationships with other faculty who then are willing to read or comment on one's research and scholarly work, (2) to learn about the institution, and (3) to try to change the criteria/standards being used to open up space for non-conventional candidates, for challenging ideas that a single individual embodies "excellence," and for suggesting that excellence is the sum of the individuals we hire. Even when the "minority-preferred" candidate is not hired, incremental transformation can occur over time as a result of the relationships that are established. On the other hand, without allies on the committee, such participation can be both meaningless and alienating.

54. Many of these ideas, especially the importance of redefining what counts as a means to a guiding end, were inspired by the benchmarking and bootstrapping approach of "democratic experimentalism." Michael Dorf and Charles Sabel, "A Constitution of Democratic Experimentalism," 98 *Columbia Law Review* 267, 285–288 (1998). "These principles enable the actors to learn from one another's successes and failures while reducing the vulnerability created by the decentralized search for solutions."

55. William Simon, "Visions of Practice in Legal Thought," 36 *Stanford Law Review* 469, 489 (1984).

56. See Archon Fung, "Street Level Democracy" (Ph.D. dissertation, Massachusetts Institute of Technology, 2000), ch. 13.

57. Robnett, "African-American Women in the Civil Rights Movement" at 1662–1665, 1678. Of course, SNCC, which was created with Ella Baker's help, never had a woman leader even as Baker's philosophy became the cornerstone of community mobilization. Nevertheless, the organization functioned as a bridge among students throughout the South as well as between the student organizers and local communities. "The idea was for SNCC to build leadership within a respective community but not to become its leader."

58. For example, Bernice Reagon, a member of SNCC, stated, "So that one of the things that happened to me through SNCC was my whole world was expanded in terms of what I could do as a person. And I'm describing an unleashing of my potential as an empowered human being." This idea was echoed by "most of the women" Robnett and others interviewed. They felt their experiences in the movement to be liberating rather than constrained by their gender. Ibid. at 1676.

59. Charles Payne, "Men Led but Women Organized: Movement Participation of Women in the Mississippi Delta," in *Women in the Civil Rights Movement* at 158 (Vicki Crawford, Jaqueline Rouse, and Barbara Woods, eds., 1990).

60. C. Cryss Brunner and Paul Schumaker, "Power and Gender in the 'New View' Public Schools," 26 *Public School Journal* 30, 35, 37 (1998). They interviewed three applicants for a position as school superintendent in a small midwestern community called "New View." The two men "acted under a social control model of power," whereas the woman applicant "acted under a social production model of power." Mary Osburn, the woman applicant, was also task-oriented, but she wanted to solve problems through a decision-making apparatus that yielded policies everyone could support. See also C. C. Brunner, "The New Superintendent Supports Innovation with Collaborative Decision-Making," *Contemporary Education* (in press) (study of 47 school superintendents throughout the United States, including multiple interviews with 25 male and 22 female superintendents,

revealed that 60 percent of the men, but only 9 percent of the women, had "power-over" orientations; 77 percent of the women but only 24 percent of the men had "power to" orientations; the remaining 16 percent of the men and 14 percent of the women in the sample had mixed conceptions).

61. Brunner and Schumaker, "Power and Gender" at 39, 41. Brunner and Schumaker do not argue that all political communities respond to fragmentation by seeking stronger forms of democracy. They recognize that many communities in transition seek centralizing and controlling leadership that "can reestablish the old social order." But the outcome of social fragmentation is not always predictable. In New View, which went from having 50 percent of its citizens as natives of the state in 1980 to one-third natives in 1990 (20 percent of the newcomers were minorities), the social fragmentation created a "functional need for collaborative leadership." Because changes in the community power structure and in the method for selecting leaders were accompanied by increasingly democratic norms, leaders with a collaborative "power to" style were allowed to emerge. For example, in New View, "many people came to believe that elected officials can share power-with other actors in an urban regime, but that their power must be more than simply 'overseeing' a policy process dominated by others." Ibid. at 40.

62. Ibid. at 41.

63. Fifty-eight Latinos ran for elected office in Massachusetts between 1968 and 1994. Fifty-seven percent of the Latinos elected to office have been women. Of the women who ran for office, 47 percent were elected; 15 percent of the men who ran were elected. *Directory of Latino Candidates in Massachusetts* (Center for Women in Politics and Public Policy 1995) (Principal Investigator: Carol Hardy-Fanta) at 4. See also Carol Hardy-Fanta, *Latino Electoral Campaigns in Massachusetts: The Impact of Gender* (1997).

64. Hardy-Fanta, *Latino Electoral Campaigns* at 30, 31.

65. Her findings echo those of other observers who discern similar patterns. See Gail Collins, "Why the Women Are Fading Away," *New York Times Magazine,* October 25, 1998, at 54, 55, in which she pursues the notion that women in politics are different. Harriet Woods, the former president of the National Women's Political Caucus, concludes, "Most women begin with community concerns, not ambition," both as candidates and as voters (the latter are more willing to support social spending and activist government and the former are "miraculously devoid of ego"). Two different sets of researchers—Susan Carroll and Wendy Strimling, and Edmond Constantini and Kenneth Craik—conclude that "women's participation is more often motivated by public-serving considerations, while men's participation is more often motivated by self-serving considerations." Hardy-Fanta, *Latino Electoral Campaigns* at 31–32.

66. Carol Hardy-Fanta, *Latino Electoral Campaigns* at 32: "The guys are there to advance their careers; the women are there as issue advocates. They care about something. Or they really want to serve the public."

67. Carmen Rosa, for example, "saw her success as due to the nature of her campaign: 'It was grassroots, *mano a mano,* People came together.'" Hardy-Fanta, *Latino Electoral Campaigns* at 36–37.

68. This is also consistent with the literature on women's political style. Ibid. at 40, citing Sherman, Cardozo, and Rohrback, "Draft Report for the Women Elected Municipal Officials" at 33; and Linda Witt, Karen M. Paget, and Glenna Matthews, *Running as a Woman: Gender and Power in American Politics* at 266 (1994).

69. Hardy-Fanta, *Latino Electoral Campaigns* at 44–45.

70. On the other hand, Jennifer Gordon and the Workplace Project in Long Island found, in part because immigrant Latinas often labor in isolation as domestics and carry the double burden of work and family, that "men are much more likely than women to participate in our organizing and educational efforts." Gordon, "We Make the Road by Walking" at 431.

71. Thomas B. Edsall, "Poll Finds Peril to House Democrats' Edge," *Washington Post*, May 1, 2001, at A5 (finding that men tilted toward the GOP 39 percent to 36 percent, while women leaned Democratic 42 percent to 31 percent; but the nature of that gap shifts dramatically when only white voters are polled: white men gave Republicans an advantage of 14 points and white female voters gave them a 1 point advantage; the GOP's "gender disadvantage" in congressional voting "is very much driven by minority voters," according to Ed Goeas, head of the Tarrance Group).

72. Ibid. (working women favor Democratic congressional candidates by 15 points, whereas women at home favor the GOP 49 percent to 26 percent).

73. Evelyn Brooks Higginbotham, "African-American Women's History and the Metalanguage of Race," in *We Specialize in the Wholly Impossible: A Reader in Black Women's History* at 7–8 (Darlene Clark Hine, Wilma King, and Linda Reed, eds., 1995).

74. The work of Stanford psychologist Claude Steele on stereotype threat, cited in Chapter 3, note 45, and Mano Singham, "The Canary in the Mine" at 9, 14 (discussing black students who condemn others who study for "acting white") are certainly relevant here.

75. Higginbotham, "African-American Women's History and the Metalanguage of Race" at 18.

76. Carol Gilligan's work relinks gender to narratives of healthy psychological and political resistance in order to protect girls from this loss of confidence and to make them more resilient in the face of social stress or failure. See Carol Gilligan, "Women's Psychological Development: Implications for Psychotherapy," in "Women, Girls, and Psychotherapy: Reframing Resistance," 11(3–4) *Women and Therapy* 5, 14 (1991) (evidence suggests that some girls respond to the psychological crisis of adolescence by devaluing themselves and feeling themselves to be worthless). See also Lyn Mikel Brown and Carol Gilligan, *Meeting at the Crossroads: Women's Psychology and Girls' Development* (1992) (describing an inter-generational cycle of silencing which undermines the potential for resistance and politics among girls and women); Lani Guinier, Michelle Fine, and Jane Balin, *Becoming Gentlemen: Women, Law School and Institutional Change* (1997) (finding that some women law students internalize their failures in law school and think they are stupid, whereas many more male students just think law school is hard). Students of color are not immune from this dynamic either.

77. Carla O'Connor, "Dispositions toward (Collective) Struggle and Educational Resilience in the Inner City: A Case Analysis of Six African-American High School Students," 34(4) *American Educational Research Journal* 593 (Winter 1997). Many of these kids say that they are learning (directly and indirectly) how to effectively and responsibly resist from their parents or other trusted adults. And in the beginning of her most recent book, the black baby boomer parents of adolescents that Ward interviewed also confirm that they believe it is important to talk about racism with their kids and teach their kids how to resist and fight back (though they may not have used these words exactly). See Janie Victoria Ward, "Resistance and Resilience," in *Souls Looking Back: Life Stories of Growing Up Black* (Andrew Garrod, Janie Victoria Ward, Tracy Robinson, and Robert Kilkenny, eds.,

1999); and Janie Victoria Ward, *The Skin We're In: Teaching Our Children to Be Psychologically Strong, Socially Smart, and Spiritually Connected* (2000).

78. Anna Yeatman, "Feminism and Power," in *Reconstructing Political Theory: Feminist Perspectives* at 148, 149 (Mary Lyndon Shanley and Uma Narayan, eds., 1997).

79. Many women of color, including Angela Harris, Kim Crenshaw, and Patricia Hill Collins, have criticized feminists for generalizing from the experience of white middle-class women, promoting a false unity of "women's lives." Others, such as Iris Marion Young, have pointed to the dangers of basing feminist visions on a unitary notion of women that fails to consider "univocal concepts of power" that are not rooted in enforcing homogeneity or conformity.

80. See Collins, "Why the Women Are Fading Away" at 54 .

81. We by no means suggest that white women should not benefit from affirmative action. Nor do we intend to minimize the tremendous challenges women still face in the workplace as well as in society as large. Our argument is limited to the reasons we focus first on race and then on gender and class.

82. It may reduce some understandings of the need to mobilize publicly for political and collective responses to systems of injustice. In other words, "personal is political" suggests that politics occurs in private spaces, which is true. But it does not articulate a clear mandate for a public politics as well. Catharine MacKinnon, *Toward a Feminist Theory of the State* (1989).

83. "It is not too late for predominantly white feminist organizations led by women of my generation to make issues of social justice that are attuned to the severity of racial bigotry and class as well as gender hierarchies the centerpiece of their own activist agendas. Not just in feminist but in so many other precincts of American society these days, the question of what a just society requires has been virtually eclipsed. But ultimately, I do not put my full faith in voluntarist politics, in politics motivated by altruistic convictions. What drove feminism several decades ago was a sense of self-interested possibilities and of personal justice denied. Similarly now, it will be the women [of color] in the first four rows of today's classrooms, the women that are hellbent to become the lawyers, the judges, the political and community leaders of tomorrow that will lead this struggle towards a successful conclusion. And when these women are ready to lead, we better be ready to follow." Mary Fainsod Katzenstein, "Remarks on Women and Leadership: Innovations for Social Change," sponsored by Radcliffe Association, Cambridge, Massachusetts, June 8, 2001.

84. Feminists have also sought to explore this dimension of power. See notes 14 and 21 to this chapter.

6. The Problem Democracy Is Supposed to Solve

1. The position of the "enfranchised mass" is still that of the "audience in a court of justice" rather than the jurors who have decision-making authority or "the political elites in legislatures and administrators who stand as judge and jury." Archon Fung, "Taking Democracy Seriously," in "Street Level Democracy," ch. 2 at 18 (Ph.D. diss., Massachusetts Institute of Technology, 2000), borrowing John Stuart Mill's analogy.

2. Andy Card, general cochairman and chief conceptualizer of the $63 million Republican event in Philadelphia, as quoted by Peter Marks, "A Plan to Accentuate the Positive and (at Least) Minimize the Negative," *New York Times,* July 25, 2000, at A18 (describing how Republican convention abandoned rituals of a political party gathering and adopted instead those of a marketing convention); Lynda Gorov, "Activists Plan to Counter the Con-

ventions: Wits, Reformers Target Traditional Party Fare," *Boston Globe*, July 3, 2000, at A1 (describing genesis of shadow conventions in activists' dismay that major party conventions have become coronations; in the words of one organizer they are "scripted events addressing themselves to a shrinking audience, a shrinking voting public, a shrinking engaged public").

3. Despite the warning of many in the generation that wrote the Constitution of the corrosive effect of a two-party system, the current Supreme Court has, in recent years, acted more strongly than ever to preserve it, ironically—given the state of political parties—finding those parties to have "associational interests" that trump innovations designed to enhance voter turnout or to broaden the range of ideas and the number of parties who can participate in meaningful and interactive forums for robust political debate. See *California Democratic Party v Jones*, 530 U.S. 567 (2000); *Arkansas Educ. Television Comm'n v Forbes*, 523 U.S. 666 (1997); *Timmons v Twin Cities Area New Party*, 520 U.S. 351 (1997).

4. These contemporary ideas have their origins in the framers' eighteenth-century aristocratic conception of political leadership. See Bernard Manin, *The Principles of Representative Government* at 121 (1997) (both the Federalists and the Anti-Federalists agreed that representatives should not be like their constituents). The touchstone of electability was "character," reflecting the classical republican ideal that "legislators were supposed to be disinterested umpires above the play of private interests." Gordon Wood, *The Radicalism of the American Revolution* at 258 (1992). Thus, extending the suffrage was not intended to include more people in the class of leaders. The ballot played the role of ratifying social and political hierarchies. Samuel Issacharoff, Pamela Karlan, and Richard Pildes, *The Law of Democracy* at 19 (1998). According to the historian Robert Wiebe, "leaders still assumed political office as their right and instructed the people as their duty." Robert H. Wiebe, *Self-Rule: A Cultural History of American Democracy* at 29 (1995). Voting was not the genuine collective choice between competing candidates in competitive contests; it was "a ritual of acclamation, a public act that recognizes (and reconstitutes) the superior status of the candidate." Don Herzog, *Happy Slaves* at 197 (1989).

5. Robert E. Pierre and Peter Slevin, "Fla. Vote Rife With Disparities, Study Says," *Washington Post*, June 5, 2001, at A01; Glen Johnson, "Balloting was unfair to blacks, report says," *Boston Globe*, June 9, 2001, A2.

6. Douglas J. Amy, "Plurality voting is consistently the worst at encouraging turn-out," in *Behind the Ballot Box: A Citizen's Guide to Voting Systems* at 170 (2000). See also voter turn-out window for all elections in all countries between 1945 and 1998 at http://www.idea.int/voter_turnout/voter_turnout2.html (visited August 26, 2001).

7. *Shaw v Reno*, 509 U.S. 630 (1993); *Miller v Johnson*, 515 U.S. 900 (1995); *Shaw v Hunt*, 517 U.S. 899 (1996) ("Shaw II"); *Bush v Vera*, 517 U.S. 952 (1996); *Abrams v Johnson*, 521 U.S. 74 (1997) at 98–99; *Hunt v Cromartie*, 526 U.S. 541 (1999).

8. Justice O'Connor explicitly notes in her opinion for the Court in *Shaw v Reno*, 509 U.S. at 647, that this "is one area in which appearances *do* matter."

9. Although the representational harms rhetoric seems to have been dropped from more recent decisions, the notion remains an implicit concern.

10. Race-based districting "makes it unnecessary, and probably unwise, for an elected official from a white majority district to be responsive at all to the wishes of black citizens; similarly, it is politically unwise for a black official from a black majority district to be re-

sponsive at all to white citizens." *Holder v Hall,* 512 U.S. 874, 907 (Thomas, J., concurring) (1994).

11. In the wake of Shaw and its progeny, Richard Pildes and Richard Niemi argued that the constitutional injury reflected "expressive harms," a characterization subsequently adopted by Justice O'Connor, writing for the Court in *Bush v Vera,* and by Justice Souter, writing the principal dissent in the same case. An expressive harm "is one that results from the ideas or attitudes expressed through a governmental action, rather than from the more tangible or material consequences the action brings about. On this view, the *meaning* of a governmental action is just as important as what the action *does."* Richard Pildes and Richard Niemi, "Expressive Harms, 'Bizarre Districts,' and Voting Rights: Evaluating Election-District Appearances after Shaw v Reno," 92 *Michigan Law Review 483* (1993).

12. See Justice Kennedy writing for the Court in *Miller v Johnson,* 515 U.S. at 912, and declaring that the assumption that black voters "think alike, share the same political interests, and will prefer the same candidates at the polls" is "offensive and demeaning."

13. See April 24, 2000, opinion and judgment of a three-judge district court, reported at *Kelley v Bennett,* 96 F.Supp. 2d 1301, (M.D. Ala. 2000) (declaring that three House Districts [63, 75, and 86], and four Senate Districts [21, 25, 29, and 30] in the redistricting plan adopted by the Alabama State Court violate the Fourteenth Amendment to the United States Constitution and enjoining further elections in those districts under that plan). In a per curiam opinion, *Sinkfield v Kelley,* 531 U.S. 28 (2000), the U.S. Supreme Court vacated the judgment of the District Court on the grounds that none of the plaintiffs lived in the challenged districts and therefore did not have standing under *U.S. v Hays,* 515 U.S. 737 (1995). The lower court had tried to buttress its discovery of an irrebuttable presumption of personal harm with the passage from *Bush v Vera,* 517 U.S. 952, 980–981 (1996), which identifies the "constitutional harm" addressed by *Shaw* to be "the message" conveyed by racially designed districts "that political identity is, or should be, predominantly racial," and with the statement in *Miller v Johnson,* 515 U.S. at 916, that a *Shaw* violation is established by proof that "race was the predominant factor motivating the legislature's decision to place a significant number of voters within or without a particular district." Ibid. at 14–15. This led the district court to conclude that the "essence" of the constitutional harm in a *Shaw* case is a message of racial political identity. Ibid. at 15–16.

14. In Massachusetts, Republicans are shut out of ten House seats and two Senate seats despite Republican candidates winning 32 percent of the vote in 1996.

15. 478 U.S. 109 (1986).

16. *Whitcomb v Chavis,* 403 U.S. 124 (1971).

17. Justice White recognized this explicitly in *Gaffney v Cummings,* 412 U.S. 735, 752–753 (1973): "Politics and political considerations are inseparable from districting and apportionment . . . It is not only obvious, but absolutely unavoidable, that the location and shape of districts may well determine the political complexion of the area. District lines are rarely neutral phenomena."

18. Adam Clymer, "Old-Time Races with Outcomes Truly in Doubt: 2 House Districts Defy Rite of Incumbency," *New York Times,* July 29, 2000, A1, A10 (describing the vanishing breed of swing districts that switch from the control of one party to the other).

19. Here Justice O'Connor gets it exactly wrong and exactly right at the same time. In *Shaw v Reno,* 509 U.S. at 646, she concludes that a reapportionment statute "typically does not classify persons at all; it classifies tracts of land, or addresses." This is technically cor-

rect in terms of the formal language of the statute. But in *Bush v Vera*, 517 U.S. at 963, referring specifically to the role that incumbency protection played in the Texas Congressional districting at issue there, the final result, she concludes, "seems not one in which the people select their representatives, but in which the representatives have selected the people."

20. It is unfortunate but predictable that the Democratic or Republican minority will be submerged year after year by the "adherents to the majority party who tend to vote a straight party line." Justice White, *U.J.O. v Carey*, 430 U.S. 144 (1977).

21. *Davis v Bandemer*, 478 U.S. 109 (1986).

22. Ibid. at 153 (O'Connor, J. concurring the judgment and disparagingly characterizing the plurality opinion).

23. That the Court does not want to examine the merits of individual voting power within single districts makes sense given the Court's reluctance to pay attention to the voting preferences of constituents. In the one-person/one-vote cases—where the Court does examine the composition of individual districts—the Court is only concerned with population, not voters. The relevant question is whether each person gets a "fair share" of the pie that the representative had to distribute. No question is raised, however, about the ability of voters to influence the outcome of the individual district election.

24. Pamela Karlan and Daryl J. Levinson, "Why Voting Is Different," 84 *California Law Review* 1201, 1209 (1996).

25. Wood, *Radicalism of the American Revolution* at 258. Burke, who is normally credited with formulating the concept of "trustee" representation (although he did not use the word), combined the idea of (1) voting for the interest of the whole and (2) voting according to the representative's best judgment (not conscience—an American importation). But as Jane Mansbridge points out, the term does not really have a clear definition, and the ideas that Burke combined are not logically connected. See Jane Mansbridge, letter to Lani Guinier, August 17, 2000.

26. *Davis v Bandemer*, 478 U.S. at 144 (O'Connor, J. concurring in the judgment).

27. *Davis v Bandemer*, 478 U.S. at 149. See also Rosemarie Zagarri, *The Politics of Size* at 147 (1987) (arguing that the residents of small states still think about representation in spatial terms). For them, "geography represented the most fundamental variable in constructing representative institutions."

28. And even if those interests are not represented, the process of districting should not be investigated at all (per O'Connor) or in individual districts (per White) since it is essential to the vitality of our two-party system. Although both justices reach the same conclusion through different means, at bottom they are both equally committed to winner-take-all single-member districting and the concept of political synecdoche on which it relies.

29. The U.S. Constitution nowhere requires single-member districting for congressional elections. Thus, as Justice Thomas has observed, "The decision to rely on single-member geographic districts as a mechanism for conducting elections is merely a political choice—and one that we might reconsider in the future." *Holder v Hall*, 512 U.S. at 908 (Thomas, J., concurring). See also *Davis v Bandemer*, 478 U.S. at 159 (O'Connor, J., concurring in the judgment) ("Districting itself represents a middle ground between winner-take-all statewide elections and proportional representation for political parties").

30. It is no worry for legitimacy (or efficacy) that multiple communities of divergent interests may be contained within a district. The elected representative within the district presumptively represents everyone within it, whether the individual voted for the district

winner, voted at all, or is even legally entitled to vote. Every individual is represented because he or she lives within the physical boundaries captured by the often-artificial district lines. See *Wells v Edwards*, 347 F. Supp. 453 (M.D.La. 1972) (three-judge court), aff'd, 409 U.S. 1095 (1973) (per curiam) (primary purpose of one-person/one-vote is to make sure "that each official member of an elected body speaks for approximately the same number of constituents"). In this sense, the one-person/one-vote cases should be renamed one person/one representative who may be picked on your behalf by those who do vote or by those whose votes count. See Judge Kozinski's dissent in *Garza v Los Angeles*, 918 F.2d 763 (9th Cir. 1990), cert. denied, 498 U.S. 1028 (1991) (pointing out that the doctrine known as one-person/one-vote is really about equalizing population within districts and has nothing to do with the number or the activity of voters).

31. Until 1842, the states experimented with various systems of districting. In that year, for the first time Congress required representatives to be elected from districts even though a third of the states then used an at-large method of election. Issacharoff, Karlan, and Pildes, *Law of Democracy* at 771, 772. Within state legislatures, as in Illinois, alternative election methods, including cumulative voting, were used to elect members of the lower house until 1980. See U.S. Const., Art. I, sec. 4.

32. The language of one of the Justices of the Supreme Court of the United States takes as a foregone conclusion the propriety of both geographic districts and winner-take-all elections within those districts. Such districts, in the words of Justice O'Connor, who seems to be spelling out the implicit theory of representation that the Court now is using, promote "stability and measured change." See Justice O'Connor, concurring in *Davis v Bandemer*, 478 U.S. at 145.

33. The one-person/one-vote principle requires almost mathematical equality of population for congressional districts. See *Karcher v Daggett*, 462 U.S. 725 (1983); but see *Abrams v Johnson*, 521 U.S. at 99–100 (approving less than mathematical equality in drawing of congressional districts to accommodate state interest in preserving local communities of interest). The standard for state districting is more generous but is still based solely on population. See *Mahan v Howell*, 410 U.S. 315 (1973).

34. Justice O'Connor continues in *Shaw v Reno*, 509 U.S. at 648: "The message that such districting sends to elected representatives is . . . pernicious. When a district obviously is created solely to effectuate the perceived common interests of one racial group, elected officials are more likely to believe that their primary obligation is to represent only the members of that group, rather than their constituency as a whole. This is altogether antithetical to our system of representative democracy."

35. Justice Harlan concurring in *Whitcomb v Chavis*, 403 U.S. at 168n2: "The only relevant difference between the elementary arithmetic on which the Court relies and the elementary probability theory on which Professor Banzhaf relies is that calculations in the latter field cannot be done on one's fingers."

36. See Issacharoff, Karlan and Pildes, *Law of Democracy* at 19.

37. See Lani Guinier, *The Tyranny of the Majority* (1994).

38. Each state is awarded a certain number of the 435 congressional seats, based on the state's census population. See *Wesberry v Sanders*, 376 U.S. 1 (1964), and *Reynolds v Sims*, 377 U.S. 533 (1964). Many commentators suggest that the one-person/one-vote standard of apportionment was chosen by the Supreme Court because it was judicially manageable. District court judges could easily enforce it, especially in congressional districting, to assure uniform approaches from state to state. In other words, the one-person/one-vote rule

is actually a state-based population standard for creating the units of representation for a national legislature.

39. *Garza v Los Angeles County Board of Supervisors.* The majority affirmed the basic principle that "the people, including those who are ineligible to vote, form the basis for representative government." In a separate dissent and concurrence Judge Kozinski attempted to impose a rule that would count voters, not just people. Because elected officials "are able to obtain benefits for their districts in proportion to their share of the total membership of the governing body," the principle of equal representation, based purely on equal population, "assures that constituents are not afforded unequal government services depending upon the size of the population in their districts." The principle of electoral equality was also necessary because "electors—persons eligible to vote—are the ones who hold the ultimate political power in our democracy."

40. Indeed, 13 percent of black men in the United States are now disenfranchised because of felony convictions. In Florida and twelve other states, a felony conviction can result in disenfranchisement, generally for life, even after an offender has completed his or her sentence. See Jamie Fellner and Marc Mauer, "Losing the Vote: The Impact of Felony Disenfranchisement Laws in the United States," Human Rights Watch and The Sentencing Project, October 1998.

41. Beverly Gage, "Prisoner Nation," *The Nation,* July 17, 2000, at 5. As a recent report from City Project, a New York based urban advocacy group, sums up, "The state's prison policies effectively transfer . . . public funds and electoral influence . . . from low-income inner-city neighborhoods of color to white, rural upstate areas . . . With voting representation determined by population, every extra inmate means added political influence. Even better, inmates can't vote—so their presence simply enhances the clout of local residents." See also State of New York, Department of Correctional Services, "The Hub System: Profile of Inmates Under Custody on January 1, 2000" (65.5 percent of state prisoners are from New York City and 82.1 percent of the New York State prison system is black or Latino). Prisoners boost the population of rural communities, bringing in millions more in federal funds that are doled out on the basis of population size. For example, in the small rural town of Coxsackie in New York, the 2,800 inmates housed there account for nearly a third of the population, "skewing the town's demographic picture in a way that benefits Coxsackie beyond imagination." And, because the Census tabulates the town's per capita income by averaging in the salaries of inmates—which range from zero to $3,000 a year per inmate—Coxsackie appears poorer, thus qualifying it for federal assistance programs. Cindy Rodriguez, "Census Seen as Captive to Jail Population: Loophole Said to Skew Funding to Rural Areas," *Boston Globe,* January 26, 2001, at A2.

42. For example, in *Karcher v Daggett,* the Court rejected the idea of a de minimus standard set to the census undercount. Assuming, for example, the census failed to count everyone and overlooked 5 percent of the population, a de minimus standard would mean that the Court would tolerate 5 percent deviations between the population in a district and the ideal district size. By rejecting this argument, the Court restated its commitment to zero tolerance of population (but not voter) deviations in congressional districting.

43. If you were back in the amphitheater in Verona, a political benefit would be construed, according to the Supreme Court's one-person/one-vote jurisprudence, as the ability to "hear" what the representative repeats through a megaphone, thus assuring even those in the outer seats of the amphitheater are informed about what is going on below. A political benefit also assumes that if there are questions or concerns about the quality of

seating, each representative will have the same number of constituents for whom he is responsible, thus equalizing everyone's chance of getting their seats repaired or maintained throughout the stadium.

44. F. R. Ankersmit, *Aesthetic Politics: Political Philosophy Beyond Fact and Value* at 44 (1996). Even to the extent specific and anticipated legislative votes are considered relevant at the time of the election, they are often resolved through choices made at a single election in which the choice is based on guesses or beliefs about individual attributes of the candidate, some of which may prove irrelevant to the policy issue as it subsequently evolves.

45. *Hunt v Cromartie et al.*, 532 U.S. ___, 121 S. Ct. 1452 (April 18, 2001), dissenting opinion by Justice Thomas.

46. The language of some recent decisions suggests that the Court may be abandoning an explicit representational harm analysis, relying primarily on the "racial classification is evil" principle. This seems to reflect the conservative view that race is only one fixed thing and cannot function as a proxy or representative of other closely related phenomena. Their preoccupation with "formal race" and their concern that race-based representation raises issues of stigma and essentialism remain at the core of the analysis that race should not predominate in drawing district lines.

47. *Davis v Bandemer*, 478 U.S. 109 at 145 (O'Connor, J., concurring in the judgment).

48. Jennifer Hochschild and Reuel Rogers, "Race Relations in a Diversifying Nation," in *New Directions: African Americans in a Diversifying Nation* at 13 (James Jackson, ed., 2000): "African Americans attach more political significance to their racial identity than do other groups. More precisely, perceived racial interests strongly shape blacks' political evaluations and choices, whereas other groups either see fewer racial/ethnic interests, or do not use them to shape their policy values so strongly." Still, political identification based on race is hardly limited to black Americans. This can be seen in the huge range of research confirming the existence of racial bloc voting—the tendency of blacks and whites to vote for candidates of their same race. See Issacharoff, Karlan, and Pildes, *Law of Democracy* at 497: "There is substantial evidence of systematic racial differences in political attitudes, policy preferences and actual voting behavior." For extensive documentation of these differences, see Donald R. Kinder and Lynn M. Sanders, *Divided by Color: Racial Politics and Democratic Ideals* (1996), and David Lublin, *The Paradox of Representation* at 72–78 (1997). There is also evidence that in certain regions of the country, blacks and Hispanics have joined together as a politically cohesive coalition, a "functionally cohesive" minority. See *Badillo v Stockton*, 956 F.2d 884 (9th Circuit 1992); *Campos v City of Baytown*, 849 F.2d 1240 (5th Cir.) cert. denied, 492 U.S. 905 (1989). There are of course jurisdictions in which they are not. Blacks and Cuban Americans, for example, have fought bitterly over how to allocate political power in South Florida. See *Johnson v deGrandy*, 512 U.S. 997 (1994).

49. *Hunt v Cromartie*. The evidence is "undisputed" that "racial identification is highly correlated with political affiliation in North Carolina." Justice Stephen Breyer's opinion finds evidence that in this particular case the legislature acted "consistent with a constitutional political objective, namely, the creation of a safe Democratic seat." The legislature's motives were therefore political and not predominantly racial, according to Breyer.

50. Although the case raises the interesting question whether political associations formed by individual black voters themselves may negotiate districts that aggregate their constituents, the Supreme Court did not address this issue when the case came before it. In *Sinkfield v Kelley*, the Court vacated the judgment on the grounds that the white plaintiffs,

who did not live in the challenged districts, lacked standing pursuant to *U.S. v Hayes*, 515 U.S. 737 (1995).

51. The court in *Kelley* concluded that the redistricting agenda of the ADC, a local black political organization in Alabama, constituted impermissible, proxied-race speech instead of political speech, based solely on the fact that supporters of ADC and other predominantly black political organizations in Alabama do not register as members. In their jurisdictional statement to the U.S. Supreme Court, appealing from the adverse ruling in *Kelley*, the black litigants [the Sinkfield defendants] argue that "the federal court decision treats race solely as a stigmatic and involuntary association. It disregards the axiom that the First Amendment protects 'the freedom to join together in furtherance of common political beliefs,' which 'necessarily presupposes the freedom to identify the people who constitute the association,'" *California Democratic Party v Jones*, 530 U.S. 567 (2000), slip. op. at 6–7 (quoting *Tashjian v Republican Party of Connecticut*, 479 U.S. 208, 214–215 (1986); *Democratic Party of United States v Wisconsin* ex rel. La Follette, 450 U.S. 107, 122 (1981)). They further argue that the support black voters give the agenda of the ADC and other black political organizations at the polls "fairly can be described as an act of affiliation," *Jones*, slip op. at 10n8 (quoting La Follette, 450 U.S. at 130n2 (Powell, J., dissenting)). They suggest that if the state imposed a registration requirement on ADC to identify its members, that restriction itself might be subject to strict scrutiny, "because it burden[s] the 'associational rights of the Party and its members.'" *Tashjian*, 479 U.S. at 217 (quoted in *Buckley v American Constitutional Law Foundation, Inc.*, 525 U.S. 182, 119 S.Ct. 636, 650 (Thomas, J., concurring)). In other words, the Sinkfield defendants argue that the *Kelley* decision "threatens to subvert the free and vigorous political processes of democratic government . . . and would outlaw the unstereotyped, grass-roots, inter-racial, coalition-building politics constitutional law aims for."

52. *Sinkfield and Rice v Bennett*, Civil Action No.93–689-PR (Cir. Ct. Montgomery County, Nov. 20, 1997), appeal dismissed as moot, *Rice v Sinkfield*, 732 So.2d 993 (Ala. 1999). The court found that these organizations were the product of black Alabamians' "free political association" and that the efforts of their leaders to aggregate them were protected by the First, Thirteenth, Fourteenth, and Fifteenth Amendments, so that, like other politically designed districts, the majority-black districts they negotiated were not subject to strict scrutiny. The Alabama State Court found that black voters give their undisputed, overwhelming support to the ADC and ANSC at the polls.

53. *Hunt v Cromartie*. "Race must not be 'the predominant factor' motivating the legislature's districting decision." Citing *Hunt v Cromartie*, 526 U.S. 541, 547 (1999) and *Miller v Johnson*, 515 U.S. at 916.

54. *Adarand Constructors v Pena*, 515 U.S. 200, 239 (Scalia, J., concurring in part and concurring in the judgment). The implication of Justice Scalia's pronouncement is that the experience of being an abstract individual is the experience of the whole. In the same passage, Justice Scalia stated his view that racially-conscious government measures to redress past discrimination against groups is impossible because the "concept is alien to the Constitution's focus upon the individual."

55. *See Gaffney v Cummings*, 412 U.S. at 735 (articulating a political fairness standard for geographic districting). See also post-trial briefs filed by attorney James Blacksher in the *Sinkfield* case, *Kelley v Bennett*, 96 F. Supp. 2d. 1301 (arguing that blinkered reading of the *Shaw* cases can result in suppression of political association by black citizens). The Public Policy Institute of California's study, "The Effect of Minority Districts and Minority

Representation on Political Participation in California," found that voter turnout among California's Latino and black communities is far higher in majority-minority congressional districts. Latino and black voters participate when they believe their votes matter. For full report see www.ppic.org/publications/CG0601R/ppic147.fulltext.pdf (visited June 21, 2001).

56. Like the Alabama Democratic Conference, for example, the Progressive Party had local, county-based chapters that conducted get-out-the-vote campaigns; they recruited and investigated candidates; distributed sample ballots marked with their endorsed candidates; and provided voting assistance and monitoring on election days. Indeed, as the federal court recognized in *Kelley v Bennett*, "Thanks to the efforts of the ADC, the NSC, and other such groups, black voter participation rates in Alabama are often comparable to, if not higher than, white rates." 96 F. Supp. 2d. 1301 at 1312. This thought experiment was suggested to us by Rob Mikos, "Comments on 'The Miner's Canary,'" Legal Theory Workshop, October 20, 2000, University of Michigan Law School.

57. Certainly those who would argue that this is partisan rather than racial gerrymandering would have a point. The conventional approach to all districting treats voters in the same way the Progressive Party did; politicians seek to correlate expectations about the voting pattern of their constituents with the design of the districts. This is precisely the point Justice White makes in dissenting in *Shaw v Reno.* "It can hardly be doubted that legislators routinely engage in the business of making electoral predictions based on group characteristics."

58. Robert G. Dixon, Jr., *Democratic Representation: Reapportionment in Law and Politics* at 462 (1968) (describing how the Court's decisions did little to resolve the issues inherent in districting: "The primary difficulty is that in a generic sense all *districting is gerrymandering*").

59. This view is, of course, inconsistent with the *Bush v Gore* opinion in which the Court leapt into the thicket before it looked. See Bruce Ackerman, "The Court Packs Itself," *American Prospect,* February 12, 2001, at 48; David A. Strauss, *"Bush v Gore*: What Were They Thinking?" 68 *University of Chicago Law Review* 737 (2001); Cass R. Sunstein, "Order without Law," 68 *University of Chicago Law Review* 757 (2001).

60. Richard Briffault suggests that generally the Court does not believe losers in contemporary politics matter, because the divisions are neither significant nor permanent. In his accounting, the Court's preoccupation with race-conscious single-member districts reflects this. Racial politics, unlike partisan politics, is highly mobilizing and thus frightening to a Court committed to stability and cohesion within the structures of government rather than deeply concerned about the representational relationship between constituent and elected official. Thus, Briffault argues that the Court's view of representation is essentially one of benign neglect; they prefer to focus on issues that promote stability in governance, ignoring the nature of representation in the process. Comments at Gilbane Symposium, Brown University, November 14, 2000. See Heather K. Gerken, "New Wine in Old Bottles: A Comment on Richard Hasen's and Richard Briffault's Essays on Bush v. Gore," ___ *Florida State University Law Review* ___ (forthcoming 2001); see also Richard H. Pildes, "Democracy and Disorder," 68 *University of Chicago Law Review* 695 (2001) (to some Justices the rough-and-tumble political process threatens chaos).

61. See Cheryl D. Mills, "Talking to Oprah Isn't Enough," *New York Times,* September 30, 2000, at A27 (describing black women's feeling that they are not included in references by politicians to the greater good).

62. It is not that race-conscious districting is never appropriate. Especially under the current anti-discrimination paradigm, it may be the only way for minorities of color to gain any representation. The problem, however, is that while the anti-discrimination model is not mutually exclusive to what we advocate, it is presently held hostage by the ideology of race blindness and radical individualism; within that paradigm it is ineffective.

63. Here Richard Briffault would caution that the Court does not have a theory of representation because it is less concerned with representation than it is with governance.

64. See John Nichols, "Georgia's Cinderella Story," *The Nation*, November 11, 1996, at 26.

65. Hannah Pitkin, "Justice: On Relating Private and Public," 9 *Political Theory* 327, 344–345 (1981).

66. *Chisom v. Romer*, 115 L.Ed. ed 348, 366 (1991). The principal axis of debate around which representation theory has centered is the idea of the representative as "delegate" or as "trustee." That is, does the representative serve merely as a conduit of the people's wishes, constrained by their preferences and lacking legitimacy for independent initiative? Or is the representative a Solomonic trustee who, once elected, benevolently exercises her wisdom for the benefit of the polity? Hannah Pitkin characterized this classic debate as the "mandate-independence controversy" and concluded that there is a "duality" to the representative relationship that finds "truth in each of the two conflicting positions." Hannah Fenichel Pitkin, *The Concept of Representation* at 144–167, 153 (1967).

67. *Chisom v Romer*, 115 L.Ed. 2d at 366, 373 (Scalia, J., dissenting).

68. See Richard l. Berke, "Parties Beginning Enormous Efforts to Prompt Voters," *New York Times*, October 25, 1998, at A1 (with graph showing that only one third of Americans vote in mid-term elections and this year's "waitress moms" are less likely to vote because neither party is reaching out on issues that directly affect their lives). See also Tamar Lewin, "Crime Costs Many Black Men the Vote, Study Says," *New York Times*, October 23, 1998, at A12. In Alabama and Florida, nearly 1 in every 3 black men is permanently disenfranchised. See also Matthew Brelis, "Is It Time to Make Voting Mandatory?" *Boston Globe*, October 18, 1998, at C1: "As the 20th century—'the American century'—draws to a close, US election turnout has never been lower. According to the nonpartisan Committee for the Study of the American Electorate, 17.4 of the voting-age population went to the polls in this fall's primaries—a stunning 45 percent drop from the disappointing 31.8 percent who voted in 1966, and well below even our own lackluster average for all elections since 1990." Ibid. at C1 (graph from International Institute for Democracy and Electoral Assistance).

69. See Issacharoff, Karlan, and Pildes, *Law of Democracy* at 107.

70. Adam Clymer, "Poll Finds Voters Skeptical about Role in Nominations: Most Say Party Leaders and Donors Decide," *New York Times*, May 18, 2000, at A26 (64 percent of those surveyed said that people like themselves had "not much" to say about what government does; half of those surveyed said they wanted more choices in candidates; some questions tapped "quite deeply, into traditional reservoirs of hostility or at least skepticism about the electoral system"). See also Richard Berke, "On Eve of Election, Mostly Apathy," *New York Times*, October 28, 1998, A16. "There's nothing that affects me so much that I've got to vote on it," Cathy Scharwack, a 35-year-old math teacher who is an Independent recently told a *New York Times* reporter. "My life on November 4 is going to be the same as on Nov. 3. I don't see how voting one way will change it."

71. Politics becomes simply another forum for marketing a commodity and getting

voters to purchase it. See George Soros, *The Crisis of Global Capitalism* at 207–211 (1998) (exploring the ways that market values of individual competition have corrupted the political sphere and disabled collective decision-making to pursue a common or public interest).

72. See, for example, Steven A. Holmes, "Many Stayed at Home," *New York Times,* September 1, 2000, at A18, citing an analysis by the Committee for the Study of the American Electorate.

73. Dale Russakoff, "Cutting Out of Prosperity, Cutting Out at the Polls," *Washington Post,* October 24, 2000, at A1, A12 (describing how the absence of strong political parties increases the "cost" of voting for those who are poor and less well educated): "With both parties rhetorically targeting the same" independent and centrist voters, the costs of "just figuring out what's going on" have gone up. Working age, lower-income people interviewed in the Scranton area have the feeling "that no matter what they did, nothing was going to change." Only 28.6 percent of those earning less than $10,000 vote; 65.7 percent of those earning more than $50,000 do. But while voter turnout is much lower among poor people than among others, and the gap has grown, voter turnout has declined in all income groups since 1964. In 1964, 43.6 percent of those earning the 1996 equivalent of less than $10,000 voted. See also Richard Berke, "Voter Tune Out: Focusing on the Few, Blind to the Many," *New York Times,* October 22, 2000, at wk. 1 (describing election as a kind of drama that does not have direct affect on lives of most citizens).

74. William Greider, *Who Will Tell the People: The Betrayal of American Democracy* (1993) (describes the failure of the media to play this role and the rise instead of lawyers, hired by corporations and others, to monitor what elected officials and bureaucrats do. But this monitoring function is not played on behalf of the interests of the people. The lawyers work for their clients, who are not the American people. The journalists, who often enjoy cozy relationships with the governing elite, find themselves working for the interests of the advertisers and the media owners who seek profit, not information).

75. Adam Clymer, "Poll Finds Voters Skeptical" (quoting Annette Scott, a nurse's assistant from Miami who is a Democrat and was one of the 947 adults interviewed in a *New York Times*/CBS News Poll).

76. Indeed, even in extraordinary cases such as the U.S. presidential election of 2000, only those votes cast for the ultimate winner actually "count."

77. "As C. Wright Mills wrote, the 'mass' of citizens 'know that there are big decisions, and they know that they're not making any.'" Email to Lani Guinier from Jane Mansbridge, October 15, 1998.

78. For an excellent discussion of the role churches could play in fostering political participation in the black community, see a series of articles entitled "Faith in Politics?" in the *Boston Review,* April/May 2001, at 26. Eva Thorne and Eugene Rivers argue that black churches can use their "direct experience in . . . real-world problem solving" to empower poor black Americans. Ibid. at 5–9. In contrast, Cathy Cohen and J. Phillip Thompson argue that many churches' promotion of conservative values (including patriarchy and homophobia) diminish their capacity to lead a transformative political struggle. Ibid. at 11–14.

79. Spencer Overton reminds us of *Terry v Adams,* 345 U.S. 461 (1953), *Smith v Allwright,* 321 U.S. 649 (1944), and the other cases that tried to promote freedom of association as a value that trumped equal access to the democratic process. "Isn't it better," he asks, "to have big, highly publicized, political decisionmaking bodies that are extensively

scrutinized by the media, and accountable for most of what goes wrong?" Email to Lani Guinier, September 18, 2000.

80. Sonny Bohanan, "Voting Systems Lauded: Minority Candidates Win AISD Precincts," Web posted Monday May 8, 2000, 1:14pm CT (successful black candidate who ran for school board in a cumulative voting election said cumulative voting helped increase voter turnout because of the effort to educate voters about the new system: "It created a mind-set in Amarillo that we had to do a lot more education and be more pro-active than we usually are on an election").

81. Email to Lani Guinier from Joan Ross Frankson, Director of Communications, Women's Environment and Development Organization (WEDO), December 20, 2001.

82. The 1996 National Black Election study, according to political scientist Katherine Tate, suggests that many blacks share qualms about an overtly race-conscious redistricting process but a large majority (60 percent) endorse a change in election rules to favor the election of minorities. "Black Faces in the Mirror: African Americans and Their Representatives in the U.S. Congress" at 201 (manuscript).

83. See *Cane v Worcester County*, 874 F. Supp. 687 (Md. 1995); *Dillard v Chilton County Bd. of Educ.*, 699 F. Supp. 870 (M.D. Ala. 1988). See also Bohanan, "Voting Systems Lauded" (describing Amarillo's experience using cumulative voting, in which the first black school board member and the first Hispanic woman were elected to two of the four seats).

84. What if the goal of districting were to create competitive districts where groups have enough voting power so that polarized voting cannot shut them out of the process? What if representatives were geographically based but we abandoned the winner-take-all aspect of the current system, "providing for representative commissions" from a district rather than a single person? What if the people rather than the elite chose how districts were drawn, something that might be possible with new computer technology? Could a more dynamic notion of representation take root if territorial-based schemes were freed of their winner-take-all rules, because conversations would be going on at so many levels? Heather Gerken stimulated our thinking through these many "what if's." There are some technical fixes worth pursuing. But weak democracy feeds on itself. The problem with the above "what if's" is that they fail to provide incentives for voters to organize. It is only when voters are mobilized to remain vigilant, even after the votes are counted, that they are in a position to interact meaningfully with their representatives. Developing local grassroots organizations is necessary to monitor elections but also legislative actions, especially during the decennial task of redistricting. The development of such organizations could also fuel the development of a new era of issue-centered politics, where people are exercising their political views through advocacy groups around issues they care about.

85. Guinier, *Tyranny of the Majority* at 107–108.

86. Direct democracy has come to be seen by some reformers as a way to raise levels of citizen involvement. It is "an antidote to the entrenched power of political machines and the powers of moneyed interests at the legislative level. The major expansion of direct democracy in this country occurred in the Progressive Period at the turn of the 20th century. Initiatives and referenda were touted at the time as a means of overcoming the capture of legislatures by special interests, such as the railroads, mining companies, and other industrial interests, and of circumventing the power of ward-based political machines, in much the same way as the system of at-large elections of city and county officials was promoted during the same period. Direct participation was also thought to educate and improve the

civic virtue of citizens." Issacharoff, Karlan and Pildes, *Law of Democracy* at 667–668. Others contend that direct democracy is rather a democratic necessity for controversial minorities, serving as a check on the inherent limitations of elected legislative bodies, functioning as a "safety valve" for volatile issues that legislatures wish to avoid. See also Lynn Baker, "Direct Democracy and Discrimination: A Public Choice Perspective," 67 *Chicago–Kent Law Review* 707, 754–755 (1992) (giving women's suffrage and the eight-hour work day as examples of landmark reforms that began as initiatives in various states). Justice Scalia suggests in his dissent in *Romer v Evans*, 116 S.Ct. 1620 (1996) that public referenda are essentially democratic in furthering majority rule, because they serve as healthy antidotes to the ability of highly motivated, self-interested minorities to leverage their political strength in the local legislature through log-rolling. We remain skeptical, however, about direct democracy as the ultimate answer, because it has been conceived as a strictly majoritarian system and thus continues to make minority preferences completely invisible. Moreover, direct democracy is problematic from the perspective of political race because it ignores the significance of group-based organizing to identify and mobilize low-income or less educated citizens. See Derrick Bell, "The Referendum: Democracy's Barrier to Racial Equality," 54 *Washington Law Review* 1 (1978) (direct democracy threatens minority rights). See also James Morone, *The Democratic Wish* at 124 (1990) (arguing that referenda take organization and money to be successful, swamping rather than strengthening the hand of the "people"). It also tends to reduce politics to public opinion polls, whose focus on head counting rather than participation disables a mass electorate from engaging in negotiation or sustained, interactive dialogue with one another.

87. These forms of election structures, often called proportional or semi-proportional representation, are used in most of the world's democracies and are associated with increased turnout and citizen participation. See Douglas Amy, *Real Choices/New Voices* (1993); Lani Guinier, *Lift Every Voice* (1998), ch. 9.

88. Michael Dorf and Charles Sabel, "A Constitution of Democratic Experimentalism," 98 *Columbia Law Review* 267, 331 (March 1998).

89. Lawrence D. Bobo, Michael C. Dawson, and Devon Johnson, "Enduring Two-Ness," *Public Perspective*, May/June 2001, at 12–16 (reporting results of National African American Election Survey in October and December 2000).

90. Augusto Boal, *Legislative Theatre: Using Performance to Make Politics* (1998). The constituency groups used forum theater exercises that helped citizens "develop their taste for political discussion (democracy)" by working through the improvisation of possible solutions to locally generated problems. Boal's theater troupe traveled throughout the community enacting plays which asked citizens to step into roles and imagine solutions—solutions that were initiated by his constituents and which Boal then ultimately carried into the council and introduced as law once elected. Ibid. at 9. As Boal observed, "We are doing political work but with theatrical means." Ibid. at 98: "When I enter the Municipal Chamber building I feel like someone putting on a strait-jacket. The moment one goes in, one's identity is lost: the staff do not greet us by name, but by title. 'Good morning vereador.'" Ibid. at 104.

91. Actors and audience converged and represented one another. Things are sometimes seen as absences. The jokers, those who facilitate the conversation between the audience and the actors, deliver the audience participants into "a reality, which is not present except symbolically." This symbolic form of communication makes it possible for the participants to converse about and be part of a social activity, pedagogy, and politics. Ibid. at 76–77.

Boal developed the idea of legislative theater in conjunction with a group first established as a "Theater of the Oppressed," through which actors would pursue various theatrical methods to engage citizens on pressing problems. In "forum theater," the actors would perform a short play centered on an election issue and then ask audience members to step in to play the role of the candidate. In "invisible theater," the actors would infiltrate a crowd and stage an event in order to catalyze citizen participation. Boal on occasion has brought his political theater to the United States. For example, in 1992, his actors staged a play on littering on the Staten Island Ferry in New York City; two actors threw paper on the ground during conversation, and two others protested, catalyzing a larger conversation among the passengers about citizen responsibility for the cleanliness of the community. This kind of engagement with citizens is also practiced by such groups as the "guerilla theater" of the San Francisco Mime Troupe. Jan Cohen-Cruz, "Theatricalizing Politics," in *Playing Boal: Theatre, Therapy, Activism* at 234 (Mady Schutzman and Jan Cohen-Cruz, eds., 1994). They used techniques of the theater to engage audiences on a political as well as an aesthetic level, to "break the glass" that separated the actors and the audience. See Peter Coyote, *Sleeping Where I Fall* at 33–34 (1998) (describing development of guerrilla theater).This technique, absent the element of electoral politics, was also used quite successfully by the United Farm Workers in organizing farm workers, many of whom were illiterate. Not only did El Teatro Campesino dramatize the issues using farm workers as actors, but they developed the "Acto" as a legitimate artistic and political vehicle.

92. Boal, *Legislative Theatre* at 74. The audience is invited to substitute temporarily for the protagonist in a forum show. Members of the audience experiment with different modes of resolving the conflict as it was originally presented. See Ibid. at 45, 74, 76, 86 (describing the workshops, rehearsals and shows that formed the nucleus of his constituency theater groups and the systematic dramaturgy used by the popular theater groups to propose laws). The aesthetic space is the "creation of the audience: it requires nothing more than their attentive gaze in a single direction." Ibid. at 71–72.

93. We thank Professor Heather Gerken for clarifying this point and for pushing us not to be excessively defensive about the notion of representation itself.

94. Jennifer Gordon, "The Campaign for the Unpaid Wages Prohibition Act: Hispanic Immigrants Change New York Wage Law," 4 *Global Policy Program* 25, 26 (September 1999).

95. "These visits had a significant impact, both on the senators and their staff and on the immigrant workers . . . The unusual structure of the visit made it stand out in the legislator's mind; the impact it presented of immigrant workers as hard-working, engaged members of a community made it stay there." Ibid. at 26. "The Act was won through a campaign conceived of and led by immigrant workers, members of the Workplace Project, a nonprofit workers center on Long Island, with the support of two other workers centers, the Hispanic Workers Center and the Chinese Staff and Workers Association, and of a broad coalition of business, labor, religious and community groups." Ibid. at 1.

96. Greg Krikorian, "3 Candidates Ally in Unusual Bid to Force Svorinich into Runoff," *Los Angeles Times*, February 18, 1997, at B1, B8.

97. Ibid. at B8. See also Carla Rivera, "In Mid-City, 'We're Trying to Build Bridges,'" *Los Angeles Times*, January 15, 1999, at B3 (describing how their group went door to door for five months asking hundreds of residents what they and their government should be doing to better their lives).

98. Surely there are occasions that call for defending the importance of the representa-

tives' role as dispensers of patronage or constituent service or the notion that the district winner sometimes also represents the district loser. One could formulate these notions into a legitimate theory of representation were they to be shaped into a theory of deliberative democracy. We might even concede the value of supplementing such notions with other more interactive conceptions of representation. We are also prepared to believe that the conflicts between these ideas are valuable and the creative tensions between them may give rise to something even more interesting. Yet standing alone, such notions are too thin to support a robust conception of democracy in our view. (Again, we are indebted to Heather Gerken for her constant reminders that we should not too easily dismiss the representatives' various roles "absent evidence that they inevitably lead to vacant, sterile notions of democracy or shut out individuals from the process.")

99. Ankersmit, *Aesthetic Politics* at 255.

100. See *California Democratic Party v Jones*, 530 U.S. 567 (2000). In dissent, Justice Stevens noted that "The Court's glib rejection of the State's interest in increasing voter participation, ante, at____, 17, is particularly regrettable. In an era of dramatically declining voter participation, States should be free to experiment with reforms designed to make the democratic process more robust by involving the entire electorate in the process of selecting those who will serve as government officials." Ibid. slip. op. at 12 (Stevens, J., dissenting).

7. Whiteness of a Different Color?

1. Mirta Ojito, "How Race is Lived in America—Best of Friends, Worlds Apart," *New York Times*, June 5, 2000, at A1.

2. In a very interesting book, *Hispanic/Latino Identity: A Philosophical Perspective* (2000), Jorge Gracia attempts a historical philosophical justification for the existence of the category "Hispanic."

3. Rosa Clemente, a Puerto Rican youth organizer in New York City, in an email posting May 9, 2001, *Who Is Black?* says her racial identity is black and her cultural identity is Puerto Rican. "Often Puerto Ricans who assert our Blackness are not only outcast by Latinos/as who identify more with their Spanish Conqueror than their African ancestors, but we are also shunned by African Americans who do not see us as Black."

4. Max Sylvius Handman, "Economic Reasons for the Coming of the Mexican Immigrant," 35 *American Journal of Sociology* 609–610 (January 1930). In an earlier journal article Handman tried to identify the source of the confusion as to race and treatment. "The Mexican presents shades of color ranging from that of the Negro, although with no Negro features, to that of the white." This "problem" was perplexing because, according to Handman, "the temptation of the white group is to push him down into the Negro group, while the efforts of the Mexican will be directed toward raising himself up to the level of the white group." Max Sylvius Handman, "The Mexican Immigrant in Texas," 7 *Southwestern Political and Social Science Quarterly* 27, 40 (June 1926).

5. "Spanish origin" is the name that was and has been used by the Census Bureau to classify all Spanish-speaking ethnic groups. Within the historical charts of the 1940 Census, no "Mexican" *race* category appears under the 1930 section. Bureau of Census, Department of Commerce, *Report of the 1940 United States Census* (1942). *1950 Bureau of the Census: Special Reports* at 1A–13.

6. "The proportion of whites in the total population, which was a little over 80 percent in 1790, has increased in each succeeding census, except for a slight decline in 1810 as

compared to 1800 and a decrease of 89.0 percent (for the white population excluding Mexicans) in 1920 to 88.7 percent in 1930. The last decline is the result of a very considerable influx of Mexicans between 1920 and 1930. If Mexicans had been classed as white in 1930, the proportion would have been slightly higher in 1920." From Bureau of Census, Department of Commerce, *Fifteenth Census of the United States:* Vol. 2, *Population* at 25 (1933).

7. The 1950 census incorporated a modified one-drop rule that had been long-standing in the American judicial system but had not appeared in census materials until this point. The classification of Negro now included those persons of mixed white and Negro parentage as well as persons with mixed Indian and Negro parentage. An exception to this rule was if the Indian blood (again, in the opinion of the enumerator) "very definitely" predominates, or the individual is connected to a tribe. The modified one-drop rule was not limited to the Negro classification alone. The child of a mixed union in which one parent was white would always be classified as the race of the nonwhite parent. Should both parents be of different races, and neither was white, the race of the father was attributed to the child. "If it is known that an individual is even remotely descended from a black person, he is classified as a Negro . . . Although words like *mulatto, quadroon* and *octoroon* have been used on occasion in America, in reality they have little or no social significance." John G. Mencke, *Mulattoes and Race Mixture: American Attitudes and Images, 1865–1918* (1979).

8. See Neil Foley, "Becoming Hispanic: Mexican Americans and the Faustian Pact with Whiteness," in *Reflexiones: New Directions in Mexican American Studies* at 64 (Neil Foley, ed., 1998) (debating whether Hispanics are white is a key moment in the definition of the shape of Mexican-American political engagement in the struggle for civil rights).

9. Stan Lieberson, *A Piece of the Pie: Blacks and White Immigrants since 1880* (1981). Lieberson argues that Asians were singled out because they represented a threatening combination of economic, political, and social numbers of people with visibly different physical characteristics.

10. See Noel Ignatiev, *How the Irish Became White* (1995) (especially chs. 6 and Afterword); Neil Foley, *The White Scourge: Mexicans, Blacks, and Poor Whites in Texas Cotton Culture* (1997) (discussing the economic and social structure of the cotton culture of Texas and the accommodation to competition between poor whites, Mexicans, and blacks).

11. Until the Immigration Act of 1917, immigration from Mexico was essentially open, with Mexicans considered white for purposes of eligibility for citizenship. Asians, on the other hand—first Chinese, next Japanese, and later Sikhs—even during periods of legal immigration were denied the opportunity to become citizens. The naturalization bar was then the basis on which land ownership rights were restricted as well. Mexicans, however, wound up on the white side of this divide until their numbers became so much greater during the 1920s, a fact that prompted the deportations of the 1930s and, along with the influx of southern whites during the same period who also were competing for employment, led to the establishment of clearer lines of segregation of schools, swimming pools, and other public facilities.

12. Jennifer Hochschild, "Madison's Constitution and Identity Politics" at 19–20 (unpublished manuscript, May 18, 2000).

13. Pedro Noguera, "Anything but Black," in *Blackness and Invisibility* (Percy Hintzen and Jean Rahnier, eds., forthcoming).

14. See, for example, Tomas Almaguer, *Racial Fault Lines: The Historical Origins of*

White Supremacy in California (1994); Carlos Arce et al., "Phenotype and Life Chances among Chicanos," 9 *Hispanic Journal of Behavior Sciences* 19 (1987); Frank D. Bean and Marta Tieda, *The Hispanic Population of the United States* (1987); George Sanchez, *Becoming Mexican-American: Ethnicity, Culture and Identity in Chicago and Los Angeles, 1900–1945* (1993); Ilan Stavans, *The Hispanic Condition: Reflections on Culture and Identity in America* (1995). See also Peter Skerry, *Mexican Americans: The Ambivalent Minority* (1993).

15. The lack of specific ethnic definition (defined in terms of specific national origin) makes "Hispanic-American" in some ways the cognate category to "African-American" or to "Asian-American." See Yen Le Espiritu, *Asian American Panethnicity: Bridging Institutions and Identity* (1992), and Robert Chang, *Disoriented* (1999). "Native-Americans" do not fit into this category because they have a specific tribal definition except when spoken of casually or for purposes of popular definition. For example, the 2000 Census form which requires a specific tribal designation if the racial identity "Indian" is selected.

16. Simon Bolivar, *Selected Writings of Bolivar*, vol. 1 at 181 (Vicente Lecuna and Harold A. Bierk, Jr., eds., 1951).

17. The confrontation with race was built into the basic structure of what has come to be described as the Hispanic or Latino community. In most cases, the Latin American situation required the dominant white or European elite to undertake a strategy to manage the complex racial differences within their societies and to come to terms with the widespread miscegenation that was at the core of their national realities. When we use the term racial in the context of our discussion of Hispanics, we mean that to varying degrees these national subgroups (Cuban, Mexican, Puerto Rican, and so on) are already in a relationship with the dominant white majority that tracks the characteristics of the relationships that we explored in the context of political race. Some of these racial characteristics are historic; others are phenotypic in origin but have been given a political content that has emerged from and been reinforced by distinctive demographic associations and regional variations. Geoffrey Fox, *Hispanic Nation: Culture, Politics, and the Construction of Identity* (1996).

18. See generally David Montejano, *Anglos and Mexicans in the Making of Texas, 1836–1986* (1987); Foley, "Becoming Hispanic"; Foley, *The White Scourge;* Ignatiev, *How the Irish Became White.*

19. See Edward Lucas White, *El Supremo: A Romance of the Great Dictator of Paraguay* (1916). (In his discussion of the racial policies of Jose Gaspar Rodriguez Francia, we see that Francia wanted to make the process of mixing the races a requirement rather than a mere accidental historical process.)

20. See Walter Mignolo, *Local Histories/Global Designs* (2000); José David Saldívar, *Border Matters: Remapping American Cultural Studies* (1997). See also Foley, "Becoming Hispanic" (discussing the resistance among the Mexican-American elite to embrace an alliance with blacks in the early struggle for civil rights).

21. In Mexican culture the priority is given to the Aztec/Spanish mixture, forgetting that there were many Indians who fought with the Spanish against the tyrannical rule of the Aztec. The joke in the Chicano community when someone claimed to Aztec, was, "Oh, yeah, he's half-Aztec."

22. See Hugh Thomas, *Cuba or The Pursuit of Liberty* (1972). Yet, the current ideology surrounding Cubans in the United States is that they are all either refugees from communism or Castro's refuse (the Marielitas). Of course, this is not just ascriptive. The Cubans

of Miami dominate the popular imagination of who Cubans are. Moreover, as the Elian Gonzales episode demonstrates, they are expert at exploiting this conception. Even Cubans who were born in the United States refer to themselves as exiles. Thus the slogan, "Exiles united can never be defeated." This chant was taken up by those surrounding the house of Lazaro Gonzales to prevent the repatriation of Elian. This forgets, of course, the first big wave of Cuban immigration captured poignantly by Oscar Hijuelos in his novel, *The Mambo Kings Play Songs of Love* (1989).

23. Nicaraguans enjoyed a similar status during the Contra wars, although their number and the relative unimportance of the country to the United States does not really make them a counter example.

24. See Michael Omi and Howard Winant, *Racial Formation in the United States: From the 1960s to the 1980s* (2d ed. 1994); *Theories of Ethnicity: A Classical Reader* (Werner Sollors, ed., 1996).

25. See, for example the summary of the process described by Herbert J. Gans in "Symbolic Ethnicity: The Future of Ethnic Groups and Cultures in America," in *Theories of Ethnicity* at 425–459 (Sollors, ed.).

26. See Jennifer Hochschild, "Madison's Constitution" at 15 (identifying survey research that suggests Mexican immigrants, for example, have a "unique psychological relationship to American society").

27. See David Montejano, *Anglos and Mexicans* at xvi n49.

28. See *Hopwood v Texas*, 78 F.3d 932 (5th Cir. 1996).

29. This is characterized by the paternalistic concept of the padrone, who filled a role as economic boss, political whip, protector, and guardian in the sense of trustee in the wardship and guardian relationship.

30. See Foley, *The White Scourge:* "A close correlation existed between race and tenant status in central Texas, with most blacks and Mexicans occupying the rank of sharecroppers and wage laborers. White sharecroppers were stigmatized in Texas, as elsewhere in the South, as white trash, crackers, and rednecks, but even as marginal whites these sharecroppers came to enjoy for a brief time, the social, psychological, and economical advantages of being white. White tenants who had slipped into sharecropping were able, for example, to negotiate contracts as 'half tenants' or tenants on the halves." Ibid. at 85–86.

31. See Gerald Torres, "Local Knowledge, Local Color: Critical Legal Studies and the Law of Race Relations," 25 *University of San Diego Law Review* 1043 (1988).

32. See Foley, *The White Scourge* (exploring the different business practices that were driven by underlying racial hierarchies).

33. David Montejano explores this process in his book *Anglos and Mexicans*.

34. Foley, *The White Scourge* at 85–86: "As increasing numbers of Mexicans settled in central Texas as sharecroppers, owners no longer felt the need to rent to whites as half tenants. Rather, owners hired them to make a crop as true sharecroppers, no different in status from Mexicans and blacks."

35. See Foley, *The White Scourge*; Montejano, *Anglos and Mexicans*.

36. University of Texas historian David Montejano calls this "an accommodation between Anglo and Hispano elites."

37. *U.S. v State of Texas*, 506 F.Supp. 405, 412 (E.D.Tex.1981). Pl.-Int. Ex. 409, #735. It took this case in 1981 to finally prompt the legislature to actually begin to desegregate Mexican schools.

38. "Despite numerous examples of those who rejected whiteness and . . . White privi-

lege, many Mexican Americans must nevertheless acknowledge their complicity in maintaining the boundaries around 'blackness' in order to claim the privileges of whiteness. By embracing whiteness, Mexican Americans have reinforced the color line that has denied people of African descent full participation in American democracy." Foley, "Becoming Hispanic" at 65.

39. See Foley, "Becoming Hispanic." Quoting letter of a black El Pasoan to the editor of the local paper in 1936: "Though once pure Indians," he wrote, "Mexicans had become more mixed than dog food—undoubtedly a conglomeration of Indian with all the races known to man, with the possible exception of the Eskimos." Ibid. at 15.

40. Censuses of 1980–2000 Statistical Directive No. 15. As of 1978, the Office of Management and Budget promulgated "Statistical Directive No. 15," which was the federal government's new race classification handbook. Prior to Directive 15, the different agencies that gave grants on the basis of racial statistics did not have a standard for inter-governmental measurement of race. Since the Directive's promulgation in 1977, Directive No. 15 remained unchanged until 1988. Due to mounting pressure from groups that felt the Directive was too restrictive, OMB circulated a "draft" addition of the category "Other" to the Race question within the census. In 1993, an "Interagency Committee for the Review of the Racial and Ethnic Standards" made a series of recommendations to OMB based in part on the fact-finding nature of those meetings. The OMB made several decisions regarding adaptations of Directive 15. They accepted recommendations that there should be no "multi-racial" category, shifts within the ordering of the questions, and several terminology shifts. (62 CFR 58682 at 58582). However, the following changes were added in this finding: (1) Multiple "Race" category options could be chosen, (2) When the Hispanic Origin question is used, it should precede the race question, (3) No "Middle Eastern" racial category should be added, (4) The terms "American Indian," "Hawaiian," "Eskimo or Aleut," "Black," shall be changed, respectively to "Native American," "Native Hawaiian," "Alaskan Native," and "Black or African-American." They rejected the recommendations that: would retain the term "Hispanic" (and instead would replace it with "Hispanic or Latino") and would retain the "Asian or Pacific Islander" racial category (and instead split the categorization to "Asian" and "Native Hawaiian or other Pacific Islander"). Ibid. at 58585–58587. In addition, OMB delayed the acceptance of a rule change that would allow respondents to check more than one box for the "Hispanic Origin" question. Ibid. at 58787.

41. In the 1970s, the Federal Office of Management and Budget, in consultation with officials of Spain, created the term "Hispanic," which OMB defined as: "A person of Mexican, Puerto Rican, Cuban, or Central American or other Spanish Culture or origin, regardless of race." See 43 C.F.R. 19269 (1978). Thus the term "Hispanic" is the official term. In California, as in Chicago, the preferred pan-ethnic term seems to be "Latino." In Texas, the term with the most common usage, when not describing *just* Mexican Americans, is "Hispanic." Within the Mexican-American community, there is both a generational and political split over the use of the term "Chicano." Most progressive political activists within the Mexican-American community prefer "Chicano" and its derivative "Chicanismo."

42. Teresa Córdova, "Harold Washington and the Rise of Latino Electoral Politics in Chicago, 1982–1987," in *Chicano Politics and Society in the Late Twentieth Century* at 53–54 (David Montejano, ed., 1999).

43. Ibid. at 31.

44. Rudy de la Garza, *Latin Voices* at 16 (1992).

45. Oddly, and perhaps tellingly, the authors of this study refer to welfare as "programs

designed to help blacks." This not only mischaracterizes these social programs but insinu-
ates the dominant construction of race into the equation. The question could just as easily
have been: Are you black? The caution that is implicit here is that when looking at survey
data we need both a clear statement of the context of the study and of the social setting
within which the questions were posed.

46. Enrique T. Trueba, *Latinos Unidos: From Cultural Diversity to the Politics of Solidarity* at 22 (1999).

47. Felix M. Padilla, *Latino Ethnic Consciousness: The Case of Mexican Americans and
Puerto Ricans in Chicago* at 46–51, 58 (1985).

48. Ibid. at 72–73.

49. David Bacon, "Crossing L.A.'s Racial Divide," *In These Times,* June 11, 2001.

50. David S. Broder, "A Latino Awakening in California and Beyond," *Boston Globe,*
May 23, 2001, at A19.

51. Todd Purdum, "New Mayor of Los Angeles Wins with Black and White Coalition,"
New York Times, June 7, 2001, at A1.

52. Jennifer Hochschild and Reuel Rogers, "Race Relations in a Diversifying Nation" in
New Directions: African Americans in a Diversifying Nation at 18 (James Jackson, ed., 2000)
(describing "standard bi-racial formula" that uses racial collectivity as organizing axis, racial discrimination as exclusive analytic category and "puts too much weight on winning
positions from which blacks have historically been excluded").

53. Villaraigosa's campaign never recovered from attack ads run by his opponent linking him to a convicted drug dealer. Purdum, "New Mayor of Los Angeles wins With Black
and White Coalition" at A22. See also Harold Meyerson, "A City Hesitates at Political
Change," *New York Times,* June 8, 2001, at A27. "Dispatching Mr. Villaraigosa required the
hitherto inoffensive Mr. Hahn, a mainstream Democrat, to wage the most demagogic campaign Los Angeles has seen since the bad old days of Sam Yorty, airing an ad that made Mr.
Villaraigosa look like a cross between Marion Barry and Pablo Escobar."

54. Adam Nagourney, "Ferrer Refuses Endorsement Linked to Race," *New York Times,*
May 10, 2001, at B1, B8.

55. Adam Nagourney, "Sharpton Gives Ferrer a List of Conditions," *New York Times,*
May 9, 2001, at B1, B6.

56. Mireya Navarro, "The Latino Candidate: Yours, Mine or Ours?" *New York Times,*
May 6, 2001, at 1 of New York regional section.

57. Lani Guinier, *The Tyranny of the Majority* at 58–60 (1994).

58. As Steve Erie, a UC San Diego professor who studies Los Angeles politics said of the
campaign, "You're going to hear a lot more about equity issues, haves and have-nots and
what city government can do for the less fortunate." Matea Gold and Tina Daunt, "L.A.
Takes a Turn to the Left with Democrat in Charge," *Los Angeles Times,* June 6, 2001, at 1.
UCLA Professor Gary Blasi concurred: "Whoever wins the race [housing issues] are going
to be on the agenda." In a similar way Jaime Regalado, Executive Director of the Pat Brown
Institute for Public Affairs at Cal State Los Angeles asserted that "workers' issues will get a
full play . . . whoever gets in."

59. Hochschild and Rogers, "Race Relations in a Diversifying Nation," at 20 (concluding that electoral coalitions between blacks and other nonwhite groups have been infre-
quent, and those that have formed have proven ephemeral and susceptible to disruption).

60. Todd Purdum, "Los Angeles Race Bares Racial Division," *New York Times,* June 10,
2001, at 18 NE+. "'I've been watching what Spanish people been doing, making black peo-

ple move out their houses,' Ms. Taylor [a black woman] said, a reference to the changing ethnic makeup of some neighborhoods. 'And I thought that if that cat got in, it would just go more that way.'"

61. See also Hochschild and Rogers, "Race Relations in a Diversifying Nation" at 13 (describing how new immigrants may not interpret racially-inflected encounters as blacks typically would, so their subsequent political response (or lack thereof) may seem weak to American eyes. Black leaders may be more attuned to the racial overtones of incidents than are immigrant leaders).

62. Ibid. at 20–21. In New York City in the 1980s, for example, "black leaders were unable to relinquish the implicit claim that blacks historically have made to the most visible positions of leadership and to the right to define the policy agenda in minority-based coalitions."

63. Cathy Schneider, memo to Gerald Torres, May 23, 1997.

64. Ignatiev, *How the Irish Became White* at 179.

65. Andrew Hacker, *Two Nations: Black and White, Separate, Hostile, Unequal* (1992).

66. Yen Le Espiritu, *Asian American Panethnicity*; Chang, *Disoriented.*

67. Hochschild and Rogers, "Race Relations in a Diversifying Nation" at 13, 15.

68. Jennifer Hochschild, "Madison's Constitution" at 18.

69. Aurelio Rojas, "Asian Americans Flex Political Muscle," *Bee Capitol Bureau,* May 22, 2001.

70. Hochschild and Rogers, "Race Relations" at 18–19 (noting that "Puerto Ricans [and other nonwhites] do not respond neatly" to a bipolar racial classification, but "the notion of being a nonwhite group is a strong one and, on this basis, there appear to be many areas of public policy consensus between large majorities of Puerto Ricans and Blacks").

71. Where such leadership is absent, the black/white binary often creates a wedge between blacks and Latinos rather than forging a bond. For example, in Providence, R.I., Shannah Kurland, "Brown Power vs. Black Power," 4 (1) *ColorLines* (Spring 2001) writes that Gwen Andrade, a black political and community activist married to a Puerto Rican city council member, sees signs that many Latinos will respond to racism by more readily aligning with whites. "'In America the further away from black you get, the better,' says Andrade. 'That's the perception that's been set up—it's the historical perspective of any group of people that has African roots. If you've got that African heritage that comes out in the skin color, or in the hair, you're fighting even harder to distance yourself from it because of what black means in this country.'" Ibid. at 20–21.

72. Hochschild and Rogers, "Race Relations" at 19.

8. Watching the Canary

1. Bryonn Bain, "Walking While Black," *The Village Voice,* April 26, 2000, at 1, 42. Bain and his brother and cousin were arrested, held overnight and then released, with all charges eventually dropped, after the police in New York City, looking for young men who were throwing bottles on the Upper West Side, happened upon Bain et al. as they exited a Bodega. Bain, at the time, had his laptop and law books in his backpack, because he was en route to the bus station where he intended to catch a bus back to Cambridge. Bain's essay in *The Voice* generated 90,000 responses.

2. Tanya E. Coke, concept paper, "A Campaign Strategy against Over-Incarceration," *Open Society Institute,* July 1, 2000, at 1. See also Marc Mauer, *Race to Incarcerate* at 125

(1999) (a black boy born in 1991 stood a 29 percent chance of being imprisoned at some point in his life, compared with a 16 percent chance for a Hispanic boy and a 4 percent chance for a white boy).

3. Bruce Western and Becky Pettit, "Incarceration and Racial Inequality in Men's Employment," 54 *Industrial and Labor Relations Review* 3 (2000) (finding that high incarceration rates among black men suggest that labor force surveys overestimate the incidence of employment and underestimate employment inequality).

4. Table 1. "Percent not working and incarcerated, black and white men 1980–1999," email attachment sent to Lani Guinier from Bruce Western, May 8, 2001 (figures adapted from Western and Pettit, "Incarceration and Racial Inequality"); Bruce Western and Becky Pettit, "Some Recent Figures on Incarceration, April, 2001" (attachment to email to Lani Guinier April 25, 2001). In 1999, 16.8 percent of white high school dropouts aged 22–30 were in school or not actively seeking employment, 5.9 percent were incarcerated, and 77.3 percent were employed.

5. Edward N. Luttwak, "Will Success Spoil America?: Why the Pols Don't Get Our Real Crisis of Values," *Washington Post*, November 27, 1994, at C1.

6. Don Terry, "In Los Angeles, Tears, Confusion and a Resolution to End the Violence," *New York Times*, July 17, 2000, at A12 (describing rise in number of homicides in Los Angeles and attributing causes to drugs, turf, and too many bored and desperate young men). "Even in this booming economy, jobs for teenagers and for ex-convicts like Melvin Farmer, 43, are hard to find in the inner city, despite being so crucial in stopping the violence, many people here said."

7. "Remarks on Women and Leadership: Innovations for Social Change," sponsored by Radcliffe Association, Cambridge, Massachusetts, June 8, 2001. In her talk, Katzenstein cites David Garland, "Introduction: The Meaning of Mass Imprisonment," 3(1) *Punishment and Society* 5–9 (2001). See also Loïc Wacquant, "Deadly Symbiosis: When Ghetto and Prison Meet and Mesh," 3 *Punishment and Society* 95 (2001).

8. Mauer, *Race to Incarcerate* at 166–169.

9. Lawrence Bobo and J. Kluegel, "Status, Ideology, and Dimensions of Whites' Racial Beliefs and Attitudes: Progress and Stagnation," in *Racial Attitudes in the 1990s: Continuity and Change* (Steven Tuch and James R. Martin, eds., 1997) as quoted in Lawrence Bobo, "Racial Attitudes and Relations at the Close of the Twentieth Century," in *America Becoming: Racial Trends and Their Consequences* (Neil Smelser, William J. Wilson, and Faith Mitchell, eds., 2001).

10. See Linda Greenhouse, "Divided Justices Back Full Arrests on Minor Charges," *New York Times*, April 25, 2001, at A1, A14. The Supreme Court upheld discretion for police officers to arrest and hold in custody people who commit minor infractions that would at most subject them to a small fine.

11. Mauer, *Race to Incarcerate* at 8, 74–77, 129–132.

12. Since 1980 the number of women in prison has increased at nearly double the rate for men. There are now nearly seven times as many women in state and federal prisons as in 1980, an increase from 12,300 in 1980 to 82,800 by 1997, for a rise of 573 percent. An additional 63,000 women incarcerated in local jails yields a total of 146,600 female inmates. The Sentencing Project: http://www.sentencingproject.org/news/executive%20-summary.html.

13. Mauer, *Race to Incarcerate* at 60.

14. Cass Sunstein, "Tilting the Scales Rightward," *New York Times*, April 26, 2001, at A23.

15. As cited by Lani Guinier, *Tyranny of the Majority* (1994) at 194n9.

16. Elliot Currie, *Crime and Punishment in America* at 31 (1998).

17. "Prepared Testimony of Wade Henderson," May 21, 2000. In 1972 the population of federal and state prisons combined was approximately 200,000. By 1997 the prison population had increased 500 percent to 1.2 million. America now houses some 2 million people in federal and state prisons and local jails.

18. Ibid. "African American men are now imprisoned at a rate of 4,617 per 100,000 compared to the white male rate of 630 per 100,000. For African American women the rate is 375 compared to the white female rate of 53." Other studies suggest that black men are in prisons and jails at a rate of 7,119 per 100,000. Email from Peter Wagner to Lani Guinier, April 4, 2001: "According to the Bureau of Justice Statistics, Prison and Jail Inmates at Midyear 2000, Table 13: 4,777 per 100,000 Black males are incarcerated in prisons and jails . . . With the additional information in the online spreadsheet versions of Tables 12 and 13, I calculate an adult Black male rate of 7,119 per 100,000."

19. Mauer, *Race to Incarcerate* at 147.

20. Robert Gangi, "Upstate Prisons Blossom Amid a Field of Schemes," *Newsday* (Nassau and Suffolk editions), May 24, 2000, at A40. Gangi is executive director of the Correctional Association of New York.

21. Mauer, *Race to Incarcerate* at 152 citing 1997 study.

22. Forty-eight percent of prison and jail inmates in 1999 were black and 19 percent were Hispanic. See "Facts about Prisons and Prisoners" (sources: Bureau of Justice Statistics, *Corrections Compendium*, and The Sentencing Project: http://www.sentencingproject.org/policy/9050.htm (visited August 30, 2000).

23. The New Jersey state attorney general, John Farmer, Jr., has said, for example, that such tactics were encouraged by federal drug enforcement policies that stereotype certain ethnic groups as likely to be involved in drug activity. See, for example, David Kocieniewski, "U.S. Wrote Outline for Racial Profiling, New Jersey Argues," *New York Times*, November 29, 2000, at A1: "New Jersey officials argue that the reason racial profiling is a national problem is that it was initiated, and in many ways encouraged, by the federal government's war on drugs. In 1986, the Drug Enforcement Administration's Operation Pipeline enlisted police departments across the country to search for narcotics traffickers on major highways and instructed officers, to cite one example, that Latinos and West Indians dominated the drug trade and therefore warranted extra scrutiny." Likewise, "many of the drug interdiction policies that encouraged profiling were taught by the Drug Enforcement Administration and the federal Department of Transportation." David Kocieniewski and Robert Hanley, "Racial Profiling Routine, New Jersey Finds," *New York Times*, November 28, 2000, at A1 (quoting John Farmer). See also David Rudovsky, "Law Enforcement by Stereotypes and Serendipity: Racial Profiling and Stops and Searches without Cause," 3 *University of Pennsylvania Journal of Constitutional Law* 296, 298n25, 301n40 (February 2001).

24. Mauer, *Race to Incarcerate* at 148–149.

25. Randall Kennedy, *Race, Crime, and the Law* (1997) at 10–12, 17, 21. It may be, Kennedy concedes, that the War on Drugs "should be reconsidered" as social policy. Ibid at 386. Nevertheless, policies that might result in a "burden for those imprisoned" could still

have a positive impact on the black community as a whole since they are also "a good for those whose lives are bettered by the confinement of criminals who might otherwise prey on them." Ibid. at 375. Weighing the costs and benefits of a social policy should be done against the backdrop of a "politics of respectability," in which the goal of black leaders is to distance "as many blacks as far as possible from negative stereotypes used to justify racial discrimination against all Negroes." Ibid. at 21.

26. David Rudovsky, "Law Enforcement by Stereotypes," 296, 308.

27. Ibid. at 301.

28. David Cole and John Lamberth, "The Fallacy of Racial Profiling," *New York Times*, May 13, 2001, at Wk in Review 13: "If blacks are carrying drugs more often than whites, police should find drugs on the blacks they stop more often than on the whites they stop. But they don't." Tanya Coke, "Center on Crime, Communities and Culture Report" (unpublished manuscript, November 18, 2000) at 12 (studies comparing whites with similarly situated people of color, including research cited by the New Jersey Attorney General's office and regression-controlled research sponsored by the Building Blocks for Youth Initiative, show racial disparities at every stage of the criminal justice system, even when comparing people with similar arrest histories).

29. Mauer, *Race to Incarcerate* at 147; Diana Jean Schemo, "Students Find Drug Law Has Big Price: College Aid," *New York Times*, May 3, 2001, at A12 (citing statistics that blacks represent 55 percent of those with drug convictions although blacks are closer to 13 percent of those taking illicit drugs). See also Cole and Lamberth, "The Fallacy of Racial Profiling": "The Public Health Service reports, based on anonymous surveys, that blacks, at 13 percent of the population, account for 15 percent of illegal drug users. Hispanics are 11 percent of the population and 8 percent of illegal drug users, and whites are more than 70 percent in both categories."

30. The ACLU, which authored the report on racial profiling in traffic stops, "Driving While Black," also brought the case in Indianapolis that recently led the Supreme Court to declare random drug stops illegal. See Linda Greenhouse, "Supreme Court Bars Traffic Stops That Are Intended as Drug Checks," *New York Times*, November 29, 2000, at A1, A22. See also David Kocieniewski and Robert Hanley, "Racial Profiling Routine, New Jersey Finds," *New York Times*, November 28, 2000, at A1. "At least 8 of every 10 automobile searches carried out by state troopers on the New Jersey Turnpike over the last decade were conducted on vehicles driven by blacks and Hispanics, state documents have revealed . . . 30 percent of the searches on the turnpike turned up some kind of contraband, while 70 percent turned up nothing improper." See also Kocieniewski, "U.S. Wrote Outline for Race Profiling, New Jersey Argues."

31. Robert Gangi, "Upstate Prisons Blossom Amid a Field of Schemes."

32. Mauer, *The Race to Incarcerate* at 135 (drunk drivers are responsible for approximately 22,000 deaths annually; overall alcohol-related deaths approach 100,000 a year while drug related deaths, including violence associated with the drug trade, are estimated at 21,000 annually).

33. Cathy Shine and Marc Mauer, "Does the Punishment Fit the Crime? Drug Users and Drunk Drivers, Questions of Race and Class," in *The Sentencing Project Policy Reports* (1993): http://www.sentencingproject.org/policy/9050.htm, visited August 30, 2000; Kevin Flynn, "Violent Crimes Undercut Marijuana's Mellow Image," *New York Times*, May 19, 2001, at A1, A13 (government bore at least partial responsibility for any increase in violence, because it had made the laws that created a black market).

34. "Drunk drivers are predominantly white males; they are generally charged as misdemeanants and typically receive sentences involving fines, license suspension and community service." Shine and Mauer "Does the Punishment Fit the Crime?" (typically a drunk driver gets two days in jail for a first offense and 2–10 days for a second offense); cf. Stephen J. Dubner, "What Is Stephen King Trying to Prove?" *New York Times Magazine*, August 22, 2000, at 31, 35 (describing how in the summer of 1999, the white male driver of a minivan who hit Stephen King while King was walking on a Maine road caused King major injuries; the driver had a long history of driving violations, including a conviction for operating under the influence; yet only misdemeanor charges were pressed against him for the near-fatal accident involving King). "Once, after running several cars off the road, he pulled into his driveway and promptly passed out on his lawn, in view of the police officer who had been chasing him. In 1998, his license was suspended three times but each time was restored."

35. Shine and Mauer, "Does the Punishment Fit the Crime?"

36. Troy Duster, "The New Crisis of Legitimacy in Controls, Prisons, and Legal structures," 26 *American Sociologist* 20, 24–25 (Spring 1995).

37. California Penal Code 667(b) (Deering 1997).

38. See Chancellor Thomas J. Nussbaum, "The State of the California Community Colleges," September 19, 1997, at 3–4. This shift in priorities then costs all taxpayers not just those unlucky to be tracked to prison. As Victor Hugo said 150 years ago: Every time we build a prison we close a school.

39. See David Firestone, "North Carolina: Students Protest Budget Cuts," *New York Times* (National Briefing), May 3, 2001, at A22 (nearly 2,000 students marched to protest 7 percent budget cuts at the University of North Carolina, which will lead to the loss of 700 faculty positions and larger classes; similar reductions are also likely at public colleges in several other southern states); Andy Kanengiser, "Cuts in Higher Education Reduced," *Clarion Ledger*, March 27, 2001 (Mississippi's eight universities will see spending cuts of 8.3 percent under bills awaiting action by the governor; spending for the universities, plus programs such as the University of Mississippi Medical Center and off-campus programs will be reduced by $53.5 million).

40. Nicholas Lemann, *The Big Test* (1999).

41. "In contrast to the aloof medieval institutions of Europe and the colonies, which trained future clerics and oligarchs, American public colleges and universities . . . [were] intended to develop leaders and to hone the critical perspectives needed by citizens in a participatory democracy." Mindy Kornhaber, "Reconfiguring Admissions to Serve the Mission of Selective Public Higher Education" (unpublished manuscript, January 14, 1999). For example, the mission of the University of California is "to serve society as a center of higher learning, providing long-term societal benefits through transmitting advanced knowledge, discovering new knowledge, and functioning as an active working repository of organized knowledge." At the University of Texas, the mission "is to achieve excellence in the interrelated areas of undergraduate education, graduate education, research, and public service." The University of Michigan's mission is "Pre-eminence in creating, communicating, preserving and applying knowledge, art, and academic values and in developing leaders and citizens who will challenge the present and enrich the future."

42. Stephanie Simon, "Education/An Exploration of Ideas, Issues and Trends in Education; Working To Compete; Latino Students Preparing for the SAT Want the Opportunity to Show They Can Succeed," *Los Angeles Times*, October 1, 1997, at B2 (citing The College

Board, 1997: "SAT tests taken in California show that scores rise with the income of students' families. Two-thirds of Mexican-American high school graduates come from families with incomes of less than $25,000 annually"). The article includes a table showing that students from families with a total annual income between $10,000 and $20,000 had an average combined SAT score of 906 (437 verbal and 469 math), and students whose family income was under $10,000 annually had an average combined SAT score of 859 (409 verbal and 450 math). Meanwhile, students from families with income of $80,000 to $100,000 had an average combined SAT score of 1082 (535 verbal and 547 math).

43. See Robert Westbrook, "Public Schooling and American Democracy," *in Democracy, Education and the Schools* (Roger Soder, ed., 1996) at 125: "The relationship between public schooling and democracy is a conceptually tight one. Schools have become one of the principal institutions by which modern states reproduce themselves, and insofar as those states are democratic, they will make use of schools to prepare children for democratic citizenship." Some might argue that the exclusive or at least primary aim of schools should be to educate students "for the market." See President Bill Clinton's 1994 State of the Union message where he declared, "We measure every school by one high standard: are our children learning what they need to know to compete and win in the global economy?" Ibid. at 126. Others, such as Benjamin Barber, suggest the important yet neglected goal of "civic literacy," meaning "the competence to participate in democratic communities, the ability to think critically and act with deliberation in a pluralistic world, and the empathy to identify sufficiently with others to live with them despite conflicts of interest and differences in character." Benjamin Barber, "America Skips School," 286 *Harper's Magazine*, November 1993, at 44. Westbrook agrees with Barber that public schools are "public" not just because they are supported by public finance but because they educate every student for the responsibilities and benefits of participating in public life. Susan Sturm and Lani Guinier argue that both goals (of educating citizens for employment opportunities and for democratic participation) are critical. Susan Sturm and Lani Guinier, "From Triage to Transformation: The Role of Multiracial Learning Communities" (unpublished manuscript) (arguing that learning how to collaborate with people who are different is an essential mission of education both because the workplace of the twenty-first century will demand such "teamwork" and because complex problems are often solved only when diverse perspectives are taken into account through the process of constructive conflict). Yet, the gateway to citizenship is controlled by tests that tell us more about how much money your parents make than what kind of citizen you are ultimately going to be.

44. Derrick Bok and William Bowen, *The Shape of the River* (1998). Indeed, this is Michael Feuer's point: that high-stakes aptitude tests disadvantage low-scoring test-takers unfairly, because the test results fail to tell us whether the person has the capacity to do the job; yet we rely on the tests to deny the applicant the chance to prove what he or she can in fact do.

45. For a presentation of the study's results, see Richard O. Lempert, David L. Chambers, and Terry K. Adams, "Michigan's Minority Graduates in Practice: The River Runs through Law School," 25 *Law and Social Inquiry* 395 (Spring 2000).

46. Ibid. at 396, quoting Admissions policy adopted by the University of Michigan Law School Faculty, April 24, 1992, at 1.

47. Some may argue that we are overstating the implications of the study's results. Certainly Michigan's white students also engage in substantial pro bono and other service activities at a level that appears to the authors to go beyond what is formally required. More-

over, the negative correlation between "hard credentials" and service activities may be explained by ethnic status. That is, blacks and Latinos tend to give back more than white students, and the difference in their admissions index does not explain much of the variance. Indeed, in the authors' regression analysis the admissions index variable is not significant after ethnic status is controlled. Finally, the authors are careful to point out that many lawyers give back or feel they are giving back to society in their regular jobs. On the other hand, to the extent the school continues to rely on the so-called hard credentials to admit students, it will in fact be preferring those who are likely to do less service, meaning what lawyers do beyond their regular jobs.

48. Lempert, Chambers, and Adams, "Michigan's Minority Graduates" at 468–469.

49. Ibid. at 469. They mentor fewer young attorneys, sit on fewer community boards and do less pro bono work. This negative relationship is statistically significant among the 1970–1979 and 1990–1996 cohorts. If one compares the entry level LSAT scores of Michigan graduates with their "service" index, there is a negative relationship that is statistically significant among 1980s graduates as well.

50. Ibid. at 401.

51. The actual procedures employed should certainly be further investigated, since those criteria worked to admit students who ultimately became leaders within their profession. In particular, the criteria used to admit the first generation of black students are worth studying since that early generation gave back more to the community than those that followed. This may not simply be a function of the selection criteria but also of the experience the first cohort of black students had in the law school itself, where they had numerous occasions—outside of the classroom—to develop leadership skills.

52. Lempert, Chambers, and Adams, "Michigan's Minority Graduates" at 56. That students of color were more likely to exhibit commitment to public service may also show the correlation between race and the weak-we identity we discussed in Chapter 3. Race may be functioning here as a proxy for commitment to others, to public service, and to giving back. See discussion in State of Black America 2000 (discussing idea that those who identify as part of a community are more likely to define their own goals in community oriented ways).

53. David K. Shipler, "My Equal Opportunity, Your Free Lunch," New York Times, March 5, 1995, at E1, E10, E16 (quoting Marilyn McGrath Lewis, director of admissions for Harvard: "We have a particular interest in students from a modest background . . . We know that's the best investment we can make: a kid who's hungry"). See also National Commission on Testing and Public Policy, "From Gatekeepers to Gateway: Transforming testing in America," Boston College, Chestnut Hill, MA (1990); M. Chi, R. Glaser, and M. J. Farr, eds., The Nature of Expertise (1988); K. A. Ericsson and J. Smith, eds., Toward a General Theory of Expertise: Prospects and Limits (1991); D. Perkins, Outsmarting IQ: The Science of Learnable Intelligence (1995). In addition to the ability to prioritize and juggle tasks, it is important to understand and be able to do what is valued within one's environment. See R. J. Sternberg and R. K. Wagner, "The G-Ocentric View of Intelligence and Job Performance Is Wrong," 2(1) Current Directions in Psychological Science 1 (1993), R. J. Sternberg and W. Williams, "Does the Graduate Record Examiniation Predict Meaningful Success in the Graduate Training of Psychologists?" 52(6) American Psychologist 630 (1997). See generally Mindy Kornhaber, "Some Means of Spurring the Equitable Identification of Students for Selective Higher Education" (unpublished manuscript on file with author, November 17, 1997).

54. Asa G. Hilliard III, *Testing African American Students* (1991) at 95.

55. See Sturm and Guinier, "The Future of Affirmative Action" at 971 ("A recent study of the correlation of SAT scores with freshman grades showed correlations ranging from .32 to .36," quoting Warren W. Willingham et al., *Predicting College Grades: An analysis of Institutional Trends Over Two Decades* at 43 (1990)); see also Michael Scott Moore, "Three Hours on a Saturday Morning: UC May Drop the flawed SAT as an Admission Requirement. But Are the Other Options Any Better?" *SF Weekly,* December 10, 1997 ("According to most independent studies, the SAT's accuracy in predicting first-year college grades hovers around 30 percent, odds Ralph Nader once described as 'a little better than throwing dice'"). In terms of the LSAT (and going back to those black and Chicano students at the University of Texas), Martin Shapiro, a statistician, did an affidavit in the *Hopwood* case in which he said that the correlation between black students' LSAT scores and first-year UT law school grades was negative. See Sturm and Guinier, "The Future of Affirmative Action" at 972–973n6. Representatives of the Law School Admissions Council have said publicly that nationwide the LSAT is about 9 percent better than random in predicting variation in first year law school grades.

56. See Lani Guinier, Michelle Fine, and Jane Balin, *Becoming Gentlemen: Women, Law Schools and Institutional Change* (1997) at 8, 31 ("For students in their first and second years, the LSAT explains even less: 14% and 15% respectively"). Ibid. at 39n74 ("In other words, when LSAT is the only variable in a bivariate regression equation, it explains 14% of the variance in first-year law school GPA").

57. Of course, this is an oversimplification. The SAT and other "norm-referenced" aptitude tests do tell us something about one's capacity to do analytic thinking. The problem is that such capacity is often improved by practice; practice comes from coaching (which costs money), from experience taking the test (which means exposure to the opportunity of learning from previous mistakes), and from other kinds of exposure to travel, books, and unusual vocabulary words. Thus, while the tests do tell us something about those who do well, they often tell us less about those who do poorly; that is, they do not tell us what a poor performer is actually capable of doing, only what that person has already learned or not learned to do. See Michael Feuer, "The Changing Science of Assessment: Issues and Implications," Remarks at 1998 Symposium, Rethinking Law in the 21st Century Workplace, *University of Pennsylvania Journal of Labor and Employment Law,* January 30, 1998 (stating there is a nontrivial proportion of people who would be excluded from employment opportunities because of performance on a test who could nevertheless do the job; low scoring test takers are more likely to be misclassified; black applicants, in particular, are more likely to be misclassified). Feuer, who is director of the Board of Testing and Assessment at the National Academy of Sciences, explained that for many low-scoring individuals, differences in performance on a job are less than differences in test performance. This is because the tests only measure certain quantifiable traits and ignore "context, situation, training, teams and prior performance," which also affect job performance. Feuer mentioned Academy-supported research published as "Fairness in Employment Testing," which included a study of the performance of 3,500 air force pilots. The study found that prior performance of the pilots is the best predictor of their future performance. Feuer also gave the example of research on milk truck delivery drivers in New York who were able to do sophisticated mathematical calculations as part of their job, but the same drivers would not have been able to perform comparable calculations had they been asked first to

take a test. Feuer concludes that test-driven decision making confuses prediction with merit, especially in light of research regarding the important role of practice and skill acquisition in the workplace itself. See also Sturm and Guinier, "The Future of Affirmative Action," 84 *California Law Review* 974n82 (July 1996) and accompanying text (citing study of 300,000 recruits who failed the army battery of tests in 1976 but because of a calibration error were admitted; longitudinal study of their subsequent performance showed little difference in re-enlistment and promotion rates from those who actually passed the test).

58. Lempert, Chambers, and Adams, "Michigan's Minority Graduates" at 489. The study also suggests that the dedication necessary to achieve a high law school grade point average (LSGPA) may result in long-term career dissatisfaction, because a person with such dedication is likely not good at balancing "separate spheres" of satisfaction: "Those likely to have concentrated most on getting good grades while in law school seem to be more likely than others to dedicate themselves to their jobs to a degree that leaves them stressed by the sense that they have little time for anything other than money-producing job-related activities." Ibid. at 489–490.

59. Claude M. Steele et al., "Stereotype Threat and the Test Performance of Academically Successful African Americans," in *The Black-White Test Score Gap* (Christopher Jencks et al., eds., 1998).

60. Michael Young *The Rise of the Meritocracy, 1870–2033: The New Elite of Our Social Revolution* (1958). Jerome Karabel, "What the Deserving Deserve and Whether They Get It," *New York Times*, October 23, 1999, at A19, described this phenomenon as Michael Young's contribution to "meritocracy's dirty little secret."

61. In *The Rise of the Meritocracy*, Young argues that a test-centered ranking system would encourage the sense of "desert" among those who excelled and would possibly discourage them, as winners, from doing anything to question their success. On the other hand, Henry Chauncey and others whose commitment to testing for mental aptitude helped propel the SAT and LSAT into the credentializing machines they have become believed that testing people for mental aptitude would not only allow the selection of those who are most competent. It would also allow institutions of higher learning to recruit a leadership class who would discharge their public service responsibilities with renewed vigor. See Nicholas Lemann, *The Big Test*. As the Michigan study demonstrates, the association between leadership, service, and mental aptitude testing was perhaps the biggest flaw in the Chauncy program.

62. The study does not explicitly test the effectiveness of whole-person admissions criteria. Rather, the authors hypothesize that a plausible reason why they fail to get a correlation between the admissions index and success measures is that in accordance with Michigan's official admissions policy softer measures more indicative of the whole person were considered. One obvious next step, therefore, is for these authors or other scholars to get the resources needed to code the soft data from the admissions files for the alumni in the study in order to provide data that bears directly on the whole-person issue.

63. This study only reviewed data from a single law school. Some might reasonably argue that it would be necessary to replicate these findings at other similar institutions before launching a major restructuring of law school admissions protocols. On the other hand, the *Shape of the River* by Bok and Bowen studied students at 25 elite schools and found similar evidence that those admitted pursuant to affirmative action protocols were more likely to become leaders in their communities.

64. William Raspberry, "The Delusional Drug War," *Washington Post,* May 4, 2001, at A25 (quoting Ethan Nadelman for providing "the Vietnam analogy" which "turns out to be an interesting point to start thinking about the drug wars").

65. Troy Duster "The New Crisis of Legitimacy."

66. Beverly Gage, "Prisoner Nation," *The Nation,* July 17, 2000, at 5. Gage also notes the role of prisons in enhancing the political clout of rural legislators. "With the federal government prepared to distribute at least $185 billion a year over the next decade solely according to census figures, every warm body has become a valuable commodity." In this sense, Colin Powell was wrong in declaiming the necessity of "turning convicts into consumers." See Colin Powell, "Address to the Republican National Convention" (2000).

67. Tanya Coke, "Center on Crime, Communities and Culture Report" at 15.

68. Mary Fainsod Katzenstein, "Remarks on Women and Leadership" ("The important thing is that this is not a strangely select group of young college-going African American and Hispanic women. Their experiences are, to the contrary, shockingly normal").

69. Alan Feuer, "Making a Dent in the Demand for Illegal Drugs," *New York Times,* September 3, 2000, 4Wk (quoting Anne Swern, a deputy district attorney who runs a program called D-TAP, or Drug Treatment Alternative to Prison).

70. Indeed, that message seemed influential in the 2000 election-year passage of Proposition 36 in California, which made all first time drug offenders eligible for treatment rather than prison. See Evelyn Nieves, "California Gets Set to Shift on Sentencing Drug Users," *New York Times,* November 10, 2000, at A18. Some might argue that the passage of this proposition by a margin of 61 percent of the vote undercuts our argument that the energy for mobilization will come from communities of color. But it is also true that Proposition 36 is arguably an anomaly, in which the proponents, supported by three billionaires, outspent the opposition by more than 10 to 1. Even in such unusual conditions, movement building at the local level would help sustain the public policy outcomes engineered in such top-down fashion. In the absence of such unusual financial support, the mobilization of people of color—those most directly affected—would be crucial.

71. Feuer, "Making a Dent."

72. Shine and Mauer, "Does the Punishment Fit the Crime?"

73. This is a deep-rooted criticism of the current educational system as well as the American political system. As Mano Singham points out, for the fraction of the population who succeed, "the links between effort, credentials, and rewards are sufficiently realistic and compelling to act as an extrinsic motivator for academic [or political] effort." But "in those communities and families in which the perception of the link between effort and reward is weaker (as is the case with low-income families of all ethnicities and with involuntary minorities), these extrinsic rewards become even less compelling as motivators for academic effort and excellence, and the students' performance suffers . . . As long as society requires only a small fraction of educated people and does not care about gender or ethnic or socioeconomic equity issues, then the present system of education is quite adequate. What the academic achievement gap may really be telling us is that, while the symptoms of the education system's ills are more clearly visible in the black community than in the white, there are fundamental problems with the way education is delivered to all students." "The Canary in the Mine: The Achievement Gap Between Black and White Students," 80 *Phi Delta Kappan* 8 (September 1998).

74. "Prepared Testimony of Wade Henderson, Leadership Conference on Civil Rights,

Before the House Government Reform Committee Subcommittee on Criminal Justice," May 11, 2000.

75. Although education is a priority according to voters, state budgets for higher education are being slashed all around the country. David Firestone, "North Carolina: Students Protest Budget Cuts," *New York Times,* May 3, 2001, at A20.

76. Evelyn Nieves, "Storm Raised by Plan for a California Prison," *New York Times,* August 27, 2000, at 12; Evelyn Nieves, "A Fertile Farm Region Pays Its Jobless to Quit California," *New York Times,* June 18, 2001, at A1. More than a third of the county residents receive some form of public assistance.

77. On June 21, 2001, citizens from New York, Georgia, California, Washington, D.C., and other parts of Pennsylvania joined local residents to protest the construction of one of 30 new federal prisons in rural America. Sponsoring the protest against the federal government's seizure of the land is the Organization of Concerned Citizens of Wayne County, a local community group. It says "the prison will destroy the region's history and economy and will prove an environmental disaster for local waterways and endangered species." The land had been evaluated as eligible to be a National Historic Register District because it contained historic agricultural buildings and nineteenth-century railroad remains. Email to Lani Guinier from Samantha Bent, June 18, 2001.

78. Greenhouse, "Divided Justices Back Full Arrest."

79. Clifford Krauss, "Peru Anti-Drug Patrol Reassessed after Downing of U.S. Plane," *New York Times,* April 24, 2001, at A8.

80. Associated Press, "U.S. Monitored Peru Area Where Missionary Plane Was Hit," April 22, 2001.

81. Sam Howe Verhovek, "Augusto Pinochet, He's Not," *New York Times,* April 29, 2001, at Wk2; Sam Howe Verhovek, "Out on Parole 26 Years, Suddenly a Fugitive," *New York Times,* April 26, 2001, at A1. While in prison, he read hundreds of books; completed 31 university correspondence classes in religion, anthropology, and other fields; started a successful vacuum cleaner business with his brother; and gathered fifty recommendations for parole from guards and counselors. While serving time in Oregon for an earlier attempted robbery, his turnaround so impressed officials there that the state's governor declared Mr. Burns fully rehabilitated and blocked the extradition to California in 1975.

82. Krauss, "Peru Anti-Drug Patrol Reassessed after Downing of U.S. Plane."

83. Greenhouse, "Divided Justices Back Full Arrest."

84. Justice O'Connor added that "as the recent debate over racial profiling demonstrates all too clearly, a relatively minor traffic infraction may serve as an excuse for stopping and harassing an individual." In addition, nationwide, 13 percent of black men cannot exercise their right to vote because of felony convictions.

85. In Florida, roughly 30 percent of black men are permanently disenfranchised. Needless to say, this amounts to thousands more voters than Bush's miniscule margin of victory in that decisive state in the 2000 presidential election.

86. Diana Jean Schemo, "Students Find Drug Law Has Big Price: College Aid" (describing law passed in 1998 but being fully enforced now by Bush Administration that denies college aid to students convicted on drug charges).

87. The techniques for deciding without resorting to the crude dynamics of binaries are well known within the literature of group process.

88. Carey Goldberg, "Harvard Sit-In Over Pay Ends with Deal to Re-examine Policies,"

New York Times, May 9, 2001, at A19 ("As the protesters left Massachusetts Hall, ending what is believed to have been the longest sit-in in a Harvard building, supporters presented each with a red rose. Inside, the office workers and administrators who had played host to the protesters drank champagne. And the hall where the students sat for weeks looked immaculate except for a couple of garbage bags. 'They even vacuumed,' the university police chief, Francis D. Riley, said of the protesters").

89. Julie Flaherty, "New Kind of Test at Amherst, on the Day the Urns Went Dry," *New York Times*, May 9, 2001, at A15.

90. Andrew Hsiao, "Color Blind: Activists of Color Bring the Economic War Home, But Is the Movement Missing the Message?" *Village Voice*, July 19–25, 2000, at 43.

91. Ibid. "Hip-hop also provides the soundtrack for the ongoing 40 city 'No More Prisons' raptivists tour, whose targets include multinational Sodexho Alliance, a major underwriter of the private prison industry."

92. Ibid. Yet, when people of color are not involved early on, their voices are lost, even in some of the more spectacular mass protests against the World Trade Organization and its democratic unaccountability in 1999 and 2000 in Seattle and Washington, D.C., demonstrations that "electrified activists across the country." Historian and scholar Robin D. G. Kelley says "the lack of people of color involved in these demonstrations is a crisis."

93. Anand Vaishnav, "Students Rally to Teacher's Side: Police Stops Prompt Questions of Racism, School Protest March," *Boston Globe*, February 13, 2001, at B1.

94. In some such circumstances those raced black may eventually choose whites to lead them, when given a real choice. In a recent campaign in Los Angeles, Justice for Janitors, one of the key union organizers was a white man who played a pivotal role throughout the campaign. Once the campaign proved successful, the national union tried to send a person of color from the national staff to take over the leadership. But the union members, mainly Latino and other immigrants of color, rejected this "outsider" who shared their ethnicity but had not established the same bonds of trust or solidarity with the membership.

95. As the political theorist Peter Bachrach concludes, "political participation plays a dual role: it not only catalyzes opinion but also creates it." Peter Bachrach, "Interest, Participation and Democratic Theory," in *Participation in Politics* (J. Roland Pennock and John W. Chapman, eds., 1975).

96. See Derrick Bell, "The Space Traders" and "Epilogue: Beyond Despair," in *Faces at the Bottom of the Well* at 198–199. Racism is permanent no matter what we do; action is futile—where action is more civil rights strategies destined to fail—and yet we have the "unalterable conviction that something must be done, that action must be taken."

97. Racial literacy teaches us that racism is not simply a function of individual psychology, prejudice, or bigotry. Indeed well-meaning individuals can acquiesce in societal racism and most do.

98. We use the term racism in similar ways to Ian F. Haney-Lopez, "Institutional Racism: Judicial Conduct and a New Theory of Racial Discrimination," 109 *Yale Law Journal* 1717, 1837, 1838 (June 2000). Haney-Lopez rejects the current Court's equation of reference to race as the measure of racism. Haney-Lopez writes, "The Court seems to be developing an equal protection jurisprudence that defines racism both too narrowly (race must be openly considered) and too broadly (any consideration of race constitutes racism). The Supreme Court errs when it suggests that racism—always and exclusively—involves the open consideration of race."

99. In this way, taking race into account, by itself, is not an example of racism. It depends whether race is being taken into account in order to alleviate or reproduce racial hierarchy.

100. "The Negro in winning rights for himself produces substantial benefits for the nation. Just as the doctor will occasionally reopen a wound, because a dangerous infection hovers beneath the half-healed surface, the [civil rights] revolution . . . is opening up unhealthy areas in American life and permitting a new and wholesome healing to take place." Martin Luther King, Jr., *Why We Can't Wait* (1963) at 168.

101. Troy Duster, a sociologist at New York University who studies the interplay of race and science, delivered a speech in May 2001 to scientists at the National Institutes of Health, the nation's premier institution for medical research. The title of his talk was "Buried Alive: The Concept of Race in Science." Despite some people's wishes to the contrary, Duster said, race is not going away. "It's there," he said. "It's often buried. But I assure you, it's alive." Sheryl Gay Stolberg, "Skin Deep: Shouldn't a Pill Be Colorblind?" *New York Times*, May 13, 2001, at Week in Review 1.

102. Letter from Larry Blum to Lani Guinier, July 29, 2000: "For example, some organizations, such as US Action (which organizes around bread and butter issues such as health care coverage for prescription drugs)" are committed to organizing grassroots political power in service of social, racial, economic, and environmental justice. They are committed to organizing in a way that reflects the nation's diversity with a clear dedication to racial balance in leadership. US Action works on political programs organized around bread-and-butter issues that have a universal appeal and disproportionately affect people of color. Email from Larry Blum to Lani Guinier, January 2, 2001.

103. Jennifer Hochschild, Comments at Gilbane Symposium, Brown University, November 14, 2000.

104. Jennifer Hochschild, "Madison's Constitution and Identity Politics," in *Defining the Conditions for Democracy* at 14, 21 (Theodore Rabb and Ezra Suleiman, eds., forthcoming) (analysis by Hochschild from data in National Opinion Research Center, 1999, #11 questions 515, 519) (acknowledging that "everything in the United States is deeply racially inflected" and concluding that a structure of racial hierarchy once in place continue). "Even the values of political liberalism itself can reinforce racial hierarchy. Conceiving of rights as the property of individuals rather than of groups, legislating in accord with principles of symmetry and moral reciprocity, celebrating tolerance for all viewpoints—all permit, even encourage, a structure of racial domination to continue once it is in place."

105. Jennifer Hochschild and Reuel Rogers, "Race Relations in a Diversifying Nation" (manuscript, June 22, 1999): "Black pursuit of political incorporation and inclusion often leads to zero-sum conflict, unless blacks can refrain from guarding their political gains against encroachment."

106. Hochschild studies the isolation of blacks within cross-racial coalitions dominated by whites as well as the inability of blacks within other cross-racial coalitions to obtain group visibility and descriptive representation. She is worried by what she sees blacks doing within these failed coalitions. In an article co-authored with Reuel Rogers, she criticizes black "insistence on descriptive representation" that "comes at the expense of other political and policy goals that can be shared across groups."

107. James Phillip Thompson, "Universalism and Deconcentration: Why Race Still Matters in Poverty and Economic Development" at 39 (undated draft manuscript). "There

is no reason to expect African Americans to abandon their particular demands and place their trust in political strategies that offer vague promises of whites embracing African Americans at some undefined point in the future."

108. When 2,500 Americans were polled from April through July 2000 for the Markle Foundation and Oxygen Media, 40 percent of black women, almost twice the portion in any other group of women or men said they prefer a politician who will keep campaign promises to one who "will do what is right for the country, even it is means breaking a campaign promise." Asked why in focus groups black women made it clear that when politicians talk about the "greater good," they usually don't include what's good for black Americans. Cheryl D. Mills, "Talking to Oprah Isn't Enough," *New York Times*, September 30, 2000, at A27.

109. Viewed from our perspective, universal appeals are inadequate because they support the present reality that many whites and other people of color are reluctant to identify with blacks. And yet blacks are the one group willing to stand up for justice against claims of social peace. See James Carroll, "Black Caucus Sends a Message about Justice," *Boston Globe*, January 9, 2001, at A19 (describing role of black members of the Congress as truth tellers whose commitment to justice trumps their commitment to enforcement of rules). "Perhaps the Black Caucus registered its protest (when the electoral college votes were counted and when they could not get a single Senator to join in their written objection) as a way of bringing forward an ancient epiphany . . . those who sit atop the social and economic pyramid always speak of love, while those at the bottom always speak of justice."

110. Hochschild analogizes her position to the behavioral therapist who advises patients seeking family counseling to stay away from major traumas until they first build a long history of trust. Comments at Gilbane Symposium.

111. Francis X. Clines, "In Aftershock of Unrest, Cincinnati Seeks Answers" *New York Times*, April 23, 2001, at A11 (about issues lurking beneath surface for years).

112. Martin Luther King, Jr., "Letter from a Birmingham City Jail," *Testament of Hope: The Essential Writings of Martin Luther King, Jr.*, at 289–302 (James Melvin Washington, ed., 1986): "I have almost reached the regrettable conclusion that the Negro's great stumbling block in the stride toward freedom is . . . the white moderate who is more devoted to 'order' than to justice; who prefers a negative peace which is the absence of tension to a positive peace which is the presence of justice."

113. As cited by William Jefferson Clinton, "Erasing America's Color Lines," *New York Times*, January 14, 2001, at Wk 17. See also Martin Luther King, *A Testament of Hope* (published posthumously, January 1969): "Justice for black people will not flow into society merely from court decisions nor from fountains of political oratory. Nor will a few token changes quell all the tempestuous yearnings of millions of disadvantaged black people. White America must recognize that justice for black people cannot be achieved without radical changes in the structure of our society. The comfortable, the entrenched, the privileged cannot continue to tremble at the prospect in the status quo."

114. Anthony Pratkanis and Marlene Turner, "Persuasion and Democracy: Strategies for Increasing Deliberative Participation and Enacting Social Change," 5 *Journal of Social Issues* 187, 191 (Spring 1996) (describing a vanguard approach as one whose leaders believe they have special knowledge that needs to be communicated to the masses).

115. See Susan Sturm, "A Second Generation Structural Approach," 101 *Columbia Law Review* 458 (April 2001). See also Reed Abselson, "By the Water Cooler in Cyberspace, the Talk Turns Ugly," *New York Times*, April 29, 2001, at A1 (reporting comments that confirm

Sturm's insight—in the workplace discrimination complaints often correlate with poor la-bor-management practices more generally).

116. Greenhouse, "Divided Justices Back Full Arrest." All in all, said Gail Atwater, the soccer mom arrested for not having her children in seatbelts, it has been a tough four years. "We've made a large sacrifice trying to help people," she said, "but you don't live in a free society for free."

117. It bears repeating that our analysis is historically specific to the United States at the turn of the twenty-first century. At other times in U.S. history, and certainly in other countries around the world, class is associated with a collective and visible language of struggle and resistance.

118. Evelyn Brooks Higginbotham, "African-American Women's History and the Meta-language of Race," in *We specialize in the Wholly Impossible: A Reader in Black Women's History* (Darlene Clark Hine, Wilma King, and Linda Reed, eds., 1995).

119. Nicholas Lemann, "The New American Consensus: Government of, by and for the Comfortable," *New York Times Magazine*, 37 (November 1, 1998) (suggesting selfishness animates most American voters, but not blacks and Latinos, in part because neither party has made the case for a broader, shared vision that goes beyond market values; arguing that emerging bipartisan consensus reflects concerns of voters, not citizens).

120. Fredrick C. Harris, *Something Within: Religion in African-American Political Activism* at 37 (1999) ("Biblical scriptures, sacred icons, and prophetic insights framed political opposition . . . and expressed possibilities" for political action and success).

121. Russ Rymer, "Integration's Casualties," *New York Times Magazine*, November 1, 1998, at 48, 50 (integration destroyed a segregated community but failed to build a truly multiracial one; instead it offered individual blacks the freedom to shop). "Integration has helped to redefine success toward a surface (and mainstream) materialism that has helped to undermine the sense of thrift, community service and self-sufficiency that traditional black businesses once exemplified and championed . . . [We need to] broaden integration from the corrosive and incomplete consumer revolution it turned out to be into a produc-tion revolution as well."

122. Harvard Law School graduate and civil rights attorney Rose Sanders, as quoted in Lani Guinier, *Lift Every Voice* at 184 (1998).

123. For example, when we presented our argument to a workshop at NYU sponsored by the Africana Studies Department, one participant, a public defender, said our claims resonated with her experience. When she has a black defendant, a gay white man as a po-tential juror often makes the best sense for her client because he can understand being the object of police hostility. On the other hand, we are not making "like race" arguments. We are not pushing that legal approach regardless of its probability or unlikeliness of success. We are not urging that women or gays pitch their arguments by comparison to racial mi-norities. See Janet Halley's argument in "Gay Rights and Identity Imitation: Issues in the Ethics of Representation," in *The Politics of Law: A Progressive Critique* at 115 (3rd ed., Da-vid Kairys, ed., 1997).

124. Martin L. King, Jr., *Strength to Love* (1963). See ch. 11: "History has thrust upon our generation an indescribably important destiny—to complete a process of democrati-zation which our nation has too long developed too slowly."

ACKNOWLEDGMENTS

We speak throughout this book about children, but, as one friend noted, we do not say much about ourselves as adults. Many colleagues also expressed curiosity about how a black and a Latino, living in different regions of the continent, could or would collaborate in writing a book about race. Did the "technology" of our own collaboration, they wondered, illustrate the challenges or benefits of the political race project? What did we learn from this effort to create an intermediate space in which to rethink the idea of race and politics? In fact, we discovered many things, including that solidarity is reinforced by a sense of shared risk as well as trust and respect.

The two of us began our collaboration in 1990, when Lani sent Gerald a draft of a quasi-autobiographical article she had written as she navigated the transition from civil rights litigator to academic. Gerald completely rewrote the first three pages and returned the draft otherwise unmarked. At first, Lani was taken aback at his presumptuousness. But after she saw that he had improved the short article, she then wondered why his dramatic style of revision stopped abruptly at page 3, and she called to discuss it. Gerald admitted that his discomfort in flouting the conventions of the legal academy had caused him to abandon the rewrite. It was against the background of this conversation that our collaboration began.

That exchange ultimately led us to pursue the opportunity to deliver the Nathan Huggins Lectures together. We had originally conceived of the project in conjunction with a third colleague, but she withdrew in response to early difficulties in getting institutional support for a three-way partnership. The lecture invitation gave us a chance to work through ideas each of us had thought about individually, and it galvanized us into pulling all of the material we had previously experimented with across the country into a coherent argument. It forced us to hone our analysis and to settle on an approach that would be accessible to as wide an audience as possible. It enabled us to embody an idea that we think is foundational to the political race project—that collaboration can nurture a willingness to take greater risks and explore more innovative ideas than an individual might feel comfortable doing alone. Furthermore, our collaboration was not limited to the two of us; it included many others whose comments greatly influenced our thinking.

Before the Huggins Lectures, we began our early experimentation with the Yale Law School Critical Race Theory Conference in 1997 and three months later at Stanford's Graduate Symposium on Race and Miami's Legal Theory Workshop. In 1998 Lani gave The Tanner Lectures at Harvard, and much of the feedback she received there helped form the substance of Chapters 4 and 5 in this book. Even after we jointly delivered the Huggins Lectures in 1999, we continued to try out different formats as individual lecturers and sometimes together in venues around the country, including the Conference on Gender and Race at Simmons College School of Management, the School of Criticism and Theory at Cornell University, the Salzburg Seminar on Race and Ethnicity, New York University's Africana Studies Black Culture and Testimony Seminar, Glenn Loury's Institute on Race and Social Division research workshop at Boston University, the University of Michigan Legal Theory Workshop, and The Gilbane Lectures at Brown.

One of our goals was to create, within each lecture hall, a space to engage debate in a way that invited more voices to enter. We often structured our lectures as responses to each other's arguments in order to encourage members of the audience to participate in the critique. These critiques sharpened the differences between the two of us and helped minimize misinterpretation. They also revealed philosophical fissures and temperamental disjunctures that became more obvious as our collaboration moved to the writing stage. On the other hand, experimenting with different stories or different concepts was actually much easier after we delivered a lecture and heard from the audience, no matter who it was.

At every step in this collaboration, we were aware of the potential for conflict with our audience, as well as the actual conflict between our respective personalities and perspectives. What we were saying was unfamiliar and destined to make each of our readers uncomfortable for different reasons. We were occupying unmapped territory. But we self-consciously embraced the creative act as a fundamentally social act, and as a result we learned more from the lectures than we taught. The book itself became something very different as we ingested this ongoing critique throughout the writing and thinking process.

The list of people who deserve lengthy explanations of their distinctive role in this collaboration is long. We would include, if we could, all of the people who were in the audiences during the times these ideas were developed; we would especially thank the audience at the Huggins Lectures themselves. And if space permitted we would detail the contribution of our magnificent editors at Harvard University Press, Susan Wallace Boehmer and Kathleen McDermott, whose encouragement, support, extraordinary talent, and craft helped this book take shape. We have benefited enormously from the many colleagues who read and responded to drafts as we wrote and rewrote. We are grateful to the unwavering allies, unfriendly critics, skeptical students, diligent and resourceful research assistants, and patient friends whose reactions pushed us to see the weaknesses in what we had done.

We settled on listing the names of these many people as a tribute to the idea of collaboration. We worry that some readers will nevertheless construe this unceremonious format as an inability to recall, with heartfelt gratitude, the specific contributions of those we list. That is not the case. Rather, the people who appear below expressed their support for our work and generously offered their assistance in so many forms that a short explanation attached to each name would not begin to do them justice. We also believe that this long list of names best illustrates the sheer number of people who were willing to give of their time to collaborate with us, even when they objected to parts of what we were doing or saying. Some of those listed are working to implement the ideas outlined in this book; through their struggles on the ground they are writing the most important chapters of our project. And finally, by listing all of these names, we hope to underscore the paradox at the heart of our political race experiment: that it is simultaneously provocative and mainstream, drawing both from converging currents of established thought and from groundbreaking action. We are deeply grateful to have had the opportunity to work with, and learn from, such a diverse and dedicated group of free and courageous thinkers.

Above all we express our loving appreciation to our families who tolerated and actively encouraged this undertaking, with which we were each preoccupied for the past several years.

Adam Ambrogi	Michael Dawson	Jennifer Klar
Bryonn Bain	Aida Donald	Dominick LaCapra
Nick Bath	Soffiyah Elijah	Travis LeBlanc
Valerie Batts	Beth Elliott	Sara Lawrence
Carol Bell	Andrew Erhlich	Lightfoot
Derrick Bell	David Estlund	Martha Mahoney
Seyla Benhabib	Neil Foley	Jane Mansbridge
Samantha Bent	William Forbath	Frank Michelman
James Bernard	Marshall Ganz	Martha Minow
James Blacksher	Jorge Garza	Tim Mitchell
Larry Blum	Henry Louis Gates	Rachel Moran
Larry Bobo	Heather Gerken	Charlene Morisseau
Niko Bowie	Jennifer Gordon	Melissa Nobles
Nolan Bowie	Christian Grose	Pedro Noguera
Richard Briffault	Penda Hair	Charles Ogletree
Anthony Brown	Morgan Hankin	Steig Olson
Peggy Burlett	Evelyn Brooks	Eden Osucha
Tanya Coke	Higginbotham	Spencer Overton
Kate Cook	Jennifer Hochschild	Rob Richie
Dayna Cunningham	Mort Horwitz	Jennifer Ring

Tricia Rose
Nancy Rosenblum
Jose David Saldivar
Ian Shapiro
Sam Spital
Randy Stakeman
Susan Sturm

Jeannie Suk
Kendall Thomas
Dennis Thompson
Bennett Torres
Maria de Los Angeles
    Torres

Eric Yamamoto
Lucie White
David Wilkins
David Wong